GW00383542

History from the Sources
General Editor: John Morris

ARTHURIAN PERIOD SOURCES
VOL. 3

ARTHURIAN SOURCES

Vol. 3
Persons

ARTHURIAN PERIOD SOURCES

1 **Arthurian Sources, Vol. 1**, by John Morris
  Introduction, Notes and Index
    How to use *Arthurian Sources*; Introduction and Notes;
    Index to *The Age of Arthur*

2 **Arthurian Sources, Vol. 2**, by John Morris
  *Annals (**A**) and Charters (**C**)*

3 **Arthurian Sources, Vol. 3**, by John Morris
  Persons
    Ecclesiastics (**E**) (alphabetically listed)
    Laypeople (**L**) (alphabetically listed)

4 **Arthurian Sources, Vol. 4**, by John Morris
  *Places and Peoples (**P**), and Saxon Archaeology (**S**)*
    Places and Peoples (alphabetically listed)
    Saxon Archaeology:
      The Chronology of Early Anglo-Saxon Archaeology;
      Anglo-Saxon Surrey; The Anglo-Saxons in Bedfordshire

5 **Arthurian Sources, Vol. 5**, by John Morris
  *Genealogies (**G**) and Texts (**T**)*
    Genealogies
      Editions by Egerton Phillimore (1856-1937): *The Annales Cambriae*
      and Old-Welsh Genealogies from B.L. MS. Harley 3859; Pedigrees
      from Jesus College (Oxford) MS. 20; Bonedd y Saint from N.L.W.
      MS. Peniarth 12
    Texts discussed
      Gospel-books; Honorius's Letter; Laws; Martyrologies; Muirchú's
      Life of St. Patrick; *Notitia Dignitatum*; *Periplus*; Ptolemy; The 'Tribal
      Hidage'; Welsh Poems

6 **Arthurian Sources, Vol. 6**, by John Morris
  Studies in Dark-Age History
    Celtic Saints—a Note; Pelagian Literature; Dark Age Dates; The Dates
    of the Celtic Saints; The Date of Saint Alban; Christianity in Britain,
    300-700—the Literary Evidence; Studies in the Early British Church—a
    Review; Gildas

7 **Gildas**, edited and translated by Michael Winterbottom
    The Ruin of Britain; Fragments of Lost Letters; Penitential or Monastic
    Rule

8 **Nennius**, edited and translated by John Morris
    'Select Documents on British History'; The Welsh Annals

9 **St. Patrick**, edited and translated by A.B.E. Hood
    Declaration; Letter to Coroticus; Sayings; Muirchú's Life of St. Patrick

ARTHURIAN SOURCES

Vol. 3
Persons:
Ecclesiastics and Laypeople

JOHN MORRIS

PHILLIMORE

1995

Published by
PHILLIMORE & CO. LTD.
Shopwyke Manor Barn, Chichester, Sussex

ISBN 0 85033 759 3

Printed and bound in Great Britain by
HARTNOLLS LTD.
Bodmin, Cornwall

CONTENTS

NOTES AND ABBREVIATIONS

After each name follows the date; when no year-date is known, an approximate generation is indicated: e.g., VI (the century) E(arly), or M(iddle), or L(ate). The day of the saint's death is given when known and acts as a reference to the lives printed in *Acta Sanctorum* (ASS) and other collections arranged by calendar-order.

The country of origin is shown, followed by the countries in which the saint worked, indicated by the letters:

A	Armorican (Breton)
B	British
C	Continental
E	English
I	Irish
P	Pictish
S	'Scot' (i.e., Gael) of Dal Riada in Britain

Thus 'Modwenna VII M/L ?6 July. E;I.E.P.' means that the most likely date is the mid- to late seventh century; that lives relevant to the saint are normally published under 6 July in ASS etc.; that she was English by origin, but is held to have worked in Ireland, and among the English and the Picts.

In the text of each entry, names printed with a bold capital, e.g. **F**elix, refer to another entry in **E** where the reference for the statement may be found; names are so marked only on their first mention in each entry. At the end of each entry is printed the reference to other entries where the ecclesiastic concerned is mentioned.

Numbered Lives
When more than one Life of a saint is extant, the Lives are numbered (1) etc. In the text of the entry italic figures refer to these Lives, roman figures to the chapters within them. Where chapter-figures alone are given, the reference is to the Life numbered (1). Thus, in the text, (2) means the second chapter of the first Life; (*2*) refers to the second Life; (*2*, 2) refers to the second chapter of the second Life.

Abbreviations

AA	See MGH.
AB	*Analecta Bollandiana*, Brussels, 1882-
AC	Annals of Clonmacnoise
ACm	*Annales Cambriae* (ed. E. Phillimore: see **G**; see also Rolls)
Ad.	Adomnán, Vita Columbae
Adam King	Forbes
Add.	*Additamenta*: see Tírechán.

vii

AG	Albert Le Grand, *Les Vies des Saints de la Bretagne Armorique*, 1636 (ed. 5, 1901)
AI	Annals of Inisfallen
Ant.	*Antiquity*, 1927-
Ant. Jl.	*Antiquaries Journal*, 1921-
Arch.	Archaeologia, 1770-
Arch.Camb.	*Archaeologia Cambrensis*, 1846-
Arch. Jl.	*Archaeological Journal*, 1844-
Arnold-Forster (F.)	*Studies in Church Dedications*, London, 1899, 3 vols.
ASC	Anglo-Saxon Chronicle: see Rolls, 2 vols.
ASH	J. Colgan, *Acta Sanctorum Hiberniae*, 1645
ASS	*Acta Sanctorum* (Bollandists), 1643-
AT	Annals of Tigernach
AU	Annals of Ulster
b.	born
BArm	*Book of Armagh*, ed. John Gwynn, Dublin, 1913 (diplomatic edition); *Patrician Documents*, ed. Edward Gwynn, Dublin, 1937 (facsimile)
BB, BBal	*Book of Ballymote*: facsimile, Dublin, 1887
BBC	*Black Book of Carmarthen*, ed. J.G. Evans, Pwllheli, 1906; facsimile, ed. J.G. Evans, Oxford, 1888
BBCS	*Bulletin of the Board of Celtic Studies*, 1921-93
Bethu Phátraic	(=*Tripartite Life*): ed. K. Mulchrone, Dublin, 1939; cf. CPL 26, p.36; cf. VT.
BFen	*Book of Fenagh* (1516), ed. W.M. Hennessy etc., Dublin, 1939
BHL	*Bibliotheca Hagiographica Latina*, Brussels, 1898-1901, Supplement, 1911 (Subsidia Hagiographica, 6; 12)
Birch CS	W. de G. Birch, *Cartularium Saxonicum*, London, 1885-93, 3 vols.
BLec	*Book of Lecan* (1399): cf. ZCP 12, 1918, 434; facsimile, Dublin, 1937
BLis	*Book of Lismore*: facsimile, Dublin, 1950; cf. Lismore.
Boniface	Letters: ed. M. Tangl, *Die Briefe des heiligen Bonifatius und Lullus*, 1916
Brev.Ab.	PE, PH (*Pars Estivalis, Hyemalis*) (1509-10), London, 1854
BRG	P. Jaffé, *Bibliotheca Rerum Germanicarum*, 1-6, Berlin, 1864-73
BT	*Book of Taliesin*, ed. J.G. Evans, Llanbedrog, 1910 (with facsimile)
Bury *Patrick*	J.B. Bury, *The Life of St Patrick*, London, 1905
ByS	*Bonedd y Saint*: VSB 320-3; see also **G**.
CA	*Canu Aneirin*, ed. Ifor Williams, Cardiff, 1938
Cart. Land.	Cartulary of Landevennec
Cart.Q.	Cartulary of Quimper
Cart.Ql.	Cartulary of Quimperlé
Cat.	*Catalogus Ordinum Sanctorum in Hybernia*: Sal.161.AB
Celt and Saxon	*Celt and Saxon*, ed. N.K. Chadwick, Cambridge, 1963 (rev. 1964)
CGH	*Corpus Genealogiarum Hiberniae*, Vol. 1, ed. M.A. O'Brien, Dublin, 1962 (rev. 1976), where 'LL' = Book of Leinster

Chron.	Chronicle, *Chronicon*
CIIC	*Corpus Inscriptionum Insularum Celticarum*, ed. R.A.S. Macalister, Dublin, 1945, 1949, 2 vols.
CIL	*Corpus Inscriptionum Latinarum* (Berlin)
CL	Caradoc of Llancarfan
CLH	*Canu Llywarch Hen*, ed. Ifor Williams, Cardiff, 1935 (rev. 1953)
Coll.	*Collectanea*: see Leland, Tírechán.
Cormac	Glossary (ed. and trans. J. O'Donovan and W. Stokes, 1868)
CPL	L. Bieler, *Codices Patriciani Latini*, Dublin, 1942
CPNS	W.J. Watson, *The History of the Celtic Place Names of Scotland*, Edinburgh, 1926
CPS	*Chronicles of the Picts and Scots*, ed. W.F. Skene, Edinburgh, 1867; cf. Lebor Bretnach.
CS	*Chronicum Scotorum*, ed. and trans. W.M. Hennessy, Rolls Series, 1866
CT	*Canu Taliesin*, ed. Ifor Williams, Cardiff, 1960
CWT	*Transactions of the Cumberland and Westmorland Antiquarian and Archaeological Society*, 1866-
David Camerarius	Forbes
DCB	*Dictionary of Christian Biography* (cf. numerous comparable works)
DEPN	E. Ekwall, *Dictionary of English Place Names*, Oxford, 1936 (ed. 4, 1960)
Doble	G.H. Doble, *Lives of the Cornish Saints*, pamphlet-series, fragmentarily reprinted in *The Saints of Cornwall*, Truro, 1960-70, 5 vols.
Drummond Calendar	Forbes
Duchesne (L.)	*Fastes épiscopaux de l'ancienne Gaule*, Paris, 1907-15, 3 vols.
Dumfries Trans.	*Transactions of the Dumfriesshire and Galloway Natural History and Antiquarian Society*, 1862-
ECMW	V.E. Nash-Williams, *The Early Christian Monuments of Wales*, Cardiff, 1950 (including all inscriptions of the fifth and sixth centuries found in Wales)
EHR	*English Historical Review*, 1886-
Ep.	Epistula, Letter
EPNS	Publications of the English Place Name Society (County Volumes)
Epp.	See MGH.
Ériu	Dublin, 1904-
FAB	*Four Ancient Books of Wales*, ed. and trans. W.F. Skene, Edinburgh, 1868, 2 vols.
fl.	*floruit*, flourished, lived
FM	Annals of the Four Masters: ed. and trans. J. O'Donovan, Dublin, 1856, 7 vols., ed. 2
Flodoard	*Chronicon* (ed. P. Lauer, Paris, 1905)
Forbes (A.P.)	*Kalendars of the Scottish Saints*, Edinburgh, 1872
FW	Florence of Worcester: see MHB.
Greg.Tur.	Gregory of Tours; see HF.
HA	*Historia Abbatum* (Bede; Anon[ymous])

HBS	Henry Bradshaw Society (London)
HE	Bede, *Historia Ecclesiastica Gentis Anglorum*
HF	Gregory of Tours, *Historia Francorum*: MGH SRM 1
HH	Henry of Huntingdon, *Historia Anglorum*: see Rolls.
Hogan (E.)	*Onomasticon Goedelicum*, Dublin, 1910
HS	A.W. Haddan and W. Stubbs, *Councils and Ecclesiastical Documents relating to Great Britain and Ireland*, Oxford, 1869-78, 3 vols.
HW	J.E. Lloyd, *A History of Wales*, London, 1912, 2 vols., ed. 2
Iolo MSS	Taliesin Williams (Iolo), Welsh Text Society, Liverpool, 1888; cf. MA.
Itin.	Itinerary: see Leland.
ITS	Irish Texts Society (London)
JThS	*Journal of Theological Studies*, 1899-
Kenney (J.F.)	*The Sources for the Early History of Ireland*, Vol. 1, *Ecclesiastical* (all published), New York, 1929 (rev. 1966)
Labbé	Concilia
LBS	S. Baring-Gould and J. Fisher, *Lives of the British Saints*, Cymmrodorion Society, 1907-13, 4 vols.
Leland	John Leland († 1552): *Collectanea*, Itinerary, *Scriptores Britannici*
Lebor Bretnach	See Todd, Irish Nennius.
Lebor Gabála	See ITS 34, 35, 39, 41, 45; 1938-56, ed. and trans. R.A.S. Macalister.
LH	*The Irish Liber Hymnorum*, ed. J.H. Bernard and R. Atkinson, London, 1898 (Henry Bradshaw Society 13, 14), replacing J.H. Todd, *The Book of Hymns of the Ancient Church of Ireland*, 1855, 1869
LHEB	K.H. Jackson, *Language and History in Early Britain*, Edinburgh, 1953
LIS	*Lives of the Irish Saints (Bethada Naem nÉrenn)*, ed. and trans. C. Plummer, Oxford, 1922, 2 vols. (rev. 1968)
Lismore	*Lives of Saints from the Book of Lismore*, ed. and trans. W. Stokes, Oxford, 1890
LL	*Liber Landavensis, The Book of Llan Dâv*, ed. J.G. Evans, Oxford, 1893, text replacing ed. and trans. W.J. Rees, Welsh Manuscript Society, 1840
M	Martyrology
MA	*The Myvyrian Archaiology of Wales*, Owen Jones (Myvyr), Edward Williams (Iolo Morgannwg), W.O. Pughe (Idrison) 1801; ed. 2, 1870
Mansi	*Concilia*
Mart.Ab.	Martyrology of Aberdeen: see Forbes.
M.Don.	Martyrology of Donegal
MGH	*Monumenta Germaniae Historica*
	AA *Auctores Antiquissimi*
	Epp. *Epistulae*
	PLAC *Poetae Latini Aevi Carolini*
	SRM *Scriptores Rerum Merovingicarum*
	SS *Scriptores* (in folio)

M.Gor.	Martyrology of Gorman: see HBS.
MHB	*Monumenta Historica Britannica*, ed. H. Petrie and J. Sharpe, vol. 1 (all published), London, 1848
MHH	C. Plummer, *Miscellanea Hagiographica Hibernica*, Brussels, 1925 (Subsidia Hagiographica, 15)
M.Oeng.	Martyrology (*Félire*) of Oengus: see HBS.
M.Tal.	Martyrology of Tallaght: see HBS.
Muirchú	*vita Patricii* (BArm), in VT and AB 1
NLA	C. Horstman, *Nova Legenda Anglie*, Oxford, 1901, 2 vols.
Notitia Britanniarum	*Periplus*: see **T**.
NSA	New Statistical Account (Scotland)
Num Chron	*Numismatic Chronicle*, 1838-
O'Curry (Eugene)	*Lectures on the MS Materials of Ancient Irish History*, Dublin, 1861, 2 vols.
O'Donnell (Manus)	Life of Colum Cille (Columba of Iona), 1532: ZCP, 3, 1901, 518-70 (ch. 1-64); 4, 1903, 276-330 (ch. 65-111); 5, 1905, 26-86 (ch. 112-56); 9, 1913, 242-86 (ch. 157-203); 11, 1916, 114-46 (ch. 233-61) incomplete; Latin translation of part, Colgan, vita quinta Columbae, TT, 389-446; Kenney, 442; MHH no. 27
O'Hanlon (J.)	*Lives of the Irish Saints*, Dublin, 1875-1904, 8 vols.
Passio Albani	BHL nos. 206-213, Passiones 1-4
PE	Pars Estivalis, Brev.Ab.
Pen.	Peniarth (MS)
PH	Pars Hyemalis, Brev.Ab.
PL	J.-P. Migne, *Patrologiæ (Latinæ) Cursus Completus*, Paris, 1844-64, 221 vols.
PLAC	See MGH.
PRIA	*Proceedings of the Royal Irish Academy*
Prosper of Aquitaine	MGH (AA)
RBH	*Red Book of Hergest*, ed. J.G. Evans
RC	*Revue celtique*, 1870-1934
RCHM	Royal Commission on Historical Monuments
Rolls	Rolls Series
Sal.	*Codex Salmanticensis* (of Salamanca), ed. C. de Smedt and J. de Backer, as *Acta Sanctorum Hiberniae*, 1887; replaced by W.W. Heist, *Vitae Sanctorum Hiberniae*, Brussels, 1965 (Subsidia Hagiographica, 28)
SB	*Commentarii de Scriptoribus Britannicis*, J. Leland, ed. A. Hall, Oxford, 1709, 2 vols.
SCSW	E.G. Bowen, *The Settlements of the Celtic Saints in Wales*, Cardiff, 1954 (ed. 2, 1956)
SD	Simeon of Durham: see Rolls, 2 vols.
SEBC	*Studies in the Early British Church*, ed. N.K. Chadwick, Cambridge, 1958
SEBH	*Studies in Early British History*, ed. N.K. Chadwick, Cambridge, 1954 (rev. 1959)
SG	*Silva Gadelica*, Standish O'Grady, London, vol. 1 (text), vol. 2 (translation), 1892
SRM	See MGH.
SS	See MGH.

T	Triad: see TYP.
Tig.	See AT.
Tir.	Tírechán: see VT.
Todd, Irish Nennius	*The Irish Version of the Historia Britonum of Nennius*, ed. and trans. J.H. Todd and A. Herbert, Dublin, 1848; cf. A.G. van Hamel, *Lebor Bretnach*, Dublin, 1932.
TT	J. Colgan, *Trias Thaumaturga* (Patrick, Brigit, Columba), 1647
TYP	Rachel Bromwich, *Trioedd Ynys Prydein*, Cardiff, 1961 (ed. 2, 1978)
Usuard	Martyrology
v.	*Vita* (Life of), (1) is 1st life, (2) is 2nd, etc.; (*1*, 3) is 3rd chapter, 1st life, (2, 3) is 3rd chapter, 2nd life.
VSB	*Vitae Sanctorum Britanniae et Genealogiae*, ed. and trans. A.W. Wade-Evans, Cardiff, 1944
VSH	*Vitae Sanctorum Hiberniae*, ed. C. Plummer, Oxford, 1910, 2 vols. (rev. 1968)
VT	*Vita Tripartita: The Tripartite Life of Patrick*, ed. and trans. W. Stokes, Rolls Series, 1887, 2 vols. (includes Muirchú, Tírechán, etc.); cf. Bethu Phátraic.
Wm	William
Wm M	William of Malmesbury: see Rolls.
Wm W	William (of) Worcester, Itineraries, ed. and trans. J.H. Harvey, Oxford, 1969
ZCP	*Zeitschrift für celtische Philologie*, 1896-

PERSONAL NAMES

In most languages the changing fashions of personal names often help to illustrate the probable date, social standing, locality of the persons who bear them. Usually the reasons behind these fashions escape detection, except when the first bearer of a name previously unknown or unusual becomes so popular that many children are named in his honour. The most familiar examples are those of modern English. The Old English elements Ed- and Os-, -ward and -bert, all remain common. The combinations Edward and Oswald remain frequent today; but Edbert or Osward, common in the Old English period, are virtually unknown in later ages. Edward and Oswald were perpetuated because the fame of notable kings prompted their subjects to give the same name to their children in successive ages. Numerous early kings called Edbert achieved a lesser fame, and none of the several royal princes named Osward became kings of major kingdoms, or achieved fame.

Similarly among the British, Cuno- (in its several meanings), Maglos, Tigernos are common. The combination Tigernomaglos is common, 'Maglotigernos' unknown, Cunomaglos (Cynfael) is relatively common, Maglocunos (Maelgwn) rare, Cunotigernos (Kentigern) unique among men, recorded two or three times for women (Cantiggerna); mentions of the same name in different texts refer to the same person, or to different people of the same name.

Similarly an individual may make an exceptional name widespread for a period. When in May 1820 the daughter of William Nightingale of Hampshire was born in Italy, he named her after the city in which she was born, Florence. Her life's work caught the imagination of the public and, from the 1860s onward, very many girls were named Florence after her. The fashion declined among well-to-do families before the end of the nineteenth century, but lasted several generations longer among poorer people, so that for a period about the 1920s a 'Flo' or a 'Flossie' became a synonym for a housemaid. By the 1960s, the name had become rare.

So among the British, the names Hywel, Alan, Griffith, not used before the eighth or ninth century, became common because they were borne by famous kings. Half a dozen princes were named Arthur in the sixth century, and the name then passed from use until revived in the twelfth century, after the French romances again made it popular. Irish genealogies and tales record about a score of persons named Foirtchernn, in all parts of Ireland; three quarters of them are datable, and all the datable ones belong to the sixth century, or its margins, beginning after the maturity of bishop Foirtchernn. After the seventh century, the name is recorded no more. Some Irish names are confined to particular districts; others are more common in some regions than others, others evenly distributed. Some last through for many centuries, some have defined common usage.

1

The frequency of a name in a particular place at a particular period is the most important indication of whether references to the same name in different texts refer to the same person, or to different people of the same name. The identity of even unusual names is by itself no more than a pointer: it becomes probable if time, place and the individual's standing agree, doubtful when they do not. Thus, among the British, the name Ceretic, in various spellings, is very common, and there are not good grounds for identifying one Ceretic with another, without supporting evidence. Patrick wrote a letter to a ruler named Coroticus, in the mid-fifth century. Several persons of this name are known at this date. Ceretic who interpreted between Vortigern and Hengest (Nennius 37) is not very likely, because there is no good reason to suppose that the interpreter ruled anybody, or that the name in Kent had any connection with Ireland. Cerdic of Wessex, probably a generation later, and, though a ruler, is far from Ireland. But Ceredig of Cardigan and Ceretic of the Clyde were both rulers geographically able to raid Ireland. On name, date, and place, the balance of probability inclines to the Clyde, because the captives taken were sold to the Picts as well as the Gaels, less likely for captives brought to central Wales, and because the earliest accounts of Patrick locate him in north-east Ireland, nearer to the Clyde. The matter is clinched by one reference (Muirchú, contents table) that names the ruler as Coirthech rex Aloo (of Alclud, the Clyde kingdom).

With a name as common as Ceredig, identification requires much supporting evidence. Rarer names carry stronger weight on their own. Only two groups of sources refer to a Hengest: the British and English accounts which know Hengest as the captain of the first English to land in Britain, and German sagas that describe Hengest the Dane, in the early fifth century or earlier. The name is otherwise unknown, and therefore by itself suggests strong probability that both were the same person. Archaeology and the names of peoples strengthen the probability. Hengest the Dane was the ally of Jutes living in Frisia. Hengest of Britain brought Jutes to Kent; and the earliest settlers brought many Frisian urns, and left their names in several places in England. The alliance with Jutes in Frisia carries a date. For the early cruciform brooches, peculiar to Jutes and Angles, are found in Frisia scarcely earlier than the beginning of the fifth century. The sagas make Hengest the Dane not later than the early fifth century, while the archaeology of his Jutish allies makes him not earlier than the early fifth century. It therefore seems extremely likely that the two men with the same unique name were both simultaneously military captains concerned with Jutes and Frisians, one on each side of the narrow seas.

So in the next century, Bridei son of Meilochon (Maelgwn) became king of the Picts about 557; Maelgwn king of Gwynedd died about 550. The succession to the Pictish throne passed through the women, and the fathers of Pictish kings were either Picts of note, or foreign princes, British, Irish or English. The name Maelgwn is uncommon, though not unique, and in theory there might have been several persons called Maelgwn alive in that generation. Pictish princesses were not married to unknown individuals, but to the sons of foreign kings or native notables. It is therefore extremely probable that the Pictish ancestress was mother or grandmother of Maelgwn the king, not an unknown private person; and one text gives Maelgwn a Pictish mother.

Frequency, time, place, position, activity concern the names of all peoples. Most other aspects of name-usage are peculiar to each separate people.

Roman Names

In the early Empire most Roman citizens used three names, C. Iulius Caesar, P. Cornelius Scipio, etc. The first two names are at all points equivalent to modern first name and family name, John Smith, Hugh Beaton, etc. The *praenomen*, Caius, Publius, was personal, normally written as an initial; the *nomen*, Iulius, Cornelius, passed from father to son and daughter. The third name, *cognomen*, came into use because the number of first and family names was too few for the population, inadequate to distinguish one man from another. Its function was equivalent to modern Welsh usage; Dai Jones Post, Dai Jones Baker, Dai Jones Squint, distinguish three people who have the same name; and the habit, once formed, prevails even when there is no risk of confusion. Mr Blenkinsop from Northumberland, the immigrant who manages the electricity sub-station, is liable to be known as Sam Tricity.

The Roman *cognomen*, however, became hereditary, and passed into the common stock of names, chosen indiscriminately at birth like first names. *Cognomina* formed from *nomina*, Iulianus, Cornelianus, denoted adoption under the consular republic. From the beginning of the Empire they originated from the name of a mother or grandmother (the emperor Vespasian was son of a Vespasia, Domitian of a Domitilla), but soon became ordinary names to be chosen at will, like Rufus, Secundus, Victor.

In the later Empire the three names are extremely rare outside the upper aristocracy. Two names, *nomen* and *cognomen*, remain common among the local aristocracies of the West. But in the early third century, all free-born inhabitants of the Roman world became citizens. New citizens normally took the first two names of the person to whom they owed citizenship, commonly the Emperor, so that in the early third century, the majority of the population acquired the names M. Aurelius from the emperor Caracalla. They ceased to be useful as names, distinguishing one person from another, and were dropped after a few generations. Romans reverted to the normal habit of one name for each person.

The single names were of three main forms: a name native to the province or region, Malchion in Syria, Theodorus in Greek, Bodicus in Britain, rare among the well-to-do, commoner among the poor, in the Western provinces; or an ordinary *cognomen*, Constans, Victor, Aurelianus; or a *signum*. The origin and behaviour of the *signum* is undetected. Sometimes father and son have different *signa*; sometimes rare *signa* are used by quite unrelated people. Sometimes it was an adjective given at birth: Ausonius's aunt was named Hilaria because she smiled prettily as a newborn baby. Sometimes it derives from a *cognomen* and inspires a *cognomen*: Constantius's name derived from Constans, and he named his son Constantius. Sometimes an Eastern provincial name, Ambrosius or Gregorius, became fashionable among well-born Latins, or Latin *signa* were formed from Greek adjectives, Gerontius from *geron*, old man. These *signa* are common to all social classes, but were most widespread among people who held public office, from private soldier to pretorian prefect or bishop, less usual among peasants.

Well-to-do Romans commonly used both one or more of the old family name and *cognomen*, and also a *signum*, usually in combination or in different contexts: C. Ceionius Rufus Volusianus was identical with Lampadius. Provincials might use both one or more Roman names and a native name. Later copyists not infrequently divided persons with more than one name into two or more people. One text of the Disputation of Archelaus and Manes, set in Syria in the third century, turns the governor (*rector*) of Syria, Claudius Cleobolus, into 'Claudius et Cleobolus rectores'; another manuscript emends to 'Claudius et Cleobolus rhetores'. One Welsh genealogy turns the emperor Octavianus Augustus into father and son, 'Octavianus genuit Augustum'. It is therefore likely that when successive Roman names of different type, *nomen*, *cognomen*, *signum*, appear as successive names in a genealogy concerning the fifth or an earlier century, they are the names of one person; Cinhil (Quintilius) son of Cluim (Clemens) is probably Quintilius Clemens, *nomen* and *cognomen*. Patricius is a *signum*. Patrick's father was Calpurnius (*nomen*), his grandfather Potitus (*cognomen*, an archaic name proper to the aristocratic Valerii of the fifth century B.C., revived in the first century A.D., and occasionally borrowed by plebeian families). The grandfather's full name was plainly Calpurnius Potitus, the father electing to use the *nomen* alone, for Calpurnii were clearly few enough in late fourth-century Britain for confusion between them to be rare. The use of such a name at such a date would be a strong indication that the man was of the social class of the local aristocracy of decurions, even if Patrick had not recorded that he was.

The nomenclature of the late fourth and fifth centuries was a welter of the debris of these different forms of names. Most persons of substance were legally entitled to the old two or three names, and most used one name, one of them, or a *signum*, or a native name, or an epithet, in common practice. The nomenclature of Britain is normal. In inscriptions Turpillius (ECMW 43, Crickhowell, Brecon) is a relatively rare Italic *nomen*, used alone; and used in a bilingual Latin-Irish inscription for the son of a British Dunocatus. Pompeius Carantorius (ECMW 198, Kenfig, Glamorgan) is a normal double name, *nomen* and native name used as *cognomen*, also bilingual. The ancestors of Coel Hen and Cunedda in the genealogies have ordinary *cognomina*, Gratus, Aeternus, Paternus. These men will also have had *nomina*, as will Agricola (Aircol), Marianus (Meriaun) and the like. Many will also have had *signa*; and men with *signa* will also have had two Roman names. Patricius was also Calpurnius Succetus, perhaps with Latin *cognomen* as well. Ambrosius the elder used *signum* alone, but Ambrosius Aurelianus used *signum* and *cognomen*. Vortigern will have had two Roman names; he was descended from Bonus of Gloucester, related to and perhaps identical with Vitalinus. Gildas's king Aurelius Conanus (Caninus) bore a *nomen* and native *cognomen*, comparable with Pompeius Carantorius. Occasionally a *praenomen* survives as in Marcus, *alio nomine Quonomorius* (Conomorus); some men used two Latin *cognomina*, Paulinus Marinus (ECMW 315), Paulus Aurelianus; sometimes a Continental and a British *cognomen* survive together, Talorius Adventus (ECMW 140), Similinus Tovisacus (ECMW 16), perhaps Lunarchus Coccus (ECMW 149), Doccus Cungarus (see **E** Docco). But from the sixth century, one name for each man, sometimes supplemented by an epithet, prevailed; the great majority of the names was native, but they included a few Latin names, Donatus (Dunawt), Ambrosius (Emrys), etc., which had become naturalised into Welsh.

Irish Names (MacNeill PRIA, 29 C, 1911-12, 59ff; *Ériu*, 3, 1907, 42ff., *cf.* 9, 1921-23, 55).
The normal pre-dynastic form is to give a man's father, and the people to which he belongs; *cf.* CIIC 244, *cf.* 245 Rockfield, Kerry 'Coillabrotas maqi Corbbi maqi mocoi Qerai'; 'Maqi-Ritte maqi Colabot maqi moco Qerai' ('son of the people of Kerry'), *cf.* CGH 374. LL 324 c 17, BB 144 c 14 variant, 'Caelboth M (R)itha (MS. Ditha, an unknown name probably corrupt) m . . . m . . . Cuirp', of the Hui Cuirc of the Muscraige, *cf.* 373. LL 324 b 31, Coelbath m (R)itha, father of Factna, *cf.* Fyachna, v. *Barri* 8 and bishop Mac Cuirp of Cork v. *Barri* 7ff. In the seventh century, in Muirchú and Adomnán, *maqi mucoi* is contracted to *moccu* translated *gente* by Adomnán (see further below).

Occasionally the people are personified in a supposed ancestor; the Dal Riadans are 'Korku Reti' Adomnán 1, 47, 'maccu Reti' in AU 677.

The dynastic form from the fifth century onward, is 'avi' in inscriptions, 'Huí' or

'Uí' (modern O) in the genealogies, regularly latinised by Adomnán and in the saints' lives as 'e nepotibus'; always followed by the name of the founder of the dynasty.

The eighth century produced a hybrid form: the kings of the Airgialla dynasty, whom the genealogists make descend from Colla Uais, become 'rex (rí) ua mac Uais'; 'nepotum filiorum Uais'; 'nepotum maccu Uais'; and 'Uais' is corrupted to 'Cuais' (summarised *Ériu*, 9, 55).

The name of the founder and of the father easily thereafter became confused. Ultán mac Huí Cunga (AT, FM, CS, *cf.* AC) become Ultán mac Caunga in AU 664. Confusion is especially frequent with common names: 'mac Uí Cairpri' easily becomes 'mac Cairpri', *cf.* **A** introduction.

Notable persons with frequent names are often distinguished by epithets, Niall Noígiallach, Niall Frossach; sometimes by their mothers' names, as Muirchertach mac Ercca; but these epithets do not become hereditary.

Of the fifty or so inscriptions which had *mucoi* (*gens*, Adomnán) followed by a recognisable name, most use the name of a *tuath*, and several use an eponymous ancestor Fer-Corp, Mac-Corp, Nia-Segamain, and the like, who also head the genealogies in CGH and elsewhere. Since many of the stones date from the fifth or sixth century, they are evidence that the tradition reproduced by the later genealogists was then already formed. *Mucoi* is discussed below.

Only one inscription appears to use *mucoi* with a historical name, CIIC 106, Deelish, Muskerry, Cork, *(Maqi muc)OI CORIBITI*, with which MacNeill compares the Dal Cairpri of Leinster; the Dal Cairpri (Músc) Loingsech of the Múscraige (Hogan 332) would perhaps be more relevant, Cairpre Músc being the eponym of the Múscraige. But both the restoration of *maqi mucoi* and the equation of the name with Cairpre are uncertain. CIIC 106, commemorating Coelbad mac Mac-Rithi, should be compared with two others, across the hills in Kerry (CIIC 243, 244), naming Mac-Rithi mac Coelbad, and Coelbad mac Corbb, both *maqi Mucoi Qerai* (Kerry). The Muscraige genealogies include a Coelbad mac Citha (perhaps Ritha, since the name Citha is not otherwise recorded), descendant of Corbb, and perhaps a Mac-Raith) CGH 373, LL 324 b 31, *cf.* 374. LL 324 c 29 [BLec., BB], apparently of the mid-sixth century, *cf.* v. *Barri* 8; CGH 371 LL 323 b 51). Elsewhere, the reading of CIIC 22, *MAQI MUC(oi) A(I)I(ni)* is very uncertain, and the restoration of the Isle of Man inscription (CIIC) 504, *MAQI MUCOI CUNAVA(li)* (=? Conaill), though more attractive, is conjectural.

Consciousness of name grew slowly. Tombstones are naturally precise, but early writers leave many names without suffix. Adomnán himself, very much a member of Uí Néill, uses them nearly always, much more often than Cogitosus, Muirchú or Tírechán. A twelfth-century genealogist (Book of Leinster 144 a 24 cited MacNeill, PRIA, 29 C, 93) complained that in his day genealogies were corrupted in six ways: by intrusion of unfree families (*daer-chland*), claiming to be free (*saerch-land*); by the migration of servile people; by the decay of princes (*tigerna*) and of free families (*saer-chland*); by the rise of tributary states; and, lastly, by falsification, either by the mistakes of the unlearned, or, as bad, by bribed scholars. The *filid* who compiled the pedigrees were not humble servants who would write what their patrons demanded, but an honoured independent corporation. However, they knew that their corporate interest lay with the ruling dynasties, and the long-established framework of their integrated pedigrees allowed only marginal freedom to a corrupt individual who was prepared to amend the received texts for personal gain.

Examples of early usage are:

COGITOSUS, v. *Brigit*, TT 518, ch. 1, p. 519, *de bona et prudentissima Etech*

(=Eochaid) prosapia. He names few persons by name, but offers no ancestry for those he does mention, Mac Caille, Brocessa, Conlaeth.

ADOMNÁN, *cf.* v. *Columbae passim*; Reeves, Anderson, indices; comment on Irish genealogies in my book *The Age of Arthur,* 143-9.

TÍRECHÁN: for example

Nepotes Neill	VT 311, 23
mons filiorum Aiellelo	VT 314, 18
but mons nepotum Aillelo	VT 131, 6
cf. nepotes Maine	VT 325, 4
but Ros filiorum Caitni	VT 327, 13
filii Amolgaid = sons	VT 309, 24; 310, 2
but filii Brioin = descendants	VT 219, 21
as also filii Heric	VT 319, 27

De genere Aillelo (VT 219, 12, 17; 321, 23) used for a bishop is natural ecclesiastical Latin. Most persons elsewhere assigned to ethnic origins are given no ancestry, but *cf.* Miliuc Maccu Boin, VT 311, 1.

MUIRCHÚ leaves most names with no ancestry, or at most a father's name, but has more *maccu* attributions, e.g. Dubthach maccu Lugil (VT 283 2), and his own name, maccu Machteni in VT 271, 18. Maccu Greccae (VT 286, 13); 'Muirchú II' has *nepotes Neill* (VT 298, 25; 299, 22) and *de genere Nothi* (VT 301, 3); *cf.* also *Colalnei fines* (VT 275, 22).

It is clear that seventh-century ancestry was still unfixed, apart from the almost universal 'nepotes Neill'.

Welsh names normally give the father's name only, with no dynastic or ethnic affiliation comparable with the Irish. Prominent persons with frequent names are also sometimes distinguished by epithets, which do not pass to their descendants. Often a territory is named from a real or supposed individual, as Reinwc, Seissyllwg, Dunoding, Glevissic; but the name normally applies to a geographical extent of land, not to a group of people.

English names also give the father's name only as the normal description, commonly with the termination -ing, in texts relating to the fifth or earlier centuries; 'Ecgfrith Osuing, Osuio Ethelfrithing' (OET 170, 79) gives the proper description of the Northumbrian kings Oswy and Ecgferth. The termination is used dynastically as in Ireland: the Aescingas, descendants of Aesc, the Uffingas, descendants of Uffa, are the dynasties of Kent and of the East Angles. The same termination is also used of peoples: the Haestingas of Hastings in Sussex; the Ecwingas of Montmartre in Paris are named from a people, the Eppings and Naesingas of Essex from the Upland and Ness in which they dwelt. Epithets were used but rarely.

The study of personal names has sometimes been confused by overstrained inferences from their linguistic origin. It is useful to know that Peter means a rock, Andrew a brave man, Gurci a man-dog; but not wise to suppose that people think of rocks, bravery or dogs when they encounter people so named. More serious confusion comes from attempts to allot divine attributes to persons named after divinities. The very many women called Brega, Brigit and the like bear the names of a Celtic divinity, Briga; but the name by itself no more confers divinity on its bearer than the name of Mary, as common among modern English women. The name of Beli was constructed from a corrupt passage in a late Roman historian, and many persons bore the name Kynfelyn (Cunobelinus). It is abundantly clear that no one associated Cunobelinus with Beli, and that no one recollected that Belinus had once been a deity honoured centuries before by Continental Celts.

Mythology-fantasy, fashionable in the early years of this century, perturbs straightforward texts. In a passage phrased throughout in enthusiastic school rhetoric (*cf. Arthurian Period Sources*, Vol. 9, *St Patrick*, 15ff), Muirchú describes how Patrick sent a convert named Mac Cuil to be bishop of the Isle of Man; before conversion he had been 'saevus tyrannus ut Cuclops', a 'fierce tyrant like a Cyclops'.

Muirchú's Classical learning inspired elaborate twentieth-century legends; Cuill is a frequent name-element, occasionally used by itself. But there is an Irish word 'goll' meaning one-eyed; and the cyclops was also a one-eyed tyrant. Patrick moreover calls Christ the 'true sun'. The bishop therefore becomes to one writer 'no mere man, but the one-eyed solar deity'. But, since the word 'coll' means hazel, another writer turns the bishop to an instance of tree-worship. To a third he and others are unquestionably to be identified 'with . . . gods . . . departmental divinities of a simple agricultural community'. The sequel ranges far. Patrick sent for him to the Isle of Man. Patrick also abolished pagan divinities, who are by definition demons; demons belong to hell; the 'Other world' is associated with the sea-god Manannán; the Isle of Man has the first three letters of his name; therefore when Patrick sent Mac Cuil to be bishop of Man, we are to understand an allegory of Patrick sending demons to hell. (References, T.F. O'Rahilly, *Early Irish History and Mythology*, Dublin, 1946, 471, 473, *cf.* note 4.)

This legend developed in the twentieth century. Muirchú's tale is itself dramatised by miracle and over-simplification; but it is pedestrian sobriety in comparison with the wonders conjured out of his single rhetorical Classical illusion, in modern times. This bizarre fashion matured at the end of the nineteenth century, and was heavily influenced by the impact of Fraser's *Golden Bough* and similar works. It was extended to a large number of historical personages and at its height served to bring the texts of early Welsh and Irish history into unnecessary disrepute, and to hinder their serious study. Although now happily on the wane, it still exerts an influence upon charitable readers who may easily suppose that these fancies rest on texts earlier than the nineteenth century. The impression tends to be conveyed by concealment: a Mac Cuill mac Cermata occurs as one of the Tuatha Dé Danann kings (Lebor Gabála 7, 22, ITS 4 [41] 233; *cf.* 7, 314, 316 [ITS 4 (41) 126, 130] whence the identification of the prehistoric Mac Cuill with hazel, 'coll'), but so do the familiar names Aed, Oengus, Cairpre, Brian; and there is not the slightest suggestion that Muirchú or anyone else connected Mac Cuill or any Aed or Oengus with names inserted into mythological Irish legend.

ECCLESIASTICS

(alphabetically listed)

AARON of Aleth (St. Malo) VI M. A;A. Maclovii. *LBS* 1, 103. Predecessor of Malo.

AARON of Caerleon III ? B?;B. *Gildas* 10. Martyr.

ABBAN of Moyarney, Co. Wexford (*S 72*) V L/VI E, Oct. 27, Mar. 16. I;I.B. *M BHL* l.s. *Vitae VSH* 1, 3 (1); *Sal.* 505 (2); *ASS* Oct. 12, 276 (3); *ASH* 610 (4); *AB* 77, 1959, 168 (5). v. *Molua*, 39. *Hist. Monast. de Abingdon* (Rolls) 1, 2-3 (Abennus) (7) *M.* including Whitford (1526), Mar. 16 (8). Nephew of Ibar, +499. Son of Cormac of Dal Mescorb (? Howth, Dublin, *0 23*) *k. Leinster* and Mella, sister of Ibar (3). Studied sacred and profane letters under Ibar from age of 12 (8-10). Sailed to Rome with Ibar (11-12) by way of Britain, where they converted a pagan king at *Abbaindun vel Dun Abbain* (13-14), the story was believed (7, 8) in mediaeval Abingdon (Abbandun, Aebbandun, *DEPN*) made two further visits to Rome (17), one with 150 clerics in three ships, on the third (prophesied by an angel) ordained by *Gregory the Great* and promised a lifetime of 310 years. Founded about 30 cells in Munster and north and south Leinster (22-34) *cf.* v. *Lugid* 39 (New Ross, Wexford, *S 72*), with one in Connacht (22) and three in Meath (27, 32). Baptised Finnian of Clonard (32; v. *Finnian* C2) (+551). Resisted ejection from Camross (*S 82*) by Cormac m. Diarmait (Lt Ui Bairrche), k. S. Lt. (33). Stopped a war (41). Visited by Columba of Iona (b. 521) and *Brendan of Clonfert* (+578) (?). Concluded fraternity with Berchan of Cluain Immurchuir in Ossory (undated) and they (i.e. their houses) formed fraternity with the houses of Brendan, Moling, Flannan, Fintan Munnu (37), all later foundations. He has numerous sea miracles; verses cited 'God has given thee power over the sea, as none before'; 'Abban's ship upon the waters, his fair family in it' (17). Govan, Lugid.

ACCA of Hexham (Nb.) (*NY 9364*) +c.740. E;E. *BHL* 25a s. Bede *HE passim, cf.* Plummer, xliv; Eddius, *passim*; S.D., etc. Pupil of Wilfred, succeeded him as bishop of Hexham, 709-31. Bede dedicated most of his works to him; his cross, bearing his name, is extant in Hexham Abbey.

ADAMNAN of Coldingham, Ber. (*NT 9066*) VII L. I;E. *BHL* 68a. Bede *HE* **4**, 25.

ADEL, *see* Aedil.

ADOMNÁN of Iona, Arg. (*NM 2723*) 628-704, Sept. 23. I;I. *BHL* 69. Reeves, *Adamnan's Columba*, 1847; Kenney, index; Bede *HE* **5**, 15, 21, *cf.* Plummer, especially 2, 301-03. Abbot of Iona 686-704. Principal northern Irish advocate of conformity with the Roman Easter; with Egbert, Aed of Sletty, Muirchú and others secured the adoption, in 697, of the *Cain Adomnain*, a code of war for the protection of non-combatants; visited Northumbria in 686, obtaining the release of 60 prisoners taken in the Northumbrian raid of 684 on Ireland; visited Ceolfrith at Wearmouth or Jarrow, where Bede was then a young monk, in 688. Wrote *de Locis Sanctis* soon after 670, *Vita Columbae c.*690, and perhaps also a *Commentary on Vergil* that bears his name, Kenney 286-7.

AE–, Ea–, *see* E–.

AEBBE of Coldingham, Ber. (*NT 9066*) VII M (+ after 681), Aug. 25. E;E. *BHL* 2359-60. *NLA* 1, 303. *ASS* Aug. 5, 196. Bede *HE* **4**, 19, 25. v. *Cuthberti* 10; v. *Cuthberti* (anon.) 13. Eddius 39. Uterine sister of Oswy (613-70), founded Coldingham and Ebchester on Derwent, named St. Abb's Head; friend of Cuthbert, interceded for Wilfred's release, 681.

AECCI, bishop of Domnoc (Dunwich),(*TM 4770*) VII L. E;E. Bede *HE* **4**, 5.

AED m. Bricc of Killare (and Slieve League, Don., *B 57*), West Meath (*N 24*), +589, Nov. 10. I;I. *BHL* 188-93. *ASS* Nov. 4, 495. *VSH* 1, 34 (1); *Sal*. 333 (2); *ASH* 418 (3). Kenney 393. Gen. (MS.), listed *VSH* xxvi, note 4; *ASH* 422, note 3, descent from Fiacha of Uisnech (*m. Neill*).

Of the seed of Conn (1, 1) (Ui Neill, 2, 1), his mother from Muskerry, Munster. As a child, met **B**rendan of Birr (+564) and **C**ainnech (516-603) (2). Brought up in Munster, without education, secular or profane. His brothers in Meath divided their father's inheritance, giving him no share, and to force them to yield, he abducted the daughter of a Meath magnate. On his way back to Munster, he came to the monastery of bishop **I**lland who rebuked him for seeking his earthly inheritance by force and offered a greater inheritance from his heavenly father; Aed yielded, returned the girl, entered the monastery (3). Founded Enach Midbren, probably Co. Tipperary (4); stopped a war between Munster and the (southern) Ui Neill (5); consecrated bishop in Meath, founded monasteries there and in Munster (6), visited nunneries (9, 11-12); restored decapitated victims of robbers (12); cured sterility of Mugain, wife of Diarmait m. Cearbaill (k. I 549-64), who then bore Aed Slane (k. I 601-7) (14); visited nuns of Ciaran of Clonmacnoise (+548) (15) and other nuns (16-17); peacefully halted an attack of king of Tethba on Meath (21); secured release of a man imprisoned for his brother's murder by the king of Meath (1, 23) (king *Neill* [? king of Ui Neill] in Connacht, 2, 31); secured release of woman enslaved by king Baithen (unidentified) (25); and of numerous slaves and prisoners who desired to enter monasteries (27-28). Prevented Ui Neill forces from raiding Munster (2, 42). Visited *Rioch* at Inch Bofin, Lough Ree (Westmeath, *N 05*), Henanus (Enoc 2, 45) of Drum Raith (Westmeath) (32), **M**oLaisse of Devenish (Ferm., *H 24*) (+564) (33). He obtained his Gospels from **B**rigit (+524) of Kildare (2, 21). Visited by **B**ec m. De (+554). Released a man of substance kidnapped by Gauls (pirates 1, 34 n.) on the coast of Meath (2; 34). His other principal church was at Slieve League (*G 57*) near Carrick, Donegal Bay, Kenney, 393. *See* **L**asrian of Devenish, **R**ioch, **R**uadan.

AED of Sletty (Co. Leix) (*S 77*) +700, Feb. 7. *M. Don., M. Tal.* I;I. Handed over his family and his church to Patrick, to bishop **S**egenus of Armagh (662-88) (Tírechán *Add.* 16). Urged **M**uirchú to write the life of **P**atrick, Muirchú, Preface. Present at Synod of Birr, 697, which probably decided for the Roman Easter, and which adopted the *Cain Adomnain* (ed. K. Meyer, Oxford, 1905). He perhaps wrote Fiacc's Hymn, MacNeill, *PRIA* 37, 1926, C 123; JRSAI 48, 1928, 18 = St. Patrick 115-18. Kenney, index. **A**domnán; **C**ogitosus.

AED, *see* Mac Cairthenn.

AEDAN of Ferns, *see* Maedoc.

AEDAN of Lindisfarne, Nb. (*NU 1242*) +651. I;E. *BHL* 190-92. Bede *HE* **3**, 3-6, 14-17. Of Kilmore in Memat Tir in Airgialla (near Tehallen, *H 73*, by Monaghan) *M. Oeng.* Monk of Iona, sent, probably as second bishop (Bede knew a report [*fertur*] that the first, unnamed bishop, quickly returned to Iona without success) to the Northumbrians, soon after the accession of **O**swald, who had been converted in exile by the Irish. He was abbot of the Columban house of Lindisfarne (Holy Island, north of Bamburgh), bishop of the Northumbrians, without a fixed urban see. Bede emphasises the single-minded simplicity of his life. Symeon of Durham's *Historia Dunelmensis Ecclesiae* preface dates the foundation of Lindisfarne, presumably under its first bishop, to 635. Died 651, Bede *HE* **5**, 24; *cf.* **3**, 14 (Oswy's ninth year beginning Aug. 5, 650). Colman m. Lenini.

AEDILBERG Tata VII E. E;E. Bede *HE* **2**, 9, 11, 20. Daughter of Ethelbert of Kent (+616), wife of Edwin of Northumbria (+633), returned to Kent on her husband's death and founded Lyminge (*TR 1640*) on the site of a Roman villa, then a royal vill (Thomas of Elmham, *Hist. Monast. St. Aug. Cant.* [Rolls 176]).

AEDILBERG of Farmoutiers VII M, Oct. 11. E;Gaul. Bede *HE* **3**, 8. *NLA* 1, 424, etc. Illegitimate daughter of Anna, k.E.Angles (+654), abbess of Farmoutiers-en-Brie, sister of Saethnyd, also abbess of Farmoutiers, and of **A**edilthryd and **S**exburgh.

AEDILBURGA of Barking, Ess. (*TQ 4483*) VII L, Oct. 11. *BHL* 2631. *ASS* Oct. 5, 649. *NLA* 1, 419. Bede *HE* **4**, 6-9. Sister of Erconwald, bishop of London *c.*674-*c.*693; *NLA* makes her daughter of Offa of Lindsey. Founded Barking, when her brother founded Chertsey. **H**ildelid.

AEDILTHRYD of Ely (*TL 5380*) +679, June 23. E;E. *BHL* 2632-2640. *ASS* June 4, 491 (5,419). Bede *HE* **4**, 3, 19. Daughter of Anna, k.E.Angles (+654), wife of Tonbert, k. Gyrwas (650-53) and Egfrid, k. Northumbria 670-85, retained her virginity, entered Coldingham, abbess of Ely (672-79).

AEDILUALD, bishop of Lindisfarne, *c.*721-40. *Cont. Bedae*, etc., *cf.* Plummer *Bede* 2, 297. Ordered the binding of the Lindisfarne Gospels by Billfrith, fo. 259 r, *cf.* prayer, fo. 89 v., both added *c.*883/970. His most celebrated craftsman was **U**ltan.

AEDILUINI of Lindsey +*c.*700? E.I;E. Bede *HE* **3**, 27; **4**, 12. Studied in Ireland at Rathmaelsighe, monastery of Colman (*M. Don.* Dec. 14), in 664 with his brother Edilhun, who died there of the plague, Egbert and others. Bishop of Lindsey for a long time, probably from 679.

AETHELRED k. Mercia 675-704, abdicated, abbot of Bardney, Lincs.

AGILBERT of Wessex VII M, Oct. 11. Gaul;I.E.Gaul. Bede *HE* **3**,7, 25-26, 28; **4**, 1, 12; **5**, 19. Eddius, 9, 10. A Gaul, consecrated bishop, probably in Gaul, studied for a considerable time in Ireland, came to Essex, appointed bishop at Dorchester 649-60, withdrew when king Coenwalh divided the diocese and appointed Wine to Winchester. Came to Northumbria, present at Whitby, 664, briefing Wilfred, returned to Gaul, ordained Wilfred at Compiègne. Theodore stayed with him on his way to Britain, 668. Bishop of Paris, 667/8-680 or later (Duchesne, *Fastes*, 2, 472-3).

AGRICOLA V E. B;B. Bishop in Britain, shortly before 429. Son of Severianus, 'revived' Pelagianism, Prosper *Chron.* 429.

AID, AIDAN, *see* AED, AEDAN.

AILBE of Emly, Tip. (*R 73*) +528, Sept. 12. I;I. *BHL* 197-9s. *VSH* 1, 46 (1); *Sal.* 235 (2). *ASS* Feb. 1, 114; Sept. 4, 27 = *TT* 200, 604. *LBS* 1, 128. *AB* 50, 1932, 142. v. *Brendan* I, 28, 31, 54; II, 23, 28, 31; *Ciaran Saigir* 7; *David* 7; *Declan* 9, 12, 14, 18, 20, 21, 34; *Columba Terryglass* 24; *Colman Dromore* 4.

   Bishop (archbishop, v. *Declan* 34), 'second patron of Ireland', after Patrick (1). Son of Cronan k. of Atrigi (? Araid Cliach, in north of Co. Limerick) and a slave girl, exposed, brought up by a wolf, rescued and brought up by certain Britons in Airther Cliach, north-east Limerick (1). Baptised by a priest sent from Rome to

Ireland *long before Patrick* (2). Went to Britain with his teachers (3), thence to study under Hilary, 'bishop in Rome' (pope 461-8), who sent him 'to the pope' (called Clemens 2, 14, 16, 17) for consecration (8-15). In Rome with Declan and Colman m. Darine of Faire Mor (VI E/M) (13) with *Patrick* *VT* 198 and *12 Finians, 12 Colmans, 12 Coemgens* and Ciaran of Saigir and Ibar (v. *Declan* 12, 18) and Enda. On his way home, established the sons of Guill (*cf*. MacCuil, MacCreiche), in a monastery among pagans (16), visited *Samson at Dol* (17), baptised David (v. *David*), took him as pupil (19). Established Colman at Killroot (Antrim, *J 48*) (20). Visited Brigit (26) (2, 23-4), miraculously aided Fintan Find, *king* of Dal Araide, to defeat Connacht (21). Going to Cashel *to meet Patrick*, took precedence over Ibar, appointed *arch*bishop of Munster by king Angus, persuaded him to grant Aran to Enda (V L/VI E). His pupil Cianan (of Duleek? +491), bishop (2, 32) established Sinchell Camm at Clonduff (co. Kildare? Plummer) (28). Cianan helped him establish his see at Emly, Imlech Ybuir (*cf*. Ibar) (29). Visited virgins in Limerick, sent one of them a scribe to write a gospel. Visited Connacht (35, 36), established his pupil MacCriche (2, 37) with whom he visited Aran and Ossory, where he was granted a site by king Scanlan (early VII) (38). Sent envoys to Rome (37) to fetch a new missal (2, 45). Prevented by King Angus from sailing to Thule (41); imported a vine from foreign sailors at Corcomroe (Co. Clare, *M 20*, Galway Bay) (46). His familia stayed 80 years on the ocean island Favoria Albei (v. *Brendan*). Declan of the Dessi recognised him as superior *arch*bishop (v. *Declan*). Decided to sail to '*insula Tile*' (Iceland?) but was prevented by king Angus of Munster, who put guards on all the sea ports. He succeeded in sending 22 men 'into exile overseas' (41).It is possible that some of the ocean exploration tradition of Ailbe of Emly derives from a lost Life of Ailbe of Shancoe; but no tradition connects these voyages, or the Emly Ailbe, with Sligo.

Colman of Dromore, Colman of Munster, Cuimine, Flannan, Govan, Kebi, Samson.

AILBE m. Ronan VI L, Jan. 30. I;S. Of the Ui Neill. *M*. Supposed to be a monk of Iona, *TT* 501.

AILBE of Shancoe, Sligo (*G 61*) +542, Dec. 30? Of the Ui Aillella, *Annals* (Tig.). *Priest of Patrick* *VT* 94; Tírechán *Add. VT* 305, 348, *cf*. *M. Gor*. Dec. 30. Otherwise unknown.

AILLEL (AILILL) (I), bishop of Armagh, 512-521, Jan. 23. I;I. *M. Book of Leinster*, 42ᶜ (sedit xiii, for ix); of the Dal Fiatach (Ulaid).

AILLEL (AILILL) (II), bishop of Armagh, 521-534, July 1. I;I. *M. Don. Book of Leinster*, 42ᶜ (sedit x, for xiii) (of Cluain Ewan *M. Tal*. by confusion with *Damtia Cluain Euant* *M.Gor*.).

ALBAN of Verulamium +208, June 22.B?;B. *BHL* 206-17s, especially 2a, *Abh. Ges. Wiss. Gottingen, Ph. H. Kl., NF* viii, 1, 1904, 35, Turin and Paris MSS., giving the date, Severus (and Caracalla), with (Geta) Caesar in independent charge of the province of Britain. See also below, vol. 6, pp. 145-53.

Germanus of Auxerre.

ALBEUS, *see* Ailbe.

ALBINUS of Angers +*c*.560, Mar. 1. Gaul;Gaul.A. *BHL* 234-7. *AG* 38. *MGH AA* 4, 2, 27 (Fortunatus, contemporary) (1). Accompanied Tudwal (and other Breton saints) to Paris to protest against Conomorus. Paternus.

ALBINUS of Canterbury VII L. Italy;E. Bede *HE* pref.; **1**, 3; **5**, 20. Pupil of archbishop Theodore, succeeded Hadrian as abbot of SS. Peter and Paul, Canterbury, encouraged Bede to write *HE*.

ALCUIN of York *c*.730-804, May 19. E;E.Gaul. *BHL* 342, *cf*. Kenney 534. Head of the School of York, 766-782, where his pupils included Irishmen, e.g. Colcu (of Clonmacnoise ?) and Joseph, as well as English; his library catalogued, *Versus de Sanctis*, 1535 ff. Head of the Palace School of Aachen 782-796; abbot of Tours 796-804, succeeded at Aachen by the Irish Clement, *cf*. Dungal and Dicuil. His works, Migne *PL* 100-101; *MGH* Epp. 4; *SRM* 3, 414; 4, 381; 7, 81; 138; 819; etc. PLAC, 160 ff. *BRG* 6 (Jaffé, *Monumenta Alcuiniana*) etc.

ALDHELM of Sherborne 639-709, May 25. E;E. *BHL* 256-9. Bede *HE* **5**, 18. Pupil of Maeldubh of Malmesbury and Hadrian of Canterbury, abbot of Malmesbury, bishop of Sherborne 705-9 on the division of the Winchester diocese. Scholar, theologian, poet, works *MGH AA* Migne *PL* 89 *cf*. Plummer, *Bede* 2, 309-14, etc.

Cellan, **H**eadde, **H**ildilid, **L**eutherius, **P**echthelm, **V**irgilius Maro.

AMANDUS of Utrecht +679, Feb. 6. Gaul;Gaul. *BHL* 332-348. *MGH SRM* 5, 395 ff.; 7, 179 ff. Aquitanian, one of the first and foremost converts of Irish monasticism in Gaul.

AMATOR of Auxerre +418, May 1. Gaul;Gaul. *BHL* 356. Pupil of **M**artin of Tours, Sul. Sev. *Dial*. 3, 1, 4. Bishop of Auxerre, *BHL*, *cf*. Duchesne *Fastes* 2, 244-5. Amatorex, bishop (near) Auxerre, ordained **P**atrick, (Muirchú and derivate sources, who frequently write 'Amatho Rex').

AMBROSIUS of Milan 374-397, Dec. 7, Apr. 4. Italy;Italy. *BHL* 377-381. *DCB*. Principal author of the independence of the Latin church, and of the Latin hymn.

ANGUS, *see* MacNissi.

ARMAHEL, *see* Tigernmaglus.

ARTHMAEL of Ploermel VI M, Aug. 16. B;A. *BHL* 678-9. *ASS* Aug. 3, 298. *AG* 522. *LBS* 1, 170. Son of a noble of Pennychen (Glevissig), schooled 'en pension au Monastère d'un saint Personnage de ce Pays, qui faisait école à nombre de jeunes enfants de maison' (Illtud's or a similar school) (1). After leaving school, took orders; later, after discussion with *Caroncinalis* (*cf*. v. *Cadoci*) abbot of the monastery where he had studied, and near relative of **P**aul Aurelian, decided to abandon his property and emigrate, attracting a number of young men as followers. Founded Plouarzel in Leon; when Conomorus killed Jonas of Domnonie and raided Leon, he withdrew with Judwal of Domnonie (and **S**amson and others to Childebert in Paris) (2). On his return, settled at St. Armel, near Rennes (3-4). The places that he named are more widespread than those of any other Armorican saint, and include more district centres.

ASAPH of Llanasa, near Prestatyn, Flint (*SJ 2472*) VI L? May 1. B;B. *BHL* 721; v. *Kentigerni* 25; 31. Named Llanasa, and a few nearby topographical features in Tegeingl (Flint). *LBS* 1, 182. The *Martyrology of Usuard* of Paris (+876/7) enters (May 1) 'In Scotia S. Asaphi episcopi, de cuius nomine nunc vocatur episcopatus S. Asaph'. The see was presumably created after Offa's conquest of Tegeingl, *c*.795; it is doubtful whether the conquest or the see extended across the river Clwyd to include Llanelwy, *cf*. Lloyd, *HW* 242, *cf*. 201, and doubtful if Offa's see survived the Scandinavian invasions. The seat of the bishop will have been Llanasa.

A Welsh see was established at Llanelwy (*SJ 0374*) before the twelfth century; 'Bedwd vero noster (sc. ep. Meneviensis) ordinavit Melanum Lanelvensem', Giraldus 3, 56 = *HS* 349, letter of Bernard of St. David's to Pope Eugenius III, 1145. The date is wholly uncertain, since the claims advanced use real names with wrong dates (e.g. Joseph of St. David's [+1061] is made to consecrate Morgleis of Bangor [+945]). The continuing history of the see begins with the consecration of 'Gilbertus Lanelvensis Ecclesiae' at Lambeth in 1143 (*HS* 347), and it has ever since retained the two names 'Cathedralis ecclesia a nostratibus Lan Elguensis, ab Anglis Assaphensis dicta, inter Cluydam et Elgium Fluvios', Humphrey Lhuyd, 1572, cited *LBS* 1, 181, in modern Welsh Llanelwy, in modern English St. Asaph.

In both Welsh and Scottish tradition, from the twelfth century onward, Kentigern of Glasgow is made the founder of Llanelwy, Asaph his pupil and successor; the tradition might be regarded as a wholly twelfth-century invention, were it not for the ninth-century record of Usuard, who records the festival of the bishop of St. Asaph as celebrated in 'Scotia', where a possible dedication exists in Skye (Forbes 271); if the entry is in fact the work of Usuard, and not an addition by his renaissance editor Molanus.

If the words are Usuard's, they are among the earliest instances of the extension of the term 'Scotia' to western Scotland; in native ninth-century usage, 'Scotia' could not include Glasgow or the Clyde, but a monk of Paris might have had a vaguer idea of geography. The likely explanation of Usuard's entry is that he combined two separate pieces of information; that the see of Asaph was on the river Clyde; and that the river Clyde lay in or by the territory of the Scots, without knowing that there were two rivers of that name. The source of the information is likely to have been a Life of Kentigern, containing a story that on his expulsion from Glasgow, Kentigern spent some time in north Wales, founding a monastery in which he installed Asaph, perhaps a companion who came with him from the north. The monastery is likely to have been Llanasa rather than Llanelwy, but the Life will have mentioned the Glasgow Clyde. Usuard accords the rank of bishop to Asaph, because in his day Llanasa was a bishop's name.

Whatever the explanation, it is evident that Asaph was a relatively minor saint, who left virtually no tradition, locally or elsewhere, whose name acquired prominence only when his monastery became a bishop's seat after Offa's conquests.

ATTRACTA of Killaraght, Sligo (*M 79*) VII L, Feb. 9 (Aug. 11). I;I. *BHL* 7986. *ASH* 278. *Veiled by Patrick* (1). Helped king Bec of the Lugni to expel a dragon beast (8); helped Lugni hostages to escape from the king of Connacht (11); successfully resisted the attempts of king Cennfaelad of Connacht (664-80) to conscript clerical labour to build a royal fort (13-14). With her help, the Lugni, 'feroces ac saevi bellatores', alone in Connacht rejected the authority of *Hualgarg* of the Ui Brefni (? Amalgaid m. Cennfaelad). Many unidentifiable persons and places are named. *Assessor* of Bercgus (v. *Ber.* 19) of Kilbarry, Rosc. *N 08* in a land dispute, together with Samthanna of the Tethba (VIII E). These later abbesses are presumably imported into Bercgus' lawsuit because Kilbarry is less than 20 miles from Killaraght, two miles from the Shannon border of Tethba, and their houses had interest in the territorial rights asserted.

AUDOENUS, *see* Ouen.

AUDOMARUS, *see* Omer.

AUGURIUS (Augulius) bp. London 361, Feb. 7. B?;B. Some two dozen martyrologies name, under Feb. 7, 'In Britaniis in civitate Augusta natalitas beati Auguli

episcopi et martyris'; listed *HS* 1, 27 ff., *ASH* 275, *cf. LBS* 1, 189 and *M. Gor.* Bede
reads 'Augusti' and three or four others 'Auguri', one 'Augulini'. Genebrardus and
Horolanus (*ASH* 275) read 'Auguri episcopi Hiberniae sub Valentiniano anno 361'.
None of the main Irish martyrologies know him as Irish.

No martyrology shows knowledge that Augusta was London. The title Augusta
for London is known only from Ammian, a contemporary record; it was not
bestowed before the early-, or probably mid-, fourth century, and nothing suggests
that it remained in use later than the mid-fifth, if so late. The origin of the notice
is therefore near contemporary. So also, therefore, is the exact date; but Julian, not
Valentinian, ruled Britain in 361; there were no martyrs under Valentinian, and
no tradition that could lead a commentator to place a martyrdom under him; the
name is evidently a gloss, a bad guess for the emperor in 361. Augurius might have
been martyred under Julian, more probably in an anti-Christian riot than by
deliberate government action. But it is as likely, perhaps more so, that he was one
of the 15 bishops exiled by Constantius after Rimini (359), and died before restoration; death in exile was sufficient qualification for the title of martyr. The majority
of texts read Augulius, an unknown and improbable name; Augurius is probably
the better reading.

AUGUSTINE of Canterbury +604, May 26. C;E. *BHL* 777-784. Bede *HE* **1**,
23-33; **2**, 1-7; **5**, 24. Sent by Pope Gregory the Great with other monks to convert
the English; landed in Thanet 597, converted Ethelbert and Kent.

AUGUSTINE of Hippo (North Africa) 354-430, Aug. 28. C;C. *BHL* 785-801.
DCB. Architect of Latin theology; the principal opponent of his central dogma of
original sin was **P**elagius.
Sicilian Briton.

AUSTOLUS (of St. Austell and St. Mewen) VI M/L, June 28. B;A. *LBS* 1, 189.
v. *Mevenni* 19-20, disciple and successor of Meven, who accompanied Samson to
Brittany, died a week after Meven (perhaps stated because his day is a week later).
Meven is patron of Mevagissey (*SX 0144*), adjoining St. Austell (*SX 0152*) as does
St. Mewen (*SW 9951*). It is therefore probable that Austolus names St. Austell,
adjoining Tywardreath (Castle Dore), where Samson stayed and named a chapel,
at the royal residence of Conomorus, before sailing to Brittany.

BACHAN VI E. B?;Italy.B. Teacher of **C**adoc, in Brecheniauc, 'nuper de Italia
adven(it)', v. *Cadoci* 11. He might be a Briton who had studied abroad, or a
foreigner.

BAEDA, *see* Bede.

BAETAN, *see* Baitan.

BAITAN of Iona, Arg. (*NM 2723*) 537-c.601, June 9. I;S. *BHL* 896. Sal. 871.
Adomnán, v. *Col. passim.* 'qui et Conin', *Cainnech* 21-22; *Lasren* 32; *Fintan Munnu* 5,
7; *Ruadan* 29, etc. First cousin, disciple, and successor of **C**olumba of Iona. His sites,
O'Hanlon 605. Died, aged 66, *Annals.* **A**ed m. Bricc.

BAITAN VII M. I;I. Bishop addressed by Pope John, 640, Bede *HE* **2**, 19;
neither Baetan abbot of Clonmacnoise +664, nor Baetan abbot of Bangor +667,
were yet abbots, and neither is called bishop. No abbot or bishop named Baetan is
known to have been in office in 640, and he therefore remains unidentifiable.

BAITHENUS, *see* Baitan.

BARRFIND of Drumcullen, Off. (*N 10*) and Kilbarron, Don. (*G 64*) VI M/L, May 21. I;I. *M.*; Barrind, *M. Oeng.* notes etc.; therefore probably identical with Barrinthus, v. I *Brendani Clonfert* 13 (Barrus, v. II *Br. Cl.* 3), who accompanied Ternoc on a voyage to the Land of Promise and told his experiences to Brendan. Sometimes confused with Findbarr of Cork; either he or Findbarr is probably Barrideus, last-named of the abbots of the second order, *Cat.* 2. Barrindus, companion of Columba in the Lough Earn region, O'Donnell, v. quinta *Columbae* 1, 91 (*TT* 404); of the Ui Neill, Cenel Conaill Gulban, *M*; *O'Donnell*; cognatus Columbae, *O'Donnell*.

BARRINDUS, Barrinthus, *see* Barrfind.

BARRUC, *see* Findbar.

BARRUS, *see* Findbar.

BEC MAC DE (Son of God, Son of the Faith) 554, Oct. 12 (*M. Gor., cf. M. Don.*). I;I. Of Dal Cais, Munster, *M., cf. CGH* 235 R 152 a 56. Propheta v. *Aed* 19; *Brendan* I, 2. Propheta regis, mendax magus v. *Lasrian Dev.* 28. Defended king Diarmait m. Cerbaill against Ruadan, *Lebor Breac* 260, 2, 12, cited O'Hanlon 10, 209; warned Diarmait against his assassin, Aed Dubh, text printed Reeves, *Adamnan* 67. His verses on the battle of Ocha, *FM* 478. 'He prophesied that lords would loose their chiefries and seignories, and that men of Little Estate would loose their lands.' *AC* 550 (p. 83), *cf. M.Oeng.* Aug. 29. He was evidently a druid who accepted Christianity. Aed m. Bricc.

BEDE of Jarrow, Dur. (*NZ 3265*) 672-735, May 29 (26). E;E. *BHL* 1067-1076 *Works*, ed. Giles, 12 vols., 1843-4; *Opera Historica*, ed. Plummer, Oxford, 1896; his life summarised Plummer 1, ix ff. Born in the territory of Jarrow, entered the monastery at the age of seven under Benedict Biscop and Ceolfrid, ordained deacon at 18, priest at 29, by John of Beverley. Taught, wrote works on grammar, mathematics, natural history, theology; saints' lives, letters, hymns; published the *de Tempore Rationum*, with appended *Chronicle*, in 725, the *Historia Ecclesiastica Gentis Anglorum* in 731. The *Historia* is extant in over 130 MSS., four of them eighth-century, two of them probably copied in his lifetime. Much of his work concerned Easter dates.

BELA (Beli?) of Bretona, Spain 675. Bela Britaniensis ecclesiae episcopus, at the fourth Council of Braga, *Labb.* 6, 567, cited *HS* 2,100.

BENEDICT BISCOP, Baducing 627?-690 (689?), Jan. 12. E;E. *BHL* 1101. Bede *HE* **4**, 8; **5**, 19, 21, 24. *HA* 1-16, 20, 22; Anon. *HA* 5-13, 15-18, 20, etc. Thane of Oswy, founded Wearmouth, 674, and Jarrow, 681. Visited Gaul and Italy six times, studied at Lerins, brought back books, masons, and relics. Composed a monastic rule after comparative study of those of 17 other monasteries. *See also* Eosterwine, John the Archcantor, Theodore, etc.

BENEDICT of Nursia and Monte Cassino 542, Mar. 21. Italian;Italy. *BHL* 1102 ff. *DCB*. Hermit, founder of Monte Cassino, gave his name to the Benedictine rule and order.

BENIGNUS (Bineus) of Armagh 468, Nov. 1 (9). I;I. Pupil and successor of Patrick, *Muirchú* 27, *cf.* 19; equated by William of Malmesbury, *Ant. G.*, with Beo(a)n of Feringmere near Glastonbury (VI/VII?), translated 1091, *NLA.* Mocteus.

BERACHUS of Kilbarry, Rosc. (*N 08*) VI L/VII E, Feb. 15. I;I. *BHL* 1168. *VSH* 1, 75. Pupil of **D**agaeus (+586?) (v. *Dagaei* 10) and **C**oemgen (+618) (6); cured Coemgen's pupil Faolan (+667*?) son of Colman, k. Lt. (south) (+578) (9). Acquired Kilberry from a 'minister', 'ex miraculo', and was prosecuted by a royal magus, who claimed ownership by 'ius hereditarium'. The case was referred to **A**edan m. Gabran, k. Dal Riada (574-609), who passed it to Aed Dubh of Brefni and Aedh of Tethba (+590). The magus was struck dumb, fled, and later killed; an attempt by his heirs to fire the monastery was miraculously thwarted. Berachus' assessors were a Finnian and the later saints, *Ultan*, *Samthanna*, *Attracta* (19). He was granted a fort, for use as a monastery, by Aedan, at Aberfoyle (*NN 5202*), by the Trossachs (Plummer, *Irish Lives*, Bethada Naem nErenn, 1, 35; 2, 327; cited Watson, *CPNS* 225), commanding the northern road from Loch Lomond and Dal Riada to the upper Forth, the only route by which Dal Riada armies could reach the southern Picts without violating British, Alclud, territory; and until recently the October market at Aberfoyle was known as *Feill Barachan*, Berachus' Fair (Watson, *CPNS* 225). The site was of great strategic importance to the Dal Riada kings; its grant suggests that both Aedan and Columba took kindly to Berachus. He may or may not be identical with Berachus who escaped a whale on a voyage from Iona to Tiree, *Adomnán* 1, 19. **D**agaeus, **R**onan.

BERNACUS (Brynach) VI M/L, Apr. 7. B?;A.B. *BHL* 1186-7. *VSB* 2 ff. *LBS* 1, 321. Nobly-born, visited Rome, killed a dragon. Returned through Armorica to Milford (Haven) in Dyfed, withstood attempted seduction, founded many churches, in old age withdrew to Cornovia. Resisted the demand of Maelgwn (+*c.*550) for food supplies, secured from him a grant of immunity 'ab omnia regia exactione in perpetuum', and the land of the monk Thelych. He has numerous churches in Demetia, one each in Carmarthen, Brecon, Glamorgan and Braunton (*SS 4836*) in Devon. His Irish origin, asserted in *LBS*, appears to rest only on the *Iolo MSS*.

BEUGNAI (Beoghna), abbot of Bangor (Ireland), +609, Aug. 22. I;I. Successor of **C**omgall (+605), *M.* only. Possibly a confusion with **B**euno, regarded as successor of **D**aniel of Bangor (Caernarvonshire), who lived 20 or 30 years after 605, with an Irish Beugnai, died 605, who was not an abbot of Bangor; since his name is absent from the lists of abbots of Bangor.

BEUNO VII E, Apr. 21. B;B. *VSB* 16, Welsh language Life only, translated *Arch. Camb.* 1930, 315 (1). v. *Wenefred, VSH* 288 ff. Bennonus (2). Son of Bugi of Banhenic on the Severn (unlocated) in Powys (1), schooled at Caerwent under Tangusius (3) in the old age of king Ynyr Gwent (4), granted Berriew on the Severn (*SJ 1800*), near Welshpool by Mawn *son* of Brochmail (VI M/L) (7) king of Powys, heard Saxons shouting in English 'Ker Gia' to hunting dogs, perhaps the Mercian calling of the Welsh, and withdrew westward (8). Stayed with **T**yssilio at Meifod (*SJ 1513*), founding a church on land given by Cynan, son of Brochmail, who also gave him Gwyddelwern (*SJ 0746*), near Corwen, Merioneth. Expelled by the sons of Selyf (+613) son of Cynan (10; *2, 4*), received a *tref* (11), (*villa* [2, 5]) from Temic (Teuyth) son of Eliud named Sechnant in Beluyc (*2, 6, cf. 2, 2*) in Tegeingl (Flint), with the approval of king Cadfan of Gwynedd (614-*c.*625). He replaced the head of Teuyth's daughter **W**enefred, severed by a nobleman to whom she refused to yield, so that she lived an abbess till old age, patroness of Hoywell, Flint (*SJ 1875*) (12; *2, 8 ff.*). He bought Gwaredauc in Arfon from Cadwallon son of Cadfan (*c.*625-634) for a gold sceptre given him by Cynan, worth 60 cows, cursed Cadwallon at Caernarvon when he discovered that its rightful owner had been deprived, and received his permanent home at Clynnog (*SH 4746*) in Lleyn from the king's cousin (14 ff.). Resuscitated the daughter of Ynyr Gwent, murdered by her husband, an artisan of Aberffraw who had been employed at the court of Caerwent (17 ff.). Her brother Idon came to Caernarvon to reclaim her dowry of horses, gold and silver, cut off the head of the husband, which Beuno replaced. His churches are numerous in north Wales. *LBS* 1, 208. Bowen, *Settlements of the Celtic Saints*, 85, fig. 23. He was perhaps regarded as a successor of Daniel of Bangor, *cf.* Beugnai.

BINEUS, *see* Benignus.

BIRINUS of Dorchester-on-Thames *c.*645, Dec. 3. Italian?;E. *BHL* 1360 ff. Bede *HE* **3**, 7 *cf.* **4**, 12. Sent to Britain (634 *ASC*) 'cum consilio papae Honorii' (625-638), consecrated by Asterius (of Milan and) of Genoa, converted Wessex and baptised king Cynegils in the presence of Oswald of Northumbria (635 *ASC*), given Dorcic by both kings, buried there, later translated to Winchester. Haedde.

BITHEUS, *see* Mobhi.

BIVONOI, abbot of Llantwit, VII E. B;B. *LL* index.

BLAAN of Kingarth, Bute (*NS 0956*) VI L/VII E, Aug. 10. B;B. *BHL* 1366. *Brev. Ab.* PE 77. Native of Bute, nephew of Cathan, educated for seven years in Ireland by Comgall and Cainnech, returned to Bute, in a boat without oars; struck fire from his finger ends, as from a steel, to light his lamp. Visited Rome, consecrated bishop, returned, curing a boy in a city of the northern Angles. Credited with enclosing land by erecting boundaries still visible in the Middle Ages, O'Hanlon 8, 143, citing *Registrum de Passelet*, p. 15. Dunblane, Perthshire (*NN 7801*), north of Stirling, his principal monastery, *M. Oeng.*, etc. Dunblane became the cathedral see of the Scottish kingdom under David I in 1142; Fordun (11, 21) claimed the manors of 'Appilby, Congere, Troclyngham and Malemath in England', given to Blaan by a lord whose son he revived (Forbes 281). His other sites, O'Hanlon 8, 146.

Uncle of Lasrian of Leithlin (+641), v. *Lasr.* 3, who was said to be son of *Gemma* d. of Aedan of Dal Riada. Blaan is himself made *grandson* of Aedan in Newton's life (1505), cited Forbes 281, from Reeves, *Culdees* 46.

BOECIUS of Monasterboice, Louth (*O 08*) 521, Dec. 7. I?(Italian?);P.I. *BHL* 1388. *VSH* 1, 87. The text consists of two distinct Lives run together, ch. 1-18 (1), and 19-31 (2), the latter an incomplete *de Miraculi*. Both Lives assume, but do not assert, his Irish birth; exceptionally, neither his ancestors nor region are named; 2, 22 calls his father Bronachus. Studied in Italy under abbot Tilianus (*1*, 4; *2*, 30), sailed thence to the land of the Picts, with 60 saints 'de Germani' (4), resuscitated king Nectan (Morbet) (*c.*462-486) who gave him his castellum, crossed to Irish Dal Riada and resuscitated the daughter of the king (6) (the dynasty migrated to Britain *c.*500), passed to Connacht (6-8) and Bregh, where he founded Monasterboice (9), and encountered otherwise unknown kings of Bregh (*1*, 9; *2*, 15 ff.). The Ui Neill (Cenel Crimthainn) appear to have mastered Bregh by *c.*480. His name is Italian. He was evidently either an Italian assumed to be Irish, or an Irishman educated in Italy; Plummer's emendation of Ytalia and Tylianus to Walia and Teilo (p. xxxv) is chronologically impossible, linguistically improbable, and is formally contradicted by *2*, 30, which routes him 'ad Gallias' (plural and early) on his way to Ytalia. His name might underlie Kirkbuddo in Forfar, near Dunichen (Dun Nechtain), Watson *CPNS* 313, and the Byth Market at Aberdeen (Forbes, *Calendars* 292, citing *NSA* xii 273).

BOISIL +*c*.664, Feb. 23. E;E. Bede *HE* **4**, 27-28; **5**, 9. v. *Cuthberti* 4-8, Sacerdos, praepositus.at Melrose, Roxb. (*NT 5434*) under abbot Eata in 651, when Cuthbert entered the monastery. Taught Cuthbert, laying special emphasis on the gospel of St. John. Died in the plague. Appeared in a dream to a disciple whom he charged to tell Egbert not to evangelise Germany, but to go to Iona. Named St. Boswell's (*NT 5931*), near Melrose, and the church of Tweedmouth (*NT 9952*).

BONIFACE of Mainz 680/689-755, Jun. 5. E;Germany. *BHL* 1400 ff.; *Die Briefe des heiligen Bonifatius*, ed. Tangl, 1916. Born 'on the farthest borders of Germany', near Exeter, where he was educated (Willibald, 1), at Crediton (Bishop Grandisson of Exeter, 1327-1369), archbishop of Mainz, founder of Fulda, etc., apostle of Germany, *DCB*. Cuthbert of Wearmouth, Cuthbert of Canterbury, Daniel of Wessex, Egbert of York, Hwaetbert, Pechthelm.

BOTULF of Icanhoe VII M/L, June 17. E;E. *BHL* 1421-4. Founded Icanhoe (perhaps Boston, Lincs., *TF 3400*, or Iken, Saxmundham, *TM 4060*) *ASC* 654. Taught Ceolfrid. Named Boston and other places. His 60 odd sites include Cambridge, Colchester, Lincoln, the gates of London, etc., Arnold-Forster 2, 52; 3, 343.

BREACA V L/VI E, June 4 (Dec. 26). I;B. Leland, *Itin.* 3, 4 (1, 187), (cited *LBS* 1, 229), 'Barricius (Findbar) socius Patricii, ut legitur in vita (lost) Sti. Wymeri (? Guiner). Sta. Breaca nata in partibus Lagonia *vel* (MS., et) Ultoniae. Campus Breacae in Hibernia, in quo Brigida oratorium construxit et postea monasterium, in quo fuit Sta. Breaca (*cf.* Briga, mater ancillarum, in Brigit's time, v. *Brigit* 3, 30 [*TT* 530]; *4*, 60-61 [CS 55-57]). Breaca venit in Cornubiam, comitata multis sanctis, inter quos fuerunt Sinninus Abbas (Senan of Inis Cathy, Shannon, and Sennen (Land's End) (*SW 3425*), qui Romae cum Patricio fuit; Maruanus monachus; Germochus rex; Elwen; Crewenna; Helena. Breaca appulit sub Rivyer (Hayle Bay, St. Ives) (*SW 5438*) -- cum suis, quorum partem occidit Tewder(ig). Breaca venit ad Pencair (unidentified). Breaca venit ad Trenewith (*SW 6522*). Breaca aedificavit eccl(esias) in Trenewith et Talmeneth, ut legitur in vita (lost) St. Elweni'. The parish of Breage (*SW 6128*) adjoins Germoe (*SW 5829*), Crowan (Sta. Crewenne) (*SW 6434*) and St. Elvan in Helston (*SW 6527*). The tradition makes these saints part of the Irish invasion checked by the elder Theodoric in the first years of the sixth century. Fingar, Guiner, Runon.

BRENDAN of Birr, Offaly (*N 00*) +564 (or 573), Nov. 29 (May 9). I;I. *AB* 55, 1937, 96 (1). *Adomnán* 3, 3; 3, 11 (2-3). *TT* 462 (4). v. *Aed* 2 (5); *Brendan C.* 1, 94 (6); *Ciaran C.* 15 (7); *Ciaran S.* 30 (8); *Ruadan* 16 (9); *Barri* 5 (10); *Finnian C.* 19 (11).
Pupil of Finnian of Clonard (11, 7, *cf.* Catalogus 5); friend of Brendan of Clonfert (6) and of the two Ciarans (8) and of Cainnech (4), *cf.* the agreement between the two Brendans and two Ciarans v. *Ciaran S.* (CS) 18. Taught the youthful Aed (5) and Barri (10) *cf.* v. *David* 39-40. His ascent, 561. Successfully opposed the proposed excommunication of Columba at Tailltiu, but urged Columba to go into exile (2-4). Accompanied Ruadan to Tara (9) to oppose king Diarmait. Colman m. Lenin.

BRENDAN of Clonfert, Galway (*M 92*) 486-578, May 16. I;I. *BHL* 1436 ff. *VSH* 1, 98; 2, 270. *AB* 48, 1930, 103. Lismore 99=247. *Sal.*, *VSH*, index nominum, Kenney, index, etc. Pupil of bishop Erc (of Kerry) and of Ita (+570), his greatness foretold by Bec m. De (+550). The navigator, sailed to Iceland and thence westward to a fair land beyond the fogs, vitae; with Malo across the ocean to Ima; and to the Fortunate Islands (Teneriffe) (the *Kalendar*, cited Espinoda, *Hakluyt Society*, 1907,

28, Plummer *VSH* xli n.; *Brev. Ab.* PH 98v). Visited Gildas in Britain (vita *1*, 83-87). Founded Clonfert, aged 77 (vita *1*, 91), in 561 opposed king Diarmait (*1*, 95). The ocean voyages are placed in the years before 560.

Abban, Barrfind, Cainnech, Columba (Iona), Cormac Ua Liathain, Cuimine, David, Flannan, Foelan, Gildas, Gurwal, Iarlaithe, Ita, Kebi, Lasrian of Devenish, Malo, Mobhi maccu Alde, Mo-Luoc, Ruadan, Senan, Ternoc.

BRIAC, *see* Brioc.

BRIDE, *see* Brigit.

BRIGIT of Kildare (*N 71*) 455-524, Feb. 1. I;I. *BHL* 1455 ff. Colgan, *TT* 515 ff. Kenney, 356 ff. *Lismore* 84 = 182. *VSH, Sal.* indices, v. *Gildae* (R) 10, etc. The most important Lives are those of Cogitosus, mid VII (1), of Ultan (2), Animosus, VIII or early IX (3), and Laurence of Durham, XII (4). The basis of 2 is very early, when the normal position of prayer was still standing, with the arms outstretched (91; *TT* 538). Daughter of Dubthach (*1*) of Leinster (*2, 3*), veiled by bishop Mac-Caille (*1*), presented by him to the British-born bishop Mel (and Melchu) (*3*).

The circumstances of the foundation of Kildare and allied houses are not described; but 'de ecclesiis multarum provinciarum sibi adhaerentibus sollicitans, et secum revolvens quod sine summo sacerdote, qui ecclesias consecraret, et ecclesi-asticos in eis gradus subrogaret, esse non potest, illustrem virum (Conlaed) (+518) . . . convocans . . . ut ecclesiam in episcopali dignitate cum ea gubernaret . . . semper Archiepiscopus Hibernensium episcoporum' (*1*, prolog., *cf.* 29). In time of famine, Ibar (+499) supplied her with 12 wagon loads of corn, miraculously provided (*2*, 54). Her miracles are predominantly concerned with dairy farming. Cogitosus makes no mention of Patrick; Ultan and Animosus make her his counterpart, and stress her protection of the secular state of north Leinster. Her patronage enabled king Illan (493-512) to defeat the Ui Neill and win nine battles in Britain (*3*, ii, 12; *2*, 90). She was succeeded by her favourite pupil Darlugdach. Her name is exceptionally widespread outside Ireland; some 20 places in Wales (mapped Bowen *ECSW* 98, fig. 26) bear her name as Sanffraid, rather more in western England, with St. Bride's in London, with 30 to 40 in Scotland and as many in Brittany, *LBS* 1, 283, Arnold-Forster 3, 344, Forbes, *Kalendars*, 290. O'Hanlon, 211; she is widely honoured in Europe.

Darerca, Darlugdach, Finnian of Clonard, Gildas, Ibar, Ita, Muirchú, Tigernach, Ultan of Ardbreccan, Vougay.

BRIOC of St. Breock, Co. (*SW 9771*) and St. Brieuc, Brittany *c.*468-*c.*559, May 1. I.B;B.A. *BHL* 1463-4. *AB* 2, 1883, 2 *cf.* 23, 1904, 264. *LBS* 1, 288. The MS. is tenth-/eleventh-century, and was then composed, *cf.* ch. 58 (an addendum), written long after the translation of the relics to Angers *c.*850, but before the retranslation of 1210. The extant Life is presumably earlier than 850. It rests, however, upon a much earlier original; the orthography of ch. 2. 'Briomaglus, Coriticianae regionis indigena' can hardly be later than VII, if so late, and normal prayer with hands outstretched to heaven (ch. 32) is scarcely later. The testimony of Simaus, present at the saint's funeral, is cited (57). The name is normally Brioccius, variant Briocus; Briomaglus, variant Briocmaglus (2); Briomelus, lost life quoted by Leland, *Collectanea 1, 430*, *cf.* App. I.

Born in the land of Coritic, probably Cardigan, conceivably Alclud, son of Cerpus and Eldruda (2); the father's name is Irish, the mother's English. An angel foretold his birth on the occasion of an annual three-day festival on January 1, involving games and songs (2-4). Educated by *Germanus of Paris* (555-575) (not Germanus of Auxerre, +*c*.447) with *Patrick* and *Illtud* as his fellow pupils (8-9). Ordained by *Germanus* (18), sent home, landing at the river Scene (unidentified) (21-22), at the age of 25 (*c*.493). Refused to participate in the January Festival, healed the broken thigh of a dancer, converted his family and fellow countrymen, founded 'Landa Magna' (? Llandyfriog Fawr), Card. (*SN 3341*) (24-29), where his miracles concern building, the rescue of stag from the hunt of a tyrannus, and a famine. Sent abroad by an angel, with 168 companions, landed at a port (? in Cornwall, Padstow area) and converted a king Conan and his people (35-39). Crossed 'mare Britannicum', sailing 'recto cursu dextroque navigio' to land at the port of Achim on the Ioudi river (Jaudi, the river of Tréguier) (40). Hearing of a great plague (*c*.547-550) in Coriticiana, he returned home to comfort his people and expel the plague, entrusting his monastery to his nephew Papa Tugualus (**T**udwal, the founder of Tréguier) (41-42). On his return the monks of Tréguier refused to receive him back, and he passed on to St. Brieuc (44-49) where his miracles mainly concern the clearing of woodland and scrub. Visited Childebert at Paris with other saints, *c*.557, Leland, above (during the episcopate of Germanus, whence doubtless the story of his *education* by Germanus). At the age of 90 gave last unction to the dying Rigual of Dumnonia (*c*.558) (50-52). Died soon after; Simaus, from Coriticiana, attended his funeral (53-58).

He is patron of Llandyfriog (whence Saint 'Tyfriog' of the Welsh calendars, May 1) and of St. Briavels, Glos. (*SO 5504*); of the huge Cornish parish of St. Breock, south of Wadebridge; of the diocese of St. Brieuc, and three or four other Breton churches; of Rothesay, of Bute (*NS 0864*), of Inchbraoch near Montrose (*NO 7056*), and of Dunrod in Kirkcudbright (*NX 6850*) LBS 1, 300; Forbes, *Kalendars*, 291.

BRYNACH, *see* Bernacus.

BURIANA of St. Buryan, Land's End (*SW 4025*) VI E? May 29. I;B. 'S. Buriana an holy woman of Irelond sumtyme dwellid in this place and there made an oratory', Leland, *Itin*. 3, 5 (Toulmin Smith 1, 189). Identified *LBS* 1, 341 with Bruinsech Cael (wrongly printed as Bruinech) 'venerated in a town bearing her name in England', cited from a scholiast on *M. Don*. May 29; with a Bruinet who, Leland says, came to Cornwall with Piran (**C**iaran of Saigir); and with Bruinech, v. *Ciaran Saigir* 8-9, who 'lived long in her profession' as a nun after escaping an unwished marriage by death and resuscitation. I have not been able to verify the reference to *M. Don*. and Leland.

CADFAN of Bardsey Island (*SH 1221*) VI M/L. A;B. Day unknown (assigned to All Saints' Day, Nov. 1, by recent writers, *LBS* 2, 7). v. *Paterni 4*, the young **P**adarn joined a migration from Brittany to Wales, 'ducibus Ketinlau, Catman, Titechon'; Breton breviaries (*LBS* 2, 2 *cf. AG* 245) give name variants Hetinlau, Tinlatu, Quilan; Cathinam; Techo, Techucho (=**T**ydecho). Catvan Sant en (ynys) Enlli (Bardsey), son of *Eneas Ledwic of Lydav (Armorica)*, followed by Hewyn (Hetinlau?) and 17 other saints, including **P**aternus, Tedecho and Mael, companions or cousins of Cadvan, *ByS* 19 ff. A Catman, glossed *sanctus*, is listed as witness after Cethig (of Llandough), before Cadoc, in a grant placed in VI M/L, v. *Cadoci 57*. A Caduonus,'vir caritativus', gave a site in the Vannetais to **M**evennus (placed in or about the 540s), v. *Mevenni 6-9*. Late legend makes much of these saints, and adds **B**aglan and a few others. The principal centres of his cult were Bardsey and Towyn, Mer. (*SH 5800*). The dedications of his followers are mapped, Bowen *SCSW* 93, fig. 25, where, however, the later additions are conflated with the saints named in v. *Paterni*, ByS and the Breton Breviaries; these are confined to

Merioneth and Lleyn, with Llandrinio (*SJ 2817*) in Powys and the churches of Sulien in Powys and Tegeingl. Hewyn (Hetinlau? named first in v. *Paterni* and the Breviaries) is remembered only at Aberdaron, Lleyn (*SH 1726*), (*LBS* 3, 264), the port of embarkation for Bardsey; the veneration of Cadfan as leader of the whole party may be due to the prominence of Bardsey. The essence of the tradition is a migration from the Vannetais to the northern coasts of Cardigan Bay; the only indication of date is that of Paternus. It is possible that king Catman of Gwynedd, born *c*.580, was named after the saint.

CADOC of Llancarfan (Nantcarvan) (*ST 0570*) *c*.580, Jan. 24. B;B.I.A. *BHL* 1491 ff. vitae *VSB* 24 (Lifris, XI); *AB* 60, 1942, 45 (Caradoc of Llancarfan XII) (2); v. *Gwynlliw VSB* 172 (3); *AG* 665 (from breviaries based on a life stolen in XII or earlier from Quimperlé, *Cart. Quimperlé* 101 [1904. 255] [4] is a version of [1] and [2] with Welsh localities and incidents replaced by Armorican).

Son of Gwynnliw of Glevissig, *nephew* of Paul Penychen, Petroc, Etelic (and *six others* named from places) *1*, prolog. = v. *Petroci* prolog.; *cf. 3*, 1; and of Gwladus, daughter of Brychan (*c*.500), *1*, prolog. and 1; *2*, 2 ff.; *3*, 2 ff. Called Catmail *1*, 1, Cathmaelus v. *Fin. Clon.* 4 ff. Educated at Caerwent v. *Tathei 12* by Tatheus (Meuthi, *1*, 1 ff.) for 12 years, 'Donato Priscianoque necnon aliis artibus' (*1*, 6). After refusing to forsake religion for the royal sceptre of Penychen, was granted Llancarfan by Paul Penychen *1*, 8, where he built Castil Kadoci (? Castle Ditches by Llancarfan, *ST 0570*) becoming 'plurimorum agrorum possessor' (*1*, 9). Granted Neath (*SS 7597*) by rex Arthmail *1*, 20 = 2, 13. Went to Ireland to study for three years at *Lismore* (founded 636) of *Mu-Chutu* (Mo-Chuta, Carthacus, +637) (*1*, 10). Settled at Inis Fail (Begerin, Wexford Bay, *T 02*), named Mo-Chattoc, with Conoc (of Brecon?) (Mo-Chonoc), as in Cornwall later (see below), first named of a group of seven south Leinster saints (Augustine of Inis Beg (Begerin) (with Erdit), Tecan, Diarmait, Naindid, Paul, Feidelmid), annexed to the Patrician legend, Tírechán *Add.* 13, *cf.* index Hibernicus (*AB* 2, 1883, pp. 228-9, 235. *L. Ard.* f. 18 r. 19 3.; Stokes *VT* 344, 349), *Bethu Phátraic*, Stokes *VT* 190, 192. Llancarfan claimed land on the Liffey and hospitium with Clonard in XI (*1*, 43). Returned with numerous Irish and British pupils, including Finnian (conflated in Irish tradition with *Finnian of Clonard*) studied in (11), and Cainnech of Archadboe (+603), v. *Cainnech* 3, named (Ca)docus. Studied in Brecon under Bachan, recently come from Italy (11), recovered and rebuilt Llancarfan, which had been destroyed (12). Inherited and extended his father's temporal kingdom; 'abbas . . . et princeps super Gunliauc post genitorem' (*1*, 18 *cf. 2*, 16), 'regimine concesso . . . Cadoco . . . filio suo ar regendum (Gundleius)' (*3*, 4), utrumque tenens regimen et abbaciam Nant-cabarnice vallis' (*3*, 7). Maintained 100 soldiers, as well as many clergy, workmen and poor, and a familia of 300 (*1*, 18 *cf.* v. *Illtud 11*). Confounded the 'lictor Caradauc Pendiuin' (15), dux Sauuil (Samuel) Bennuchel (16), *king Arthur* (22), Maelgwn (23) and his successor Run (24) and Rhain of Brecon (25). His disciple Finnian routed the Saxons (v. *Fin. Clon. 8*), probably in or soon after 577. Surrendering the political control of 'the whole region, except Gwynlliog' to Mouric filius Enhinti (*c*.580), stipulating that the levies of Gwynlliog should not serve more than three days at their own charges (25). Left Llancarfan to Elli of Llanelli, Carm. (*SN 5000*), and moved to *Beneventum* where he was visited annually by Elli and became bishop under the name of *Sophias* and was martyred by the soldiers of a cruel king (*1*, 37-39). The place might be a British 'Bannaventa', conceivably Gobannium, Abergavenny; 'Sophias' perhaps translates

Cato Sapiens, a VII/VIII moralist whose sayings Welsh mediaeval tradition ascribed to Cadoc (*LBS* 2, 41).

Visited Rome (in the time of Pope John III, 560-572, *4*, 3) and Jerusalem (*1*, 26; *1*, 32), Cornwall (*1*, 30-32), where he is commemorated at Padstow, with Conoc (*LBS* 2, 269) of Boconnoc and St. Pinnock, adjoining St. Keyne, by Liskeard; at Harlyn Bay; at St. Just in Roseland, at St. Michael's Mount (idiomate Din Sol appellatur, *1*, 31), with St. Keyne, *daughter* of Brychan (Doble, 4, 58); Brittany (*1*, 35), where he was called Catbodu (Caduonus *4*); Scotland (*1*, 26), where he is patron of Cambuslang, near Glasgow (*NS 6460*) with Machan, his pupil, trained in Ireland, who has several dedications on or near the Clyde, Forbes, *Kalendars*, 292; 380 (whence perhaps the story that Catwallaun of Gwynedd [*c.*625-634] gave Nantcarfan to Kentigern, v. *Kent. 23*); and in Aquitaine (*4*, 3). Acquired Gildas' bell which Gildas refused to surrender until ordered by Pope *Alexander*, and Gildas' Gospel book (*1*, 27; 33-34); which Gildas wrote while 'studium scolarum . . . rexit' at Nantcarvan for a year, during Cadoc's absence in Scotland (v. *Gildae*, CL. 8); lived on Ronech (Barry Island) while Gildas lived on Echni (Holm), (v. *Gildae*, CL. 9); with Gildas and David when Finnian awarded supremacy to David, v. *Fin. Clon.* (Lismore) 2527 ff. While Cadoc was abroad, David convened the synod of Brefi, to his intense anger (*1*, 13; *1*, 17, *cf.* v. *David* 49). *Converted Illtud* (*1*, 19); (1) is the remnant of a Gospel book, in which the Life is followed by posthumous miracles, a list of estates, genealogies and grants; some 70 properties are claimed.

Cadoc has more dedications than any other Welsh saint except David, *cf.* Bowen, *SCSW*, 42, fig. 92a, but in a restricted area, the vale of Glamorgan, Brecon, the Usk and Wye Valleys, Brittany, especially in the Vannetais, with the Scottish and Cornish sites, *cf. LBS* 2, 37 ff. He is exceptionally prominent in both Welsh and Breton fable. He is hardly Docus (*Catalogus* 2), who with David and Gildas provided the liturgy of the second order, but *see* Docco. Findbar (Barrucius), Mac Moil, Ibar, Illtud.

CAEDMON of Whitby (*NZ 8911*) 657/680, Feb. 11. E;E. Bede *HE* **4**, 24. Leland *SB* 86. Northumbrian at Hilda's monastery of Whitby, composed and sang (to the harp, OE Bede) the principal stories of the Old and New Testaments in English verse. For the extant verses attributed to him, *see* Plummer, *Bede*, 2, 251, ff. The name is Welsh, Cadfan (Catman).

CAELAN, *see* Mo-Choe.

CA(I)DOC and Fricorius VII E. B?;Gaul. *Irish* priests, converted a nobleman of Picardy, Richarius (+645), who founded St. Riquier (Somme), Alcuin, v. *Ricarii*, *MGH SRM* 4, 1902, 381. The names are British, not Irish, Kenney 490, *cf.* 500.

CAINNECH of Achad Bo, Aghaboe, Co. Leix (*S 38*) 516-603 (both dates *Annals*), Oct. 11. I;I.S.P. *BHL* 1519. vitae *VSH* 1, 152 (1); *Sal.* 361 (2); Adomnán v. *Col.* (3); Aed (4); Coemgen (5); Colman Elo (6); Comgall (7); Fintan (8); Lasrian (CS) (9); Mo-Lua (11); Munnu (12); Columba (CS) (13); Catalogus (14); Finian Clon (15), etc. Son of a poeta (*1*, 1; *2*, 1), mocu-Dalon (*3*, 3, 17: Corco Dalann 2, 1, C(ia)nna(c)ht *1*, 1) in northern Ireland (*1*, 1; *2*, 1), baptised by bishop of Luyrech (*1*, 1). Studied in Britain under (Ca)docus (*1*, 3); pupil of Finnian of Clonard (*14*, 5; *15*, 11); visited Rome (*1*, 5), returned to his mother's country of Airgialla (macc Cuais *2*, 1; mic Nais *1*, 1; 7). Travelled (ambularet cum populo suo *1*, 9) in a two-horse carriage (*1*, 8). Visited Comgall (+605) (*1*, 14; *7*, 20). With Comgall and Columba, helped Eogan of Ardstraw (+549). Attended a convention with Columba, Aed m. Ainmire, Aed Slane (*6*, 3+ ? Drumceat ? AM. L.). Established fraternitas at Uisnech with Columba, Comgall and Coemgen (*5*, 27). Went to Columba in Iona (*1*, 15-26) with Comgall, Brendan of Clonfert, and Cormac Ua Liathain (*3*, 3, 17, *cf. 3*, 1, 4; *3*, 2, 13); visited Brudeus king of the Picts (555-584) (*7*, 51; *13*, 12 *cf. 1*, 20, *2*, 25); stayed as a hermit (*1*, 17), penetrated 'trans dorsum Britannie' (*2*, 24); saw Land of Promise with Columba, Brendan and Fintan Munnu (*12*, 28). Returning to Ireland, helped Aed m. Bricc (+589) against Colman Bec kg. Meath (+589), rescued Colman's soul from hell on his death (*1*, 27; 31). Columba sent Baitan to him for penance (*1*, 22). Preserved a child sentenced to the *gall-cherd* death by kg. Cormac of the Ui Bairrche (*1*, 34), visited Munster (*1*, 38). From Aghaboe, helped Colman of Ossory (+608) against a besieging army (*1*, 39); advised Mo-Choemog on his dealings with Colman and princes of Eile, *c.*590 (*10*, 18; 27-29), and replaced the severed head of the child Dagan of Ennereill (+641); met Mo-Choemog, Mo-Lua (Lugid +609) and Mo-Fecta (? Fechin of Fore +666) (*10*, 29). Miraculously provided Brendan with gold to make a chalice (*1*, 44) and saved Columba from a storm (*1*, 45; *3*, 2, 13). Died, aged 84 (*Annals*; *M. Tal*). He persuaded Fintan to relax the extreme rigour of his rule (*8*, 5), and renounced Columba's friendship because of his cruelty to Fintan Munnu (*2*, 26). Died, aged 84 (*Annals*); shriven by Fintan Maeldubh (+632).

One of the principal saints of the second order, *14*, 2. He named Kilkenny, and has many dedications in Ireland (O'Hanlon, 10, 164), and in Scotland (as Canice, Kenneth or Kenzie) (O'Hanlon, 10, 167; Forbes, *Kalendars*, 297; *LBS* 2, 60-61; MacKinlay 61), where they are said to be more numerous than those of any other Irish saint except Brigit and Columba.

Blaan, Cadoc, Docco, Finan of Swords, Findbar of Cork, Fintan of Clonenagh, Lasrian of Leighlin, Mobhi, Ruadan.

CAIRLAN, bishop of Armagh, 579-589, Mar. 24. I;I. *M*. Of the Ui Neill, *Book of Leinster* 42ᶜ, (sedit iv, for x). Revived by Dagaeus, v. *Dagaei* 23.

CAIRNECH Coem (Dear) of Dulane (Tuilen) Meath (*N 77*) V L, May 16. I;I.B. Exhumed Niall Noigiallach and re-buried him at Tuilen, near Kells of the Kings (*M. Oeng.*), Nov. 25, p. 246. Of the Cornish Britons, *M. Don.*, *M. Gor.* Identified with Carantocus, son of Cereticus (v. I *Carantoci* 1, *VSB* 142), of Ceredigiaun, son of Cunedda (v. II *Carantoci*, *VSB* 148), refused to succeed his father, and settled at Guerit Carantauc (v. II, 4), crossed to Ireland and changed his name to Cernach, 30 years before the birth of David (=*c.*496) when the Irish overcame Britain, under (Aed) Briscus (of Demetia) and three other chiefs and founded many churches in Leinster. Called 'carus (dear) Cernacus'; thus Carantocus led the Irish against the opposition of the 'magi' (druids). (v. I, 2). Returned to Cardigan, crossed the Severn Sea (v. I, 3); Carantoc founded Carrum (Carhampton, So., *ST 0143*, near Minehead) (Carrum, *ASC* 830, 840 *cf. DEPN* 87) when Cato and Arthur ruled at Din Draithov; Arthur wickedly tried to use his altar as a table, granted Carrum when confounded (v. I, 4), giving 'xii partes agri' to Carrow at the mouth of the Guellit (v. I, 5). Cernach returned to Ireland and died on May 16 (v. I, 6). Perhaps originally identical with Cairnech, March 28. v. *Caradoci*, *BHL* 1560, May 16 = v. II *Carantoci*, the name changed, with a migration to Ireland, the conversion of a king, and the education of his pupil Tenenan, who accompanied Senan to Brittany. Named Karentec in v. *Tenenan* 4 (*AG* 401). The principal churches of Carantoc are Llangranog, Card. (*SN 3154*), Crantock, Co. (*SW 7960*), and Carantec and Tregaran-tec in Brittany (with St. Tenenan), *LBS* 2, 99. Cianan of Dulech.

CAIRNECH Coir (the Just) 438. I;I. One of the authors of the Senchus Mor, *FM*, etc.

CAIRNECH of Drumleen, nr. Raphoe, Don. (*C 20*) V L, March 28. *M. Don., M. Gor., M. Tal.* I;I.B. vita (Book of Ballymore) Skene *CPS* 52 = Todd, *Irish Nennius* 178, *cf.* ci (1); poem, *Death of Muirchetach Mac Erca* (Book of Lecan), *RC* 23, 1902, 195 (2). Son of Saran (*1; 2*) of Dal Araide of Airgialla (CF) *M. Don.*; of Cenel nEogain (2), of (D)uachaill, Dundalk, Lough (J 00), on the southern border of Dal Araide and Airgialla, *M. Gor.* Patron of Cenel Eogain, first at Ailech, then Drumleem (*2*). His brother Luirig, kg. of Alba, built a fort in a monastery he had founded in Alba. Mac Erca, who had been exiled from Ireland and from Alba, was blessed by Cairnech for killing Luirig and bringing him his head. Attended a council at Tours; built an underground church at Carnticeon among the Cornish Britons. Increased the strength of the exile Mac Erca, who returned to Ireland to destroy the power of the provincial kings. Returned to Ireland before Mac Erca, to become the first bishop of the Clann Neill and of Tara, the first martyr, monk and brehon of Ireland (*1*). Colgan *ASH* 782, *cf.* 713 is a digest of these tales. Buried Mac Erca at Dulane (*2*). Blessed the Cenel Conaill and Cenel nEogain as perpetual coarbs of Ailech, Tara and the Ulaid, bequeathed them the battle insignia of the Cathach, Patrick's Bell, and the Misach (*2*), perhaps the Gospel bookcase preserved at St. Columba's Dublin (Reeves, *Adamnan*, 328, *cf.* O'Curry. 600). St. Carnac's, Turiff, Aberdeen (*NJ 7249*) may be named from him or from Carnocus, ep. Culdaeus (IX or later), Forbes *Kalendars* 238 (David Camerarius). The Drummond Calendar in Scotland names him in May 16, Forbes 13. Possibly identical with Cairnech Coem.

CAIRPRE, *see* Coirpre.

CALPURNIUS IV L. B;B. Father of Patrick, 'patrem Calpornium diaconum, filium quendam Potiti filii Odissi presbyteri', Patrick, *Confessio* 1. Potitus is a personal name (*cognomen*), Calpurnius a hereditary family name (*nomen*), borne by all the ancestors male, in full Calpurnius Potitus, Calpurnius Odysseus. These double names, normal in the early empire, were in the fourth century characteristic of old-fashioned curial classes, local notables, in the western provinces. Calpurnius Odysseus, born about the end of the third century, will be one of the earliest-known British priests.

CANAUC, *see* Conoc.

CANICE, *see* Cainnech.

CARADOC, *see* Cairnech Coem.

CARANTOC of Cardigan, *see* Cairnech Coem.

CARANTOC of Saul. Haute Saone, Burgundy (? . . . monasterio cui Salicis nomen est). VI L. B;Gaul. Jonas *Columban* 1, 7. Abbot who sustained Columban in his first winter, *c.*590, evidently previously established, by name British.

CARANUS, *see* Mo-Chua of Tuirahoe.

CARTHACUS of Saigir VI E/M, March 5. I;I. v. *Ciaran Saigir* (1), *Carthaci* (Mo-Chutu) (2). Grandson (son *M.*) of Angus Mac Nadfraich, kg. of Munster (+492) (*1*, 13; 15 *M.*). Favourite pupil of Ciaran, exiled for attempted fornication, welcomed back (*1*, 24, 29). On his death, Ciaran 'dedicated' Saigir to him (*M. Don.* only). Teacher of Mo-Chutu (*M. Oeng.*). Carthacus senior, teacher of Mo-Chutu (Carthacus junior)(*2*, 6; 9; 10; 12-14), with *Moel Tulus, chief of Kerry, son-in-law of Mael Duin of W. Munster, +642*. Bishop (*2; M. Don.*).

CARTHACUS (Mo-Chutu) of Rahan, Off. *(N 22)* and Lismore, Waterford *(X 09)* +639, May 14. I;I. *BHL* 1623-4. *VSH* 1, 170 (1); *Sal.* 779 (2); *ITS* 16, 1914, 74 (3); of the Ciarraige Luachra (1), pupil of Carthacus of Saigir and of Comgall of Bangor (15). Visited Mo-Lua (18), Colman Elo (29) and others. Established at Rahan in the time of kg. Cairpre m. Crimthainn (541-580) (37) and Cathal m. Aeda (619-628) (39); Columba visited him there and foretold his expulsion. Two British monks tried to murder him; he foretold that the British monks in his monastery would be for ever 'ridiculosi' (45). He had 867 monks at Rahan, including many British, and his rule at first forbade the use of animals for ploughing or transport (20), but was later relaxed on the demand of Finan (? Finnian of Moville) 'who came from Rome' (46). Made bishop of the Ciarraige (20); his monks were not clergy (20). Maintained a water-mill (27). Expelled from Rahan (638), by Diarmait and Blathmac, kings of the southern Ui Neill from 636, of Ireland 655-664 (53 ff.). Was *succeeded by* Constantine 'rex Cornubiensis'. Received Lismore from Maelochtraig, kg. of the Dessi +645 and his father-in-law Failbe kg. of Munster 628-639. Died 18 months later (639) (68), in old age, 'decrepitus antistes' (55). The tradition that Cadoc (+c.580) studied at Lismore suggests that Llancarfan and Lismore had close relations; the ridicule of British monks at Lismore suggests that they were numerous when the tale was set down.

Cadoc, Finan of Cenn Etigh, Finan of Swords, Ita, Lugid.

CASSIANUS Iohannes *c.*440-450. Eastern? Gaul. *DCB.* Travelled widely among eastern monasteries, ordained by Chrysostom, founded twin monasteries for men and women, on the Egyptian model at Marseille, *c.*410. Wrote *Institutiones* and other works, resisted Augustinianism and pioneered 'semi-Pelagianism'.

CASSIODORUS *c.*470-*c.*565. Italian;Italy. *DCB.* Minister of Theodoric the Ostrogoth and his successors, retired *c.*540 to found the monastery of Vivarium in southern Italy, where hermits, in the 'monasterium castellense' were distinguished from the scholars, who studied and copied secular and sacred texts; he maintained *operarii* and *pauperes.*

CATALDUS of Tarentum VII? May 10. I;Italy. *BHL* 1652-5. Munsterman, studied at Lismore, bishop of Tarentum.

CATBODU, *see* Cadoc.

CATGEN, abbot of Llantwit, VII E. B;B. *LL* index.

CATHAN VII, Feb. 1 (May 17). I;I.S. Teacher of Blaan (+710) *M. Don.* Feb. 1. *ASH* 233; abstinent, *M. Gor.* Feb. 1. Uncle of Blaan, *Brev. Ab.* May 17, Scottish Calendars, May 17. Patron of Bute, numerous dedications in SW Scotland and some in NE Ireland, Forbes, *Kalendars*, 299, O'Hanlon 2, 239; 243, and perhaps of Llangathen, Carm. *(SN 5822)*, *LBS* 2, 91.

CATHMAIL, *see* Cadoc.

CEADDA (Chad) of Lastingham, Yk. *(SE 7290)* 672, March 2. E;E. *BHL* 1716-7. Bede *HE* pref.; **3**, 21-28; **4**, 2, 3; **5**, 19, 24. Brother of Cedd studied in Ireland, founded Lastingham, disciple of Aidan, consecrated bishop of the Northumbrians, replacing Wilfred, by Wine and two British bishops, *c.*665, reconsecrated and assigned to the Mercians, *c.*669, fixing his see at Lichfield. Winfrith.

CEDD of Lastingham, Yk. (*SE 7190*) 664, Jan. 7. E;E. *BHL* 1716-7. Bede *HE* pref.; **3**, 21-28; **4**, 3. Brother of Ceadda, trained at Lindisfarne, evangelised the Middle Angles, bishop of the East Saxons, baptised king Swidhelm at Rendlesham, Sf. (*TM 3353*), founded monasteries at Ythan Caestir (Othona), Bradwell-on-Sea, Essex, and Tilbury (*TQ 6476*). Succeeded by his brother Cynbill. Died of the plague at Lastingham.

CELESTINUS, Pope, 422-432 *DCB*. Vigorous opponent of the Pelagians and of Nestorius, sent Palladius and Patrick to Ireland.

CELLACH, *c.*660. Irish, second bishop of the Middle Angles, withdrew to Ireland, succeeded by the Englishman Trumhere, Bede *HE* **3**, 24.

CELLAN, abbot of Peronne, +706. I;Gaul. Correspondent of Aldhelm, Kenney 507.

CERMAIT, *see* Germochus.

CERNACH, *see* Cairnech.

CERPAN, bishop of Tara, +503, day unknown. I;I. *Annals* (Tara *AU*, *cf.* Tírechán. *Coll.* 13).

CETHIG, abbot of Llandough, VII E. B;B. *LL* index.

CHAD, *see* Ceadda.

CIANAN of Duleek, Meath (*O 06*) +491, Nov. 24. I;I. vitae Lectiones, *AB* 73, 1955, 363 (1); Colgan *ASH* 443, n.11, citing Ussher, *Prim. Eccl. Brit.* 1070 (2); v. *Mo-Chua* 8-10, *VSH* 2, 187 (3); his office, *AB* 73, 1955, 363 (5); *M. Oeng.* (*cf. M. Don., M. Gor.*) (4). Kenanus (*1*; *2*; *5*); Kyennanus (*3*); Ciann (*4*); Kynanas (*5*).

Of Connacht ancestry (*1*, 1; *2*; but Munster parents *1*, 1), Ciannacht *M. Don.*, one of 60 boy hostages given to Loegaire (+463). *c.*460 (MS. 406) (*1*, 1, *5*), rescued the hostages (*2*); educated by nuns (*1*, 2) and Nathan (*1*, 3; *2*), visited Tours (*1*, 3; *2*, *5*) and Jerusalem (*1*, 3), visited Connacht and Leinster (*2*), returned to Duleek to build the first stone church in Ireland (*1*, 4; *3*, 8-10, *5*), obtaining dry weather for his 'cementarii', to allow cement to mix, through the prayers of Machotus (? Mocteus; wrongly identified with Mo-Chua, VII E/M) (*3*; 5) (*1*, 4; *cf. 3*, 8). Visited by Cairnech (Coem) of Dulane V L/VI E (*1*, 6; *4*). Visited the Luigni Tirconnel, curing a son of king Amalgad, Tirowen, Dal Araide (*1*, 7-8). Sent disciples to Gaul to import relics, books and vestments; imported corn from abroad during a famine (*1*, 9; *5*). Buried at Duleek (*1*, 9; *5*), his body incorrupted (*4*; *Irish Nennius*, p. 221). An outstanding scribe, better than Patrick, exchanged gospels with Patrick (*4*); Patrick gave him his own gospel (*A. Tig*). He is confused with Kenan of Armorica (*2*), *cf. LBS* 2. 118; and is distinct from bishop Kyenanus, v. *Ailbe* 28-29. **A**ilbe.

CIARA, *see* Piala.

CIARAN of Clonmacnoise. Off. (*N 03*) 521 (515)-548, Sep. 9. I;I. *BHL* 4654-6 vitae *VSH* 1, 200 (1); *Sal.* 155 (2); *Lismore* 117 = 262 (3).

Son of a plebeian chariot-maker in Meath, who, to escape the tributes of kg. Ainmire (Cenel Coirpri, brother of Tuathal Maelgarb k. Ireland 532-548), emigrated to Connacht. Baptised by Diarmait, 'postea nominatus . . . *Justus*' (1 *cf. M. Oeng.* May 5). Studied under Justus (*cf.* Fuerty, Rosc. *M 86, M. Oeng.*) (3-4), Ninnid of Lough Erne (20n., *cf. ASH* 111, *M. Don.* Jan. 18; 2, 14), *Enda and Senan of Inis Cathy (20-21)?*, Finnian of Clonard (15) with Ciaran Saigir, the two Brendans and Columba (*cf. Catalogus* 5; v. *Fin. Clon.* 11), taking a cow as his fee. Taught a king's daughter reluctantly, until Finnian could establish a separate house for women (16). Freed a woman unjustly enslaved by Tuathal Maelgarb (19) and another in Connacht (20). Visited Senan of Slattery and gave him his cloak (22, *cf.* 29, but *cf.* Ciaran of Saigir). Removed a fort near his cell (24). Expelled Daniel, a British hermit, from Hare Island (W. Meath, *N 04*) (25). Founded Clonmacnoise (547) (28), a year before his death (32). Helped the exiled Diarmait m. Cerbaill, subsequently high king (*3*, 4376; *cf. Aided Diarmada*) (*Silva Gadelica* 1, 72; 11, 82); *Bethu Phátraic VT* 88, *TT* 182; and *AC* 547, *cf. AB* 68, 1951, 96 (posthumous miracle). Died young (34), aged 33 (*Annals*). 'Half Ireland his portion' (17); 'omnes praecellit suos coetaneos', v. *Lasrian* of Devenish. Columba said of him 'Blessed be God, who called St. Ciaran from this world in his youth; if he had lived to old age he would have aroused the envy of many, for he would have made all Ireland his parish' ('valde enim parrochiam Hibernie apprehenderet', where the sting lies in the verb, making 'parrochia' mean the territory of a single priest's authority) (33). In *3*, 4472 the last phrase is altered to make Columba say, 'he would not have left room in Ireland for a pair of cart horses that were not his'. In the preface to his death-bed poem (*cf. M. Don.*, Sept. 9), 'the saints of Ireland fasted that his life might be shortened, for otherwise Ireland would belong to him alone', *AB* 69, 1951, 104. In the Columban tradition, Columba renounced for the love of God 'the sceptre of Ireland', but Ciaran abandoned only the tools of his father's trade (Colgan, v. quinta) (O'Donell 1, 44, *TT* 396).

He was credited with a monastic rule, Ussher, *Brit. Eccl. Ant.* 1050, cited O'Hanlon (9, 228), *cf.* the law of Ciaran, *AU* 743, whose text is extant in verse (O'Curry 374), his rather than Ciaran Saigir's and with several poems and hymns, O'Hanlon 9, 22; 232. His miracles are principally concerned with the improvement of arable farming: he used a horse-drawn plough (10), a water-mill (11), and a corn-drying oven, called a 'zabulum', 'in the western manner, that is of Britain and Ireland' (12). In later years, his monks imported wine from Gaul ('mercatores cum vino Gallorum venerunt') (31), for use at harvest time, when Columba visited Clonmacnoise, *c*.585/589 (31; Ad. v. *Col.* 1, 3).

He names a dozen churches in Ireland (O'Hanlon 9,236) and as many in Scotland (Forbes, 435; O'Hanlon 9, 235), but none in Britain or Brittany.

Aed m. Bricc. Coemgen, Cuimine, Dagaeus, Lasrian of Devenish, Mobhi, Nin-nidh.

CIARAN m. Echach of Tubbrid, Tip (*S 01*) (*VSH* 2, 341) V L / VI E, Nov. 10. (*M. Don., M. Gor.*) I;I. Baptised by Declan, v. *Declan* 31; accompanied Tigernach on his return from Rome to Tours and Ireland, v. *Tig.* 5.

CIARAN of Saigir (Seirkieran), Off. (*N 10*) V L / VI E (?*c*.440-*c*.520), March 5. I;I. (B). *BHL* 4657-9. vitae *VSH* 1, 217 (1); *Sal.* 805 (2); *ASH* 458 (3); *NLA* 2, 320 (4); *AB* 59, 1941, 225 (cod. Gothanus) (5).

Kyaranus (*1*), Keranus (*2*), Kieranus (*3*), Piranus . . . Keranus vocatur (*4*), Pyranus, nunc Pieranus, nunc Kyeranus (*5*).

Born in Ossory (*1-5*), son Lugneus (*1-3*), of Domuel (*4-5*). Lived *30 years* unbaptised in Ireland (Clear Island), because the Irish were pagan (*1, 3, 4, 5*). Went to Rome, consecrated bishop, stayed *20 years*, met *Patrick* (*1-5; 2* omits Patrick); in Rome with Ailbe, Declan, Ibar (v. *Declan* 12, 18) and Enda, in the time of Pope Hilary (461-468). Gave a cow annually to Brendan of Birr (*4:5*, 4). Established a double monastery, with his mother in charge of the women (*1-5*) (Liadain *1-3*; Wingella *4-5*). He, Ailbe, Declan and Ibar were the four bishops of southern

Ireland who preached before Patrick (*1*, 7). Ransomed a prisoner of Angus m. Nadfraich, k. Munster (+492) (*1-3*). Protected the virgin Bruinech (**Buriana**)(*1*, 8). Abused by Ailill k. Munster (Angus' brother and predecessor) (*1*, 28; *2*, 9; *3*, 30); stopped a war between Ailill and the high king Loegaire (+463) (*1*, 18; *2*, 11; *3*, 21). Resuscitated Angus' harpists (citharistae) (*1-5*), who had been killed by the plebs. 'Omnis enim regio Osraighi parrochia sancti Kyarani est' (*1*, 16). Angus killed in battle (*1*, 16, *cf. 2-5*). Very many incidents in Ireland with detail of place and person (*4-5*); others (*1-3*), some common to (*1-5*). In extreme old age ('ad decrepitam etatem') attended the school of **F**innian of Clonard (*1*, 36). Rescued **C**iaran of Clonmacnoise from imprisonment (*1*, 30, *cf. 2; 3*). Teacher of **C**arthacus senior, grandson of Angus (*1-5*). Entertained **G**ermanus peregrinus (*1-5*); his bell (*1-5*) made by faber **G**ermanus (*5*, 3; so Irish language Lives). Fraternitas with St. **C**ocha (*4-5*; *cf. 5*, p. 270) and her pupil Geranus presbiter; with Ciaran of Clonmacnoise and the two Brendans (*2*, 18); **R**uadan (*1*, 33-34, *cf. 4, 5*, 11) 'Comes semper et socius' of **S**enan (vitae *Senani*). Visited Tours and died in Cornwall (*4-5*); (*1-3* make no claim that he died or was buried at Saigir or in Ireland); aged 300 (*1-5*; 360 *M. Don.* citing an Irish language Life). An illuminated MS. entitled 'Ciaran's Travels' was preserved at Saigir in the Middle Ages, *M. Oeng.*

(*1-3*) and (*4-5*) make different selections from a common original, exceptionally detailed; they, with the Irish language versions (Plummer *MHH* 18-20), deserve exhaustive study. He might have visited Tours and Cornwall in his old age; but his numerous British sites could as well have been due to his followers and Senan's, whether or not he personally crossed the sea.

He names several churches and places in Ireland, where he is closely associated with relics of St. Martin (of Tours), O'Hanlon, 3, 144 ff.; in Wales (as Caron, Calendars, March 5) at Tregaron, Card. (*SN 6759*) and Cardiff (Piran), at Exeter (Kerian) and in Cornwall (Perran), *LBS* 2, 135 ff.; Arnold-Forster, 445.

CINAUC, bishop, +608 (*ACm*). B;B. Possibly **C**onoc, possibly a different person.

CIRYCUS, *see* Curig.

CLITAUC VI L, Nov. 3 (Aug. 19). B;B. 'rex filius Clitguin', king of Brecon who 'invaded all South Wales'; m. Clytwyn m. Brychan, brother of Dettu (Dedyu). Killed by one of his *sodales*, who desired the girl to whom he was betrothed; named Merthir Clitauc (Clodock, Hereford, *SO 3227*), *LL* 193.

COCHE, *see* Lugid.

COELAN, *see* Mo-Choe.

COELESTIUS + after *c.*420. I?;Italy. *DCB*. Principal colleague of **P**elagius, monk, lawyer in Rome from *c.*405; probably the Irish Pelagian denounced by Jerome (*cf. JTS* 16, 1965, 41-60).

COEMAN of Inis Daire (Wexford Harbour, *T 02*, Hogan 329) V L / VI E. I;I. Taught **F**innian of Clonard (v. *Fin. C.* 4, 11); perhaps a successor of **I**bar; possibly identical with one or other of the Coeman of the martyrologies. **C**olman Elo.

COEMGEN (Kevin) of Glendalough, Wicklow (*T 19*) +618, June 3. I;I. *BHL* 1866-8. vitae *VSH* 1, 234 (1); *Sal.* 835 (2); *ASS* June 1, 312, *AB* 74, 1956, 143 (3), *cf. AB* 63, 1945, 122, *cf.* 70, 1952, 313; Kenney, 403. Nephew of **E**ugenius of Ardstraw (v. *Eugenii* 3), trained by **P**etroc (*3*) and others, friend of **C**omgall, **M**unnu and others, formed fraternitas with **C**olumba, **C**omgall and **C**ainnech at Uisnech; visited Clonmacnoise *three days* after Ciaran's death. Founded Glendalough,

near the royal seat of king Brandub (+608) of North Leinster. Taught Colman Elo.
Died, aged *120*, shriven by his neighbour, a British hermit. Mo-Chorog (Mo-
Cuaroch) (? Warocus). Encountered numerous kings and saints of c.600; cured the
blind 'sanctus senior Berchanus' (30). Brother of Nathcomi, abbot of Terryglass,
died 589, May 1, (*FM* 584).

Ailbe, Berachus, Maedoc, Moling.

COEMGEN, *see* Mo-Choemog.

COEMOG, *see* Mo-Choemog.

COENRED, king of Mercia. E;Rome. Abdicated 709, monk in Rome, with king
Offa of Essex, Bede *HE* **5**, 19.

COGITOSUS VII E/M, Apr. 18. I;I. Sapiens *M. Tal.* The virtue of Cogitosus
the Just *M. Gor.* 'In hoc periculossum et profundum narrationis sanctae pylagus
. . . a nullis adhuc lintribus, excepto tandem uno patris mei Cognitosi expertum
atque occupatum, ingenioli mei puerilem remi cymbam deduxi' ('I have launched
the baby bark of my innocent oar upon the deep and dangerous sea of saintly tales,
that has so far been tested and used by no vessels, save one, my father Cognitosus'),
Muirchú, preface; Muirchú knew of no previous Life of a saint, other than one
written by his father. Secunda Vita S. Brigidae, authore S Cogitoso, ex MS. Codice
S. Amandi, Prologus sancti Cogitosi, Colgan *TT* 518, *cf.* n. 1, p. 524.

Both names, Cogitosus and Muirchú, are unique. Cogitosus' *Brigit* is a list of
miracles, with little narrative content, simpler than the main run of Lives. It shows
no knowledge of Patrick or of other saints, and the prologue presses the claim of
the bishops of Kildare to be 'archbishops' of Ireland. Such a claim is unlikely to
have been advanced before c.625-630, when controversy over relations with Rome
first posed the problem of a hierarchical episcopal organisation, nor later than Aed's
submission of Sletty to Armagh, c.670. Muirchú was still alive in 697; his father is
therefore likely to have written c.630/660.

The Life of Brigit contains a detailed description of the church of Kildare in
Cogitosus' time.

COILBRIT, abbot of Llantwit, VII M. B;B. *LL* index.

COIRPRE, bishop of Coleraine, Derry (*C 83*) VI M. I;I. Student at Rosnat with
Eugenius and Tigernach.

COITTRICE, *see* Patrick.

COLLEN VI? May 21. B;B.A. vita (Welsh language) *LBS* 4, 375, an excessively
devolved mediaeval romance, in treatment analogous to Albert le Grand's Armorican lives. *Descendant of* Caradauc Vreichvras and the 'earl of Oxford', went
eastward from Glastonbury, and worked wonders against Caradauc at Southampton
(Porth Hantwn). He names Llangollen, Denbigh, (*SJ 2141*); Castell Collen, Radnor,
(*SO 0562*); St. Colan, Co. (*SW 8661*); Langolen, Finistère, Brittany *LBS* 2, 161.

COLMAN of Dromore, Down (*J 25*) VI M, June 7. I;I. *BHL* 1878-9. *Sal.* 827.
Of Dal Araide, baptised by his uncle, bishop Colman, educated by Caelan (Mo-
Choe) of Nendrum (+498), Ailbe (+528) and MacNissi (+509). Visited Rome; on
his way home, revived the still-born child of a British king, who became St. David
(born c.525?), whom he taught. Welcomed king Diarmait m. Cearbaill (548-565).
Helped Aedan of Ferns (Maedoc) to revive Brandub k. S. Leinster (c.560-608).

Confounded druids. He may be the Colman who names a few places in Wales, *LBS* 2, 164. Macarius, Mo-Choe.

COLMAN Elo (Land Elo, Lann Ela), Lynally, Off. (*N 22*) (558)-613, Sep. 26. I;I. *BHL* 1180. *VSH* 1, 258. *Sal.* 415. Of the southern Ui Neill of Meath, pupil of Coeman, attended a convention (Drumceat?), visited Columba in Iona in 597, and on other occasions (Ad. v. *Col.* 1, 5; 2, 15-16). Died at 55, *A. Tig.* Kenney 309; 472. Visited Clonard and Clonmacnoise (after their founder's death) and Mo-Chutu (Carthacus) at Rathin. Had an irascible British monk at Lynally; liberated a prisoner of Aed Slane, k. Meath, +607. Coemgen, Lugid, MacNisse, Mo-Chua, Ruadan.

COLMAN of Cule (Coole, West Meath, *N 47*) VI E, Aug. 18. I;I. Teacher of Columba of Terryglass, v. *Col. T.* 4. Finnian of Clonard.

COLMAN m. Lenini 504-606, Nov. 24. I;I. Of the Ui Liathain. Poet. Cormac, *Glossary*. Converted by Brendan of Clonfert, *then a child*, v. I. *Brendan* 8; confused by v. *Brendan* with Colman of Cluain, +613. He is probably Mo-Cholmog Cenn Eich (MS. Cain Eich) (Kinneigh, probably Co. Cork, *W 35*), pupil of Findbarr of Cork, v. *(Find)barri* 13. He and Columba of Iona are said to have written on Patrick's miracles, *Bethu Phátraic* (*VT* 60), thus the earliest recorded biography of Patrick. Senan.

COLMAN, abbot of Clonard, +653, Feb. 8, I;I. *Annals, M.*; perhaps Columbanus to whom Pope John IV wrote in 640, Bede *HE* **2**, 19.

COLMAN, bishop in Munster, V M. I;I. A priest, later a bishop, baptised Declan (+ V L/VI E), sent him at the age of seven to study under Dymma, v. *Declan* 5; 7. Probably identical with Colman, who accompanied Ailbe and Declan to Rome. v. *Ailbe (1)*, 13, wrongly called Colman f. Derane (=Daire) in v. *Ailbe (2)*, 15. He perhaps named and lived at Kilcolman near Ardmore, Waterford *(X 17)*, P. Power, v. *Declan* (Irish), *Irish Text Soc.* 16, p. 161. He is the earliest recorded priest of Munster, perhaps Declan's predecessor as bishop of the Dessi.

COLMAN m. Daire of Derrymore, near Leamakevogue, Tip. (*S 25*) VII E, May 20. I;I. Colman filio Dare of Dayre More in Eile on the borders of Leinster and Munster, not more than four miles (Irish life, a mile and a bit) from Leamakevogue, *cf. VSH* 2, 324). A bishop, welcomed Mo-Choemog (+654) on his arrival at Leamak-evogue and prepared him a bath, v. *Mo-Choemog* 15. He and Mo-Choemog forced Failbe (Fland) king of Munster (628-639) to give way, v. *Mo-Choemog* 21. Sent butter to a nearby monastery of Ruadan (+587), v. *Ruadan* 25. *Nephew of Enda, son of his sister Darinea, *wife of Angus of Munster* (+492), v. *Endei* 12, evidently equating Enda's alleged sister with Colman's father Daire, followed v. *Ailbe (2)* 15, equating Colman f. 'Derane' with bishop Colman of Munster.

COLMAN, bishop in Dal Araide, V L. I;I. Baptised his nephew Colman of Dromore, (VI E/M) taught Finnian of Moville, *NLA* 1, 444.

COLMAN of Melk, Austria +1012, July 17 (translated 1014, Oct. 13). I;Germany. *BHL* 1881-2. *MGH SS* 4, 674, Kenney 613. Irish monk murdered while on pilgrimage to Jerusalem, at Stockerau, near Vienna, translated to Melk by the margrave Henry in 1014. His cult is extremely widespread throughout Austria, Bavaria, the Palatinate and Hungary, and he remained patron of Austria until 1663, Gougaud, *Saints Irlandais* 47. It is not easy to understand why so extensive a cult should attach to an apparently unimportant simple pilgrim, nor why it should be accepted by the Hungarians, standing enemies of the Austrians, within a few decades of his death, unless he were personally concerned with the Benedictine conversion of Hungary in 1001, sponsored by Pope Silvester II and politically directed against Austrian domination; for which there is neither evidence nor probability. Nor is it easy to see why the Hungarian king Koloman (1095-1116) should receive the name of a recent Austrian saint, even if he were born as early as the time of the Austrian nominee to the Hungarian throne, Peter, c.1045.

It does not seem probable that so extensive and important a cult arose so quickly from the murder of a casual pilgrim, within the lifetime of the contemporaries of the murder. It is likely that there already existed a cult of an earlier Colman, not hitherto specifically associated with the Austrian dynasty, which the margrave Henry and his successors attached to Colman of Melk; it may have originated with Colman of Wurzburg.

COLMAN of Wurzburg +689, July 8. I;Germany. Martyred with Kilian of Wurzburg, *BHL* 4660-3. It is possible that his name initiated the cult which concentrated from the eleventh century on Colman of Melk.

COLMAN of Hanbury, nr. Droitwich, Worcs. VII M.

COLMAN of Lindisfarne (*SU 8036*) +675, Feb. 18. I;E.I. *BHL* (1880/1). Bede *HE* **3**, 25-27; **4**, 1, 4; **5**, 25. Bishop of the Northumbrians, sent from Iona, in succession to Finan, championed Irish usage at Whitby 664. On his defeat, withdrew to Iona and thence to Inishbofin, Mayo (*L 56*) with Aidan's bones, most of the Irish and about thirty of the English monks of Lindisfarne. Established the English in Ireland at Mayo (*M 27*). Called Archbishop of York (Eboracae civitatis episcopus metropolitanus) by his contemporary, Eddius (10).
Aedeluin, Eata, Geraldus, Tuda.

COLUMBA of Iona (*MN 2723*) 521-597, June 9. I;I.S.P. *BHL* ff. vitae, *Adamnan*, ed. Reeves, 1857, also Anderson, 1961; Colgan, *TT* 321 ff.; Bede *HE* **3**, 4. *cf.* Kenney, index, especially 428 ff. The fullest collection of traditions is that of O'Donnell, 1522, chief of Tirconnell, head of Columba's *Cenel*. This extraordinary repository of legend ranges through the whole spectrum from the highly probable to the impossible; but it is only available in the 60-page extract that was translated in Latin by Colgan in 1647 (Vita Quinta, *TT* 389 ff.); the text is published with translation in *ZCP* 3-5 (1901-1905), 9-11 (1913-1916).

The essentials of his life are embedded in the work of Adomnán, a relative and later abbot of Iona, who wrote about a century after his death, and collected his information well within living memory. Adomnán's work is not a biography, but a collection of wonders, arranged by type, without chronological framework.

Columba was born a prince of the northern Ui Neill; two of his first cousins obtained the throne of Ireland in his life, to which he was born eligible. The tradition of the Columban houses represents him as hostile, in his twenties, to the overriding influence of the plebeian Ciaran of Clonmacnoise; the Clonmacnoise tradition concurs. He is said to have founded some 40 houses in Ireland, the first of them at Derry, hard by the dynastic capital of his family at Ailech. He is said to have copied, without permission, the Gospel Book of Finnian of Moville, who obtained judgement against him from king Diarmait m. Cearbaill; who also executed the king of Connacht's son, who had killed a noble youth at the games and sought sanctuary with Columba. Columba therefore is said to have rallied both the monks and the regional kings against Diarmait's centralised monarchy, and to have won military victory, by prayers on the battlefield, at the unusually bloody battle of Cuil

Dremhne, in 563.The consequence was exile, imposed by a monastic synod, which deplored the involvement of monks in secular political warfare, after a proposal of excommunication had been rejected, on the advice of Brendan of Birr. Adomnán (Bref. ad Fin. *cf.* 1, 7) associates his exile with the battle of Cuil Dremhne, and is the authority (3, 3) for the statement avoided by much of the later tradition, that he was actually excommunicated by the synod of Telltown, whose enforcement Brendan stayed (Brendan is reproachfully asked 'Quare coram excommunicato surgere et eum exosculari non renueris?'). Adomnán indirectly substantiates the charges; Columba was excommunicated 'wrongly, for trivial and pardonable offences'; Adomnán defines his own concept of offence and excellence by listing among Columba's virtues that 'in the terrible clash of war, his prayers won victory for some kings from God, defeat for others' (1, 1 [8a]). Such prayers were the substance of the offence with which tradition reproached Columba. All sources emphasise his transformation into the 'dove of peace' in exile.

There are slight discrepancies in the sources about the date of Columba's exile to Britain. The *Annals* give 563, his death in 597, his birth in 521. The main MSS. of Bede (*HE* **3**, 4) say that he died at the age of 77, 'about 32 years' after he came to Britain; and attach his arrival to the year of Justinian's death, 565. Adomnán (summarised Reeves 310) fixes his death to 597 by a whole number of calendar coincidences, at the age of 76, 34 years after his arrival, when he was 42, giving the *Annals* date of 563. Bede's MS. variants also read 76 and 34, as Adomnán; and Bede in any case is careful to make his date approximate 'circiter'. Adomnán was a scholar as careful as Bede, and, in this particular, much better informed. His date must stand.

Settled in Iona, converted Brudeus, king of the Picts; consecrated Aedan king of the Scots of Dal Riada; and accompanied him to the convention of Drumceat (Roe Park, Newtown Limavady, Derry (*D 62*), Reeves, *Adamnan* 37), presided over by his cousin king Aed m. Ainmerech, where he secured the independence of Dal Riada of Britain, and the regulation of the profession of scholars in Christian Ireland. He and his successors at Iona appointed monks as bishops to communities in Britain, who, as monks, remained subordinate to the abbot's authority. He visited Ireland on a number of occasions, and travelled widely among the Irish colonists in and about Dal Riada of Britain, making at least two journeys to the northern Picts. His closest Irish associates were Brendan of Clonfert, Cainnech, Comgall, and Cormac Ua Liathain. He quarrelled with Cainnech, remained at odds with Finnian of Moville, and, just before his death, refused to accept Fintan Munnu, who had announced his intention of settling in Iona. Died on Sunday, June 9, valid for 597, Reeves, *Adamnan* 309 ff.

Numerous other monks, not connected with Columba in their tradition or his, settled among the Picts and northern British, but Columba remained the principal ecclesiastic of Aedan's Dal Riada. In or about 573 Kentigern obtained an influence at the court of Riderch of Alclud, comparable with Columba's position in Dal Riada. Kentigern is said to have met him, and Adomnán (1, 15) reports a message sent to Riderch to assure him that he would not be killed by his enemies, but would die in his bed at home, presumably implying a guarantee against attack by Aedan, hardly given without Aedan's authority. During his lifetime, warfare between the British, Scots and northern Picts is not recorded, though wars between the Scots and southern Picts broke out after the death of Brudeus. It is probable that Columba's influence prevailed to keep the northern kingdoms at peace.

He is said to have written on Patrick's miracles, *VT* 60, of Colman m. Lenin. A colophon in the Book of Durrow (*cf.* Patrick), originally written not long after his death, attests an early tradition of his reputation for calligraphy and scholarship, and perhaps also of his respect for Patrick. Adomnán's work depicts the stern vigour of his character, his towering ability, and Bede comments that, whatever the character of the man himself, the church that he founded in northern Britain set and maintained an example of discipline and restraint that was later to shape the Christianity of England and Europe.

His churches and monasteries in Ireland and Scotland are listed, Reeves, lxvii, 276-298, 462; O'Hanlon 6, 550 ff.; Forbes, *Kalendars* 306; in England (Westmorland and Cornwall), Arnold-Forster 3, 349; 2, 144, *cf. LBS* 2, 166 ff., where the suggestion that the Cornish churches should belong to Columba of Terryglass, though possible, lacks evidence, and conflicts with the days. The fairs (June 9) commemorate Columba of Iona, the feasts (Nov. 15) of Columban (Nov. 23 OS). There appear to be no dedications in Wales, but there are a couple in Brittany, *LBS* 2, 166.

His principal teachers were Finnian of Clonard, and Gemman, his immediate successor, his cousin Baitan.

Abban, Carthacus, Colman Elo, Constantinus rex Cornubiensis, Farannan, Fechin, Fergna of Hinba, Finan of Swords, Gildas, Ita, Lasrian of Devenish, Macarius, Mobhi, Mocteus, Mo-Luoc, Naille, Ninian, Ruadan, Ternan, etc.

Modern traditions, largely under the influence of Bede, see Columba above all as the apostle of the Picts. Adomnán, his relative and successor, presents him as the spiritual guide of the Dal Riadan Scots. The Irish Lives see him as the greatest monk, whose *paruchia* included more houses in Ireland than that of any other monk; and they mention his work in Dal Riada in passing.

Columba visited the court of the northern Picts at least twice, and was the principal ecclesiastic, whom Brudeus most heeded. But the perspective of Iona, given by Adomnán, and of the insular Irish, given in the Saints' Lives, differs from Bede's. To them, the Picts were incidental to Columba's main work; Adomnán records the visits, and says that Brudeus honoured him, but has little to say of priests and bishops sent from Iona to the Picts. But the scattered notices of the rest of the Irish saints name some two dozen other monks, including Cainnech, Comgall, and other outstanding leaders, who established houses among the Picts and Scots, which no tradition links with Columba.

COLUMBA of Terryglass (Tirdeglas), Tip. *(R 89)* + 551, Dec. 13. I;I.E. *BHL* 1897. vitae *Sal.* 445; unpublished, *cf. AB* 72, 1954, 343. A Leinsterman (Ui Crimthainn), educated by Colman Cule and Finnian of Clonard, visited Rome and Tours. On his way home, he passed through those parts of Britain that were inhabited by pagan Saxons, and resuscitated the king's recently dead children, baptising them and returning them quickly to Heaven at their own request. In so doing 'conversus ad cinerem iterum oravit . . . de cinere suscitavit ad vitam' (10). I have not met any other reference to the ashes of the dead in Saints' Lives; the usage is not biblical. The story is a conventional consolation miracle, where the bereaved are assured that the deceased are happier in Heaven, and the deceased brought back confirm their joy themselves, and receive baptism in assurance of Heaven. It appears that the original version concerned ashes and a cremation burial; the ashes are unlikely to be a later addition since, though many saints revived many corpses, Columba is unique in reviving a burnt body, yet the hagiographer makes nothing of his exceptional claim. Gave last unction to Finnian of Clonard, died soon after nearby (both died in the plague, *Annals*), there buried, subsequently his relics translated to Terryglass against the opposition of the southern Ui Neill, headed by Colman Bec (+589) (26-31).

Erc of Kerry, Fintan of Clonenagh, Luchtigern, Mobhi maccu Alde.

COLUMBAN of Luxeuil and Bobbio (Burgundy and Lombardy) +615, Nov. 23. I;Gaul.Italy. *BHL* 1898 ff. vita, *MGH SRM* 4, 1902, 1 ff., ed. Krusch, *cf.* 7, ii, 1920, 822 ff., contemporary, by Jonas, who entered Bobbio in 618 and was secretary to successive abbots. Eleven of Columban's letters are extant (*MGH* Epp. 3, 1892, 154 ed. Krusch), with several sermons (Migne *PL* 80, 229), his rule (*PL* 80, 209), penitential (*PL* 80, 223) and a Commentary on the Psalms (*PL* 26, 863) and other works that may be his, Kenney 186, ff. Born *c.*545 (Ep. 10, where 'ad 18 Olympiadis venimus annos': means 'I am nearly 68', not 69/72 as Kenney 194. Jonas' statement that he crossed to Gaul 'vicensimum ergo aetatis annum agens' (4, inferior variant 'Tricesimum') is certainly corrupt, but could mean after 20 years as a monk; he had been 'many years' at Bangor (Jonas 3). Studied under Sinell (+605) (3-4). Entered the monastery of Benechor (Bangor, founded 558) under Commogellus (Comgall +605), crossed to Gaul, by way of Britain with 12 companions (including, *cf.* Jonas 11, Gallus), *c.*589/590 (Jonas 20, *cf.* Kenney 187, 101), in the time of *Sigibert* (+575) of Burgundy (Jonas 6), settled at Annegray (Haute Saone), succoured by bishop Carantocus 'de Salicis' (Saulx ?) (Jonas 7), moved to Luxeuil (10). His miracles chiefly concern arable farming and brewing (16). Called king Theodoric an adulterer to his face, compared his all-powerful grandmother Brunhild with Jezebel, and the 'ancient serpent', denounced the heirs to the throne, in a royal vill in the presence of the court, as illegitimate (18-19), and threatened the queen with excommunication. The king accused him of disrupting civil society ('ab omnium saeculorum mores disciscat'; 'cur ab conprovincialibus moribus discisceret', 19), and ordered his expulsion, with his Irish and British monks, leaving his Gallic converts behind (20). Sent under guard to Nantes, and ensigned on a 'ship engaged in the Irish trade' (Navis quae Scottorum commercia vexerat, 23); en route, an officer attempted to murder him at Avalon (20), and, when forbidden to buy food in Orléans, was succoured by a Syrian trader, a woman with a blind husband, long established on the Loire (22). The ship, however, was forced to put back to port, and Columban made his way to the territory of Theudebert, where he established the monastery of Bregen (27). He considered, but rejected, a proposal to move eastward and convert the Slavs (27). Adjured Theudebert to resign his crown and become a cleric, to the ribald amusement of his courtiers. When Brunhild and Theuderic deposed and tonsured Theudebert (612) (28), migrated to Lombardy to Bobbio, where he died (29).

His total disregard of the conventions of church and state electrified Gaul, and initiated a massive recruitment in the east and centre to monasteries on the Irish, and subsequently Anglo-Irish model. It perturbed the church; his polite but firm exposition to Gregory the Great of the pope's mistakes was difficult to repress or accept; argument therefore shifted to externals, in particular the divergent date of the Irish and Roman Easters (*cf. AB* 64, 1946, 200; Kenney 210, etc.). His Latin was considerably more vigorous and literate than that of contemporary Gaul, as though 'a product of the Gaul of Sidonius Apollinaris (fifth century) had dropped in the Gaul of Gregory the Great' (Kenney 189) and Bobbio became a major centre for the study and preservation of classical texts. He may name St. Columb, Co. (*SW 9163*) and Culbone, Somerset (*SS 8448*), *cf.* Columba of Iona.

COMGALL of Bangor, Down (*J 58*) 515 (525)-605, May 10. *BHL* 1909-1910, vitae *VSH* 2, 3 = *Sal.* 773, *cf. AB* 52, 1934, 348; Kenney 396. Of Dal Araide, foretold by MacNissi of Connor. Served in a levy, baptised by presbyter Feidlimid, studied for a long time with Fintan of Cluain Eduech and Ciaran of Clonmacnoise. Returned home, ordained by Lugid (?bishop of Connor, died 546). Settled on Ely Island, Lough Erne, Ferm. (*H 15*). Relaxed his excessively austere rule under pressure of other abbots, after seven of his monks had died of hunger. He then resolved to emigrate to Britain, but was dissuaded by Lugid, and founded Bangor (558) and dependent houses, containing 3,000 monks. Established fraternitas with **C**ainnech, **C**oemgen and **C**olumba at Uisnach (v. *Coem.* 27). Visited Britain in 565, founded monastery in Tiree (Heth), sustained a raid by Picts (22), visited Columba with Cainnech, **B**rendan of Clonfert and **C**ormac Ua Liathain (Ad. v. *Col.* 3, 17); visited Columba (31) and by Columba (33-34) after the convention of Drumceat (Ad. v. *Col.* 1, 49). Accompanied Cainnech and Columba to the court of Brudeus of the Picts (51). Visited by, and outlived Finnian (Findbarrus) Moville (+580) (28, 30). Cormac m. Diarmata of the Ui Bairrche, king of the Ui Cennselaig, became a monk at Bangor; Bangor monks drowned in Belfast Loch (Ad. v. *Col.* 3, 13). Asked by queen Cantigern of Dal Araide to try a slave girl accused of trying to poison her, sentenced her to freedom and penance (52; *cf.* penance substituted for civil punishment, e.g., v. *Brigit* [Ultan 59] *TT* 533, corn thieves) v. *Ita* 25 (murderer). Received pupils from **S**inell (+605), including Aedan of the Ua Dunlaing (kings of north Leinster) (54) and **C**olumban of Luxeuil. Died and buried at Bangor; his arm taken as a relic by abbot Fiachra of Airard (57), who gave him last unction. He is celebrated in the hymns of the Antiphonary of Bangor, composed in the seventh century, the first perhaps not long after his death (Kenney 265; *Ulster Journal of Archaeology*, 1, 175). Aged 90, *M. Don., M. Tal., A. Tig.*: 80 *CS M. Tal.* dates the foundation of Bangor to Feb. 1, 556. He has churches in Scotland, at Dercongal, Holywood (*NX 97*) and Durris, Kincardine (*NO 79*). Forbes, *Kalendars*, 309, O'Hanlon 5, 184. The Irish Bangor was probably modelled on the British Bangor-on-Menai of **D**aniel, since *AU* 631 (=634) describes it as 'Bennchoir Moer in Britannia', 'The Great Bangor, in Britain'; and because in the Irish tradition, Comgall founded Irish Bangor when he was prevented from emigrating to Britain to join holy men he admired. He sent out numerous missionaries, including Columban, **F**indbar, Lactean, **L**uchtigern, Molua (**L**ugid), (v. *Mo-Choemog* 10); in three teams, v. *Lugid* 18.

Blaan, **C**oemgen, **D**agaeus, **D**aniel, **E**ugenius, **F**inan of Swords, **F**innian of Moville, **F**intan of Dun Blesc, **F**intan Munnu, **L**ugid, **M**ac Nisse, **M**aelrubha, **M**obhi, **M**o-Choemog, **M**o-Chua, **M**o-Luoc.

CONAIDUS, *see* Meven.

CONAN, *see* Cynan.

CONCENN, abbot of Llancarfan, VII M. B;B. *LL* index.

CONGAR, *see* Docco.

CONGEN, abbot of Llantwit, VI M. B;B. *LL* index.

CONIGC, abbot of Llancarfan, VI L. B;B. *LL* index.

CONIN, *see* Baitan of Iona.

CONINDRUS (Cynidr?) V M. B;Man. British bishop, consecrated **M**ac Cuil to Man, with **R**umilus (Romelius?) and **P**atrick, Muirchú 22, who understood them to be already bishops in Man.

CONLAED of Kildare +518. I;I. Bishop of **B**rigit; baptised **T**igernach. One of the three chief artisans of Ireland, together with Tassach and **D**agaeus, *M. Oeng.*

CONOC, 'son' of Brychan, VI E, Nov. 18? B;B.I.A? Colgan *ASH* 311. Assigned to Feb. 11 by Colgan, without calendar authority *LBS* 2, 270. He may or may not be identical with the Irish Mo-Chonoc, companion of Cadoc in Ireland and Cornwall, Nov. 18 in *M. Don., M. Gor.*; or with Quonococ, follower of Paul Aurelian in Brittany, v. *Paul Aur.* 11. He is remembered in south-west Ireland (O'Hanlon 2, 476), at Padstow (*SW 9175*), Boconnoc and perhaps St. Pinnock (*SX 2063*) in Cornwall, with Cadoc, and Llangynog in Carmarthenshire, Brecon and Denbigh (*SN 3316*; *SO 0245*; *SJ 0526*); *cf.* Cinauc (+?*c*.593).

CONOCAN of Quimper VI M, Oct. 16. A;A. *AG* 623 (Guenegan), native of Landerneau, student at Landevennec, contemporary of Winwaloe and Childebert, *Cart. Landevenec* 41, p. 19 (Conocanus), bishop of Cornouailles after Corentin.

CONOTIGIRNUS, *see* Kentigern.

CONSTANS Caesar, monk, +409. B;B.(Gaul, Spain). 'Constantinus (III, Emperor 406-411) Constantem filium suum, pro dolor, ex monacho Caesarem factum . . . in Hispanias misit' Orosius 7, 40, *cf.* Zosimus 6, 4 ff. The elder of Constantine's sons, he took Terentius as his magister and Apollinaris (probably grandfather of Sidonius Apollinaris, *cf.* Sid. Ap. *Ep.* 3, 12, 5) as his praetorian prefect to repress a revolt by the relatives of Honorius. He succeeded, and returned to his father in Gaul, Constantine sending his own magister Gerontius to Spain. Constans was then sent back to Spain with Iustus as his magister, but was killed by Gerontius.

CONSTANS VII L. I;I.'anchorita qui est in Eoinis' (Eanish, L. Oughter, Cavan, *H 30*? Hogan *Onomasticon* 399) *c.*670. 'Haec Constans in Gallis invenit', *Muirchú II*, addenda, Book of Armagh 8ᵛ, *AB* 1, 1882, 584, Stokes *VT* 300, cited as authority for Patrician legends.

CONSTANTINUS rex Britto, abbot of Rathin 635 – after 638, March 11. B;I. Monk of Mochuda (Carthacus), obtained three years' respite before Carthacus' expulsion from Rathin (638), *M. Oeng., cf.* Keating 2, 13 (ed. Dineen 3, 121), etc. Succeeded Mochuda at Rathin, *M. Oeng., M. Gor.*, scholiast, *Cathal Maguire* (cited *LBS* 2, 173; *Calendar of Cashel*, cited *ASH* 574, Forbes 312). Formerly king of the Britons, *M. Oeng., M. Don., Maguire*, etc.; Britto also *M. Gor., M. Tal.* 'as others say', son of Fergus king of the Picts, king of Alba, *Maguire, M. Oeng., M. Gor., M. Don., M. Tal.*, etc. by confusion with king Constantine m. Fergusa, died 820, builder of Dunkeld. Cleared woodland to establish 'Ceapach Cusantin' (Constantine's clearing), near Rathin, poem ascribed to Ruman m. Colmain (optimus poeta, died 747, *A. Tig.*) cited Forbes 312, *LBS* 2, 174 (reading Ruman m. Duach), *M. Oeng.* Visited Alba, with Mochuda's permission, to see his 'children and kin' (a clainni 7 a ceneil), *M. Oeng.*, perhaps echoing confusion with Constantinus rex Cornubiensis.

The successor of Mochuda at Rathin in 638 is very unlikely to be identical with Constantinus rex Cornubiensis, who had become a monk 50 years earlier, and is said to have had an adult son before conversion. It is theoretically possible that a second Cornovian king became a monk; but Constantinus of Rathin was contemporary with Constantinus of Alclud, born in the last decades of the sixth century, who is said to have been a saint, and was replaced as king of Alclud some years before 643, when the next known king died; he may therefore be identical with him.

CONSTANTINUS rex Cornubiensis, monk of St. David's, +*c.* 596/600, March 11. B;B.(I.S.P.). *BHL* 1932. 'Conversio Constantini ad Dominum', 589, *Annals.* 'Audita . . . fama David agii reges . . . eius . . . monasterium petunt . . . Constantinus

Cornubiensium rex sum desereret regnum, ac . . . in huius patris cella subiugaret; ibique diu fideli conversatus servitio, tandem in aliam longinquam patriam monasterium fundavit', v. *David* 32. The Life expressly does not say that he served at St. David's in St. David's lifetime. 589 is independently given as the year of David's death; *AT* and *AC*, who give both entries, place the conversion before David's death.

'Constantinus, Paterni regis Cornubiae filius' married the daughter of a king of Britannia Minor. Inconsolable on her death, he consigned his kingdom to his son, and crossed to Ireland, where he stayed seven years in 'quandam domum religionis', (Rahan of Carthacus, founded before 580), carrying corn from the granary to the mill. He was ordained, went to Columba (of Iona) and was sent by Kentigern to preach in Galvedia (Galloway); he died of wounds inflicted by sea-borne raiders in Kintyre, 'about the year *576*', *Brev. Ab.* PH 67. Succeeded Carthacus at Rahan (638). A dozen sites that bear his name in Pictish and in Scot territory are listed, Forbes 314. He also names several sites in Cornwall and Devon, Constantine (*SW 7329*), near Falmouth, Constantine (Bay) (*SW 8674*), near Padstow; and Milton Abbot (*SX 4079*), near Tavistock, whose dedication to Constantine and Elidius (Teilo), confirms the association with David, whose mother Nun is patron of the adjoining parish of Bradstone. Constantine's dedications and place-names in North Wales, Herefordshire, Shropshire, and Staffordshire might derive from him, or from Constantine of Wroxeter, with whom he might be identical. He is distinct from Gildas' Constantine of Dumnonia, and from Constantine of Rathin and Constantine the Culdee, both also kings. The prominence given to his conversion in the *Annals* suggests that it was regarded as a major event; and Constantine, son of Riderch of Alclud, born at about the time of his conversion may therefore have been named after him. The *Annals* entry also confirmed the Brey, Aberdeen tradition that he was a monk in Ireland as well as at St. David's.

CONSTANTINUS, king of the Scots, abbot of the Culdees of St. Andrews, +*c*.945. S;S. m. Aeda m. Cinaeda m. Alpin, *CPS* lists, *cf.* index, etc. He may possibly be responsible for some of the places and churches named Constantine in Scotland, listed under Constantine rex Cornubiensis.

CONSTANTIUS, presbyter of Lyons, *c*.410-*c*.480, *DCB*, encouraged Sidonius Apollinaris to publish his letters, which he dedicated to Constantius, then very old, publishing book 1 *c*.478. Biographer of his elder contemporary, Germanus of Auxerre. Lupus.

CORCODEMUS, *c*.310.

CORENTIN of Quimper V L/VI E? Dec. 12. A;A. *BHL* 1954-7, vitae *AG* 798 (1); ed. Plaine, *Bull. Soc. Arch. de Finistère* 12, 148 (13, 118) (2), (late IX) cited, with discordant references, *BHL* 1954, *LBS* 2, 182. Doble 2, 45. Born in Armorica, hermit at Plomodiern, bishop of Cornouailles; Quimper is commonly called Kemper Courentini, *Cart. Quimper, Quimperlé, Landevenec*, indices. Ordained at Tours (*1; 2*). He is made contemporary with king Gradlon, mid to late V, and also patron of *Winwaloe* and *Tudy*, visited by *Paternus* and *Malo*, hardly earlier than the 540s. He has nothing to do with Chari(l)ato, bishop in Armorica at the Council of Angers, 453, Mansi, 7, 899 (as *LBS*); consecration at Tours is proper and normal before the third British migration of the 540s, not the prejudice of a late writer 'adverse to the independence of the British church', as *LBS* 2, 183. It is just possible that he had a long episcopate, *c*.490-540; but more probable that he was a late V bishop, patron of Cornouailles and therefore claiming for his successors a traditional authority over its monks. His association with them is not recorded in their lives, save in an association, not necessarily chronological, in the verses attached to v. *Winwaloe* (*AB*) 2, 19. *Accompanied **S**amson and Malo to Paris, *c*.556*.

He is patron of Cury, Co. (*SW 6721*) (S. Corentini, 1234, 1302, *DEPNS*), and of numerous places in Brittany, especially in the diocese of Quimper, *LBS* 2, 184.

CORMAC Ua Liathan VI M/L, June 21. I;I. Adomnán, v. *Columbae* 1, 6 (1); 2, 42 (2); 3, 17 (3). Poems, Reeves, *Adamnan*, 264 (4); 270 (5); 276 (6). *M.* Made three unsuccessful voyages in search of desert in the ocean (*1; 2*): the first started from Broadhaven Bay (Eirros Domno [Irrus Domnann; Erris (Head) of the Damnonii], beyond the Mo, *F 74*) (*1*). He accompanied **C**olumba, **B**rendan of Clonfert and **C**ainnech to the court of Brudeus king of the Picts, *c*.565/578 (*3*), and on the second voyage Columba asked Brudeus, in the presence of the 'regulus' of the Orkneys, whose hostages he held, to see that 'our people', who had set out to seek a hermitage in the uncrossable ocean ('desertum in pilago intransmeabili'), came to no harm if they landed in the Orkneys. On the third voyage, they sailed north for 14 days and met dangerous swimming creatures the size of frogs whose sharp stings pierced their coracle skins (? pack ice) (*2*). Abbot of Durrow, *M. Don., M. Gor.* (*4; 5*); *cf. M. Tal., M. Oeng.* He is commemorated near Durrow, in Wexford, and in Ayrshire and Galloway, O'Hanlon 6, 760-1, Forbes 316.

CORMAC m. Eogain VI E/M, Dec. 13 (*M. Oeng., M. Gor., cf. M. Don.* Dec. 23) I;I. Irish Life, *Book of Lecan*, f. 60b, *cf. Ballymote* 233a (*MHH* 135 and 29), paraphrased in Latin, *ASH* 751.

A Munsterman, given numerous brothers. Founded many churches in Connacht in the time of Eogan Bel (502-546) and Ailill Onbanda (546-551), especially in Tirawley and among the Luaigni and Galenga. The Life is a mass of genealogical and local tradition concerning the origin of Connacht houses.

CORMAC, bishop of Armagh, 491-498, Feb. 17. I;I. *Book of Leinster* 42[c] (sedit xii, for xvii); 'primus abbas'; 'de Clan Chernog' (in northern Ui Maine, Connacht?). Confused with the eighth-century Cormac of Trim.

CORMAC m. Cuilennain, king and bishop of Munster, *c*.885-908. I;I. O'Curry, index; Kenney, index, especially 11. Author of numerous learned works, including, probably, the first (lost) version of the Book of Rights, and the 'Sanas Chormaic', Cormac's *Glossary*, partially published, Stokes, *Three Irish Glossaries*, O'Donovan and Stokes, Calcutta, 1868; and elsewhere (corrected proof sheets in Stokes Library, University College, London, marked 'Irish Archaeological Soc.'). Much of the MS. material about Cormac appears to be unpublished. The available portions of the *Glossary* are the work of a scholar of high standard.

CREWENNA VI E, Feb. 2 (1). I;B. Came to Cornwall with **B**reaca and others, Leland, *Itin.* 3, 15, cited *LBS* 1, 229. Patron of Crowan, Co. (*SW 6434*), festival Feb. 2 (*LBS* 2, 188; Feb. 1, Doble 1, 99). Possibly identical with Croine of Kilcrony, Wicklow, *M.* Jan. 27.

CRONAN of Balla, *see* Mo-Chua.

CRONAN of Roscrea, Tip. (*S 18*) +640, Apr. 28. I;I. *BHL* 1995. *VSH* 2, 22. *CS* 541. Munsterman, studied in Connacht, monk at Clonmacnoise, visited **M**o-Choemog (+654), gave the viaticum to Lugid in 612; encountered king Fingen of Munster (607-619). Distinct from Cronan bishop of Nendrum +645, and Cronan abbot of Moville +649. **F**ursey, **L**ugid.

CRONAN of Moville +649, Aug. 7. I;I. *M. cf.* Cronan of Nendrum.

CRONAN of Nendrum +644, Jan. 7. I;I. Pope John's letter, 640, was addressed, among others, to bishop Cronan and a priest Cronan, Bede *HE* **2**, 19.

CUANU of Kilcoona, Galway (*M 34*) VII E/M? Feb. 4. I;I. *CS* 931 = *ASH* 249. Brother of Carthacus (Mo-Chutu) (+639)?, scholiasts, cited *ASH*. Followed by 1,746 monks (8), received Fursey's bell (9, 10). Abbot of Lismore, *M. Don., M. Gor.*, etc. He is possibly identical with Cuana, cited frequently by the annalists as a source for events up to 640. Fintan Munnu.

CUIMINE Albus (the white) (Cummeneus), abbot of Iona, 657-669, Feb. 24. I;S. *ASH* 408, author of a Life of Columba, cited by Adomnán v. *Col.* 3, 5. Took relics of SS. Peter and Paul to Roscrea (*ASH* 411, 26).

CUIMINE (Cummianus), bishop at Bobbio, VIII E. I;Italy. Epitaph, erected by king Liutprand (712-744) *MGH* Poet. Lat. aevi. Carol. 1, 1887, 107, Kenney 516.

CUIMINE (Cummianus) VII. I;I. Convened the successors of Ailbe, Ciaran of Clonmacnoise, Brendan of Clonfert, Nessan and Lugid (Mo-Lua) at Mag Lena near Durrow to discuss the Easter problem, 633, and reported the results to Segene of Iona. His report is extant. Migne *PL* 87, 969, *cf.* Kenney 220. Possibly abbot of Durrow, identical with any of the score or so of seventh-century Cuimine listed in the martyrologies.

CUIMINE Foda (the tall), abbot of Clonfert, 596-661, Nov. 12. I;I. Scattered stories, *cf.* Kenney 242.

CUIMINE (Cummian) (of Durrow?) VII E. I;I. *PL* 87, 969. Kenney 220, *cf. ASH* 409. Wrote, *c.*633 to abbot Segene of Iona and to his own blood-brother Beccan, an anchorite (? Beccan Ruim [of Rum, *NM 39*?] March 17 *M*), to explain the development of the Easter controversy. Bede *HE* **2**, 19 mentions its initiation, in a letter from Pope Honorius (625-638). Cummian relates that he convened a synod of the abbots of Ailbe (of Emly), of Ciaran 'Colonensis' (Clonmacnoise), of Brendan (of Birr?), of Nessan (of Mungrit, Limerick *R 55*) and of Lugid of Clonfert Mulloe 'in campo Lene' (Mag Lene, Moylen, Offaly, the plain and heath which includes Durrow, *N 33*). They decided to celebrate the same Easter as the universal church in the next year, but a 'whited wall', probably Fintan Munnu, arose to lead a conservative opposition after the meeting. A delegation was therefore sent to Rome, and came back in the third year, having learnt the practice of the universal church, and discovered that the Irish and the Roman Easter differed by a full month, which implies the year 631. The delegation was doubtless headed by Lasrian of Leighlin who 'brought the new order from Rome to Ireland' and defended it at the synod of Mag Ailbe, presumably after Cummian's letter was written, since the letter mentions only the delegates' return, but not the second synod. The delegation and the synod were decisive, since Bede *HE* **3**, 3 noted that the southern Irish had accepted the Roman Easter before Aidan came to Northumbria, *c.*637. Cummian lists a number of Easter cycles which conflict with the Irish, including that brought by St. Patrick, 'noster papa'.

Cummian is doubtless one of the several Cuimines named in the martyrologies. Since he convened a number of major abbots, he was probably himself a major abbot. Since he wrote to Segene, and had a brother in Ionan territory, his was probably a Columban house. Since he convened the synod at Durrow, it is probable that he was abbot of Durrow. The names of the seventh-century abbots of Durrow are not recorded.

The southern Irish decision was followed by a letter addressed by Pope John IV in 640 to a number of northern ecclesiastics, quoted in full by Bede *HE* **2**, 19; but the northerners did not accept the change for another two generations.

CUMMIAN (Cummene) *see* Cuimine.

CURIG VI, Feb. 17. B;B.A. *LBS* 2, 192, known only from place-names and post-reformation legends, one of which, *Buchedd Ciric*, may be a fragment of a mediaeval Latin Life. Contemporary of Maelgwn in Gwynedd, attacked by Maelgwn, but prevailed. In the Middle Ages, he was identified with the Cilician Diocletianic martyr Cirycus (with Julitta), June 16, *BHL* 1801, ff. He has numerous dedications in north and south Wales, Cornwall, Devon and Brittany, and perhaps Scotland (Grigg), Forbes 319, *LBS*, sufficient to suggest that he was a major saint, ill-recorded because he was from north Wales, whence extremely few Lives or traditions have survived. He is perhaps St. Cyri(a)c of Laycock, Wilts., South Pool, Devon (*SX 7740*), and Swaffham Prior, Cambs. (*TL 5764*), Arnold-Forster 350. David, Decuman.

CUTHBERT, archbishop of Canterbury, 740-760. E;E. *DCB* correspondent of Boniface.

CUTHBERT of Lindisfarne (*NU 1242*) +687, March 20. E;E. *BHL* 2019-2032. *DCB*. Bede *HE* pref.; **4**, 26 – **5**, 1; **5**, 24. Anchorite of Farne, monk of Melrose and Ripon, consecrated bishop at York by Theodore; failed to dissuade Egferth from aggression against the Picts. More than any other native ecclesiastic, he shaped the character of the English church in the north after Whitby, deeply influencing contemporaries and future generations.

CUTHBERT of Wearmouth VIII E/M. *DCB*. Bede's abbot, correspondent of Boniface and Lullus.

CYBI, *see* Kebi.

CYNAN Colledauc VI E, Oct. 3 (Nov. 5). B;B.A. *AG* 675; *LBS* 2, 224. Doble 3, 89. Son of *Ludun and Tagu* (Leudonus), established at Ros-Ene (? Roseland peninsula, opposite Falmouth, Co., *SW 8032*). Received a bell from Gildas, came to an arm of the sea Hildrech (? Truro river). At Gudrun (Goodern, *SW 7843*), near the forest of Ros-Ene, lived king Theodoric, who seized Cynan's oxen, was blinded and healed, and gave the saint land. Cynan crossed to Brittany, at Landegu, and founded his monastery of Cleder. He returned to Britain to make an unsuccessful attempt to negotiate between *king Arthur and Modred* and went home to die at Cleder. Numerous dedications in Cornwall and Brittany. *LBS*, Doble.

CYNDEYRN, *see* Kentigern.

CYNGAR, *see* Docco.

CYNIDR of Glasbury, Radnor (*SO 1739*) VI, Dec. 8. B;B. Grandson of Brychan. Grouped with Maedoc as major saints in the Usk valley, v. *Cadoci* 22, *cf.* 25, 70. Possibly identical with Enoder in Cornwall. His cult is restricted to Brecnock, Radnor and Herefordshire, *LBS* 2, 258.

CYNIDR, *see* Conindrus.

CYNOG, *see* Conoc.

CYR(I)AC, *see* Curig.

DABIUS, *see* Mobhi of Iona.

DADO, *see* Ouen.

DAGAEUS of Inishkeen, Monaghan (*H 90*) +589, Aug. 18. I;I. *BHL* 2119. *Sal.* 891. *M*. Of the Ciannachta of Bregh (Cenel Eogain *M. Don.*). Baptised by Lasrian of Devenish (+563), pupil of Mocteus (+533), to whom he gave last unction (3; *cf.* v. *Moctei* 20), and of Ciaran of Clonmacnoise (+548); monk of Lasrian and Comgall of Bangor (588/605) (1-6), then of Clonmacnoise (7), *in Ciaran's lifetime*. Founded a large number of small monasteries (9 ff.). He is credited with more houses for women than any other mid-sixth-century saint, against the strong criticism of abbot Oenu of Clonmacnoise (548-570) (16). He was the outstanding scholar and craftsman of the sixth-century monasteries, in charge of 'the little monastery called the School' at Devenish, where he 'taught intensively literature, calligraphy and the plastic arts':'Huic . . . monasterio . . . secretum adiacet monasteriolum quod Scola dicitur, in quo Daygaeus literalem scientiam et scribendi notitiam atque fabrilem artem ad plenum didicit' (5). Craftsman of Bangor (6), brought vestments and books to Clonmacnoise (7). Worked for all the saints of Ireland for whom he 'made ecclesiastical utensils of iron and bronze, gold and silver and wrote many books' (3). Later, he 'made ingenious and wonderful things for the abbots and other saints of Ireland, bells large and small (*campanas, cimbala*), croziers, crosses, desks, caskets, pyxes, chalices, platters, small altars, chrisms, and book covers, some plain, some set out with gold and silver and precious stones, all for the love of God and the honour of the saints, without earthly payment' (3, *cf. M. Don., M. Oeng., etc.*). His pupils included Berachus (10) and Diarmait, king of the Ui Alilla of Connacht, who entered his monastery. The Life names an exceptionally large number of minor monks and nuns, most of them otherwise unknown outside the calendars. He revived many corpses, and died aged 140 (29). A bishop, *M. Oeng*. His water-mill (10). Conlaed, Ruadan.

DAGAN of Ennereilly, Wicklow (*T 28*) +641, Sept. 13. I;I. *ASH* 584. *M*. Of Dal Meisi Corb, Leinster, pupil of Mo-Choemog, beheaded as a boy, his severed head replaced by Cainnech, v. *Mo-Choemog* 26-27. Abbot of Inbyr Dayle (Ennereilly, Hogan *Onomasticon* 457) v. *Mo-Choemog* 26. *M*.

DAGAN of Achad-Dagain, Leinster VII E, Mar. 12. I;I. Took Mo-Lua's rule to Gregory the Great; died soon after Mo-Lua (609); abbot v. *Mo-Lua* (Lugid) *VSH* 47, 50; bishop *Sal*. I, 64, 68. Perhaps identical with bishop Dagan who visited Laurentius in Canterbury soon after 604, but refused to eat or lodge with the English and the Roman mission, Bede *HE* **2**, 4.

DAGAN, abbot of Llancarfan, VII L. I?;B. *LL* index. The name is Irish.

DAGAN of Padstow VI M, June 4. I;B. Studied under Petroc in Ireland, accompanied him to his British monastery. Leland *Script Brit.* 61. Probably named St. Degan's chapel, Trehowel, Llanwnda, Pemb. (*SM 9339*) (*LBS* 2, 284).

DAGA(N)US of Bangor (Ireland), uncertain date, May 29. I;I. Forbes, 320, confused with Dagan of Achad Dagain.

DAGOBERT II +679. Gaul;I. The last independent Merovingian king, tonsured and exiled to a monastery in Ireland, 656-676; the story summarised by Kenney, 496, *cf.* Wilfred.

DAIRCHELLUS, *see* Moling.

DAMASUS, Pope, 366-384, *DCB*. Received the title 'Pontifex Maximus' from Gratian, negotiated the aftermath of the Arian controversy, instituted the cult of the martyrs in the catacombs, impressed external pomp upon the Roman bishopric.

DAMIANUS, bishop of Rochester, *c*.655-*c*.664. E;E. Bede *HE* **3**, 20; **4**, 2. Native of Sussex.

DANIEL of Bangor (Caern.) (*SH 5771*) +584, Sept. 11 (*M*). B;B. Vita (lectiones) *LBS* 4, 387. British-born, hermit at 'Mons Danielis' near Pembroke (2) 'Capella S. Danielis', 1535, *cf. LBS* 330, Windmill Hill (*SM 9800*), living in a hut with 'animals and servants suitable for agriculture', where 'now stands a church of wonderful beauty and size named in his honour' (3), using plough oxen (7). Cured a man 'de partibus Oxoniis' and a woman of 'Caerwy in the diocese of Menevia (St. David's)' (9); made a pilgrimage to Jerusalem (9). When 'the cathedral church of *Bangor* (Gwynedd) was vacant through the death of its bishop', he was invited to fill the vacancy (4), protesting that he was virtually illiterate (5), but was miraculously transformed so that 'there was no one like him then in Britain for learning and literature' (6).

He was regarded as the outstanding bishop of the north, on a par with **D**ubricius in the south (e.g. *LL* 3, 71; v. *David* 50; *B. Dewi* 15), bishop and patron in the thirteenth-century version of Maelgwn's grant of Llanelwy to **K**entigern (*LBS*, 4, 385). His was the greatest monastery of north Wales, and made the name **B**angor synonymous with a large monastery. Since, unlike most of the greater abbots, he was particularly represented as bishop, it is probable that he was a hermit summoned to a vacant bisopric, of the kingdom of Gwynedd, as **S**amson to the Severn bishopric; who subsequently founded a monastery, as Martin and many other Gallic bishops. The date is probably before 558, since **C**omgall founded the Irish Bangor when he was deterred from joining holy men he admired in Britain, and Irish tradition regards the Welsh monastery as 'the great Bangor', *cf.* Comgall; and probably after the death of **M**aelgwn (*c*.551), since the only major native saint of his reign, **C**urig, emigrated, and Maelgwn appears in innumerable southern lives, and in Gildas, as the enemy of monasticism, powerful enough to prevent its large-scale success. His churches, in north and south Wales, *LBS* 2, 328, *cf.* **D**ubricius.

DANIEL of Brittany, named in a few places *LBS* 2, 331; Ploudaniel and Ploudenoual may take their names from king **D**aniel Dremrud, S. Denoual from a saint.

DANIEL of Hare Island, L. Ree (*N 04*) VI E/M. B;I. Hermit evicted by **C**iaran of Clonmacnoise (v. 25); do Breatnaibh, *Lismore* 4344.

DANIEL, bishop of Wessex (Winchester), 705-744. E;E. Bede *HE* pref.; **4**, 16, 18; **5**, 23. *ASC* 709, 721, 731, 744. Source of Bede's information on Wessex and Sussex, visited Rome 721, correspondent of **B**oniface, retired to Malmesbury, died there 745; a native of Wessex; *cf.* Plummer, *Bede* 2, 307-8. **H**aedde.

DANOC, abbot of Llancarfan, VII L. B?;B. *LL* 197c *cf.* v. *Cadoci* 62, distinct from Dagan.

DARERCA (Mo-Ninna) of Killevy, Armagh (*J 02*) +516, July 6. I;I. *BHL* 2095-2100, vitae *Sal.* 165 (1); by Conchubran, *ASS* July 2, 297 (2); by Geoffrey of Burton, abridged *NLA* 1, 198 (3). M. *cf.* O'Hanlon 2, 56; 2, 80. Born in Mag Coba, the Killevy region near Newry, daughter (? pupil of) Mochta (*1-3*). Consecrated by Patrick, trained by **F**aencha (v. *Faenchae cf.* v. *Endei*). With eight other young women, placed herself under the care of bishop Ibar of Wexford (+499); entered Kildare, *portaria hospitalis* of Brigit (+524). Established her own house (near Wexford? [8]), left it, after a dispute, with 50 nuns (11), to return home to found Killevy. Sent one of her nuns, Brignat, to study at Rosnat, Whithorn (25). Died under Eugenius f. Conayll, then ruler of three provinces (later king of Dal Araide and the Ulaid, died 554). The original version of (*1*) was apparently written by a contemporary of the fourth abbess, not later than the early seventh century, and may contain one of the earliest references to Patrick. (*2*) and (*3*) confuse her with the seventh-century English Modwenna, and give her houses in Scotland, *cf.* also Morwenna.

DARLUGDACH. The mention of Brigit's little-known disciple is curious; she has no known association with Scotland, and has left little trace in Ireland. She died a year after Brigit (Ultan, v. *Brigit*, 131, *cf.* 99; *TT* 541, *cf.* 539-540). Either some tradition close enough to Kildare to remember Brigit concerned Nectan, or she has some forgotten connection with the Strathmore region.

DARLUGDACH of Kildare +525, Feb. 1. I;I.P. v. *Brigit*, Ultan 99, 132; Animosus 65, 97 = *TT* 539, 541; 560, 562 = *ASH* 229. Successor of Brigit, died a year later. When young, slipped out of Brigit's bed to meet her lover, torn between desire and devotion, put live coals in her slippers, so that 'one fire extinguished the other' and virtue prevailed. Visited Nectan, king of the Picts, third year of his reign (*465*); Nectan dedicated Abernethy, Perth (*NO 1916*) to her and Brigit. She is said to have been venerated at 'Freysingen in Bavaria' (O'Hanlon, 2, 225; *cf.* 228? Freising, 15 miles north of Munich?).

DAVID *Dewi* of Menevia (St. David's), Pemb. (*SM 7525*) (523?)-589, March 1. B;B. *BHL* 2107-2112. vita, Ricemarchus, *VSB* 150 (whence derivatives, a few with variants or additions, *cf.* *LBS* 2, 286, D. S. Evans, *Buched Dewi*, Cardiff, 1965, xxvii ff., etc.). Ricemarchus (+1099) selected 'a few items' from 'a number of ancient MSS.', many of them barely legible (66 *cf.* 54). The items are drawn from two or more distinct lives; abstracted from the lives of other saints; and from local legends, where Welsh names are fancifully Latinised.

Born 'a xxx post discessum Patricii *de Menevia*' *ACm* *458* (expanded vita 3-4). 'Discessus' means death, the words 'de Menevia' being evidently a gloss. The later *Annals* death-date for Patrick, 493, was plainly intended, given 523; so v. *Carantoci* I, 2, born 30 years after Carantoc (*cf.* Cairnech Coem) crossed to Ireland (*c.*500), giving *c.*530. Died 589, *AI, AT, AC, CS;* (*ACm* 601 'David ep. Moni Iudaeorum', whatever its meaning, does not concern David's death). Died Tuesday, Mar. 1, which fits the calendar of 589, *LBS* 2, 306. Aged 147 (58; evidently drawn from *ACm* 458-601 = 143).

Son of 'Sanctus', *king of Cardigan*, and of Non(nita) virgo, daughter of Cynyr (Conaire?) (2-4), in the time of 'king Triphunus and his sons', *cf.* Agricola, VI E (5, *cf.* v. *Gildae* [CL] 4). His father hunted at Lin Henlanu on the Teifi, gave gifts to 'Maucanni ... nunc Depositi (Welsh *Gwystl*) monasterium' (2; Lin Henllan a Liton Maucan, B. *Dewi* 1); his mother lived in Pepidiauc (northern Pembrokeshire *YC* 9, 330) at 'maritima ecclesia' (v. *Gildae CL* 4; Ka[ir] Morva, Giraldus [Rolls 3, 381]: the White House, *Buchez Santez Nonn*, cited *LBS* 2, 293). Baptised by Ailbe (+528) (7; *cf.* v. *Ailbe* 19) of Munster. Educated at 'Vetus Rubus' (= Henllwyn, Old Bush), (*under Illtud* v. *Paul Aur.* 3, v. *Illtud* II), sent to Paulinus (Cynwyl Gaeo, Carm., *SN 6537*, tombstone); returned to Vetus Rubus, under bishop Guistlianus *his cousin* (9-14), seceded to establish Vallis Rosina (also called Hodnant) (now Merry Vale), by Portus Magnus (Porth Mawr, Whitesand Bay) on the Alun

(2; 15, 16), rightly glossed 'id est Menevia . . . modo ecclesia cathedralis' *NLA* 1, 254, St. David's (Mynyw, Cill Muine). These are traditions of identifiable localities; Guistlianus presumably named *Llan Gwystl*; his Hen Llwyn *LBS* 2, 293 translates Hen Fynyw, which is near Aberaeron, Card. (*SN 4562*). Henllan is east of Newcastle Emlyn (*SN 3040*). *LBS* 2, 289 equates the 'White House' with Tywyn on Whitesand Bay (*SM 7227*), where ruins of an unexcavated chapel and cemetery are said to have been visible in modern times.

He was harassed by Boya (*P*) (*B. Dewi* 7, Giraldus; Baia, 16 *NLA*), an Irish chief (16, *B. Dewi*; Pict, v. *Teilo LL* 100; the name is Germanic) who paraded naked women before his monks, but was killed by Lisci (Loisc?) (19), *cf.* Porth Llisky (*SM 7223*) and Clegyr Boia (*SM 7425*), Caer Fai (*SM 7524*).

He established an austere rule (21-31), 'Egyptios monacos imitatus', refusing gifts of land, the use of animals in agriculture, with a diet of vegetables and water, earning him the name David Aquaticus, and a routine of work, reading, writing, and prayer. The rule, described as that of the so-called 'meliores', was fiercely attacked by Gildas, *Epp.* 4 ff., citing v. *David* 22 verbatim, and is therefore a version of the original. Visited Jerusalem, with Teilo and Paternus (44, 48; *cf* v. *Teilo LL* 103 v. *Paterni* 20) where the Patriarch consecrated him.

At the Synod of Brefi, Card. (*SN 6454*) (49-54), convened to debate Pelagianism, he stood on a pile of clothing to address the assembled clerics, and his oratory swayed them, to the extreme anger of Cadoc, then absent abroad. Its conclusions were ratified later, by the Synod of Victoria (55), 569 *ACm*, to which a part of David's Penitential rulings are ascribed (*HS* 1, 118). Daniel, *Dubricius* and *Paulinus* attended.

Gildas denounced David's extremism; British tradition emphasises the antagonism between David's austerity, and the secular power and comfort of Cadoc, and Irish tradition makes Finnian of Clonard adjudicate between Cadoc, Gildas and David, awarding primacy to David. The Synod of Brefi is represented as a decisive victory for David. It was followed by the foundation of new houses following the rule of David 'all over the country' (56), and David's tradition acclaimed him as 'archbishop', 'head' of all Britain (especially 53, 56, 57) until his death (58 ff.).

His notable disciples included Aedan of Ferns (Maedoc) (15, 35, 36, 42), through whom 'a third or a quarter of Ireland followed David' (Irish tradition praises Finnian of Clonard for austerities comparable with David's, but in the next generation records instances of the successful pressure of a majority to persuade extremists to abandon excessive asceticism, *cf.* e.g., Cainnech, Comgall, Fintan); king Constantine (32); Mo-Domnoc (41, 43); and Scutinus, Scolanus, who tried to 'poison' him (37-38). His colleagues and allies included Teilo, Padarn, Brendan (of Clonfert?) (40) and the 'Irish abbot Barre' (39, *cf.* v. [Find] Barre 9 and Lugid [Mo-Lua]).

David is named more frequently than any other British saint except Gildas, in a dozen Irish Lives (*VSH, CS* indices; *ASH* 147, etc.) as well as British, often occurring out of due time and place to honour the saint concerned.

The cult of David (Bowen *SCSW* 52, fig. 13; *cf.* 12, *LBS* 2, 316 ff.; O'Hanlon, 3, 48; Arnold-Forster 3, 350, *cf.* 432, Nun) is exceedingly widespread in Demetia, Brecon and the Wye Valley, scattered in Cornwall and western Brittany. In England it stretches up the Fosse Way to Nottinghamshire, with churches in or close to most of the small Roman towns on the road, and extends to the West Riding of Yorkshire (Airmyn and Holme Bridge). It is wholly absent in Scotland, north Wales, and almost entirely absent in Glamorganshire, where Cadoc and Illtud are well remembered. Ricemarchus (13) includes among David's houses: Glastonbury, Bath, Crowland, Repton, and Leominster. There were British monasteries at Glastonbury and in the West Riding (Eddius 17) before the English conquest. There is no evidence for or against the existence of British houses, of David or any other monk, at the other places named. Outside Yorkshire, Devon, Cornwall, and the borders, the ancient dedications in England are Barton, Somerset (*ST 5431*), Moreton in the Marsh, Glos., Newbold-on-Stour, Wo. (*SP 2446*), Holme (*SK 8059*), and Farnsfield (*SK 6456*), Notts; Wettenhal, Ches. (*SJ 6261*), Caldecote, War. (*SP 3594*), near Mancetter. Samson also has dedications on the Fosse Way and at York. His dedications and David's are not found in areas settled by the English before *c*.580; if they are of later origin, an occasion must be found to explain a movement of Welshmen up the Fosse Way to Trent and Humber. The simpler inference is that they originated while the northern British kingdoms were in being, in contact with Gloucester and South Wales along the Fosse Way, in the years between about 560 and 580, when houses of the rule of David multiplied after Brefi, but were 'deserted by the British clergy, fleeing from the sword of the English enemy' (Eddius 17) thereafter.

Constantinus rex Cornubiensis; Declan; Findbar; Finnian of Clonard; Finnian of Llancarfan; Ismael; Justinian; Lugid; Paul Aurelian; Senan.

DAVID of Armagh *'David m. Guaire Ua Forannan episcopus Ardmacha et legatus totius Hiberniae'*. *Annals* 552 (*AU* 550, *cf*.552; *FM* 550). Probably Duach (died 547) is intended. The Ua Forannan were located in the north of Co. Tyrone (Hogan 672), in or near the territory of the Ui Tuirtre, whence Duach is said to have come. The confusion probably arises from a spelling Dui (for Duach), interpreted as Deui (David). The term 'legatus' implies that Duach discharged, or claimed, a papal mission, or endorsement. Mobhi of Inch is sometimes called David, but is not connected with Armagh.

DECLAN of the Dessi V L/VI E, July 24. I;I. *BHL* 2116. *VSH* 2, 32; *ITS* 16, 1914, 2. Son of Erc, *descended from high kings of the remote past*, born when 'Christians were rare individuals' in a pagan world (4), baptised by Colman of Munster, later a bishop (5). Sent, aged seven, to be schooled by Dimma, recently returned to Ireland after study abroad, Cairpri m. Colmain, a future bishop his fellow pupil (7 ff.). Went to Rome, under Ailbe (+528), consecrated by bishop Hilary (461-8), met *Patrick* (8-9), returned by the sea of Ycht and Britain (11), with Lunan (Irish, Runan) *son of the king of the Romans*, to become one of the four southern bishops, with Ailbe of Emly (Munster), Ciaran of Saigir (Ossory) and Ibar of Wexford (S. Leinster), who preached in (southern) Ireland before (the followers of) Patrick (12). Given licence to preach by king Angus (+492), *his stepfather*. Visited *David at Cill Muine* (15); received Ardmore, Waterford (*X 17*), from the chief of the Dessi against the will of the inhabitants (15-17). When Patrick *came to Cashel*, Ciaran and Ailbe accepted him as patron, Declan as an equal, but Ibar rejected him (18 ff.). Installed Fergal m. Cormaic (22) as ruler of the Dessi in place of a pagan. Freed hostages from Angus of Cashel (23). Visited Tara (26), expelled by force of arms from Ossory (subject to Leinster after 492) (27). Accepted Ailbe as 'archbishop of Munster' (34). His disciple and successor Ultan turned raiding pirate pagans to stones still visible (36). Received a 'legatio' from *Patrick archbishop of the Irish* (37). Received last unction from bishop Mac Liag, *cf*. Kil Macleage (Tramore) (*T 60*), died, in old age, buried at Ardmore (28-30). His cult does not appear to extend beyond Dessi Territory. Ciaran of Tubbrid.

DECUMAN of Dunster So. (*SS 9943*) VI E/M? Aug. 27. B;B. *BHL* 2118. *NLA* 1, 263. Native hermit in Wales, practised moderate abstinence, ill-educated, preferred labour to letters. Meeting too severe opposition at home, crossed the Severn sea to 'castrum Dorostorum', martyred; names St. Decuman's (St. Decombe's), Watchet (*ST 0743*), near Dunster. His name occurs in Cornwall, Brecon and Pembroke (*LBS* 2, 324) and at Llandegfan in Anglesey (Beaumaris *SH 5673*); the texts cited *LBS* 4, 216 are contrived, and do not distinguish Tegfan from Decuman. *LBS* 2, 324, gives a date, 706, but cites no authority. Though he might have been a late hermit killed by the incoming English, he sounds more like an expelled northerner, like Curig. His Pembrokeshire site was one of the 'seven bishop churches' in Demetia, and he may have been of greater importance than the fragmentary record suggests.

DEGA, *see* Dagaeus, Dagan.

DEINIOL, *see* Daniel.

DENOI, *see* Thynoy.

DERLUGDACH, *see* Darlugdach.

DEWI, *see* David.

DIARMAIT, *see* Justus.

DICU(I)L of Bosham, Sx. (*SU 8004*) 680. I;E. Bede *HE* **4**, 13. Irish abbot at Bosham, with five or six monks, living, without influence on the population, when Wilfred arrived in 680.

DICUIL, the geographer and astronomer. *c.*745-830. I;Gaul. Kenney 545 ff. Monk under Suibne (? abbot of Iona +772) in Ireland before 767. Settled at the Carolingian court, perhaps at Aachen, *c.*800, perhaps on the sack of Iona in 806, published his *Geography*, a major work of mediaeval scholarship, in 825.

DIMMA, bishop of Connor, +657, Jan. 6. I;I. Perhaps Dimma, addressed by Pope John IV in 640. Bede *HE* **2**, 19.

DINOI, *see* Thynoy.

DINOOT, *see* Dunawt.

DISIBOD of Dissenberg *c.*675, July 6. I;Germany. *BHL* 2204-5, O'Hanlon 7, 143. Irish bishop, emigrated, probably mid-seventh, to found Dissenberg on the Nahe, later a Benedictine and Cistercian house, about ten miles south-west of Bad Kreuznach, south of Bingen on the Rhine. Resigned the abbacy, 674/5, *Annales S. Disibodi, MGH SRM* 17.

DIUMA of Mercia +*c.*659. I;E. Bede *HE* **3**, 21, 24. Irishman, first bishop of the Middle Angles and Mercians, 653-*c.*659, died at In Feppingum (not identified).

DOBIUS, *see* Mobhi of Inch.

DOCCO (Cyngar) of Congresbury, So. (*ST 4363*). 473, Nov. 27 or 6 or 7) B;B.I. *BHL* 2013. *AB* 42, 1924, 105; *2* (p. 106) vitae *NLA* 1, 248 (1), translated *Ant.* 19, 1945, 37 (summary), *cf.* 85; *JThS* 20, 1918/19, 97, (*cf.* 23, 1921/22. 15 and *AB* 42, 1924, 100) (2); v. *Kebi*, 9 and 11 (3); v. *Cadoci* 22 (4); v. *Samson* I 45 (5); *Catalogus 2* (6); in the name of his monastery, v. *Cadoci* 65, 67 (7), *LL, passim, see* index (8). *LBS* 2, 248, Doble 4, 105, *Ant.* 19, 1945, 32. Doccus, *AU*; Docus, *AC* (*6*); Docco (*5*); Dochou (*4; 8*); Doccuinus, etc. (*1; 4, 7; 8*); Doccovus, Docto (*8*-variants). Cungarus, Kengar, Kyngar, (*1; 2; 3*). Cungarus ' . . . *apud Angligenas* . . ., Doccuinas apud Britannigenas' (*1*, 249, 28, *cf.* 253, 8).

Bishop of the Britons, *AU, AC*, +473. Son of *Luciria* and of Constantinus imperator (*1; 2*); of the family of Custennin Gorneu (? Constantine III). Consobrinus senex of Kebi (*3*). Born therefore, *c*.400/410, he was of age to be son of Constantine III or of one of his sons, one of whom was a monk, the Caesar Constans. Came from Italy to found Congresbiria in Somerset (*1*, 249, 28, *cf. 2*, 101; Cungaresbyrig in 1065, Cungresberie *DB, DEPN* 120). 'Doctor' (*2*, 249, 29, *cf. 1*, 101), his teaching spread throughout the land; a monk, following 'Pauli primi heremite et Antonii vestigia' (*1*, 250, 13; *2*, 102). Congresbury endowed by kings Ine (in 711) and Edgar (*1*, 250-1; *2*, 103). Crossed to 'portu Camensi' in Glamorgan (*1*, 251, *cf. 2*, 99), founded a monastery in the territory of Paulentus (Penychen), against the opposition of Pebiau (of Ercig) (*1*, 253). Visited Ireland, and Enda on Aran (*3*). With the licence of Dubricius, visited Rome and Jerusalem, where he died, whence he was translated (*1*, 253-4) to Congresbury.

Patron at Badgworth, adjoining Congresbury; of St. Kew (Do)Cheu, Lan Deho, 1259, S. Doquinus 1400 (*LBS* 2, 253, *cf.* Doble 104-6) (*5*); Hope, Flint (*SJ 3058*); Llangefni (*SH 4575*) and Ynys Cyngar, near Caer Gybi (*SH 2482*), in Anglesey; of Llandough by Cowbridge and by Cardiff, Glam. (*SS 9972*), (*ST 1673*); *cf.* Llandogo, Mon. (*SO 5204*), Llandawke, Carm. (*SN 2811*); and half a dozen Breton sites, *LBS* 2, 252, Doble 106 n., *Ant.* 19, 1945, 32, *AB* 42, 1924, 109. He perhaps named Achad Cuingire (Hogan, *Onomasticon* 8), perhaps Achonry, (*G 51*), the later episcopal see of Sligo; his name may be concealed in Congham, Nf. (*TF 7123*) (Congreham *DB*), Congerstone, Leics. (*SK 3605*) and Congleton, Ches. (*SJ 8562*). In *B.C.* he is brother of Yestin, *cf.* St. Just of Cornwall (May 5, *LBS* 3, 238, also of Llanwrin, Montg. (*SH 7803*) and Llaneast, Pemb. (*SM 9635*); Justus, or Justinus, *M. Oeng.*, May 5, *cf.* p.428, of Fidarta (Fuerty, Athlone, Rosc. *M 86*. Hogan *Onomasticon* 416, a deacon from France who baptised Ciaran of Clonmacnoise); *cf.* 'Iusti', Latin and Ogam tombstone, *CIIC* 484, St. Kew.

Docco, David and Gildas are the only British ecclesiastics remembered in the Irish *Annals*. The monks of the second order, headed by Finnian of Clonard, also received their 'ritum celebrandi missam' from 'sancto David et sancto Gilda et sancto Doco' (*6*); the emendation (Ca)doco is improbable, since Cadoc was too young to have inspired Finnian, and figures in his story (where the Finnian tradition awards the primacy to David) only through confusion with his pupil of the same name, and is otherwise known in Ireland only as the teacher of Cainnech. In south Wales, the 'chief leaders' (principales proceres) of the 'three regions' were David and Teilo (in Demetia), Illtud and Dochou (in Morgannwg), and Cynidr and Maedoc (in east central Wales) (*4*) (later tradition, v. *Cadoci* [*CL*] 26 and v. *Cadoci* [Lifris] 70 substitute 'Cannou' for 'Dochou'). As (Do)Cheu he is probably the origin of place-names St. Quio, Kewe and the like, whence the 'Ciwa' of *LBS* 2, 139 (unhappily explained as an Irish Cuach) whose sites in Brittany and Wales (listed Doble 108 note) include Cynwyl Gaeo, where Paulinus, teacher of David, was buried; *cf.* also Llancaeuch, Gelligaer, Glam. (*ST 1196*); Llancaes, Mon. (*SO 3603*).

He has more early major houses than any other British saint. Congresbury survived to be refounded, with Glastonbury, by Ine; St. Kew is the earliest-known Cornish monastery, already long-established when Samson visited it (*c*.540), before the arrival of Petroc of Bodmin; Llandough was one of the three great houses of sixth- and seventh-century Morgannwg, in the *LL* grants (*8, cf. 7*), but disappears at the beginning of the eighth century. Paulinus is the only teacher recorded on a surviving contemporary inscription, and he and Iuniavus of St. Kew are, with Illtud, the only abbots recorded to have lived before the monastic upsurge of the 530s. In Ireland, Achonry, if it be his, survived to become a bishopric. His tradition is ill-recorded and much distorted because all his houses declined, or passed from Welsh control, before the monasteries recovered or re-wrote their founders' lives in the eleventh and twelfth centuries. His date makes him the earliest of the monastic teachers; it also means that, unlike any other, except possibly Illtud, he was educated in a society still fully Roman, a younger contemporary of the Sicilian Briton, who was perhaps no more than ten or fifteen years older. The genealogists place him among the Cornovii; he will have been adult at the time of their migration to Dumnonia. Congresbury, like Llantwit, lies close to a Roman villa whose great house was gone by the fifth century, but whose estates will have survived. It lies in territory into which the Cornovii moved; the Midland sites that may be his lie in old Cornovian territory. He may, therefore, have been one of the migrants, establishing a personal monastery on his own estates, in the manner of other fifth-century noblemen in Italy and Britain. His see is likely to have been either Exeter, Gloucester or Caerwent.

DOMNECH VI M/L. B;A. Hermit, surrendered his cell to Malo (v. *Malo* [Bili] 44-45) at St. Domneuc, Ile et Vilaine, *LBS* 2, 353.

DOMNOC (Mo-Domnoc) VI M, Feb. 13. B;B.I. v. *David* 41; 43. *M. ASH* 326. Disciple and bee-keeper of David, left David to settle in Ireland, and introduce bees to Ireland. Of Tibberaghny, Carrick-on-Suir, Tip. (*S 42*), and Llanrhaeadr, Denbigh (*SJ 0863*), Machynlleth, Montg. (*SH 7400*), also traced to Caernarvonshire and Radnorshire, *LBS* 2, 353 (Domnoc); 2, 286 (Dyfnog.). The day is the same in Wales and Ireland. The name is British, not Irish; his descent traced from Saran m. Tigernaig, is a hagiographer's contrivance. The scattered Welsh sites might be named from more than one individual. **F**elix.

DOMNOC VI ? B;E. Of Dunwich, Suffolk (*TM 4770*), called 'civitas Domnoc', Bede*HE* **2**, 15; *cf.* Dyfnauc Sant m. Medraut, *ByS* 51. Dunwich is more likely to have taken a name that the English had retained from a monk than a lay ruler. He will therefore be one of the few British monks recorded in eastern Britain.

DONATUS, *see* Dunawt.

DROSTAN of Aberdour, Buchan (*NJ 8664*) VI L/VII E (or later), Jul. 11, Dec. 14. P?;P. *BHL* 2338. *Book of Deer*, p. 19, Forbes, *Kalendars* 326, O'Hanlon 7, 201 (*Brev. Ab.* PH 19 and *M*). Made a companion of Columba, of Irish royal origin. The name is Pictish, and he may well have been a Columban monk, conventionally made contemporary with Columba.

DUBRICIUS VI E, Nov. 14. B;B. *BHL* 2338-2341. v. *Samson, passim* (1); v. *Leonori* (2); *LL* 78 (3); *NLA* 1, 267 (4). Bishop whose visitations included Llantwit, Glam., Caldey, Pemb. (*1*), Monmouthshire (v. *Gwynlliog* 5; 10). Patron of **S**amson and **I**llltud (1), of Morgannwg and Gwent (*LL passim, cf.* index), v. *Illtud* 11, 15, bishop, or *archbishop* of *Llandaff*. Treated as the principal bishop of the south, bracketed with **D**aniel (*at Brefi*), v. *David* 50, etc. Consecrated Samson as bishop by the Severn Sea (as his successor?). (*3*) and (*4*) attach him to the dynasty of Ercig (south Herefordshire and north Monmouthshire), and his very numerous churches (English, Devereux) concentrate in Ercig (mapped *LBS* 2, 368). He will therefore have been bishop of Ariconium. In (*1*), written within living memory, he is the first and only episcopal patron of the monks of the civitas Silurum, in and about the 520s; he ordained **L**eonorus *c.*525 (2); either he was also bishop of the Silures, or else extended a patronage which their bishop withheld. In Gaul the interference of bishops in neighbouring dioceses is frequently reported, and was frequently forbidden; in the chaotic and corrupt episcopacy described in Britain by Gildas, it was doubtless as frequent. It is equally possible that the established bishops refused to accept bishops uncanonically consecrated on the initiative of local rulers of Gwent and Morgannwg, or that those rulers accepted the episcopacy of a neighbouring bishop duly ordained; episcopal legality is unlikely to have been less confused than in Northumbria in the mid-seventh century. Dubricius' general date is established by (*1*); in the *ACm* entry 612 'Conthigirni obitus *et Dibric episcopi*', the last words are a mistaken gloss. It is unlikely that *ECMW* 301, Caldey (Ogam) 'Magl . . . Dubr . . . inb' refers to him.

DU(BTH)ACH, bishop of Armagh, 534-547; *Book of Leinster* 42ᶜ (sedit xii), of the Ui Tuirtri, north of Lough Neagh (Colla Uais *FM*); probably identical with 'David' of Armagh (*Annals* 552), 'legatus totius Hibernie', suggesting a claim to papal authority or approval.

DUBTHACH, bishop of Armagh, 498-512; *Book of Leinster* 42ᶜ (sedit xiii). Revived by **T**igernach. He and Du(bth)ach may be identical with one, or two, of the several Dubthach named in the martyrologies.

DUNAWT, abbot of Bangor (on Menai?), *c*.603. B;B. Bede *HE* **2**, 2 (Dinoot).

DUNGAL of Pavia *c*.825. I;Italy. Principal director of the schools of northern Italy, Kenney 538, *cf*. 531.

DYFNAUC, *see* Domnoc.

DYMPNA of Brabant VII? May 15. I;Belgium. *BHL* 2352-5. Daughter of an Irish *king*, apostle of Brabant, martyred, *cf*. O'Hanlon 5, 284.

EA-, *see* Ae-, E-.

EADFRID, bishop of Lindisfarne, 698-721. E;E. *DCB* (SD, Fl. Worc., etc.), Bede, vita *Cuthberti*, dedicated to him. Wrote ('avriten') the Lindisfarne Gospels (Colophon, f. 259ʳ, and prayer, f. 89ᵛ, both added *c*.883/970), in his own hand, SD 2, 12, *cf*. Bruce-Mitford, *Lindisfarne Gospel Facsimile*, Olten, Switzerland, 1960, 5 ff. The book was bound by his successor **A**ediluald.

EANFLED 626-685 or later. E;E. Bede *HE* **2**, 9, 20; **3**, 15, 24, 25, 29; **4**, 26; **5**, 19, 24. Daughter of Edwin, born Easter 626, first baptised of the Northumbrians, queen of Oswy; joint abbess of Whitby, with her daughter Aelbfled.

EANSWITH of Folkestone (*TR 2235*) *c*.610-*c*.650, Aug. 31. E;E. *NLA* 1, 296. Daughter of king Eadbald of Kent (616-640), established a house for women at Folkestone, under her aunt **A**edilberg of Lyminge.

EARCONWALD, *see* Erconwald.

EATA of Lindisfarne and Hexham +686, Oct. 26. E;E. *BHL* 2356-7. Bede *HE* **3**, 26; **4**, 12, 27, 28; **5**, 2, 9, 24. *NLA* 1, 300. Pupil of **A**idan, abbot of Melrose, abbot of Lindisfarne 664 after **C**olman; bishop of the Bernicians, 678, with his see at Lindisfarne, at Hexham from *c*.684.

EBBA, *see* Aebbe.

EDIUNET, *see* Idiunet, Ethbin.

EFFLAM VI, Nov. 6. I;A. *BHL* 2664. *AG* 696. Irish hermit, settled at Toul-

Efflam, Plestin, Tréguier, Cotes du Nord; other Armorican dedications, Gougaud, *Saints Irlandais* 81.

EGBERT of Iona *c*.640-729, April 24. E;I. *BHL* 2430. *NLA* 1, 364. Bede *HE* **3**, 4, 27; **4**, 3, 26; **5**, 9, 10, 22-24; (Plummer, 2, 285), Alcuin v. *Willibrord* 4 and other Lives of English monks in Germany.
Left Britain (with Colman in 664 *NLA*). Wished to evangelise Germany, but sent Willibrord instead. Close colleague of Adomnán, aided him to establish the *Cain Adomnain* (Kenney 245, Reeves 178, etc.); at Iona from 716 until his death (729 *Annals*), a principal author of the conversion of Iona to the Roman Easter. Aediluini, Boisil.

EGBERT of York +766, Nov. 19 (*ASC*). E;E. Northumbrian prince, disciple of Bede, received letter of Bede (Plummer 1, 405), archbishop of York, elected 732, *Bedae Continuatio*, received pallium from Rome, 735; founded its schools and library, correspondent of Boniface, *cf.* Plummer, *Bede*, index, 2, 456.

EGBIN, *see* Ethbin.

ELIGIUS +659, Dec. 1. Gaul;Gaul. *BHL* 2474 ff., *MGH SRM* 4, 634, *cf.* 746; 5, 88; 7, 842. Mint master of Dagobert I, convert of Columban's successors, bishop of Noyon 640. Patron of gold- and other smiths, hence his English dedications, Arnold-Forster 1, 475.

ELIUD, *see* Teilo.

ELLI(NUS) of Llanelli, Carm. (*SN 5000*) and Brecon (*SO 2314*) VI M/L, Jan. 23. B;B. Pupil and successor of Cadoc, v. *Cadoci* (L) 14, 15, 26, 37, 38, 49, 53, 63. Finnian of Llancarfan.

ELOI, *see* Eligius.

ELTUTUS, *see* Illtud.

ELUGED, abbot of Llantwit, VII L. B;B. *LL* index.

ELWYN of St. Elwyn, Hayle, Co. (*SW 5537*) VI E, Aug. 28? I;B.A. Companion of Breaca, Leland, *Itin.* 3, 15, and Hia, with dedications in Cornwall and Brittany, *LBS* 2, 449.

ENDA of Aran, Galway (*L 90*) V L/VI E, Mar. 21. I;I. *BHL* 2543. *ASH* 704. *VSH* 2, 60. *Of Airgialla* (1), of Meath *M. Tal.*, *cf. VSH* 1, lxiv. Returning from a raid on his neighbours, he was denounced by the virgin Faencha, *c*.460; to his defence that 'I hold my father's inheritance and must therefore fight my enemies', she replied, 'Your father is in hell; his inheritance is sin and crime'. (2). He was converted, entered her house, and helped to build it, was transferred as 'yconomus' in charge of the builders of a new house at Kell Ayne (Killany, Ardee, Louth, *N* 99) (5). When enemy raiders engaged his people near the site, he seized a timber and prepared to help; Faencha reminded him of his tonsure, and told him, 'You must get away from this country and your kin, lest you hark back to the vanities of the world; go to Britain, to the monastery of Rosnat (Whithorn, Galloway) to be the humble disciple of its master Maucennus'. When he asked, 'How long must I stay there?' Faencha answered, 'Until I get good reports of you.'(6). Went thence to Rome (7) with Ailbe and Pubeus (? Kebi) in the time of Pope Hilary (461-468), who allotted primacy to Enda over Pubeus (20-21). Founded the monastery of *Latium in Italy* (7). While he was away, Faencha, with Darerca, came to Killany

(9-11). Returned from Rome (12) with Ailbe and Pubeus (22) to found numerous monasteries in Meath (11, 22). Asked for Aran from king Angus of Munster (+492), his *brother-in-law* (12), who objected that 'St. Patrick laid down that I must offer to the Lord only good fertile lands near my royal residence', but consented (13) *cf.* v. *Ailbe* (25). Enda established Aran, against the opposition of a local pagan chief, Corbanus (14-18). A council debated who should be 'princeps ac maior in ipsa insula'; Pubeus was 'principalior', 'senior', 'auctoritate dignior' but 'debilis ac senex'. He and Enda deferred to each other, and the council sent envoys to Rome, Finnian junior (*cf.* Fintan Crumthir), Mac Crichi and Erlatheus (of Armagh +481), who returned with a chasuble and gospel book (*cf.* 19), confirming the primacy of Enda (23). Finnian of Clonard was with him on Aran (32-33), Ciaran of Clonmacnoise was *his* pupil (25-32), *cf.* v. *Ciaran C.*,20-21. *Brendan of Clonfert* visited him and Pubeus, v. *Br.* I 14, 71. Brendan and Ciaran are too late; the Brendan story collects tales of others, including earlier travellers under his patron's name; Ciaran may well have studied in Aran, but hardly in Enda's time. Colman m. Daire; Docco; Mocteus; Rochath.

ENDELIENTA of St. Endellion, Co. (*SW 9978*) VI E, Apr. 29. I?;B. *Daughter* of Brychan.

ENODER of St. Enoder, Co. (*SW 8957*), perhaps Cynidr, *cf.* Wethenoc.

ENODOC of St. Enodoc, Rock. Co. (*SW 9377*), *cf.* Wethenoc, bishop at Padstow VI M.

EOCHAID, bishop of Armagh, 589-601. I;I. *Book of Leinster* 42[c] (sedit iii, for xii), Domnach Rig Druim (? Rigdoen in Hui Tuirtre).

EOGAN, *see* Eugenius.

EOSTERWINE of Wearmouth +686, Mar. 7. E;E. *BHL* 8968 ff. Bede, *HA*; *NLA* 1, 407 etc. Cousin of Benedict Biscop, who appointed him joint abbot of Wearmouth.

ERC of Kerry VI E, Oct. 31? I;I. Bishop established by Senan (Lismore 2189) on Inismor in the Shannon estuary; *cf.* 'insula Erci', near Limerick (*R 45*) taken over by Columba of Terryglass, v. *Col. T.* 23-24. Bishop Erc baptised Brendan of Clonfert, near Tralee, Kerry (*Q 81*), brought him up, entrusted him to Ita (v. *Br.* I 1, 3 ff., 11, 71, 96). He may be one of the numerous Erc in the calendars. He is probably Herygh in Cornwall (Wm. of Worcester, *LBS* 2, 459) of St. Erth, Hayle (*SW 5535*) and Lanner; Cornwall, Oct. 31.

ERC of Slane, Meath (*N 97*) (of Lilcach, *cf.* Hogan, *Onomasticon*, 490, *M. Gor.*) +512, Nov. 2. I;I. 'Ercc filius Dego, cuius nunc reliquiae adorantur in . . . Slane' *Muirchú* 16, converted by Patrick at Tara, before *c.*460. Bishop, *Annals* 512, *M.* Brehon of Patrick, *FM* 448, father of Eugenius of Ardstraw, *M. Oeng.* etc.

ERCONGOTA VII L, Feb. 23. E;Gaul. *BHL* p. 389. Bede *HE* 3, 8, *cf.* Plummer 2, 144. Daughter of king Erconbert of Kent (+664) and of Sexburg, daughter of Anna, king of the East Angles (+654). Abbess of Brie, founded by (Burgunde) Fara. Ermingilda.

ERCONWALD, bishop of London, 674-693, Apr. 30. E;E. *BHL* 2600 ff. *NLA* 1, 391. Aedilberg; Waldhere.

ERLATHEUS m. Trene, bishop of Armagh, 468-481, Feb. 11. I;I. Probably he, rather than Iarlaithe of Tuam, went to Rome with Mac Criche and Finnian

(Fintan?) and obtained a ruling against the primacy of Pubeus (? **K**ebi), v. *Endei* 23. *Book of Leinster* 42ᶜ (sedit xiv), o Cluain Fiada, Clonfeade, Tyrone (*H 85*).

ERLATHEUS, *see* Iarlaithe.

ERMIN(G)ILDA VII L, Feb. 13. E;E. *BHL* 2611-2. *NLA* 1, 405, etc. *M*. Daughter of Erconbert of Kent and **S**exburg. Sister of **E**rcongota, wife of king Wulfhere of Mercia, mother of St. **W**erburga of Ely, succeeded her mother as abbess.

ERNAN, Ernin, *see* Ternoc.

ERN(I)ANUS VII M, Aug. 17? I;I. Addressed by Pope John IV in 640, Bede *HE* **2**, 19, perhaps abbot of Tory Island.

(H)ERNIN of Locarn, Carhaix VI M, Nov. 2. I?;A. *AG* 668. Came from Britain, befriended by **C**onomorus, who built his church for him; British born, but the name is Irish; a dozen Ernin named in the martyrologies.

ERTH, *see* Erc of Kerry.

ETHBIN VI M, Oct. 19. B;A.I?Gaul? *BHL* 262, *NLA* 1, 368 *cf. LBS* 2, 466. Follower of **S**amson and **W**inwaloe, withdrew from Brittany, after Frankish raids, to Ireland, to 'Silva Nectensis'. He served abbot Similianus in 'Tauraco monasterio', probably Similinus 'apud Tarvam vicum' (Tarbes, Bigorre, Hautes Pyrenees), Greg. Tur. *Glor. Conf.* 48; 'Silva Nectensis' is Senlis, near Paris, whose bishop in VI M was Conotigirnus, *cf.* **K**entigern. 'Ireland' a hagiographer's gloss. Idiunet.

ETHEL, *see* Aedil.

ETHERNANUS +669, Dec. 2. I;P. *BHL* 2652, *cf.* Forbes, *Kalendars*, 333, dedications.

EUGENIUS of Ardstraw, Tyrone (*H 38*) VI M, Aug. 23. I;I. *BHL* 2677. *Sal.* 915. Son of **E**rc of Slane. Leinsterman, taken prisoner by pirates from Britain together with **T**igernach of Clones, liberated at the request of '**N**ennyo qui **M**aucennus dicitur de **R**osnatensi monasterio' and entered the monastery. Some years later, pirates from Gaul took them prisoner, with **C**oirpre, future bishop of Coleraine; after a miracle on the king's mill, they were set free and returned to Rosnat. Returned to Ireland with Tigernach, founded Ardstraw. Failed to deter king Amalgaid from the *gall-cherd* cruelty (*cf.* **C**ainnech). Lent his gospel book to Coirpre. Foretold **C**olumba of Iona. Died. Called bishop in the martyrologies; Ardstraw was a later bishopric. Visited by Cainnech and **C**omgall, v. *Cainnech* 22. *AC* 617 'Owen Bishop of Ardstrathy died' is an error for Eogan of Rashee, other *Annals*. **C**oemgen; **R**uadan.

EUNIUS, bishop of Vannes, fl. 578. A?;A. Sent as legate by Waroc of Vannes to Childcric, king of the Franks, who exiled him. Waroc later refused to have him back. He ended up as an alcoholic in Paris. Greg. Tur. *HF* 5, 26; 29; 40.

EUNY of Uny-Lelant, Co. (*SW 5437*) VI E, Feb. 1. I;B. Companion of **E**rc of Kerry, Wm. of Worcester, *LBS* 2, 470, patron of Redruth etc., *cf.* Gougaud, *Saints Irlandais* 83.

EUTIGIRN, abbot of Llandough, VII L. *LL passim, cf.* index.

FAELAN, *see* Foelan.

FAENCHA of Rossory, Ferm. (*H 24*) V M/L, Jan. 1. I;I. v. *Endei* 2-4, 6, 8-12.

M. Converted and trained **Enda**, *her brother*, *c*.460, sent him to **R**osnat; friend of **D**arerca. Her date places her among the numerous girls whose conversion **P**atrick claims in the *Confessio*; but she is not named in the Patrician legend, since she left no foundations to attract the interest of its seventh-century authors.

FAILBE, abbot of Iona, 669-678, Mar. 22. I;S. Ad. v. *Col.* 1, 1; 1, 3, *cf.* Reeves. *ASH* 719.

FARA (Burgundofara) of Farmoutiers-en-Brie (east of Paris) +*c*.665, Dec. 7 (Apr. 3). Gaul?;Gaul. *BHL* 1487 ff. Bede *HE* **3**, 8. Convert of **C**olumban, founder of Farmoutiers, also called Evoriacum, *c*.617, a double monastery under the patronage of Bathildis, the English-born queen of Clovis II; many of the nuns were English, several of the subsequent abbesses English queens and princesses.

FARANNAN of Alternan, Sligo (*G 43*) VI M/L? (or VII L?), Feb. 15. I;S.I. *ASH* 336. *M*. Of the Cenel Eogain, accompanied **C**olumba when he left for Iona, to convert the Picts, and because he could not pacify the northern Ui Neill, returned with Columba to **D**rumceat. Columba then founded Drumcliff, Sligo (*G 64*), and held a synod of his own at Easdra (unlocated), attended by 25 named clerics, most of them otherwise ill-recorded, several of them long dead, all claimed as 'de genere Cumne'. Columba was received by *Tibraid* and his son *Dunchad* (Muirisce, king of Connacht, +638) of the Ui Fiachrach Aidni; and gave Alternan to Farannan. The Life is a detached fragment of the local Columban tradition in Sligo; Farannan could be a late-VII saint attached to Columba's time by the hagiographer, or a contemporary brought into contact with the only Muirisce chief who attained the kingship of Connacht. **M**obhi of Inch.

FARANNAN, *see* Forannan, bishop of Armagh.

FASTIDIUS V E. B;B. *DCB*. Bishop in Britain, dated about the 420s (Gennadius); probable author of the Pelagian tract *de Vita Christiana* published in or about 411. Migne *PL* 40, 1031; R.S.T. Haslehurst, *The Works of Fastidius*, Westminster, 1927, with English translation, *cf. JThS* 16, 1965, 26 ff.

FAUSTUS of Riez, Provence *c*.408-*c*.495. B;Gaul. *DCB*. British-born monk of Lerins, abbot of Lerins, bishop of Riez, friend of **S**idonius Apollinaris. His extensive writings are a principal foundation of later Gallic theology. *Son of Vortigern*. **H**ilary of Arles; **L**eo I; **R**iocatus.

FECC, *see* Fiacc.

FECHIN of Fore, W. Meath (*N 57*) +666, Jan. 20. I;I. *BHL* 2845. *VSH* 2, 77. *ASH* 130 (1): 132 (2), *cf.* O'Hanlon, 1, 356. The original of the Life is attributed to his contemporary, Aileran Sapiens (Kenney 279; +666). Foretold by **C**olumba, abbot of 300 monks, encountered king Diarmait (+664), *cf.* v. *Geraldi* 12, proposed prayer for limiting the population by plague in time of famine, opposed by **G**erald, died of the plague. His miracles are concerned with agricultural improvement; he built a water-mill by draining a lake (14), tamed a wolf (7), and, thanks to his 'Columbine innocence', successfully milked a bull's genitals. The MS. adds the urbane mediaeval comment 'a remarkable innovation ... but such a thing is possible in a land where honey is produced from stones, oil from the hardest rock' (8). Adomnán credited Columba with the same miracle. Named St. Vigeans, Arbroath, Angus (*NO 64*), and Ecclefechan, Dumfries (*NY 17*), Forbes 456, 458. **L**ugid, **M**o-Choemog, **M**o-Chua, **T**írechán.

FEIDLIMID, bishop of Armagh, c.567-579. I;I. *Book of Leinster* 42ᶜ (sedit xv, for ? xii), of Hua Faelain, (of the Ui Bresail, Co. Armagh).

FELIX, bishop of the East Angles, c.630-c.647, March 8. Gaul;E. *BHL* 2859. *NLA* 1, 439. Bede *HE* **2**, 15; **3**, 18, 20, 25. Burgundian, sent by Honorius of Canterbury to evangelise the East Angles, c.630, under king Sigebert, with his see at Dunwich (civitas **D**omnoc); helped king Sigebert to establish a school on the Frankish and Kentish model.

FERGHIL, *see* Virgilius.

FERGNA Brit, abbot of Iona, 608-624, March 2. I;S. Ad. v. *Col.* 3, 19; *ASH* 448. *M.* Son of bishop (?) Failbe of the Cenel Enna Bogaine (northern Ui Neill), a young man in **C**olumba's lifetime. The name suggests a connection with Britain; possibly his maternal ancestry, possibly his education. His nephew, **C**olman, was one of Adomnán's informants.

FERGNA of Hinba VI L/VII E. I;S.I. Ad. v. *Col.* 3, 23. A young monk in Ireland, who crossed in 597, when he heard of **C**olumba's death, served many years in Hinba, then 12 years in Muirbulc Mar (perhaps Irish Dal Riada), a monk of Columba till his death; plainly distinct from Fergna Brit.

FERGUS the Pict VIII E, Sept. 8. P;I? 'Fergustus episcopus Scotiae Pictus'. Attended a council at Rome in 721 with '**S**edulius Britanniae episcopus de genere Scotorum', and a Spaniard and many Italians, Mansi 8, 109. 'Fergus Cruithnech' Sept. 8, *M. Don., M. Gor., M. Tal.* 'Scotia' at this date meant Ireland; it is, however, possible that the uncertain geography of Rome included the *paruchia* of Iona within the territory of Ireland. Possibly a Pict, perhaps a monk of Iona, who was a bishop on Dal Riada.

FERGUS of Strageath (*NN 8918*), near Crieff, Perth. VI/VII? Nov. 18. I;P. *BHL* 2899. *Brev. Ab.* PE 164. Irish bishop, settled at Strageath (in or by the Roman fort), evangelised Caithness and Buchan, dedications Forbes 337. Possibly a companion of **F**oelan of St. Fillans.

FIACC of Sletty, Leix (*S 77*) V M/L, Oct. 12. I;I. 'adoliscens poeta', student under 'Dubthoch maccu Lugil, poeta optimus', who alone of magi of Loegaire accepted Patrick, 'nomine Feec, qui postea mirabilis episcopus fuit, cuius reliquiae adorantur hi Sleibti', Muirchú 18. He plays a large part in the Patrician legend, but is ignored in the tradition of the Saints' Lives. **A**ed of Sletty.

FIACHRA of Aberdeen and Perthshire VI/VII? I;P. Known from place-names only, Forbes 339. The Aberdeen Breviary summarises the Life of Fiachra of Breuil because it had no other record of a Fiachra.

FIACHRA of Breuil-en-Brie, east of Paris +670, Aug. 30. I;Gaul. *BHL* 2916 ff. *NLA* 1, 441. Lectiones and hymns of Meaux, reprinted Forbes 339 ff., *Brev. Ab.* PE 94. Son of Eogan, an Irish king, (*hymn*, Forbes 340). Irishman, settled under bishop Faro of Meaux (+c.672), *brother* of Syra, abbess of Chalons, visited by **K**illian. His cult was exceptionally popular in the Middle Ages in northern France, from Brittany to Luxemburg, *cf.* Gougaud, *Saints Irlandais* 87, Kenney 493, O'Hanlon 8, 437 ff., expressed in festivals, calendars and relics, but not in the dedication of churches or place-names.

FILLAN, *see* Foelan.

FINAN of Aberdeenshire VI/VII ? March 18, Scottish Calendars. I;P. Numerous dedications, mostly in Aberdeenshire and Perthshire, Forbes 347. Since the feast day is so close, they might be due to Finan of Swords, a pupil of Columba, or his pupils; but a distinct Finan is as likely.

FINAN of Cenn Etigh (Kinnitty, Off., *N 10*) VI L/VII E, Apr. 7. I;I. *BHL* 2979, 2980. *VSH* 2, 87; *Sal.* 305. Pupil of Brendan of Clonfert (+578), who 'saw many wonders in the ocean'; Munsterman of the Corco Duibhne. Had his monks construct a huge ship for the king of Lough Leane (Killarney, *V 99*). Cured an illness of Carthacus (+639), persuaded king Failbe Fland of Munster (628-639) to remit the taxation of his 'gens', against the opposition of the king's 'proconsul'.

FINAN of Lindisfarne (*NU 1242*) +661, Feb. 17. I;E. *BHL* 2981. Colgan *ASS* 43 *cf.* 357. Bede *HE* **3**, 17, 21, 22, 25-27. Irishman from Iona, successor of Aidan, baptised Peada of Mercia and Sigebert of Essex, consecrated Diuma to the Middle Angles, Cedd to Essex, built a wooden church at Lindisfarne, defended the old Easter against Ronan.

FINAN (the Leper) of Swords, Dublin (*O 13*) VI L/VII E, March 16. I;I. *ASH* 627. Pupil of Columba (of Iona), Comgall and Cainnech, friend of Carthacus, forbidden by Columba to visit Rome. Perhaps identical with Finan of Aberdeenshire.

FINAN VI E? I;I.B. Disciple of Senan, v. *Senan* 12; perhaps named Carwynnen, Co. (*SW 6537*).

FINDBAR nUa Bairdene +438.

FINDBAR, alternative spelling of Finnian (of Clonard, and of Moville).

FINDBAR (Barrus) of Cork (*W 67*) VI M? Sept. 25. I;I.B? *BHL* 2983. *VSH* 1, 65 (Barrus, etc.). Son of Amargen, of the Ui Briuin of Connacht, 'faber ferrarius' to Tigernach of Rathlen (Cork), who sentenced his pregnant mother (*cf.* Thynoy) to be burnt at the stake (in most versions because he was illegitimate; legitimate *VSH*), but released her when the infant protested from the womb that the execution was immoral *VSH*; that it was wrong to condemn the innocent child with the guilty mother, *Brev. Ab.* PE 115 = *AB* 69, 1951, 337. Baptised by bishop Mac Cuirp under the name of Lochan (Luan), Irish Lives, *VSH* 2, note. Hermit in Munster (in the time of Brendan [of Clonfert] ? *VSH* 5) and *Leinster* (6). Visited Rome, with Mac Cuirp, in the time of *Gregory the Great*, (*VSH* 7 ff.), on his return visited St. David (+589) (v.*David* 39, 40, 'fidelissimus ille abbas Hibernensium cui nomen Barre', in the time of Brendan of Clonfert [?]: *VSH* 10 [MS. R]), returned to Cork. His pupils (*VSH* 13) included Cainnech (+603) and Sinell (+603), and (MS. R) *Colman m. Lenin* (+606), and others, *ASH* 607. The texts are disturbed by paragraphs intruded from the Lives of Findbar of Fowey; *cf.* also Mac Cuilin of Lusk, Breaca, Fursey, Hia, Lasrian of Leighlin, Ruadan, Senan.

FINDBAR (? Barricius) of Fowey, Co. (*SX 1251*) VI E? July 31? I;B. Patron of Fowey (St. Fimbarrus, Wm. of Worcester, 1478, cited Gougaud, *Saints Irlandais*, 93; *LBS* 3, 20; Leland *Itin.* 1, 3, 203; Barrianus in 1170. The feast was Sept. 26, Wm. of Worcester (*LBS*); July 31, Truro Calendar, Arnold-Forster 2, 278. 'Barricius socius Patricii, ut legitur in vita Sti Wymeri (Fingar). Sta. Breaca . . . venit in Cornubiam' Leland, *Itin.* 3, 15, *LBS* 1, 229. Leland's lost Life of Fingar and the Fowey dedication attest a tradition that a Findbar came to Cornwall, but do not connect him with Findbar of Cork. In the *lectiones* of Cork (*AB* 69, 1951, 333, nos. 7-8, *cf.* Lusk no.6, p.340) Fynbarrus 'Albaniam petiit' and killed a dragon, 'ob quod etiam beneficium Albani S. Fynbarro quandam civitatem cum magna parochia contulerunt', in which he left disciples of S. Rudicuno (no.6, p.341). It is however also possible that he derives from Barius, companion of the ninth-century St. Neot (*SX 16*), ten miles to the north.

FINDBAR (Barrucius) of Llancarfan VI M. I;B. Disciple of Cadoc, drowned with *Walees*, *named Barry Island* (*ST 1168*) v. *Cadoci* 29. *ECMW* 150 (*CIIC* 368) cf. Docco of Llandawke, Carm. (*SN 2811*). 'Barrivend filius Vendubari hic iacit' is the tombstone of a Findbar, monk or layman of Llancarfan or elsewhere; it explains the interchangeability of Barr and Findbar and Barrfind.

FINDBAR (Fimbarrus, Barr, Finbar) of Scotland VI? I;S.P. Has a widespread cult from the Orkneys to Ayrshire, Forbes 275. The Aberdeen Breviary (PE 115 = *AB* 69, 1951, 337) reprints an abstract of the life of Findbar of Cork, with whom nothing else links him.

FINDLUGAN of Tamlacht Finlagan, Derry (*C 62*) VI L, Jan. 3. I;I.S. Saved Columba's life from an assassin on Hinba, Ad. v. *Col.* 2, 24. Fingola, brother of Fintan of Dunblesc, left Dunblesc for Albania, where he lived and died, v. *Fint. D.* 14. Brother of Fintan of Tamlacht Finlagain in Ciannachta Glinne Geimin; 'in peregrinationem exiit in aquilonem', *M. Oeng.* Tamlacht Finlagan adjoins **D**rumceat, Newtown Limavady. There is a church of Finlagan on an island in Loch Finlaggan, Ilarro, Islay (*NR 3867*), Reeves, *Adamnan*, 136, O'Hanlon 1, 56. Forbes 348.

FINGAR of Gwinnear, Co. (*SW 5937*) VI E, March 23. I;B.A. *BHL* 2988. vita by Anselm (*of Canterbury*) (perhaps of St. Michael's Mount, Cornwall). *ASS* March 3, 456 (454) = *ASH* 387, cf. *TT* 202, xx, xxi. = Migne *PL* 159, 325 (1); *AG* 812 (2); lost Life, cited Leland, *Itin.* 3, 4 (1, 157: App. 1) (3). (*2*) sometimes distinguishes Fingar from his companion Guiner (Wymerus, *3*), sometimes equates them. (*1*) equates them. Neither name is easily rendered into Irish.
    Son of an Irish king *Clyto*, who alone honoured Patrick when he came to his father's court in Ireland (*2*; in Cornwall, *1*), disinherited (*1, 2*), emigrated to Armorica, where he founded monasteries, returned to Ireland on his father's death, renounced the earthly throne (*1*; omit *2*). Set sail for Britain (*1*; for Armorica by way of Britain *2*) with his sister Piala (Ciara) (of Phillack, Hayle) and 770 companions and seven bishops (*1*), accompanied by St. Hia (**I**a), of St. Ives, who travelled by herself on a leaf (*1*) by Barricius (**F**indbar), socius Patricii (*3*). Landed at Heul (Hayle, *SW 5537*) (*1*); associated with **B**reaca and **S**enan, who landed at Riviere, Hayle (*3*). Entertained by a religious woman Coruria at Conectonia (Connor Downs, *SW 5939*) (*1*). Attacked by king **T**heodoricus (*1, 2*), a *pagan* who feared the conversion of his subjects (*1*); who had been warned by the king (Clyto) that his son, prince Guiner, had sailed with 300 men in support of his *uncle* **M**axentius to attack him (*2*). Theodoric set a watch on his coasts to catch the expected fleet (*2*), separated the invading forces (*1; 2*), fell on the rear of one party (*1*), Fingar's party of 200 (*2*) and cut them to pieces. The other party, Fingar's (*1*), Guiner's, with 300 men (*2*), surrendered and were massacred, their leader beheaded (*1; 2*), replacing his severed head, and performing numerous miracles (*1*); 'Breaca appulit sub Rivyer cum suis, quorum partem occidit Tewdr(ig)' (*3*).'Haec ego . . . Anselmus . . . digessi' (*1, 28*). 'Ryvier castle . . . was Theodore's castle' (*3*, cited Doble, 1, 107). Leland visited Cornwall in 1538, just before the dissolution of the monasteries, and had access to at least four lives (Breaca, Elwen, Ives, Guiner) which did not survive. Tradition evidently associated **G**within with Gwinnear.

The name Guiner (Guinier) is British, *cf.* e.g. *LL* 174, Guigner in Breton place-names. Fingar, despite its deceptive appearance, is not known in Irish tradition. The older among the varying traditions may therefore have been that he was a companion of an Irish ruler in Cornwall, expelled first to Brittany, thence to Ireland, returning with a large invading army. The approximate date is given by the career of Theodoric.

The saints concerned named many places and parishes in western Cornwall, *cf.* Breaca, *LBS* 1, 231-2; Arnold-Forster 2, 263-270; and Guigner has many in Brittany, *LBS* 3, 30; Doble, 1, 108; *AG* 81.

FINGOLA, *see* Findlugan.

FINIAN, *see* Finnian; Fintan; Winninus.

FINNIAN of Clonard, Meath (*N 64*) +551, Dec. 12. *BHL* 2989. *Sal.* 189 = *ASH* 393, *cf. TT* 457, 604. Kenney, 374. Of the Ui Loscain (in Ossory, Hogan, *Onomasticon* 674) (1), baptised by Abban (V L/VI E), taught by Foirtchern (V L) (2), and Coeman of Inis Daire (Wexford Harbour) (4; 11). Chapters 4-11, are a Life of Finnian of Llancarfan (wrongly incorporated into that of Finnian of Clonard). Visited Enda in Aran, v. *Endei* 32-33; Britain, with Mobhi (Biteus) and Genocus (11). Given a site at Achad Abla (Aghowle, Wicklow, *S 96*, Hogan, *Onomasticon* 5) by Muiredach, king of south Leinster, opposed by the sons of Diarmait of the Ui Bairrche (12-13), seven years at Mugny (Dunmanoge, Kildare [*S 78*], Hogan, *Onomasticon* 544, correcting p. 8, Moone, Kildare [*S 79*]). Visited Brigit (+525) (15). Accepted the church of Cassanus f. Nemain (March 1, *M.*; follower of Brigit, *ASS* Feb. 1, 116) among the 'Forthortenses' (Fortuatha of Co. Wicklow?), giving the local king an ounce of gold (a ring) 'ut permitteret servos Dei in pace' (15). Built and fortified (in circuitu eius fossavit) the church of Escayr Branan (Ardsallagh, Navan, Meath [*N 86*], Hogan, *Onomasticon* 395) (16) and founded Clonard (18) where he encountered the magus Fraychan. His mother founded a house for women, with the mothers of Ciaran (of Clonmacnoise) and Colman (of Cule?) (21), *cf.* v. *Ciaran* 16, whose outstanding pupil was Lasra (22). The inevitable occasional scandal caused 'diversae opiniones'. The bard (carminator) Gemman composed a 'carmen magnificum' in his honour (23). Visited his pupil Ruadan at Lothra, drank the juice of his lime tree (24-25), and demanded that Ruadan follow the common 'vivendi modus' (26). Visited the Ui Aililla of Connacht (Tirerrill, Sligo), established the priest Nathi at Achad Chonayri ('Aghaconary in Mayo' = Achonry, Sligo [*G 51*], probably also Achad Cuingire, *cf.* Docco, Hogan, *Onomasticon* 7-8), later the bishopric of the Lugni (27-28), also Aghanagh, Sligo [*G 71*], future seat of the bishops of Elphin, then the cell of Maine (Maneus) senex, who had been baptised by Patrick (30), and also Craeb Mor (Creeve, Rosc. *M 89*) under his disciple Grellan (31).

'Teacher of the saints of Ireland'; 'archidoctor sapientissumus', etc., *M. Gor., M. Don.*, etc.; 'optimus sanctorum secundi ordinus abbas' (13). First of the saints of the second order, which began under king Tuathal Maelgarb (532-548) (*Catalogus* 2). His 12 pupils (19 and *Catalogus* 5) were the two Ciaran, two Brendan, two Columba, Mo-Laise, Cainnech, Ruadan, Mobhi, Sinell, and Ninnidh; with Genoc, and his successor at Clonard, Senach; Ciaran of Saigir in old age attended his school (v. *Ciaran* [*VSH*] 36); episcopus, magister of 'iuvenis' Columba (of Iona), Ad. v. *Col.* 1, 1; 2, 1; 3, 4 (Findbarrus; Finnio; Viniavus), wrongly equated with Finnian of Moville, Irish Lives. He is named in the Lives of most of his other pupils and others, Colman, Enda, Ibar, Lasrian of Devenish, Lugid, Senan, Molua (v. 25;

27), **D**agaeus (v. 12) and some dozen other saints are also made his pupils, *cf. VSH, CS* indices.

He was full of learning, a 'scriba doctissimus', compassionate. His diet was bread, vegetables and water, with no meat, save a little fish occasionally on feast days, with a cup of beer or whey. He slept on the ground with a stone pillow; 'omnibus erat misericors, sed sibi tantum durus et austerus' (34). The tradition recalls the rule of **D**avid, without the harshness and arrogance attributed thereto. In an Irish Life (*Lismore* 2527) he is made to adjudicate a contention for the 'headship and abbacy of Britain' between David and **G**ildas, and awarded the island to David. Confused with Cadoc's pupil **F**innian of Llancarfan, received the last unction from **C**olumba of Terryglass (20; v. *Col. T.* 26), died in the plague, *Annals*. His office, *AB* 73, 1955, 356, *cf.* 75, 1957, 337.

FINNIAN of Llancarfan VI M/L, Feb. 23? (so *ASH* and a few Calendars, *cf.* O'Hanlon 2, 686). I;B. v. *Finnian Clonard* 4-11 (1); v. *Cadoci* (2).

In youth (effebus, *2*, 12), with Mac Moil and Gnouan, accompanied **C**adoc on his return from Ireland (*2*, 11), helped to rebuild Llancarfan, where he had a chapel (*2*, 12). Welcomed by Cathmaelus (Cadoc), *with David and Gildas*; given the two sites of Melboc (unidentified) and Nont (*1*, 5. 'Lann Gharban no Gabran', Irish Life seeking to translate Llancarfan into Irish; Carbayn, alio nomine Nant, *1*, 10). Visited Echni (Flat Holm, *ST 2264*) (*1*, 7). Broke the news of David's Synod of Brefi to Cadoc, returning from pilgrimage abroad (*2*, 17). Sent with Gnouan and **E**lli as representatives of Llancarfan to negotiate with Gwynlliw (*2*, 53). Witness of a grant, named after Cadoc (*2*, 57) (Finian Scottus). Negotiated with an invading Saxon army (*c.*557/584 ?), unsuccessfully, on behalf of the British; on his advice, the British ambushed the Saxons in a defile, and the Saxons were destroyed by rocks from the hilltop (*1*, 8). Cathmael, Finnian and Bitheus (**M**obhi) were dissuaded by an angel from visiting Rome (*1*, 9). Cured Elni (Elli), then a youth, when he lost his head ('amens') through 'cogitatio dyabolica' when a girl touched his hand, near Llancarfan (*1*, 10).

The only association between Finnian of Llancarfan and of Clonard is Bitheus in *1*, 9; which may be a tale proper to Clonard, wherein Cathmael is imported. It is evident that a lost Life of Finnian of Llancarfan was used by both the author of a Life of Finnan of Clonard and the author of a v. *Cadoci*. (*2*) does not identify its Finnian with Clonard; the source of (*1*) incorporated the Llancarfan Finnian's Life at a fairly early date, since *2*, 45 claims hospitalitas with 'Clunerert . . . monasterio beati Finiani', glossed as 'discipuli sui' (Cadoci). **M**aedoc, **M**obhi.

FINNIAN of Moville, Down (*J 57*) +580, Sep. 10. I;I. *BHL* 1990; 3173 ff. *ASH* 634 (1); *NLA* 1, 444 (2); *Liber Hymnorum* 2, p. 11, reproduced *LBS* 3, 14-15 (3). *ASH* 638 (4) Fridianus of Macbili (*1*), MS. of Lucca in Tuscany, confusing him with Fri(gi)dianus, bishop of Lucca (so also *4*); Finanus, Wallico nomine Winninus, (*2*); Findbarr Maige Bili, *M. Oeng.* Vennianus, Columban, *Ep.* 1. Of Dal Araide (*2*), of Ulster (*4*), trained by bishop **C**olman of Dal Araide and *by Caelan (**M**o-Choe)* (+498), at Nendrum (*2*), sent to Britain, to 'civitas . . . Candida' (Whithorn) (*1: 4*) under abbot **N**ennio (*2*), **M**ugentius (*1: 4*), where he cured a demoniac Greek (*2*). At Whithorn a fellow student was Drusticc, daughter of king Drust (528-544 or 548), who promised him Mugint's whole library if he could get a student named Rioc into her bed; he sent another student, Talmach (*cf.* March 14, *ASH* 601, pupil of Findbar of Cork) in his guise, by whom she conceived Loman de Treocit (Nov. 1) (*3*); the king's daughter tried to seduce Finnian, who sent her home, where she died, but was resuscitated to a chaste life (*2*). Mugint was angry (iratus) and had

Finnian beaten (*1: 4: 3*) with 'securibus' (*1: 4*), 'securi' (*3*) (the rods of a lictor's axe?) but stopped the punishment 'quia putavit inimicos populum populari' (*3*), was himself beaten (*1: 4*). Finnian was sent away to Rome (*2*), to Moville (*1: 4*). Quarrelled with king Tuathal, who refused fat for his lamps, foretold his immediate death (548) (*2*). Stayed seven years in Rome (*2*), under Pope Pelagius (555-559) (*4*), outshouted a hostile crowd who tried to drown his preaching with musical instruments (*2*). Returned, with a marble altar (*2*); brought to Ireland the law of Moses, the first whole gospel, Colman's gospel, *M. Oeng.* Refused to lend his gospel to Fintan of Dunblesc (v. *Fint. D.* 6), then at Bangor (founded 558), who, on the advice of Comgall, obtained it, thanks to a pirate raid on Moville. Lent the codex to Columba of Iona, who transcribed it without his knowledge, while staying at his monastery of Dromin (Louth, *O 08*), and knocked out the eye of a monk sent to his room to reclaim it. Finnian prosecuted Columba before the high king Diarmait (549-564), *c.*560, who gave judgement for Finnian, enouncing the rule that, 'The copy is to the book as the calf to the cow'. Columba made an impassioned attack on copyright, proclaiming, 'Whatever I find in anyone else's book I may freely put to my own use, and copy it to make it freely available to others for the glory of God' (ut que praeclara in alieno codice reperaram, et commodius in alios ad Dei gloriam derivarem); and denounced the judgement as 'irrational, plainly wrong . . . an arbitrary miscarriage of justice that cannot long remain unavenged' (absonam et aperte iniquam . . . tantam arbitrii obliquitatem non diu abituram inultam) (v. quarta *Columbae* [O'Donnell, excerpted and translated into Latin by Colgan] 2, 1, *TT* 408 [misnumbered 402] -- 409 *cf. ASH* 644; *cf.* Keating 2, 10 [Irish Texts Soc. 3, 88, citing the Black Book of Molaga (probably earlier than 1100, O'Curry 20-21)] and numerous other shorter versions). At the battle of Cuil Dremhne, 561, where the northern Ui Neill and Connacht armies, organised and prayed for by Columba, defeated Diarmait, Finnian prayed on Diarmait's side (v. quarta *Columbae* 2, 3, *TT* 409); Columba regained the book, held to be the 'Cathach', an early Latin MS. of Psalms 31-106 preserved in a silver case as a battle relic of the O'Donnells, Reeves, *Adamnan*, 233; a late sixth-century date is 'palaeographically possible' (E. A. Lowe, *Codices Latini Antiquiores* 2, 1935, 41, *cf.* 52, cited Anderson, *Adomnan* 90).

Blinded and cured Diarmait, who refused a favour asked for a friend (*2*). Killed a son of king Deman (of Airgialla, +564) with a blow of a hammer, that fell from heaven at his prayer (*2*); killed and resuscitated the followers of king Arth (? Artrach) of Airgialla, who seized ecclesiastical lands (*1: 4*). Drained a lake to supply a water-mill (*1: 4*), drowning but rescuing its architect. Visited Comgall at Bangor, v. *Com.* 28, placed about the time of Columba's emigration. King Ainmire invited Gildas to restore order in the Irish church (v. *Gildae* [R] 11-12) in 565 (*Annals*), after Columba's departure; Columban, who will have been at Bangor at the time of Finnian's visit, reported to Gregory the Great, *c.*595 'Vennianus auctor Giltam de his (monks who leave their houses without permission in search of perfection) interrogavit, et elegantissime ille rescripsit', (*MGH Epp.* 3, 158-9, letter 1); the fragments of Gildas' extant letters 4 and 5 deal with this problem; their content justifies their description as an 'elegant rescript'.

Died 580, *Annals*; before Comgall (+603), v. *Comgall* 30; *at Cunigham . . . wallico nomine Kilwinnin* (*2; cf.* Winninus). Succeeded by Sinell, +607. Bishop of the Ui Fiatach, *Annals*. Carthacus.

FINNIAN, *see* Finan.

FINNIAN, *see* Winninus.

FINTAN of Cluain Ednech (Clonenagh, Leix, *S 39*) +606, Feb. 17. I;I. *BHL* 2993. *VSH* 2, 96; *Sal.* 289. Leinsterman (1). As a boy, met Columba of Iona, then 'iuvenis' (2). Pupil of Columba of Terryglass (2), established Clonenagh, rejecting animals for farm work, and all animal food, including milk and butter (3). Cainnech came with a delegation of other saints and persuaded him to relax his excessive rigours (4). Sinchell his pupil (11). Some of his monks migrated to Britain without his permission; one returned (12). Buried human heads left behind by passing raiders in his cemetery (13). Freed Cormac m. Diarmata of the Ui Bairrche, then a youth, from imprisonment by Colum (Colman) (m. Cairpri) m. Cormaic, king of north Leinster (554-578). Cormac reigned long, and in old age became a monk of Comgall's at Bangor (17). Visited by *bishop* Brandub of the Ui Cennselaig, three years before he died; Brandub died a fortnight after Fintan (19); the original perhaps concerned king Brandub of the Ui Cennselaig, +608. Columba of Iona sent Columbanus (? Colman Elo) to him from Iona (21). Died in old age, after naming Fintan Maeldubh as his successor. (22). The lost Book of Clonenagh, used by Keating in the seventeenth century, is believed to have been in existence at Ballyfin House, near Clonenagh, early in the nineteenth century, O'Hanlon, 2, 591; O'Curry 21. Mobhi maccu Alde.

FINTAN of Dun Blesc (Duleng, Doon, Limerick, *R 85*) VI L, Jan. 3. I;I. *BHL* 2995. *Sal.* 225. Lived 360 years in southern Ireland (3). The king of 'Calathmag', 'now Eoganacht' resisted Fintan 'cum turba sanctorum comitum', telling his harvesters 'non est bonum ut illi seductores ad nos veniant', and put up a road block. Fintan called down a violent thunderstorm that set the crops and barricade on fire; the king then handed over his property, his sons, grandsons and great-grandsons to Fintan 'in sempiternum in servitutem' (4). Studied 'in scolis sancti Comgalli' (at Bangor) (5); Finnian of Moville refused to lend him his gospel book to read; Comgall advised him 'If you have faith, you will get it'. Pirates plundered Moville and stole the book, sailed on to Bangor, where a storm blew a tree on to their ships, and Fintan rescued the book from the wrecks (6). A very fat man called Lotraid burdened his subjects by taking a daily bath that had to be filled by ten jars of water; Fintan turned the water to salt, so that the fat man died and his servants (servi) were freed from the task (8). At Tulach Bennain (unidentified) seven British pilgrims who lived there refused to surrender to him, but were later supplanted by the virgin Ernait (April 10), daughter of a king (of) Connacht (9). Settled at Dunblesc, with his brother Finlog, received by Columbanus, son of Kynchada (unknown) (13). Declined to feed travelling actors (mimis et histrionibus) (16), at Terryglass. His water-mill worked for three days and nights on end on the occasion of a visit by Columba, 'amicus noster' (? of Iona) (15). Never angry or agitated (17). Brother of Findlugan.

FINTAN (Munnu) of Taghmon, Wex. (*S 91*) +637, Oct. 21. I;I. *BHL* 2996-9. *VSH* 2, 226. *Sal.* 393; (2) 489 (3). Son of Tulchan, of the Ui Neill, a monk of Iona, v. *Cainnech* (2) 26, Cenel Conaill, and of Feidlimid of the Ui Maine of Tethba. Mocu Moie, Ad. v. *Col.* 1, 2. As a boy, met Columba of Iona; who threw him into the sea, because his father loved him too much, v. *Cainnech*.

Studied under Grellan of Achad Broan (near Uisneach?). Studied under Comgall, and at Columba of Iona's school at Kilmore, Roscommon (Moyglass) (*cf.* Reeves, *Adamnan* 99), under Sinell of Devenish 'the most learned of all Ireland and Britain', went to Iona when still young, just after Columba's death (597), but was not accepted by his successor, Baitan, on Columba's orders because he was needed in

Leinster. Settled for five years in Eile, with 50 monks, surrendered his site to the virgin Ciara (Kyera, Kera, Emher) with five nuns, from whom it passed to Tailli maicc Segeni. Moved to Ard Crama (Bargy, Wexford, *T 00*), among the Ui Bairrche where he displaced Aed Gobban, a monk of Comgall's who went into exile for 12 years. His mill, v. *Lasrian of Leighlin* 4. His people were raided by Guaire m. Eogain in an unsuccessful attempt to seize the throne of south Leinster. After Comgall's death (605), Bangor offered him a choice between *succeeding Comgall as abbot of Bangor*, accepting confirmation at Ard Crama under the supremacy of Bangor, or expulsion. The date should be 615. Aed Gobba returned and Fintan went to Achad Liacc Ech Dromma, apparently Taghmon (Hogan, *Onomasticon* 9) among the Fotharta. Visited by Maedoc, v. *Maedoc* 29. A son of king Dimma of the Fotharta became a monk of Fintan's; his brother, a monk of the hermit Cuain, killed Aed Slane, son of king Crundmael (Bolc Luatha) of south Leinster. King Dimma escaped with the aid of Fintan's magic cloak, but 80 of his men were taken, including his son, who was executed; Fintan miraculously secured the release of the prisoners and confirmation of his site. An angel of the Lord used to visit Fintan on Sundays and Thursdays; the angel missed one Thursday because all angels had to attend the reception into heaven of Mo-Lua (Lugid) (612, Aug. 4). A leper from 612 till his death; for seven years, v. *Mo-Chua* of Timahoe, 5-6. At the synod of Mag Ailbe he defended the 'old order' of Easter against the 'new order, that recently came from Rome', championed by Lasrian of Laighlin (+641), who had 1,500 monks; king Suibne of the Ui Bairrche called him a leper, but was rebuked by Lasrian, and was killed by his nephew next month. He offered Lasrian a trial by ordeal or by miracle, but Lasrian declined. He is presumably the 'whited wall' of the letter of Cummian, who rejected the Synod of Magline. He visited a British monk whose house was on the edge of his 'civitas' and made carts for the community: and took off his shoes to warm his toes at the forge fire. The British monk saw sand in the shoes and asked how it got there. Fintan replied that he had just returned from the Land of Promise, which he had visited with Columba of Iona, Cainnech and Brendan of Clonfert; Columba's site there was called Ath Cain (Fair Ford), Fintan's Port Subi (Port Joy), Cainnech's Set Bethath (Path of Life), Brendan's Aur Phardus (Brink of Paradise). If the British monk was tempted to sail there, he might take 12 carts and 12 bronze cauldrons to Slieve League on the Donegal coast (*G 57*), there kill his oxen for supplies, and use their hides to make boats to sail to the Land of Promise. The British monk told the tale after Fintan's death, showing the sand in evidence. When Fintan died, all heaven rejoiced to receive him. A leper, *M*: with 230 monks, *M* (150, Pilgrim Litany, *AB* 77, 1959, 318 no.10). A hostile satire 'O little vassal of a mighty God' against him is attributed to Columba of Iona *M. Oeng.*, to Maedoc of Ferns, Cormac, *Glossary*, p. 110. The story of his rejection at Iona is his own, told by him to one of his monks, who recounted it personally to Adomnán, v. *Col.* 1, 2. He has several churches in Scotland, Forbes, 416. Succeeded by Foelan.

Abban; Cainnech; Lasrian of Devenish; Lugid; Mo-Choemog; Vougay.

FINTAN the priest (Crimthir Fintan) V L, Jul. 13. I;I. Cruimther Fionntainn, Cille Airthir (eastern cell) *M. Don., cf. M. Gor.* Mocteus of Louth (v. *Moct.* 11 [*Sal.* 909]), celebrating Easter *with Patrick* 'in monte Cruachan' (? Croghan Hill, Daingean [Philipstown], Offaly, *N 43*, Hogan 310) revived his disciple Fintan, 'ab adversariis per rupes in profunde vallis ima detrusum et in multa frustra divisum'. Fintan later became abbot of Cella Orientis (eastern cell) (West Meath, Hogan 175). Crubthir Fintan's enmity drove Kengar (Docco) and Kebi from Aran, despite

Enda's attempts at pacification; an angel told Kebi to 'go east' (ad orientalem plagam), so he built Mo-Chop in Meath, but Crubthir Fintan evicted him, claiming 'ista terra mei iuris est'. Kebi then settled in Bregh, and then 'Vobyun', but was again evicted by Fintan, who expelled him from Ireland (v. *Kebi* 10-15). There is a Killartery (Cell Airthir) in Mayne, Clogher, Louth (*O 18*), O'Hanlon 7, 225; another in West Meath, Hogan 175. Crimthir Fintan of the Irish tradition and Crubthir Fintan of the Welsh tradition are contemporaries, in the same region of Ireland, both in violent conflict with enemies, and both have a monastic site called 'orientalis'. These are presumably two versions of the same tradition.

FLAND FEBLA, bishop of Armagh, 689-715. I;I. *Book of Leinster* 42c (sedit xxvii). Accepted Sletty from Conchad, successor of Aed, Tírechán *Add.* 16; omitted by the *Annals*.

FLANNAN of Killaloe, Clare (*R 67*) VII E/M? Aug. 28. I;I. *BHL* 3024. *Sal.* 643 (1); *AB* 46, 1928, 124 (2); 122 (3); 117 (4). Kenney 405. *Son of king Theodoricus, of Dal Cais, ancestor of Brian Boru* who became a monk in old age under Colman of Lismore (698-702) (14) and died of pleurisy (22). 'Theodoric' is a latinisation of Toirdelbach, characteristic of the Dal Cais genealogies (O'Clery 1948). A monk at 'Laoniensis civitas' (Killaloe) under its founder, a Mo-Lua, whose mill he worked, and whom he succeeded (4-8); Brendan (of Clonfert) 'among the other wonders in the islands of the ocean that he saw and described' foretold that Flannan would found numerous congregations 'In Hibernie seu Scotie, verum etiam in Anglia' (7). (Britannie 2, 3). Against the advice of St. Bracanus and all his own friends and relatives, he went to Rome. On the way he was given a site in Gaul (*2; 3*), where he left a disciple Cochid (Eochaid?) (*3*). Met Pope John, brought 14 invalid Roman disciples (12; 23), lepers (*2, 7*), settled on 'insula Ferdinea' (unlocated) 'and nova instituta . . . de curia Romana' (8; 13); the context implies an early stage in the Easter controversy, and the pope will therefore be John IV, 640-642; the Roman 'instituta' were no longer new in southern Ireland under John V, 685-6. Theodoric's brother defeated enemies in their territory, near Imelac, then deserted, with the help of 'the demon Albe' (18-19); perhaps Imlech Ailbe, Emly, the see of Ailbe. Prophesied the durability of a wooden church built by 'vir sanctus Fedelminus' who 'tota Hyberniam . . . regebat' as 'sanctus rex' (king and bishop of Munster 824-847 identified in 2) *whose pupil he had been* (28); he might have been the pupil of a Feidelmid. Turned nine 'iaculatores' (actors?) to stone in the Isle of Mananch (Manand, Man) (29); had monks in the 'islands of the great ocean' (32). Enjoined that his see be held not by his kinsman but by any learned chaste cleric. 'Cuiuscumque conditionis sive ingenuus sive liber, sive media de plebe' (29). In his day, there was no agriculture in Ireland (inarata tellus, ac nullo semine iecta) (31); many of the miracles concern the clearance of land and construction of roads (e.g. 23; 15). The Irish chiefs are cattle thieves, 'as in Spain' (13). The Life, written soon after 1162 (10), is plainly the work of a monk trained in Europe, unique among Irish texts. Kenney's conjecture that Flannan was himself foreign seems unwarranted. The name is Irish, and [2-4] are normal Irish Latin Lives. Abban.

FLANNAN of the Flannan Isles, Lewis (*NA 74*). I;P. Forbes 350, perhaps identical with Flannan of Killaloe.

FOELAN of Fosses, near Namur, Belgium +c.655, Oct. 31. I;E.Gaul. *BHL* 3070-8 (*NLA* 1, 447). Brother of Fursey and Ultan, succeeded Fursey as abbot of Cnobheresburh (Burgh Castle, Suffolk). Expelled, crossed to Peronne, received at Nivelles in Brabant by Ita, widow of Pepin the elder (of Landen, +639), who gave him the site of Fosses. Murdered by bandits. Nivelles was a double monastery of Irish inspiration, founded on the advice of St. Amand.

FOELAN of Scotland VI/VII ? Jan. 9. I;P. *BHL* 297. David Camerarius, = *ASH* 49 = *Brev. Ab.* PH 26. Son of Kentigerna (+734), baptised by *Ibar* (+499), successor of Fintan Munnu (+637) (as abbot of Taghmon). Came to Scotland, where his festival is kept on Jan. 9, on which day the Irish Martyrologies name Foelan of Fertullagh in West Meath. The martyrologies list some 20 saints named Foelan (indices, *cf. ASH* 104). The account is a pastiche of other Saints' Lives, contrived in the absence of a tradition: the story that Foelan wrote at night, using the miraculously illuminated fingers of his left hand as a torch, and caused a crane to peck out the eye of an abbot's messenger who observed him, is taken from the story of Columba's transcription of Finnian of Moville's book. His name is Irish.

He has a widespread cult in Scotland, especially in and about Perthshire, Forbes 345, O'Hanlon 1, 139, his principal centre at St. Fillans, at the lower end of Loch Earn (*NN 6924*); and is made nephew of St. Congan of Turiff (Oct. 13), Aberdeen (*NJ 7249*), Forbes 310, O'Hanlon 10, 236, whose cult is as wide, whose tradition equally lost. Fillan's relics were credited with bringing victory to the Scots at Bannockburn (Hector Boethius, cited *ASH*, Forbes, O'Hanlon). The Life of Congan (*Brev. Ab.* PE 126) equates Foelan with Foelan of Fosses.

FOIRTCHERN of Trim, Meath (*N 85*) and Leinster V M/L, Oct. 11. I;I. Tírechán *Additamenta* 1; (*AB* 2, 1883, 213 ff.); = *Bethu Phátraic* (Mulchrone 43) = Stokes *VT* 334-336; 66. *cf. FM* 432. Son of Feidelmid, son of king Loegaire, high-king 428-463, and of the daughter of the king of the British (*i Scott, *BP*; id est Scoth Noe, Tír. *Add.**), and therefore spoke British. Converted by Lomman the Briton, to whom his father made over his fort of Trim. On Lomman's death, Foirtchern surrendered Trim to Cathlaid peregrinus. Patrick's smith, *FM* 446.

Of Trim and of Cill Foirtchern in Ui Drona (the southern part of County Carlow, in Ui Cennselaig territory) *M. Don.*, *M. Oeng.*; and of Cill Foirtchern in Ui Trea (? Ui Trena in Ui Cennselaig) *M. Oeng.* Telach Foirtcheirn (Tullow, Carlow, *S 87*, Hogan 628) *M. Oeng.* June 12. 'Fortkernus episcopus Roscurensis ecclesiae' educated Finnian of Clonard (+551, elderly, born *c*.480/490), v. *Finn. C.* 2. Roscuire, where Finnian had three churches, is Myshall, Carlow (*S 86*), in Ui Drona territory eight miles south of Tullow, Hogan 585 (rather than Roscore Wood, near Rahan, Offaly). Finnian, baptised by Abban, was reared in south Leinster; the martyrologies equate the south Leinster Foirtchern with Foirtchern of Trim; Foirtchern, grandson of Loegaire abandoned Trim, his future whereabouts unstated. The two are contemporary in differing traditions, and therefore probably identical.

The name is an Irish transliteration of Vortigern, and it is therefore likely that his maternal grandfather, a British king contemporary with Vortigern, was Vortigern (*see* L). The name spread in Ireland; on two Ogam inscriptions, *CIIC* 297, Knockboy, Waterford (*S 20*), near Lismore, 'Vortigurn' and 97, Ballyhank, Cork (*W 58*), a re-used stone ' . . . lli maqi Vorrtigurn'. Both stones formed one among a considerable group, suggesting cemeteries, perhaps monastic; *CIIC* 100 from Ballyhank 'Ab Ulccagni' perhaps commemorates an abbot. The name occurs several times in the genealogies with a rich layman in Scotland, Ad. v. *Col.* 2, 17, and a bishop Foirtchern attended the synod of Drumceat in the later sixth century. All these persons are later than bishop Foirtchern, with the theoretical exception of the Knockboy stone, whose date is unknown. The name is not known to have been used after the sixth-century, and therefore owed its short-lived popularity to a well-known individual. It is therefore likely that these persons were named in honour of bishop Foirtchern, perhaps under the influence of Finnian of Clonard, his pupil, who became the greatest of the early sixth-century monks.

FORANNAN, *see* Farannan of Alternan.

FORANNAN, bishop of Armagh, 688-689. I;I. *Book of Leinster* 42ᶜ(sedit i); omitted by the *Annals*.

FRIDIANUS, *see* Frigidian.

FRIDOLIN of Saeckingen, Baden, Upper Rhine VII M, March 6. I;Germany. *BHL* 3170-2; *ASH* 479. Kenney 497. Irishman who reached the Rhine by way of Poitiers, founded a major monastery, earned a wide cult in Wurtenburg, Alsace and Switzerland, *cf.* O'Hanlon 3, 171, Gougaud, *Saints Irlandais* 105.

FRIGIDIAN of Lucca, northern Tuscany VI L, Nov. 18. I;Italy. *BHL* 3173-7. *ASH* 633. A Life of Finnian of Moville is attached to the beginning of the Life, Frigidian's name (Fridian) applied to Finnian. Irishman, came to Italy, appointed bishop of Lucca, held the see for 28 years. Built very many churches, in honour of SS. Vincentius, Stephen, Laurence, with miraculous help to the builders. Miraculously diverted the course of the river, with the aid of an earth-levelling machine of his own invention. The Lives are twelfth-century or later. The river miracle is narrated by Gregory the Great, *Dialogue* 3, 9, on the authority of bishop Venantius of Luna, who told him the tale 'ante biduum', the day before yesterday. The monasteries of his order are listed *ASH* 647.

FURSEY of Peronne +649, Jan. 16. I;I. Gaul. *BHL* 3209-3221. *ASH* 75 (1). *NLA* 1, 461 (2). *Sal.* 77 (3). Bede *HE* **3**, 19 (4). Kenney 500.
A Munsterman (1); of Dal Araide, his mother from Connacht. Visited Findbar's tomb in Cork, v. *Findbar* 15; bishop, superior to Cronan, v. *Cr.* 17: friend of Mo-Choemog, v. *Moch.* 31. Nobly-born Irishman, abbot of Louth, founded by Mocteus, succeeded by Ultan of Ardbreccan (+655), *M. Oeng.* (perhaps intending Ultan, brother of Fursey). Welcomed by Sigebert of the East Angles, built his monastery at Cnobheresburh (Burgh Castle, Suff., *TG 4805*); had a dramatic vision of the underworld, *cf. Annals* 639; after many years in Ireland, emigrated 'per Brettones' with his brother Foelan, but since his monastery was disturbed by pagan raids, crossed to Gaul, where he was received by the mayor Erconwald, leaving Foelan in East Anglia (4). His brother Ultan was already in Gaul. Founded Lagny, died, buried at Erconwald's church at Peronne, where Ultan presided. (2) and (3) are versions of the vision, which became a favourite mediaeval tale. He is one of the few Irishmen abroad who was remembered at home, in the Annals, Saints' Lives and martyrologies; some, but not all, of these records are due to the popularity of his vision.
Cuana, Gobban.

GALLUS of St. Gall, Switzerland +c.630, Oct. 16. I;Gaul. *BHL* 3245-3258. Companion of Columban, established a hermitage and oratory, on whose site the major monastery of St. Gall was founded nearly a century later. His cult is widespread in eastern Switzerland, southern Germany, northern Italy, Gougaud *Saints Irlandais* 115.

GARMON, *see* Germanus of Auxerre.

GAVIDIUS IV M. Gaul;Gaul. Aquitanian bishop, who disapproved of the attitude of some British bishops to the government at the Council of Rimini, 359, Sulp. Sev., *Chron.* 2, 41.

GEMMAN V L/VI E. I;I. Aged magister of Columba of Iona, then a young deacon, in Leinster, Ad. v. *Col.* 2, 25. Carminator, who composed a 'carmen magnificum' in honour of Finnian of Clonard, also probably in Leinster, v. *Fin. C.* 23. Both stories relate to the late 540s; *cf.* Germanus peregrinus.

GENOC VI E, Dec. 26. B;I. Pupil of Finnian of Clonard, a Briton who returned to Ireland with him, with Biteus (Mobhi), v. *Fin. C.* II, *cf.* 19 and *Catalogus* 5 (Mo-Genoc); Mo-Genoc of Cell Duma Gluinn (unidentified) in southern Breg. Lomman.

GERALDUS (Gerhard?) of Mayo +726 (*c.*696), March 13. E;E.I. *VSH* 2, 107. Son of *Cusperius* Anglie rex and regina *Benicia* (? comitis regis Berniciae); in his youth *abbot* at Winchester. Disciple of Colman (of Lindisfarne), followed him to Ireland (i.e. 664), landing in Connacht in the territory of Ailill (Ui Fiachrach?). Given land by rex Ragallus (*Rhaghallach +648, for his son rex Cellachus 654-703) king of Connacht, and built 'Maguncia' (Magh Eo, Mayo). Sent a third of his party to England to fetch supplies. Attended a synod convened at Tara by the kings Diarmait and Blathmac (+664), on the occasion of a great famine, who proposed that each 'colonus' should be allocated seven or nine 'iugera' of 'terra plana', eight of 'aspera', nine of woodland. The 'maiores terrae' proposed that the people should meet, and all, lay and clerical, should pray that God should remove by a plague a part of the 'multitudine onerosa populi inferioris' so that the rest should live more easily. Fechin of Fore (+666) argued that excess population was the cause of famine; that there was not enough agricultural land for the multitude of men; and that it was right that the 'maiores terrae' should pray that the excessive 'multitudo vulgi per infirmitatem aliquem tolleretur'. Gerald opposed the proposition as immoral: for God can feed many men from a few grains sown in the earth. An angel appeared in a dream to a certain saint, and announced that 'God can multiply food as easily as men'; the 'maiores' who seek 'mortem inferiorum de populo' act against the will of God, and will die. So it proved. The plague killed the two kings, with the kings of Ulster and Munster, and Fechin, but spared Gerald (12). He returned to Connacht, where his sister 'Sigresia', who presided over 100 nuns, with 50 of his followers, at the monastery of Elitheria (? Alither: pilgrims, foreigners), had died of the plague with all her flock. He died some years later, and Adomnán presided over his monastery for seven years, writing a gospel book with his own hand, before returning to Iona. Mayo was destroyed later by 'Turgetius Norvagensis' (Thorgisl, *AU* 844). Died 726 *FM* (731 *AU*, many of whose eighth-century ecclesiastical obits lag by five years, *cf.* Virgilius), named Garaalt Maige heo.

The Life compounds two distinct individuals. Adomnán was away from Iona, in Ireland, from 696 to 703; and may well have supervised Mayo. The Life therefore deals with an English follower of Colman who became abbot of 'Mayo of the Saxons', established by Colman's English followers, unable to agree with the Irish after 664, and died *c.*696. He might have been one of the half-dozen English who are known to have settled in the later seventh century at unnamed monasteries in Ireland (listed Plummer, *Bede* 2, 196), several of whom must have chosen Mayo; but is more probably otherwise unknown, and must remain nameless. This Englishman might well have been in Ireland at the time of the Tara synod (*c.*663?), joining Colman on his return, possibly a Bernician who had lived at Winchester. The Life uses the name of the later Geraldus, of whom nothing else is known. The sharp social struggle described is plainly an independent story, attached by the author to his hero, with or without good reason.

GERMANUS, bishop of Auxerre 418-*c*.448, July 31. Gaul;Gaul.B. *BHL* 3453-3464 (*cf.* Sulpicius Severus; Germanus is frequently mentioned in the literature of fifth-century Gaul). The principal Life, by Constantius, *MGH SRM* 7, 259ff. (*BHL* 3453), was written by the priest Constantius not long after 472; (ch. 12-18, 25-27 were accurately transcribed Bede *HE* 1, 17-21, with minor MS. variants and the insertion of a paragraph from *Passio III Albani* 21-22 at the end of 1, 18, and of a sentence from vita *Lupi* 12 at the beginning of 1, 21). A *dux* before he took orders and succeeded Amator, Martin's pupil, as bishop (418). He worked closely with Hilary of Arles, metropolitan of Gaul (v. *Hilary* 16). Visited Britain (429 Prosper. *Chron.*, written three or four years after the event) to combat Pelagianism with Lupus, bishop of Troyes, preached in public open places, appealing to the *plebs* rather than to the bishops. Visited St. Albans (sacerdotes beatum . . . Albanum . . . petierunt) (and opened his tomb, inserting 'membra sanctorum ex diversis regionibus collecta', Bede, from the *Passio*). While laid up after an accident to his foot, miraculously stemmed a fire which spread from one thatched house to another. Offered himself as *dux praelii* of the British army, whom a joint campaign of Saxons and Picts had 'in castra contraxerat'; 'castra' may carry the meaning of a legionary fortress, Chester. Baptised the bulk of the army, at Easter, stationed a light force in ambush above a mountain valley, whence the enemy were expected, and ordered them to shout 'Alleluia' three times when the enemy entered the valley; the rebounding echo so terrified the enemy that they fled in panic, many of them being drowned in the river which they had to cross, so that the bishops won a bloodless victory. Visited Britain again (shortly before his death), in the mid- or late-440s (for discussions of the date, *cf.* E. A. Thompson and P. Grosjean, *AB* 75, 1957, 135; 174), with Severus, bishop of Trier, received by Elafius, 'regionis illius primus', secured the deportation of some Pelagian bishops. G. de Plinval (in *St Germain*, 1950, 146) adduced an ancient tradition that he set sail to Britain from Saint-Germain-des-Vaux, 20km west of Cherbourg. On the occasion of both visits, he passed through Paris, encouraging and blessing Genevieve (Genofeva) daughter of Severus and Gerontia, then little regarded. Established or developed a cathedral monastery at Auxerre, perhaps initiated by his predecessor **A**mator, where **P**atrick is said to have been educated; he is said to have promoted the mission of Patrick to Ireland, on and immediately after his first visit to Britain. Went to Ravenna, seeking pardon for Armorican Bagauda rebels, and there died.

The story of Germanus is unusually clear and well attested in ancient sources, but was more savagely distorted by modern fantasy than that of any other fifth- or sixth-century personage of note. He brought with him to Britain the newly-ordained bishop of Troyes, Lupus (*BHL* 5087-5090) who is even better recorded. Lupus was previously a monk of Lerins, brother-in-law of Hilary of Arles, and held his episcopate for more than 50 years, to become the senior and most revered bishop of Gaul. He was also an outstanding scholar and writer, with an unusually large library; and in old age revised book six of Sidonius's letters before publication. Constantius, Germanus's biographer, was also an eminent scholar; nearly as old as Lupus, he was responsible for persuading Sidonius to publish, and several books of the letters are dedicated to him. He was well acquainted with Lupus, and almost certainly knew both Germanus and Faustus of Riez; the latter maintained contact with his native Britain. He is a contemporary source, a writer of exceptional ability and integrity, unusually well informed. Modern attempts to dodge or deny the facts which he set down go to surprising lengths; it may or may not be true that his purpose was to 'create a new popular saint to rival the cult of St Martin', but no such purpose either invalidates his report of events thoroughly well known to many of his readers, or gives any justification for dismissing his account of Germanus's first visit with the comment, 'The admirable narrative style of Constantius still to-day succeeds in imposing this fantastic story on our sober historians' (N. K. Chadwick, *Poetry and Letters in Early Christian Gaul*, London, 1955, 266; 254). To most readers of the text, the sobriety of Constantius contrasts with the fantasy of the modern critic.

The facts about Germanus are those set down by Constantius. He fought a battle in mountainous country close to a large river, impassable to non-swimmers. The well-informed contemporary statement cannot be avoided. The geography of Britain locates the engagement in the highlands, common sense in Wales rather than the north. Native traditions which coincide with Constantius deserve consideration, and may possibly be true. Traditions and embellishments ancient or modern which conflict with it must be rejected. A strong native tradition locates Germanus in Powys about the Dee. It was already a devolved tradition by the eighth century, and is independent of Constantius, since it is primarily concerned with political dispositions initiated by Germanus in association with Vortigern, not mentioned by Constantius, rather than with the battle itself. The essence of this story is possible, and may well be thought probable.

Germanus is more prominent in British hagiographical tradition than any other continental cleric. He is introduced into very many Lives, usually out of due time and place, to increase the authority of the saint concerned. In the early seventh century (vita *Samson* 1, ch. 42), Samson's monastery on the lower Severn was believed to have been founded by him. On the Pillar of Elise (*ECMW* 182), Llantysilio-yn-Ial, Denbigh (*SJ* 1943) (*c.*800), he is made to bless Vortigern (Guarthi[girn]) *father* of Brittu, founder of the Powys dynasty. In Nennius 32-35, from the *Liber Beati Germani*, Germanus destroyed by heavenly fire the fort of the wicked king Benlli (cf. Moel Fenlli, *SJ* 1660), hill-fort with a hoard of over 6,000 coins mostly Constantinian (Roman Britain in *Arch. Camb.* 2, 1847, 108; 76, 1921, 237; 78, 1923, 304) (indicating late or post-Roman use), and installed Catell as founder of the new kingdom of Powys. On his second visit, however, he is said to have condemned Vortigern, Nennius 47, *cf.* 39. In Wales he is Garmon (Jackson *LHEB* 281, *cf.* 128 n. 2, citing Bede's statement [*HE* **5**, 9] that in his day the British *corrupte* pronounced 'Germani' as 'Garmani' to disprove Sir Ifor Williams's contention [Cym. Trans. 1946-7, 53] that they only pronounced it 'Gerfawn' and that *Garmon* could not therefore be Germanus, cf. G. P. Jones, *Arch. Camb.* 85, 1930, 31) or Harmon. His sites in Wales are thickest in Powys (mapped *LBS* 3, 76), but there are a few sites in Lleyn and Arfon. These names' antiquity and validity are emphasized by their restricted distribution. Although the medieval editors of a number of south Welsh Saints' Lives imported Germanus, usually out of time and place, to glorify their heroes, he occurs rarely in southern place-names. In England he has three or four sites in the south-west (Cornwall, Devon, Dorset), rather more in the east: Bovinger and Faulkbourne in Essex; Marske, Winestead and Selby in Yorkshire; Ranby, Scothorne and Thirlby in Lincolnshire; Wiggenhall in Norfolk; St. Albans in Hertfordshire (Arnold-Forster 1, 462ff.). After William the Conqueror's re-dedication of Selby Abbey, late twelfth-century local tradition explained the dedication by making its founder an Auxerre monk, equipped with relics of St. Germanus; but the Norman foundation was a double dedication to Mary and Germanus, implying an early single dedication whose origin was forgotten. Double dedications, to Mary or

Michael and a saint revered by the British, commonly denote an English addition
to an original dedication. Selby existed before the Conquest (*EPNS* Yorks. WR, 4,
31) and will already have had a patron-saint. The St. Albans chapel might be
ascribed to readers of Constantius's *Life*. Any or all of these dedications might be
medieval, since Germanus was a well known saint, but there is no evident later
occasion for the dozen other English dedications and their distribution in small
distinct groups argues against a late fashion. The English distribution of Germanus's
names recalls those of David and Winwaloe. Present evidence does not suffice to
say whether they are or are not due to British, pre-English, Christians; taken
together, the reasons for later English dedication are not obvious. In Heiric's
devolved *Miracula Germani* 1, 54, 80, cited by N. K. Chadwick *Poetry and Letters* 266,
Britain was by the ninth century 'beato Germano peculiari devotione submissa'.

He is also noted in the Irish Martyrologies (Ciaran of Saigir had a bell made by
'Germanus episcopus, *magister sancti Patricii** [v. *Ci. S. 1,* 4; Germanus faber, 5,
3 and Irish language Lives, *cf.* Germanus peregrinus]). *LBS* 2, 52 ff. distinguishes
Germanus of Auxerre from 'Germanus of Man' and 'Germanus mac Guill'. Both
arise from a dittography in the Irish Martyrologies (amplified in *LBS* by use of the
modern concoctions of the Iolo *MSS.*). Germanus's day is 31 July. *Mart. Gorm. (cf.*
Tallaght) reads *July 30* . . . *Cobair mac Guill, German. July 31 German epscop airdirc, aiti*
Patraic primfir (bishop Germanus [of Auxerre], Patrick's excellent tutor). The
German at the end of 30 July is plainly a dittography of the German who begins
the next line but was explained as, like Cobair, son of Guill, and is so indexed by
modern editors. Mac Guill, however, is a known man, the bishop of Man appointed
by Patrick (Muirchú 22). The biographer of Kentigern, Jocelyn of Furness, therefore, in his life of Patrick (Colgan *TT* 86 and 98, Chs. 92 and 152) turned *German*
(et) Mac Guill into successive bishops of Man. Colgan (TT *230* [misprinted 228])
equates 'German of Man' with Gorman. Germanus 'religiosus peregrinus' who
visited Ciaran of Saigir at the end of the fifth century (v.29) and Germanus who
visited Reims in 509 (Flodoard 4, 9 cited *LBS* 1, 105) may both be mis-spellings of
the unfamiliar Gemman, teacher of Columba, in Leinster (Adomnán 2.25), Senex
in the late 530s, unless this name be mis-spelt in all manuscripts. One Irish secular
tale might echo a tradition about Germanus. *Lebor na hUidre* 38, 2783 ff., and
derivative versions, cited O'Rahilly *EIHM* 213, cf. Bury, *St Patrick* 354, summarised
O'Curry 284 ff., explained that the death of the high king Nath-I, killed by lightning
while on an expedition in the Alps in 428, was divine vengeance for his destruction
of the 'tower' of the hermit (holy man, *Cóir Anmann,* 146, Stokes, *Irische Texte,* 3,
352) Fermenus, who is in some versions also 'king of France' (*rí Tracia,* for Francia).
Bury's equation of Fermenus with the legendary Merovingian Faramund is improbable for, whatever its corruptions, no tale can have invoked divine lightning on
behalf of a Frankish king; and the corrupt part of the description of 'Fermenus' is
the word *rí*, 'king', the valid original 'holy man'. Fermenus the holy man of Gaul
might be a scribal corruption of Germanus, the tradition alleging a clash of some
sort between Germanus and Nath-I just before the king's death, with the hermit's
tower being destroyed. The loose annalistic date of 428 cannot of course be pressed
to mean that Nath-I died before the firm date of Germanus's visit, 429.

Germanus of Man and *German m. Guill* are twentieth-century antiquarian
fabrications, built upon a MS. dittography. Illtud, Ninnoca, Patrick, Samson, etc.

GERMAN mac Cuill, *GERMANUS of Man*. Germanus' day is July 31. In
M. Gor., July 30 ends with the line 'Cobair mac Guill German', and July 31 begins
with the lines 'German epscop' (of Auxerre, tutor of Patrick). The 'German', last

word of July 30, is plainly a dittography of 'German', the first word of July 31, fitting the scansion. *M. Tal.*, July 30, supposing an 'i German' reads 'German mac Guill', evidently supposing the unexplained name to be a brother of Cobair. Jocelyn of Furness, also Kentigern's biographer, in his v. *Patrick* (92; 152. *TT* 86, 98) makes German and Mac Cuill successive bishops of Man, and the parish of Peel (*SC 2 8*) became Kirk German; Mac Cuill was appointed bishop of Man by Patrick (Muirchú 22). Colgan emends German to Gorman. *LBS* 3, 60, aided by liberal use of the *Iolo* MSS. and similar modern fancies, separates *German of Man*, who is equated with *Germanus of Paris* in v. *Brioc* and given a fair share of the Germanus of Auxerre tradition, from *German mac Cuill*, who is no longer connected with Man, but is equated with 'Germanus peregrinus' (3, 80). The activities of the allegedly Irish Germanus (of Man) in Wales have played some part in modern writing that cites *LBS* without probing its sources.

GERMANUS 'episcopus ex Hibernensium regione transmissus a sancto Patricio archiepiscopo venit ad Brochanum regem Britannae' (**B**rychan, VI E) and converted his daughter **N**innoca, v. *Ninnoca, Cart. Quimperlé*, p. 58. Evidently intended for Germanus of Auxerre, turned from Patrick's teacher into his pupil.

GERMANUS Heliae VII? Named in a seventeenth-century Latin poem on Irish saints honoured in Belgium, line 47, *AB* 43, 1925, 121.

GERMANUS of Paris +576, May 28. Gaul;Gaul. *BHL* 3468-3481. *DCB*. Bishop of Paris *c*.555-576. Entertained **S**amson in Paris, *c*.557 (v. *Samson* 2, ii, 10 ff.). *Teacher of **B**rioc, and **I**lltud and **P**atrick before him*, v. *Brioc* 9 ff.; the inclusion of Illtud and Patrick, both elsewhere treated as pupils of Germanus of Auxerre, indicates that he was confused with his namesake. Brioc is said to have visited Paris at the same time as Samson, and was doubtless also entertained.

GERMANUS peregrinus V L/VI E. Gaul?;I. A bishop, guest of Ciaran of Saigir when Carthacus returned, v. *Ci. S.* (*1*) 29. Faber Germanus made Ciaran's bell (v. *Ci. S. 5*, 3, and Irish Lives; *Germanus of Auxerre* *1*, 4). Germanus visited Remigius of Reims with **G**ibrianus, Tressan and other Irishmen(?) in 503, (Flodoard 4, 9 = *ASS* Feb. 7, 274, cited *LBS* 1, 105). These three persons are contemporary and may be identical; some or all of them may be emendations of the unfamiliar **G**emman.

GERMOCHUS rex VI E. I;B. Accompanied **B**reaca to Cornwall, Leland, *Itin.* 3, 15, cited *LBS* 1, 229. Named at Germoe, Co. (*SW 5829*), near Breage, Sancti Germocii 1377, *DEPN* 195. The name might be Cermait, as Diarmait gives Dermocius.

GIBRIANUS of Châlons VI E, May 8. I?;Gaul. *BHL* 3526-7. 'Delata sunt etiam tunc temporibus (Remigii, *c*.457-530) ad ecclesiam beati Remigii memoria Sancti Gibriani a pago Catalaunensi, ubi peregrinatus fuisse noscitur et humatus. Advenerunt siquidem in hanc provinciam septem frates ab Hibernia peregrinationis ob amorem Christi gratia; hi scilicet, Gibrianus, Helanus, Tressanus, Germanus, Veranus, Abranus, Petranus, cum tribus sororibus suis, Fracla, Promptia, Possenna, eligentes sibi super fluvium nomine Maternam (Marne), opportuna degendi loca' Flodoard (+966) *HE Rem.* 4, 9 (cited *LBS* 1, 105); in the reign of Clovis, +511, *Brev. Rem.*; 509, Sigebert, *Chron.* (whose dates tend to be inferred rather than evidenced). Buried in a stone sarcophagus on the site of his roadside hermitage, over which an oratory was built. The later history of the shrine, notices in Usuard and continental martyrologies, summarised O'Hanlon 5, 132. The names, evidently the centre of a local cult, do not sound Irish; their Irish origin may have been the imagination of a later age, when most strange monks were Irish.

GILDAS +570, Jan. 29. B;B.I.A. *BHL* 3541-4. His own works, *de Excidio Britanniae* (1); *Epistulae* (2); *Penitential* (3), probably, and *Lorica* (4), possibly his *MGH AA* 13 (= *Chron. Min.* 3), 1894, 1 ff. (ed. Mommsen); ed. Hugh Williams, *Cymmrodorion Society*, David Nutt, 1899, with translation; lengthy excerpts, *HS* 1, 44 ff. (*1*) also *MBH* 3 ff. *Vitae*, Ruys, *MGH* 91, Williams 322 (5), Caradoc of Llancarfan, *MGH* 107, Williams 390 (6); Brev. Nantes *ASH* 176 (7). Large extracts of (*1*) are reproduced by Bede, *HE* **1**, 12 ff.

(*1*) was written before the death of Maelgwn (551), (33 ff.), but not long before, since Maelgwn had ruled, been deposed, and returned to power, and was evidently no longer young; but while the 'honi', adherents of the reform movement which Gildas championed, were still 'pauci', 'paucissimi pastores' (26; 50; 110). They could no longer be so described after the reform movement flourished in the early 540s, hardly after Samson was consecrated bishop, probably in the late 530s. It will therefore have been written about 540, or shortly before. The proper names are in late British, not yet Welsh (Jackson *LHEB* 40; 42; 188-9, etc.) appropriate to the mid-sixth century. (2, 4-5) is cited by Columban (*MGH Epp.* 3, 158) as addressed to Vennianus (Finnian, evidently of Moville) presumably on the occasion of Gildas' intervention in the affairs of the Irish church (565, see below). Wrote more than a generation after Badon (*c*.495), born then, perhaps 44 years ago (*1*, 26); in Arecluta (Alclud, Dumbarton) on the Clut (Clyde). Son of Cauuus (*5*, 1; of *Nau [Cau Prydein], also father of Cuillus who rebelled against Arthur* 6, 1; 6, 5), *brother of Mailoc, Alleccus, Egreas, Peteova* (*5*, 2). Migrated, probably in infancy, to Wales, perhaps to Caer Gai (*SH 8731*), Lake Bala. Schooled by Hildutus (Illtud), with Samson and Paul Aurelian (*5*, 3-6), then in the schools of 'Iren' (Ireland) (*5*, 6), in Gaul (*6*, 2). Preached in Pepidiauc (northern Pembrokeshire) in the time of king Tribinus and his sons (Agricola, early VI) (v. *David* 5, hence 6, 4) and renounced the district to the yet unborn David. Preached in northern Britain (*5*, 8); received a *message from Brigit* (+525) and sent her a bell (*5*, 10). Visited Rome and Ravenna (*5*, 13-15; *6*, 7); on his return, founded Ruys, in the Vannetais, in the time of *Gradlan* (450) and '*Childeric Merovei filius*' (473-481) (*5*, 16); wrote 'Ormesta' v. *Paul Aurelian* 3, 'epistolarem libellum', denouncing five kings *10 years after leaving Britain*, (*5*, 19). Arranged a marriage between Trifina, daughter of Weroc of Vannes and the evil tyrant Conomerus (+560), who cut off her head, which Gildas restored (*5*, 20-25). Called Trechmorus in Brittany (*5*, 26); wrought miracles (*5*, 26-31); the later history of Brittany and Ruys (*5*, 32 ff.).

On Columba's excommunication (562), the 'seniores Hiberniae' sent envoys to Gildas 'de genere Saxonum' with a letter 'ut charitatem mutuam nutrirent' (anonymous Life of Columba, cited from Ussher, Reeves, *Adamnan* 193, Colgan *TT* 463, *cf. CS* 221). King Ainmire (565-569, Columba's cousin) invited Gildas to 'restore the churches' of Ireland (*5*, 12 ff.); he crossed to Ireland in 565 (*Annals*), collecting monks 'tam ex nobilibus quam ex pauperibus' and subjecting them to 'norma regularis disciplinae'; his extant letters, one of them addressed to Vennianus (*cf.* Finnian of Moville), see above, are largely concerned with the relations between stricter and milder monks. Directed studies at Armagh (*6*, 5). Gildas' letters and penitential (*2; 3*) strongly defend the milder rule (credited to Illtud and Cadoc) against the stricter rule (credited to David). The tradition of Clonard assigns its founder a rule close to David's, and makes him adjudicate the 'primacy of Britain', disputed between Gildas and David, to David (*Lismore* 2527). Gildas is not named among the list of clerics who supported David at the synod of Brefi, whose convocation enraged Cadoc.

Gildas visited Cadoc on his return from Ireland (v. *Cadoci* 27). From Rome (*6, 7*), where he supervised the school for a year, writing a gospel, 'which still remains at St. Cadoc's church, encased in gold and silver' (*6, 8*), and spent a winter on Echni (Flat Holm) island (*cf. LL* 138-9), where he was disturbed by pirates *from the Orkneys*, and migrated to *Glastonbury*, while king *Melvas* ruled Somerset (aestiva regio), *where* he died (*6, 9-12*). v. *Teilo* (*LL* 99-100) also reports a 'Pictish' raid on the Bristol Channel, citing 'historia Gilde Britannorum historiographi'. His mill, on the Blavet in Armorica (*5, 17*); came to Brittany soon after the death of king Gradlon (Brev. Nant. *ASH* 176); knew Philibert *of Tournus* (+*c*.684 *BHL* 6805) or of 'insula Hoia' (Houart, Morbihan, where he died *5, 28*) (perhaps VI L, Surius, Feb. 6) (Brev. Quimper, *ASH* 226).

Visited by Brendan of Clonfert, whom he kept waiting all night in the snow outside his locked gates, and who read his Greek missal, v. *Brendan* I, 83-84. His Old Testament quotations (listed *HS* 1, 170 ff., *cf.* 175 b) consistently emend the Old Latin version from the Septuagint; either he, or the scribe of his text, knew Greek. He cites Vergil, Orosius, Juvenal, Jerome, and other Latin authors, *cf. MGH*, p. 6, *EHR* 56, 1941, 353 (C. E. Stevens), *AB* 75, 1957, 189 (P. Grosjean), etc. His Latin is a 'good swinging style in the flowery taste of his age' (Jackson *LHEB* 119), a great deal nearer to the tradition of Sidonius before him than to Gregory of Tours in the next generation. The *de Excidio* springs from a deep reading of the Old and New Testaments, coloured by some classical learning. It is a single work; sporadic attempts to divide it, on the grounds that one MS. and one glossary reproduce only the early chapters, rest on no evidence, *cf.* Stevens 353; *DAD* 178, n. 30.

He is more widely honoured in the surviving tradition than any other native. In *Catalogus 2* he, David and Docco gave the Irish their liturgy. These three are the only British saints remembered in the *Annals*. Gildas is introduced into numerous British, Armorican, and Irish Lives, almost always as a superior who honours the saint concerned by giving him a bell, foretelling his greatness, assigning him territory. His sites, however, are confined to Brittany, where they are numerous in the Vannetais and Domnonie (mapped *LBS* 3, 114). Since he left no houses in the British Isles, his reputation derived from his writing and his impact on his own generation; which extended to the English, who knew him as 'Gildas historicus' (Bede *HE* 1, 22), and 'Gyldas Britto sapientissimus' (Alcuin *Epp.* 28 and 86), which assume that he was widely known to English readers at the end of the eighth century.

Cynan Colledauc, Finnian of Clonard, Finnian of Llancarfan, Maedoc, Oudoceus, Sicilian Briton, Virgilius Maro, etc.

GNOUAN, abbot of Llancarfan, VII L. B;B. *LL* index.

GOBAN of Laon VII M, June 20. I;B.Gaul. *BHL* 3569 (*ASS* June 4, 23 [ed. 3, 5, 20]). Native of Fursey's district (Dal Araide), accompanied Fursey to Britain, stayed at Burgh Castle, with Dicuil (Bede *HE* 3, 19) when Fursey left for Gaul (*c*.640). Crossed later to France, given Mons Eremi, Laon, by Clothaire III (656-670), killed by *Vandal* invaders.

GOBBAN, *see* Govan.

GOLL, *see* Mac Cuil.

GONERIUS VI M, July 18. B;A. *BHL* 3611, *AG* 223, *LBS* 3, 134. British companion of Tudwal, settled near Rohan on land given by Alvandus, in the Vannetais.

GOUEZNOU VI M, Oct. 25. B;A. *BHL* 3608, *AG* 659, *LBS* 3, 222. Briton, crossed to Armorica at the age of 18 with his parents and his brother Maian, given land near Brest by Conomorus, succeeded Houardon as bishop in Leon; killed when a labourer dropped a hammer on his head from the scaffolding while he was supervising the building of a monastery. Possibly identical with 'Woednovius qui alio nomine To-Woedocus vocabatur' pupil of Paul Aurelian, v. *Paul A.* 11, *cf.* v. *Winwaloe* 1, 16.

GOULVEN VI M/L, July 1. B;A. *BHL* 3610, *AG* 367, *LBS* 3, 138. Briton, crossed to Leon, received land from Godianus of Villa Godiani (Ker-Gozian, near Goulven), *cf.* Guedianus comes. Succeeded Cetomerinus, the successor of Paulus Aurelian, as bishop of Leon. Died at Rennes, succeeded by Tenenan, v. *Tenenan* 10.

GOVAN VI? I;B.A. St. Govan's Head, Pemb. (*SR 9792*); Goven, south-west of Rennes(*S 5*); St. Govan at Plouguerneau, Finistère. The name is Irish Gobhan, *cf.* the artifex of Maedoc of Ferns, v. *M.* 46, 48, and of Abban, v. *Ab.* 42; Ailbe, v. *Ailbe 2*, 45; Fintan Clonenagh, v. *Fint. C.* (*CS*) 16, etc. The name means 'smith'.

GREGORY (the Great), Pope 590-604, Mar. 12. *BHL* 3636-3651. *DCB.* Bede *HE* pref.; **1**, 23-32; **2**, 1-4, 17, 18, 20; **3**, 29; **4**, 2, 27; **5**, 13, 19, 20, 24. Near contemporary Life by an English monk, *BHL* 3637, extensively excerpted, Plummer, *Bede*, 2, 389.

Born *c*.540, heir of one of the greatest Roman senatorial families; founded numerous monasteries on his estates. Left Rome for Britain to convert the English, *c*.575, but recalled by Pope Benedict, sent as papal representative to Constantinople. A scholar, reformed church music, liturgy, published Moralia, Dialogues, giving prominence and publicity to the work of Benedict of Nursia, and many other works. Elected pope in the thick of the Lombard invasion of central Italy, his defence of Rome and the Romagna shaped the future Roman territorial state. Sent Augustine to Kent, guided his mission with repeated letters, and additional priests. He is almost the only pope known to Irish hagiographers, and is made to meet saints who visited Rome at any date. See also Findbarr, Frigidian, Kentigern, Lasrian of Leighlin, Honorius and Laurentius of Canterbury, Macarius, Mellitus, Paulinus of York, Ternan, etc.

GREGORY, bishop of Tours, *c*.573-594, Nov. 17. *BHL* 3682. *DCB.* Born 538, Nov. 30, of a senatorial family of the Auvergne. Friend and counsellor of Radegundis, queen of Clothaire I and abbess, and of Ingoberga, mother of Bertha, queen of Aethelbert of Kent. His works (*MGH SRM* 1) include the *Miracula Martini, Vitae Patrum, de Gloria Confessorum, Martyrum*, and his immensely detailed *Historia Francorum*, whose narrative ends in 591. As bishop of Tours, he was in name metropolitan of the former province of Lugdunensis Tertia, which included Armorica. Though the British settlers in Armorica do not appear to have paid attention to his nominal authority, and are said to have sought confirmation of their episcopal claims from king Childebert in Paris, over his head, Gregory was well informed about his Armorican contemporaries. He also entertained visitors from Britain, including Winnocus.

GUEAN, *see* Julitta.

GUEN, *see* Julitta.

GUENEGAN, *see* Conocan.

GUENNGUSTLE, *see* Ninnoca.

GUENODOC, *see* Wethenoc.

GUIGNER, *see* Guiner.

GUILL, *see* Mac Cuil.

GUINER VI E. B?I?;B.A. v. *Fingar 2, 3*. Companion of Fingar, perhaps identical with him. Invaded Cornwall, killed by Theodoric; the name is British; he was perhaps a Demetian Briton obeying the Irish government of Demetia.

GUISTLIAN VI E. B;B. Bishop in northern Pembrokeshire in the youth of David; perhaps named 'monasterium Depositi', in Welsh Llangwystl.

GULVAL, *see* Wulvella.

GULWAL VI L, June 6. B;B.A? *BHL* 3688 ff. *NLA* 1, 501. *LBS* 3, 150. Bishop in Britain. When the wrath of the Lord afflicted Britain 'gladio, fame, et peste' (? in the second Saxon revolt of the late sixth century), he removed to a coastal monastery (in Armorica?) in his diocese, with 180 monks, where he embanked the tides, and apparently used the tides to work a water-mill. Died in 'insula Plecit', whence much later his successors 'ob infestationem barbarorum et paganorum' (Scandinavians?) crossed the sea to Francia, and settled with his relics at Blandinio (Blandinberg, Ghent, Belgium) well before 1143. He has a considerable cult in Brittany *LBS* 153.

GURHAVEL, abbot of Llantwit, VII M. B;B.

GURON (Uuron) VI M, Apr. 7. B;B. Hermit at Padstow, evicted by Petroc. Named several sites in Cornwall, *LBS* 3, 157, including Din Uurin, the episcopal see of the ninth century (*HS* 1, 674), perhaps Bodmin (Doble 4. 151); Gourin, Brittany, (*I 4*). Llanwrin, Montg. (*SH 7803*), etc. might concern him, but more easily derives from another monk of the same name.

GURTHIERN (Vortigern) VI? June 29 (July 3). B;A. *BHL* 3720-2; *Cart. Quimperlé* (ed. 1904) 42. Became a monk because he inadvertently killed his nephew in battle. A hermit for a year in northern Britain, in a valley between two high mountains. Stayed long in a cell on the Tamar. Crossed to Brittany, given Anaurot (Quimperlé) and Ile de Croix (where his relics were discovered) by *Gradlon*, Plebs Veneaca (? Ker Vignac *L 6* near L'Orient) by Waroc, for his help in time of plague (*c*.548?). Called *rex Anglorum*,*son of Bonus son of Gloui (of Gloucester)* and of Dinoi (Thynoy) through confusion with his namesake, Vortigern.

GURVAL VI L/VII E, June 6. B;A. *AG* 290. Follower of Brendan of Clonfert and Malo; successor of Malo.

GUTHLAC of Crowland, Lincs. (*TF 2310*) +714, Apr. 11. E;E. *BHL* 3723-3732. Mercian noble, settled at Crowland; disturbed by the howlings of the British in the surrounding marshes.

GWENAEL of Landevennec 533?-604? Nov. 3. A;A.B.E? *ASS* Nov. 1, 674; *AG* 670. Son of *comes* Romelius of Quimper, descendant of the British who emigrated with Conan Meriadauc (383); his personal 'hereditas' at Languenoc (Lanrivoare, *cf.* Ile Guenoc, *D 1, cf.* Kerlocguenech, Carhaix, *S 4*), *Cart. Landevennec* 39. Entered Landevennec, then newly founded, at the age of seven, succeeded **Winwaloe** as abbot, on his death (?583), 43 years later. Seven years after his accession visited Britain, founded a monastery in Britain and another in Ireland, returning after four years (594?). Welcomed by **Rigomalus** (Rualo) in Cornouailles, where he stayed six years (to 600?), before moving to the Vannetais, where Waroc granted him land after nine months. Died after four years, at the age of seventy or seventy-five. His Breton sites are given in *LBS* 3, 180. In English his name and Winwaloe's both give 'Winnell', at St.Twynnells, Pembs. (*SR 9497*), Seynt Wynelle, Wm. of Worcester, (but S. Winnoci in 1291 *LBS* 3, 180), and Wynnell's Grove, Barley, Herts. (*TL 3839*) 'capella Sancti Winwaloei' 1387, naming the Icknield Way 'Wynewalestrete' *c.*1470, *EPNS* 175. As Winwaloe's successor, he is as likely to have given Winwaloe's name as his own to his foundations. He has left no trace in Ireland. For a possible Monmouthshire site, *cf.* Gwynell, *LBS* 3, 229.

GWENFREWI, *see* Wenefred.

GWENOC, *see* Winnocus.

GWETHENOC, *see* Wethenoc.

GWYTHIAN *LBS* 3, 249, *cf.* Guedianus, layman.

HADRIAN of Canterbury +710, Jan. 9. African;E. *BHL* 3740-3. Bede *HE* pref.; **4**, 1-2; **5**, 20, 23. *Hist. Abb.* 3. *NLA* 1, 13, African abbot, offered but refused the archbishopric of Canterbury, proposed the appointment of **Theodore**, whom he accompanied. Abbot of St. Peter's, Canterbury, knew Greek; his pupils **Albinus**, his successor, and **Aldhelm**. **Tobias**.

HAEDDE, bishop of the West Saxons, *c.*674-705. E;E. Bede *HE* **3**, 7; **4**, 12; **5**, 18. Recognised Winchester as a *de jure* and a *de facto* see, since Dorchester-on-Thames had passed to Mercian control, and had been inaccessible to Wessex kings under his predecessors **Wine** and **Leutherius**. Translated **Birinus**' body to Winchester. Succeeded by **Daniel** in Winchester and **Aldhelm** in Sherborne.

HEDDE, bishop of the Mercians, *c.*679-731. E;E. *DCB*, his see at Lichfield.

HELANUS VI E, Oct. 7. *ASS* Oct. 3, 903. Visited Remigius at Reims 503 with **G**ibrianus, Tressan and others, Flodoard 4, 9, *LBS* 1, 105; perhaps identical with Helena, companion of Breaca, Leland *Itin.* 3, 15, *LBS* 1, 229. Of Lanhelin and St. Helen, near Tressaint, by Dinan, *S 2*; perhaps the Helen of West Cornish sites, *LBS* 3, 254.

HELVEUS, *see* Ailbe.

HERBLON, *see* Hermenland.

HERBOT of Berrien, Huelgoat, *I 3*, north of Carhaix. VI, June 17. B;A. *ASS* June 6, 202. A Briton, emigrated to Brittany. His cult is widespread, especially in Finistère, but the MS. of his Life was destroyed in the fourteenth century, *LBS* 3, 265.

HERMENLAND (Herblon) of Indret, Loire estuary (*T 9*) VII L, Mar. 25. German;A. *BHL* 3851-2. *AG* 774 (ad Nov. 25). Nobleman from Nijmegen on the Rhine, monk of Lambert of Fontenelle, who became bishop of Lyon in 678, founded Indret and obtained confirmation from Childebert II (695-710); sometimes confused with **H**erbot, *cf.* also St. Herblon (*W 8*) between Angers and Nantes.

HERNIN, *see* Ernin.

HERVE, *see* Hoernbiu.

HEWALD the Dark, and Hewald the White +*c*.695, Oct. 3. E;Germany. Bede *HE* **5**, 10. English priests, long exiled in Ireland (after 664?), evangelised the Old Saxons, murdered after torture, their bodies thrown into the Rhine. Buried at Cologne by Pippin (+714); *cf.* Alcuin, *de Sanctis Ebor.* v. 1045.

HIA (Ia, Ives) of St. Ives, Co. (*SW 5140*) VI E, Feb. 3 (Oct. 22). I;B. Companion of Fingar, travelling independently on a leaf from Ireland to Cornwall, v. *Fingar 1*, 12; in Cornwall before he arrived, ch. 13. Companion of Elwyn, Leland, cited *LBS* 3, 267. Perhaps from Cork, *cf.* = Cell Iae, church of Libar, pupil of Findbar of Cork, Hogan *Onomasticon*, 194.

HIERONYMUS (Jerome) *c*.346-420, Sept. 30. *BHL* 3866-3878. *DCB*. The greatest of the fourth-century Christian scholars, advocate and patron of the monastic vow, left Rome 385 and settled in a monastery at Bethlehem. His very numerous extant works include some directed against the Pelagians; the standard Latin translation of the Bible known as the Vulgate; and a translation and extension, to A.D. 378, of Eusebius' *Chronicle*, which formed the starting point and pattern for almost all later Chronicles, including the Annals of northern Europe and the British Isles. Coelestius, Manchan, Pelagius, Sicilian Breton.

HILARY of Arles 401-449, May 5. Gaul;Gaul. *BHL* 3882. *DCB*. Monk of Lerins, while still in his teens, friend of its founder Honoratus. Accompanied Honoratus when he was elected bishop of Arles, 426, succeeded him in 429. Friend of Faustus, abbot of Lerins and bishop of Riez, and of Germanus of Auxerre; championed the independence of the see of Arles, as metropolitan of the Gauls, against Pope Leo I.

HILARY of Poitiers *c*.320-368, Jan. 13. Gaul;Gaul. *BHL* 3885-3909. *DCB*. Converted to Christianity *c*.350, bishop *c*.353. Champion of the Catholics against the Arians, exiled by Constantius II, returned on Constantius' death (361). Led the Gallic churches in their rejection of the Council of Rimini, and in their opposition to Julian's paganism. Encouraged Martin, later bishop of Tours, to settle as a hermit near Poitiers. Kebi.

HILARY, Pope 461-467, Sept. 10. *DCB*. Successor of Leo. Directed his energy to constraining Leontius of Arles, and the bishops of Spain to acknowledge the supremacy of Rome. v. *Endei* 20,21; v. *Declan* (Irish) p. 17 (pope); v. *Ailbe* 8-13; v. *Declan* (*VSH*) 9 (bishop in Rome); Hilarius *Pictavensis*, v. *Kebi* 3, *cf.* Ibar.

HILDA of Whitby, Yorks. (*NZ 8911*) +680, Nov. 17. E;E. Bede *HE* **3**, 24, 25; **4**, 23, 24; **5**, 24. *NLA* 2, 29. Great-niece of Edwin of Northumbria, baptised with him, 625. Intended to follow her sister Hereswith to Chelles in Gaul, but asked by Aidan to establish a house for women, first on the Wear, then at Hartlepool, Dur. (*NZ 5032*), then at Whitby. Upheld the old Easter at the synod of Whitby, 664; opposed Wilfred. Encouraged Caedmon. John of Beverley; Oftfor; Paulinus of York; Tatfrid.

HILDILID of Barking, Essex (*TQ 4483*) VII L/VIII E. E;E. Bede *HE* 4, 10. *NLA* 2, 34. Succeeded Aedilburga as abbess of Barking, friend of Aldhelm.

HISMAEL, *see* Ismael.

HLOTHERE, *see* Leutherius.

HOAM V M/L. B;I. 'magus, magni in Britannia nominis et honoris', crossed to

Ireland with the parents of **M**octeus, v. *Moct.* 1, whom he educated in Meath. His daughter made clothes for Mocteus' monks for 30 years (8); he was betrothed to Brigit, but died (9). Possibly identical with **L**omman.

HOARNIN, *see* Ernin.

HOERNBIU (Herveus, Huerve) VI M/L, June 17. A;A. *BHL* 3859, 3860, *AG* 313. Son of Harvian (Huvarnion), British musician at the court of Childebert I (511-558), who was sent by Childebert to *Iudwal* of Dumnonie, and of Rivannon, sister of Riovarus (Rigurius) (*cf.* the several Plou or Lan Rivoare of Brittany, *L 1, D 2, E 2, E 3,* etc.), born blind. Educated by Harchian (Hadrian) and Urfoal, his uncle. Tamed a wolf. Ordained by Houardon. **M**aian.

Attended the synod of Menez Bre, *K 2*, perhaps convened it, since a chapel in his name stands on the summit, against **C**onomorus, who had married Trifina, daughter of **W**eroc and killed her child. St. Tremorus (Nov. 8) had killed king **J**onas and exiled **J**udwal; knocked down a critic at the synod. Visited comes Helenus (? Evenus) and St. Maian. Died at Lanhouarneau, *F 2*; abbots Maian, Guenegan (**C**onocan) and Mormed attended his funeral.

HOIERNIN, *see* Ernin.

HONORIUS, archbishop of Canterbury, 627-653, Sept. 30. Italian;E. *BHL* 3986. Bede *HE* **2**, 15-18, 20; **3**, 14, 20, 25; **5**, 19. *NLA* 2, 36. Consecrated by **P**aulinus at Lincoln, received his pallium from Pope Honorius. Disciple of **G**regory the Great, admired **A**idan. **F**elix.

HONORIUS, Pope 625-639. *DCB*. Bede *HE* **2**, 17-20; **3**, 7. Sent pallium to **P**aulinus, and to **H**onorius of Canterbury; wrote to Edwin of Northumbria and to the Irish on the Easter question, *c.*628; sent **B**irinus to Britain. **C**uimine of Durrow; **L**asrian of Leighlin.

HUERVE, *see* Hoernbiu.

HWAETBERT, abbot of Jarrow and Wearmouth, VII L/VIII E. E;E. Bede *HE* **5**, 24; *H. Abb.* 18-20; Anon *H. Abb.* 29-30, 39. Bede's abbot, survived him. Brought up as a monk of Wearmouth, visited Rome under Pope Sergius I (687-700). Correspondent of **B**oniface.

IA, *see* Hia.

IACOBUS, *see* James.

IACUTUS VI M/L, Feb. 8 (June 3). B;A. *BHL* 4113-4. Brother of **W**inwaloe and **W**ethenoc. He names some sites in Brittany, and may be Jacob, James in Cornwall, *LBS* 3, 333.

IAHOEVIUS, *see* Iaoua.

IAOUA VI L/VII E, March 2. I?B?;A. *ASS* March 1, 139. *AG* 44. Son of an Irish prince (?) named *Tinidorus* and of a sister of **P**aul Aurelian. Monk of Iudwal, abbot of *Landevennec*, founded his own monastery of Daoulas. Succeeded Paul Aurelian as bishop of Leon, appointed Kenan as priest of Ploucerneau. Iahoevius, successor of Paul, v. *Paul A.* 11; 20.

IARLAITHE of Armagh, *see* Erlatheus.

IARLAITHE of Tuam, Galway (*M 45*) V L, Dec. 26. I;I. 'Senior' when **B**rendan of Clonfert was 'puer', v. *Bren.* I, 8-9.

IARUMAN, bishop of the Mercians, *c*.662-665. I?;E. Bede *HE* **3**, 24, 30; **4**, 3. Reconverted the East Saxons; one of his companions described the journey to Bede. The name might be Irish.

IBAR of Bergerin, Wexford Harbour (*T 20*) +499, Apr. 23. I;I. vitae *AB* 77, 1959, 439 (1); 442 (= Book of Leinster 371, 4) (2); 168 (= Ussher 515, *cf.* 451) (3); v. *Abban 1*, 2, 3, 8, 9, 11-14, 18, *cf. 2.* (4); v. *Ailbe 1*, 24; (5), 29, 33, 38, 46 = v. *Declan* 34 = v. *Mo-Choemog* 31, 33 (6); v. *Ciaran Saigir* 7 = v. *Declan* 12, 18 (7); v. *Darerca 1*, 3, *cf. 2* (8); v. *Mochta* 12 (9); v. *Brigit*, Ultan 54, *TT* 532 = Laurentius 69, *Sal.* 66 (10).

Son of Lugna of 'terra Crimtani' (1) (Meath, *AB* 78, 1960, 370) of the Ui Echach of Ulster, *M. Oeng.*, of the Artraige of Ulster (*2*) of Leix, his mother of the Dessi of Breg, *M. Don.*, (*2*), probably of Mugdorn, in south-east Monaghan, around Lough Muckno (*H 81*), *cf.* 2, p. 444. A huge man, *18* feet tall (*1*, 3). Studied under Mochteus of Louth (*1*, 5; *2*, 13; *9*). Preached in Meath (*3 cf. 1*, 10). Stayed in the western isles of Ireland, Darerca with eight virgins under his care (*8*), moved to Bergerin (*8* and all sources). Helped Brigit in a famine (*10*). Baptised *Foelan* of Scotland. Brought up his nephew Abban 'non solum in divinis est cererarum artium, sicut nos est iuvenum . . . gustare de dulcedine et astucia disciplinarum auctorum'; innumerable monks and nuns under him. Went to Rome, reluctantly taking Abban with him; on the way, visited and converted a pagan king at Abingdon, Berkshire (*4*). Consecrated at Rome, one of the four southern bishops, with Ciaran of Saigir, Declan and Ailbe, who preached in Ireland before Patrick, with Enda, in the time of Pope Hilary (461-468) (*7*). Strongly resisted Patrick (*7*; *M. Oeng.*), so that 'the roads were full and the storehouses empty in Armagh' *M. Oeng.* Yielded precedence to Ailbe in Munster (*5*); Emly, Tip. (*R 73*), the early see of Munster, Imlech Ailbe (Hogan 454) is usually called Imlech Ibair (*6*; Hogan 455). His pupil Sethna (*1*, 8). Visited by 'germanicus heros Rotlaeb, de Germania' who gave his 'progenies' to Ibar (*1*, 12). Died aged 93 (*2*, 1), aged *404* *M. Don.*, at Bergerin (*8*, etc.) where his relics are preserved (*4*). His name means 'yew-tree', Cormac, *Glossary*, 92. Cadoc, Finnian of Clonard and others studied in Wexford Harbour after his death.

IDUNET of Chateaulin VI, Oct. 19. B;A. *BHL* 2621. *LBS* 2, 466. *Cart. Landevennec* 3 (137). *Brother* of Winwaloe, surrendered Chateaulin to him. Perhaps identical with Ethbin. He has a number of sites in Brittany, *LBS* 3, 291-3.

ILLAND VI M. I;I.B? Abbot, teacher of Aed m. Bricc (+589); perhaps Illan of Welsh dedications, *LBS* 3, 298. *M.*

ILLTUD of Llantwit (Llanilltud Fawr), Glam. (*SS 9668*) V L/VI E, Nov. 6. B;B. *BHL* 4268 = *VSB* 194 (1); *BHL* 4269 = *NLA* 52 (2). vitae *Gildae* (R) (3), *Cadoci* (4), *Leonori* (5), *Pauli Aureliani* (6), *Samson* (7).

The Life is exceptionally devolved. He was an *Armorican* (1), *cousin of king Arthur*, one of his 'curiales milites', thereafter *magister militum* of Poulentus, king of the Morcanenses (Paulinus of Penychen) (2), converted to monasticism by *Cadoc* (3; *cf. 4*, 19). In (*7*), a source of the early seventh century, just within living memory, he was 'egregius magister Britannorum . . . de disciplinis . . . Sancti Germani, et ipse Germanus ordinaverat eum in sua iuventute presbyterum' (*7* [1] 7). The last words, personal ordination by Germanus, sound like a gloss on the statement that he followed the tradition of Germanus; but it is just possible that he was baptised *c*.445 by Germanus. Established himself 'in valle Hodnant' (? Ogney Brook or Colhugh River, Llanilltud Fawr?) (6), ordained by Dubricius *bishop of Llandaff* (7) in the time of king Merchiaun Vesanus (the Wild) (8-9), king of

Glamorgan (17, *cf.* 20-21), who had given him the valley (10), his church being near 'castellum regis Merchiauni' (26). He established agriculture (11) (*cf.* 14; *7*, 12; *6*, 4), built a sea wall (13), exported corn to Armorica (24); and died *at Dol* (24). He maintained 100 familiares, 100 each of 'operatores, clericos, pauperes' (11). *Fellow pupil of **B**rioc* (born *c.*468) under ***G**ermanus of Paris*, v. *Brioc 8-9*; it is possible that he taught Brioc, or was his fellow pupil. 'de totis Scripturis . . . et omnis philosophiae generis, (geo)metricae scilicet ac rhetoricae grammatic-aeque et arithmeticae . . . omnium Britannorum compertissimus . . . genereque mag(nif)icus sagacissimus et futurorum praescius' (*7*, 7). His pupils included **S**amson (7) (*cf. 1*, 11, 14-15; *3*, 3; *6*, 3), **G**ildas (*1*, 11; *3*, 3-6; *6*, 3), **P**aul Aurelian (*1*, 11; *3*, 3; *6*, 3), ***D**avid* (*1*, 11; *6*, 3), **L**eonorus (*5*). He was also perhaps the 'praeceptor paene totius Britanniae magister elegans' who taught Maelgwn (Gildas *3*). The school was for 'plurimi nobilium filii' (*3*, 3) not primarily for monks. Education began at the age of five (*7*, 8, *5*) with the alphabet and proceeded to 'litterarum distinctiones per conjunctiones verborum' (*7*, 10); the fees were custom-ary 'donaria' (*7*, 9), a cow (*5*). His monastery was his own property, seen as 'hereditarium mundanum' by his nephews (*7*, 14). The early Lives stress his gentle understanding of his pupils, in, for example, his ban on excessive fasting for growing boys (*7*, 11), and his effort to make the 15-year-old Paul Aurelian examine deeply his motives for seeking a desert hermitage, while leaving the decision to him (*6*, 6). He was visited on his deathbed by abbots Isanus and Athoclius (*7*, 8); his death is placed before Samson left Britain (*c.*547?) (*7* [2] i, 18), perhaps 20 or more years earlier. He was still alive about 525, when Leonorus, born *c.*510, was 15 (*5*).

His principal monastery in later years, Llanilltud Fawr, confused with Caldey (*6*, 2), but confirmed by *ECMW* 222, was almost certainly the site of his school. The Roman villa, the great house of the estate was largely ruined in the third century: one wing, which remained in use at least as late as the end of the Roman period, may have been used by Illtud; or he may have lived near the present church. Post-Roman burials above the ruins of the house may be those of his pupils and monks. He names a dozen places and churches in south-east Wales, one in Merioneth, and seven or eight in Brittany, the foundations of his pupils, *LBS* 3, 315; Bowen *SCSW* 42, Fig. 9b.

ILUD of Llanilid, Brecon (*SN 8924*) and Glam. (*SS 9781*) VI E/M. I;B. *Daugh-ter* of **B**rychan, *cf.* **J**ulitta.

INDRACT of Shapwick, So. (*ST 4138*) +708(?), May 8 (Feb. 5). I;E. *BHL* 4271-2. *ASH* 253. *NLA* 2, 56. Irish monk, went to Rome, with his sister Dominica and others, visited Glastonbury on his return, murdered by a thief, Hona, at Shapwick as he left Glastonbury, buried at Shepton Mallet (*ST 6143*), by king Ine of Wessex, then lodging at Villa Pedret. May 8, Wm. Worcester *Itin.* 150, *M. Tal.* Feb. 5, Cornish Calendar and others, *cf.* Gougaud *Saints Irlandais*, O'Hanlon 2, 353. Landed in Britain at 'portus nomine Tamerunta'; honoured at St. Dominick on the Tamar (*SX 3967*), which bears his sister's name, and at Landrake (*SX 3760*), St. German's, near Plymouth, five miles to the south, *LBS* 3, 320. But the story may derive from Indrechtach, abbot of Iona, 'martyred by the Saxons while on his way to Rome' in 854 *AI*, *cf.* Reeves, *Adamnan* 390.

INDRECHTACH, *see* Indract.

IOHANNES, *see* John.

ISERNINUS, *see* Ernin.

(H)ISMAEL VI L. B;B. *Son of Budic*, king of Cornouailles, brother of Tyfei of Pen Alun (Tenby), v. *Oudocei, LL* 130. Consecrated bishop at a synod convened by Teilo after the death of David (+589), and sent 'ad consulendam ecclesiam Minuensium (St. David's, Menevia) etiam viduatam pastore' v. *Teilo, LL* 115. David is said to have bequeathed his monastery not to one of his own monks, but to Maedoc of Ferns, in Ireland. But Maedoc could not perform episcopal functions in Britain. Named St. Ismael's, Pembrokeshire.

ISSEY, *see* Ita.

ITA of Killeedy, Limerick (*R 22*) +570, Jan. 15. I;I. *BHL* 4497-8. *VSH* 2, 116 (1); v. I *Brendan* 3-4, 8, 71, 92 (2); v. *Carthaci* 30 (3); v. *Maedoc* 49 (4); v. *Mo-Choemog* 1-8, *cf.* 14, 15, 20 (5). Also called Mide (Mo-Ita) *FM* 569, etc.

Of the Deisi of Munster (1). 'Matrona gentis Hua Connaill', whom God gave to her and Senan (8). Taught Brendan (22, 2) of Clonfert. She so hated 'gold and silver and all the wealth of the world' that when her hand accidentally touched silver offered in alms by a rich man, she washed her hand clean (21). Richena of Mag Liffe (Kildare) sent her pupil, Columban, who Columba had consecrated bishop in Iona, and returned to Leinster (*cf.* Ad. v. *Col.* 3, 12, Columban [Colman] mocu-Loigse), to conduct a sick nun to her (24). Visited frequently by Luchtigern, who on one occasion brought Lasrian with him (31). Her prayers gained a victory for the Ui Conaill against West Munster (*Annals* 553), and she cured the wounded (33). At her request, Brendan of Clonfert secured the freedom and return of a nun who had fled from Killeedy when she found herself pregnant, and had become enslaved to a magus in Connacht (34, *cf.* 17). Maedoc of Ferns revived one of her nuns (*4*). Carthacus admired her (*3*). Mo-Choemog (+654), was her pupil *for 20 years* (perhaps a pupil at Killeedy) (*5*). Rebuked Brendan of Clonfert for seeking the Land of Promise in boats made of the skins of dead animals 'for that is a holy land, where human blood is not shed', and told him to build a boat of timber (*2*, 71). 'A second Brigit' (36). Suffered from an internal disease, *M*; her hymn to Jesus, *M. Oeng.* Shriven by Brendan of Clonfert (*2*, 92), her tomb at Killeedy (36). Sent holy water to the dying abbot Angus (*cf.* 20) of Clonmacnoise (+570), died herself before the messengers returned (35). Her miracles mainly concern healing, rather than agriculture. Mo-Choemog's father, Beoanus, was her artifex, who built a mill for her (*5*) *cf.* 18. She commonly gave her guests a bath (e.g. 24, 27).

Her sites are extremely numerous in Cornwall, with the name Ithney or Issey, perhaps also Sithey and Teath, *LBS* 3, 325; 331. They are presumably due to Munster immigrants, and suggest that these immigrants retained Irish loyalties until the late sixth century.

ITHAMAR, bishop of Rochester, 644-*c*.655, June 10. E;E. Bede *HE* 3, 14, 20. *BHL* 4501-2. Kentishman, first native English bishop.

ITHEY, *see* Ita.

IUDHUBR, abbot of Llandough, VII E. B;B. *LL* index.

IUDICAEL +*c*.650, Dec. 16. *BHL* 4503. *AG* 819 (1); *AB* 3, 1884, 157 (2); Fredegarius, *Chron.* 4, 78 and derivative sources. King of Dumnonie, made a permanent treaty with Dagobert I, resigned his crown and entered a monastery *c*.640; (1); monk of Mevennus (2), *cf.* v. *S. Eligii.* Father of Winnoc, brother of Iudoc.

IUDOC (Josse) +*c*.668, Dec. 13. A;A.Gaul. *BHL* 4504-4515. *AG* 806. Brother of Iudicael. Founded numerous monasteries in eastern Brittany, Picardy and Flanders.

IULITTA, *see* Julitta.

IUNIAVUS VI E. B;B. Abbot of Docheu (St. Kew, Co., *SX 07*), declined to receive Samson. **D**occo.

IVE, *see* Hia.

IWI VII L, Oct. 6. B;E.A. *BHL* 4638. *ASS* Oct. 3, 400. *NLA* 2, 91. A Briton, son of *Brano* and *Aegidia*, educated by Cuthbert of Lindisfarne, sailed to Brittany, his body a relic at Wilton. Named Loguivy, three sites in Tréguier, *J2, J1, LO* (Paimpol), perhaps also Iveston, Leadgate, Durham, *NZ 1352*; and St. Ives, Hunts., *TL 37*, for whose traditions see Arnold-Forster 1, 501.

JACOB, abbot of Llancarfan, VII E. B;B. *LL* index.

JACUTUS (James), *see* Wethenoc.

JAMES the deacon VII E/M. Italian;E. Bede *HE* **2**, 16, 20; **3**, 25; **4**, 2. Accompanied **P**aulinus to Northumbria in 625. Stayed behind in York after the British conquest of Northumbria, taught church singing to the Northumbrians, attended the Synod of Whitby (664), lived to a great age, into Bede's time. A village near Catterick preserved his name in the eighth century.

JEROME, *see* Hieronymus.

JOHN the archcantor VII M/L. Italian;E. Bede *HE* **4**, 18; **5**, 24. *H. Abb.* 6. Anon. *H. Abb.* 10. Abbot of St. Martin's, Rome, archcantor of St. Peter's, Rome. Came to Britain with **B**enedict Biscop, taught Roman singing at Wearmouth and Jarrow; died at Tours on his way back to Rome, soon after 680.

JOHN of Beverley +721, May 7. E?;E. *BHL* 4338-4351? *NLA* 2, 59. Bede *HE* **4**, 23; **5**, 2-6, 24. Bishop of Hexham, 687-705, archbishop of York, 705-721, founded Beverley 721. Ordained Bede. Educated by **H**ilda at Whitby.

JOHN of Chinon VI M, May 5. B;Gaul. *Presbiter, natione Britto*, hermit at Chinon, Greg. Tur. *de Gloria Conf.* 23. When **R**adegund left her husband, Clothair I, to found her monastery at Poitiers, she deposited her royal raiment with John of Chinon, that he might pray that she would never return to the world, v. *Radegundis* (Baldwin) 4. The story suggests that John was instrumental in aiding and encouraging her in her foundation.

JOHN Cassian, *see* Cassianus.

JULIANA, *see* Julitta.

JULIOT, *see* Julitta.

JULITTA VI E, (June 16). A;B. Mother of **P**aternus, *AG* 244. Ulitte or Uliane, patron of Tintagel, Leland (*SX 0588*), cited *LBS* 3, 336. Juliana, daughter of **B**rychan, Cornish lists. St. Juliot, the parish of Tintagel. Luid is perhaps a Welsh form of the name. Latinised and associated with **C**urig by confusion with the Diocletianic martyrs Cirycus and Julitta of Tarsus, *BHL* 1801, June 16.

JUSTINIAN VI E/M, Dec. 5 (Aug. 23). A;B. *BHL* 4576. *NLA* 2, 93. Armorican, sailed in a coracle to 'terra nomine Chormei' (variant Cormer . . .? Cornwall), thence overseas to 'insula Limeneia' (perhaps Ramsey Island, Pembroke [*SM 7023*] opposite St. David's, but hardly the 'Limnou deserta' of Ptolemy 2, 2, placed by Ptolemy off the east coast of Ireland). Found a hermit there, 'Honorius, regis

Thefriauci filius', in residence, agreed to stay with him if he sent away his sister and her servant; which he did. Killed by three of his *servi*. When his fame grew, David took him as his confessor. Named Capel Stinan on Ramsey Island, Llanstinan (*SM 9532*), near Fishguard.

JUSTUS V L? May 5. Gaul;I.B? Place-names in Cornwall, *LBS* 3, 338; *CIIC* 484, St. Kew, 'Iusti', Ogam and Latin; *M. Oeng.*; perhaps a follower of Docco. Perhaps identical with Iust(in)us, who baptised and taught Ciaran of Clonmacnoise, v, *Ciaran C.* 1; *M. Oeng.*; 'Iustus qui scottice Diarmaid', v. *Ciaran C.* 1; 'Dermicius qui et Iustus', pupil of Senan; 'of France'; equated with Eustinus of Alexandria, *M. Oeng.*; of Fidarta in Mag Ai in Connacht (Fuerty, Roscommon, *H 86*) *M. Oeng.*

KE, *see* Cynan Colledauc.

KEBI (Cybi) V L, Nov. 8. B;I.B. *BHL* 4639-4641. *VSB* 234. Son of Salomon, of the Cornovian dynasty, born between Tamar and Limar (Lynher) (Calliland, between Callington [*SX 3669*] and Saltash [*SX 4358*], south-east Cornwall). Went to school at the age of seven, on pilgrimage to Jerusalem at the age of 27. On his return stayed with Hilary *bishop of Poitiers (+368)*. Came back to Cornwall, joined by disciples Meliauc, Libiau, Paulinus, Kengar (Docco). Crossed to Etheliciaun (south-east Wales) in the time of Ethelic (son of Glivis, V L), who tried in vain to eject him, but granted Lankebi (Llangybi [Fawr], Mon., *ST 3796*) and Landeverguir (perhaps Tredunnoc, Mon., *ST 3794, LBS* 2, 205). Went to *Menevia, civitas sancti David* (to Porth Mawr, by St. David's, Whitesand Bay, *SM 7227*), whence he sailed to Ireland. Went to Aran with Melauc and his 'consobrinus senex' Kengar. Quarrelled with Crubthir Fintan (disciple of Mocteus); reconciled by Enda, but Fintan deprived Kengar of his food supplies, evicted him from Aran. An angel sent him 'ad orientalem plagam' (? Cell Airthir, West Meath or Louth, *cf.* Fintan) where he built Macop or Mo-Chop (the church of Mo-Kebi), which was taken over by Fintan, who evicted him again from Bregh, and then from 'Vobyun'. Kilmore of Mochap is distinguished from Kilmore Aedan (Monaghan, *H 63*) (Hogan 203), placed at Artane, Dublin (*O 13*), *LBS* 2, 207, perhaps related to Mochoba, Macabaeus, Oct. 11. *M. Don., M. Gor.* (Aug. 1 *M. Oeng., M. Gor.* = *BHL* 5106 ff., Macabaei of Syrian Antioch). Crossed to Anglesey (Monia), thence went to Candab (Llangybi, Lleyn, *SH 4241, LBS* 2, 208), where his disciple Caffo carried coals from the smith Magurnus in his lap, in his 'coccula, quo quippe genere vestimenti in Hibernia potitur'. Kebi quarrelled with Maelgwn; Caffo left him to found Merthyr Caffo, and be killed by the herdsmen of Rosuir (Newborough, Anglesey, *SH 4265, LBS* 2, 208). Maelgwn submitted and conveyed to Kebi his 'castellum' (Caer Gybi, Holyhead, Anglesey, *SH 2482*, a Roman fortlet) where Kebi died.

In the Irish tradition (v. *Endei* 20-23), Enda was at Rome with Pubeus and Ailbe; the Romans elected Pubeus pope, but he resigned the honour to Hilary. The three returned to Ireland, Pubeus accompanying Enda to Aran, where they disputed the supremacy, each politely deferring to the other. The dispute was settled by reference, through a delegation of a Finnian, Mac Criche, and Erlatheus (evidently of Armagh, +481), to the pope, who decided in favour of Enda. Connacht tradition also made Pubeus a major saint of Aran; when Brendan of Clonfert (v. *I. Br. C.* 71) visited Aran, he met, out of due time, Endeum et Pepeum et Rochatum (Nochatum). In the Welsh tradition, Kebius (Kepius) is evicted with Kengar from Aran and Ireland; in the Irish tradition Aran rejects the supremacy of Pupeus. For late Irish guesses on the name, *see VSH*, lxiii, note 3. Pupeus is a transliteration of Kepius from Irish into British; Kepius is itself a Welsh name, properly not in need of transliteration.

But the Irish hagiographer had no conception that the name was British; and it is probable that the form Pubeus is an attempt to render an unfamiliar name, Kebius, from a form supposed to be Irish into what seemed an appropriate British and Latin spelling. Angus the Culdee, *Mothers of the Saints of Ireland* 72, cited *ASH* 712, also knew a Libeus de Arania (*cf.* Libiau above) *brother* of Enda. Kebi's sites, *cf. LBS* 2, 211; Arnold-Forster, 2, 209.

KENGAR, *see* Cyngar, Docco.

KENNETH, *see* Cainnech.

KENTIGERNA +734, Jan. 7. I;P. Daughter of Cellach Cualan, king of Leinster (+715), sister of Muiren (+748) *Annals*. *Mother* of Foelan of Scotland, patron of a church in Loch Lomond, Forbes 373, Reeves, *Adamnan* 384. The name is British, but was brought into Ireland through Cantigerna, queen of Fiachra, king of Dal Araide, patroness of Comgall.

KENTIGERNUS of Glasgow 603? Jan. 13. B;Gaul.B. *BHL* 4645-4649. vitae, Jocelyn of Furness (1), anonymous (2), in Forbes, *Historians of Scotland*, 5, 159; Pinkerton, ed. Metcalfe, *Lives of the Scottish Saints*, 2, 1, ff., *cf.* K. H. Jackson, *SEBC* 273; *NLA* 2, 114 (3) (an abridgement of 1).
  Son of Ewen 'filius Erwegende . . . vocatur Ewen filius regis Urien' (= Owain, son of Urien of Reged) and of *Thaney (Thynoy) daughter of Leudonus 'vir semipaganus'* (*2*, 1), 'cuiusdam regis secta paganissimi' (*1*, 1), who was thrown off the top of Kepduf (in Irish) (*2*, 4), Dumpelder (in British) (*1*, 3) (Traprain Law, East Lothian, *NT 5874* [*CPNS 345*]), and cast off in a boat at Aberlessic (*2*, 6) (perhaps Tyninghame, *NT 6279*, Jackson 292-3) and was carried to Culross, Fife (*NS 9885*), where Kentigern was born, and brought by *St. Servan*, (*1*, 4; *2*, 7-8). Called Munghu (Mu Cu[ntigennus] with mutation, in British, Jackson, 300-1) and still so called in Jocelyn's day *1*, 4, also Mo Chohe (in Irish). Left Servanus, came to 'Frisicum litus', where the *river* Mallena (= high tide, Jackson 308) was flowing (8). Visited the dying Fregus (Fergus) 'in villa . . . Kernach' (Carnock, St. Ninian's, *NS 7991*), conveyed his body on an ox-cart to Cathures (Cathir Es?), now called Glasgow, and buried it 'iuxta cemiterium . . . a sancto Niniano consecratum' (9). The king and clergy chose him bishop of regio Cambria, that extended from sea to sea, like the vallum of Severus, which was later replaced by a wall 8ft. wide and 12ft. high, that reached to the Forth, and he was consecrated by a single Irish bishop 'as was then the custom of the Irish and the British' (11). His monks lived by agricultural labour, and lived in separate huts (singulis casis) (20).
  After some time, Morken acquired the country 'Cambrensis regni solium ascend-erat'; his 'a secretis', Cathen knocked Kentigern down. Morken died, at 'Thorp Morken' (21-22). 'Filii Belial . . . de cognatione regis Morken' plotted his death, so he went into exile, passing by Karleolum (Carlisle) on his way to Dewi (David) at Menevia; king *Cathwallain* gave him *Nantcharvan* (23); he founded (Llanelwy, St. Asaph's) on the river Elgu, and was attacked by 'gentilis regulus Melconde (de) Galganu' (Maelgwn of Deganwy), who was blinded, cured, and granted the site (*cf.* a fabricated thirteenth-century 'charter' [*Red Book of St. Asaph* 117, *LBS* 4, 384]) (24), where he had 965 monks (25) and appointed Asaph his successor (31, *cf.* 25). He went to Europe, visited Rome seven times, on one occasion meeting Gregory the Great, bringing back books (27). Conotigernus (Gonotigernus, Cunautigernus) attended the Councils of Orleans, 549, and Paris, *c.*557, as bishop of Senlis (Mansi 9, 127; 9, 743); during his episcopate, Saffaracus of Paris was deposed, 555, for a grave capital crime, confessed to a commission of six ecclesiastics and again to the

council, and was relegated to a monastery. The lengthy text discreetly omits precise definition of the crime; since council reports commonly state sharply the nature of serious crimes, including sexual offences, the unparallelled reticence of this text is normally interpreted as alluding to homosexuality (Mansi, 9, 739). Kentigern, while abroad, was called upon to consecrate as bishop a cleric 'natione Britannus, sed in Galliis educatus' (the plural Galliis points to a date hardly later than the ninth century, whereas the whole of the place and personal names in the story of the Welsh journey, ch. 23-26, are of eleventh or twelfth century), but his gifted vision perceived flames of sulphur and an intolerable stench that revealed the man as 'vir sui sexus perversor' (28). The coincidence of the name, otherwise unrecorded for men in either Britain or Europe (despite the frequence of the linguistic elements), of the date and place, and of the offence of homosexuality, equally unparallelled, make it difficult to suppose that two separate persons called Kentigern had the same experience in the same generation, of a homosexual bishop in Gaul. It is therefore extremely probable that Kentigern was bishop of Senlis, near Paris, from c.549 to c.560/570 (cf. Duchesne, Fastes episcopaux 3, 117. Conotigernus is the twelfth bishop; the ninth was in office in 511, the fourteenth in 584).

Kentigern's sojourn abroad (quid commoratus in terra aliena egerit) by the accession 'super regnum Cambrinum' of king Rederech (Riderch), who had been baptised in Ireland (29), probably as a consequence of the battle of Arfderydd (573). Kentigern returned to Glasgow (30-32), and founded Holdelm (Hoddam, Ecclefechan, Dumfries, NY 1573), whose adjacent parish church is dedicated to him. He taught that Woden was a mortal man, a Saxon king, not a god, and was therefore held to have attempted to convert the pagan English (32). It is possible that this tradition derives from the later Northumbrian supremacy; or that descendants of the original Frisian settlers in Dumfries remained pagan; or that he attempted to convert Bernicians. He preached in 'Pictorum patriam, quae modo Galwiethia dicitur' (cf. Wainwright, PP 40; either among the Picts, or in Galloway, is possible, the conjunction a twelfth-century gloss) and sent missions to Ibania, the Orkneys, *Norway* and Iceland (34) and was visited by Columba of Iona (39-40), who gave him a staff, still preserved at Ripon. Riderch was a friend of Columba, and on one occasion sent him a message, desiring assurance and peace (Ad. v. Col. 1, 16); Columba, in contact with Riderch, must also have been in contact with Kentigern and the two may well have met. Kentigern rescued the ring that queen Languoreth improperly gave her lover, by the miracle of the fish's belly (35-36). Riderch's fame spread to Ireland; he was visited by an 'ioculator' or 'histrio', who asked a reward of strawberries in winter, which Kentigern provided (37). Foreseeing the physical ruin of his earthly churches, he prepared to die (42). Died (43) A.D. 503, Brev. Ab. PH 64, succeeded by Baldred, perhaps intending 603 (DIII for DCIII); in ACm 612 'Conthigirni obitus et Dibric episcopi', the last three words are certainly a mistaken addendum, and the substantive entry is probably misplaced. Riderch and a notable named Morthec died late in the same year (45), as foretold by the 'homo fatuus' Laloecen, at the royal vill of Pertnech (Patrick, NS 5566). His numerous sites in Scotland and the Lake District, Forbes 372, Arnold-Forster 2, 225, mapped Bowen, SCSW 77, fig. 20.

Columba of Iona, Constantinus rex Cornubiensis, Daniel, Ethbin, Mansuetus, Paternus, Samson.

KENZIE, see Cainnech.

KEVIN, see Coemgen.

KILLIAN of Aubigny, near Arras VII M, Nov. 13. I;Gaul. Kenney 492 (no. 282). Irishman, encouraged by (Burgundo) Faro, bishop of Meaux (*c*.637-*c*.670) to settle at Aubigny. Visited Fiachra.

KILLIAN of Wurzburg +689, July 8. I;Germany. *BHL* 4660-3. Kenney 512 (no. 317). Irish bishop, evangelised Thuringia and Ostfranken, martyred, with Colman and Totnan. He has an extensive cult in southern and central German lands, Gougaud, *Saints Irlandais* 125.

KYERANUS, *see* Ciaran.

LAISRAN, abbot of Iona, 601-608, Sept. 16. I;S. Ad. v. *Col.* 1, 12; 1, 29. *M.*

LAISREN, *see* Lasrian.

LAISTRAN, *see* Lasrian.

LASRIAN of Ard mic Nasca (Holywood, Belfast Lough, Down, *J 47*) VII M? Oct. 25. I;I. *M.* Perhaps identical with Laistranus, addressed by Pope John IV *c*.640, Bede *HE* **2**, 19, *cf.* Plummer 2, 113.

LASRIAN (Mo-Laisse) of Devenish, Ferm. (*H 24*) 563, Sept. 12. I;I. *BHL* 4725. Born 60 years after Patrick (? 432 + 60 = 492?) (2). *VSH* 2, 131. Baptised and later ordained by bishop Eochaid (5), studied under Finnian of Clonard (+551) (6; *Cat.* 5; v. *Fin C.* 19), founded Devenish, on an island in Lough Erne (6), which Finnian consecrated (25), performed numerous miracles (7-13), was attacked by Conall Derg (son of Daimen, king of Airgialla, +564) with an army (14-17). Accompanied on journeys by a boy who carried his books (19); visited Tours and Rome, returning with a gospel and a bell, and relics of SS. Peter and Paul, Laurence and Clement, *which he shared with Aedan of Ferns (Maedoc +627)* (20-22), who was *his fellow pupil* (Sodalis) and *whom he helped to resuscitate (Caipre) Domangart, king of Airgialla (+511)*. Visited Aed Bricc (v. *Maedoc* 8 and 10), whom he helped in clearing timber for agriculture (v. *Aed* 33), Bangor (founded 558) (26), Tara, in the time of Diarmait (549-564) (27), disputed with Bec mac De (+554) 'profeta regis, magus mendax' (28), survived the plague (551) (29). Visited by Columba of Iona after the battle of Cuildremne (561), who sought how he might expiate the deaths of the many there killed; Lasrian 'ordered him to free as many souls from hell, as he had destroyed lives' (imperavit illi ut tot aminas a p[o]enis liberaret, quot animarum causa perdicionis extiterat) and bade him live outside Ireland in perpetual exile (ut perpetuo moraretur extra Hiberniam exilio; the words do not bear the meaning imposed upon them by some later writers, that he forbade him ever to set foot in Ireland again) (31). Columba later interpreted a dream of Baitan's of three thrones, as signifying the golden throne of Ciaran of Clonmacnoise 'qui . . . omnes precellit suos coet a neos', the silver throne of Lasrian 'qui eloquentie et sapientie nitore micat pre ceteris', and the glass throne of Columba, given him by the Lord 'quia natura sum fragilis, et carnalium amicorum et propinquorum amore frequenter occupatus' (32). Visited Brendan (of Clonfert?) (33) and died (34). Succeeded by Naille.

'Gentle, sinless Lasrian' *M. Gor.*; Devenish a house of open hospitality, common to all Ireland, *M. Don.*, *cf. M. Oeng.* One of the 12 bishops of Ireland, *M. Oeng.*; his order one of the eight orders of Ireland, 'unless it be another of the same name', *M. Don.*, citing vita Ciaran Clonmacnoise (Irish).

LASRIAN (Mo-Laisse) of Leighlin, Carlow (*S 66*) (553?)-641, Apr. 18. I;I. *BHL* 4726-7; *Sal.* 779; m. Cunnechti, *AI*; moccu Imde, *AU*; macu Dima, *AT*, *cf. CS. FM.*

mac Ua imda; m. Winge *AC*. m. Cairell (1), m. Cairell m. Ardgal m. Muiredach
Muinderg (k. Ulaid +492; descendant of Imchad of Dal Fiatach *M. Oeng.*; of the
house (shliocht) of Fiatach Finn, *M. Don.*; son of Gemma, daughter of (A)Edan,
rex Scotie (Dal Riada) (*c*.534-609) regisque Britannie neptis (1). Born *50* years
after Patrick (9) (? 1x for 1 = intended date of 493 + 60 = 553?). Nephew of Blaan
of Bute (3); studied under (Fintan) Munnu (+637; scarcely before *c*.600), and
cleared the course of his mill stream (4). His prayer put pirates to flight (5) and
also bandits (6; *cf.* 8). Moved to an island between Britain and Scotia (?Bute or
?Man). Went to Rome (8) at the request of the abbot of Clonmacnoise ('rogatu
sancti Kerani abbatis' presumably Cronan m. Ui Logde +640) and 50 bishops 'pro
institutis ecclesiasticis habendis' (13), evidently after the synod of Maglene (*cf.*
Cuimine of Durrow), *c*.630, heading the delegation thereafter sent to Rome, *c*.630-
632. Received by the pope, *Gregory the Great* (Honorius I), who gave him a
gospel and 'appointed him to preach Christ in Ireland' (8). *Visited by* Barrus
(Findbar of Cork VI E/M) (? visited Findbar's tomb at Cork) (10). Returned to
Ireland and settled at Leighlin, which abbot Gobban (perhaps Aed Gobban, *cf.*
Fintan Munnu) surrendered to him (8) where he had 1,500 monks (v. *Fintan M.*
26). In opposition to Fintan, championed the new Easter (v. *Fintan M.* 26-27), 'the
order which Mo-Laisse brought from Rome' (Irish Life of Colman m. Luachain,
cited *VSH* xlvi) at the synod of Mag Ailbe (southern Co. Carlow, Hogan 511),
about 635, evidently after the letter of Cuimine, *c*.633, before the death of Fintan
(637); 'king of the synod' *M. Oeng*. The synod was decisive; Bede (*HE* **3**, 3) asserts
that the southern Irish had accepted the Roman Easter before the appointment of
Aedan of Lindisfarne, *c*.637. Though individual objectors remained, Bede, writing
within living memory, means that the new Easter had become the normal observ-
ance of the majority.

He was visited by king Aedan *a regno suo expulsus* (12), who was said to be
half-brother of king Brandub of Leinster. Cainnech (+603) placed virgins under
him (9). His internal chest disease cured by Lugid (v. *Lugid* 31); he cured a foot
affliction of king Faelan of Leinster (629-667, text cited O'Hanlon 4, 217). His
'Vision' became a popular mediaeval text, *AB* 81, 1963, 251. It is possible that he
made two visits to Rome, one *c*.600, followed by the foundation of Leighlin, the
other 30 years later.

LAURENTIUS of Canterbury +*c*.619, Feb. 2. Italian;E. *BHL* 4741-2. *NLA* 2,
143. Bede *HE* **1**, 27, 33; **2**, 4-7. Sent by Gregory with Augustine, returned to Rome
and brought back Gregory's responses, succeeded Augustine as archbishop 604,
converted king Eadbald of Kent, visited by Dagan, who refused to eat with him.
Wrote to the British and Irish churches, his letter to Irish reproduced, buried in
Canterbury. Succeeded by Mellitus.

LEO I, Pope 440-461, Apr. 11. *BHL* 4817. *DCB*. Deacon of Pope Celestine,
+432, probably in succession to Palladius, strong opponent of the Pelagians. Pope,
Sept. 29, 440. Assumed the leadership of Rome and Italy in negotiation with Attila,
and with Gerseric, vigorously asserted the ecclesiastical primacy of Rome, in conflict
with Hilary of Arles, and bishops of Spain and Africa. Enlisted the support of
Faustus of Riez against the eastern heresy of Eutyches. Approved Patrick.

LEONORUS (Lunaire) *c*.510-*c*.561, July 1. B;A. *BHL* 4880-1. *ASS* July 1, 121
(107). Pupil of Illtud whose school he entered at the age of five; *consecrated*
(confirmed?) by Dubricius at the age of fifteen. Emigrated to Brittany with 72
disciples and many servants, landing near Dinard in the time of Rigaldus and

Childebert (+558). Cleared land by felling trees, whose trunks were carried away by a flooded river, and whose stumps his monks burnt; lost on the voyage the seed corn he had brought from Britain, and was miraculously helped by a robin, checking an attempt by his followers to abandon the site because of the initial difficulties. Excavated a golden ram. Rigaldus died and Conomorus annexed the territory; Leonorus helped Judwal to escape by sea, and was struck by Conomorus, who arrived just too late to catch him. Leonorus followed Judwal to Paris, gave Childebert the golden ram, in exchange for confirmation of his land, and died, soon after the defeat of Conomorus (Dec. 560) and restoration of Judwal, at the age of fifty-one.

LEUTHERIUS (Hlothaire), bishop of the West Saxons, 670-676 (*ASC*). Gaul;E. Bede *HE* **3**, 7; **4**, 5, 12. Nephew of Agilbert; consecrated by Theodore at Winchester, present at the Council of Hatfield 673, appointed Aldhelm abbot of Malmesbury, *c.*675. **H**aedde.

LODAN, *see* Luan.

LOMMAN of Trim, Meath (*N 85*) V M, Oct. 11. B;I. Tírechán *Add*. 1 = *Bethu Phátraic* 43 = Stokes *VT* 334-336, *cf.* 66, *cf.* Foirtchern; *M.; ASH* 362. *Nephew of Patrick*, *brother* of bishop Munis of Forgney, Longford (*N 15*), of Broccaidh, Broccan and Mughenoc (*cf.* **G**enocus). Landed in the Boyne, given Trim by Feidelmid, son of king Loegaire (+463), taught Feidelmid's son Foirtchern. Succeeded by Cathlaidus, a Briton. His other sites in Ireland, O'Hanlon 10, 171. He is perhaps identical with the 'magus Hoam', with whom the parents of **M**octeus reached Ireland, whose name is plainly a scribal corruption, possibly of (L)o(m)man.

LOUTHIERN, *see* Luchtigern.

LOVOCATUS and Catihernus 509/521. B;A. British priests who celebrated mass in Armorica, with a travelling altar, and with the ministration of women (conhospitae), to the horror of the Gallic clergy, Jackson, *LHEB* 14, Gougaud *Chrétientés Celtiques* 96 n.

LUACHAN, *see* Mac Cuilin.

LUAN, *see* Molocus.

LUGAID, *see* Lugid, Molocus.

LUGHTIERN of Ennistimon, Clare (*R 18*) VI M/L, April 28. I;I.A? Pupil of **R**uadan (+587) *ASH* 597, 14 and of **C**olumba of Terryglass (+551) v. *Col. T.* 22; visited Ita (+570) v. *Ita* 31; one of Comgall's missionaries (v. *Mo-Choemog* 10). Ciaran of Saigir (+*c.*530) rescued his swineherds (v. *Ci. S.*) (*5*) (11). Assisted **M**ac Creiche in securing a relaxation of cattle tribute, v. *MacC.* 35-37. Probably the Loutiern venerated in Brittany, *LBS* 3, 348, since the name is otherwise unknown to hagiology.

LUGID (Mo-Lua) of Clonfert Mulloe, Leix (*S 29*) 554-612, Aug. 4. I;I. *BHL* 5058-5060. *VSH* 2, 206 (1); *Sal.* 261 (2), 879 (3).
Son of Carthacus, called Coche of the Corcu Iche of the Ui Fidgenti of Munster, and of Sochla of Ossory (1), whose villa contained a mill (11); very numerous childhood miracles, mainly curative or concerned with herding cattle (2-14). Recruited by Comgall on a visit to Munster and taken to Bangor, there educated (14-17); one of the many missionaries whom Comgall sent out (18; v. *Mo-Choemog* 10) to Britain as well as to Ireland (*2*, 19). Miracles involving churns and a mill at

Bangor (20-21); ordained (23) and sent out by Comgall to Drumsnat, Monaghan (*H 64*), where he rescued swimming children from a lake beast they had not observed, without alarming them (25). Attended the school of Finnian at Clonard (25), where he produced a crop of wheat from a seed that was not wheat (26). Returned to Ui Fidgenti territory, founded monasteries (27, 29) and went to Ossory to found Clonfert Mulloe by Mount Bladma in the territory of king Berachus (*CGH* 91, R 127a34) of Leix (28), *cf.* 42. He always taught gently, leading his pupils on from one step to another, each within their own experience (*2*, 36-38); trained the 'poeta' Cronan, who was unused to manual work, to uproot (patches of) thistles with fork and knife, one on the first day, two on the second, and so on, until 'paulatim in maius crescebat opus' and a broad way was cut through the woodland (38). Visited by bishop **S**etna of Saigir (35), by **C**olman Elo (+613), and Carthacus (+639) who carried out two boxes of books to read in solitude (v. *Col. Elo* 27, *cf.* v. *Carthaci* 18). With **C**ainnech (+603) and Mo-Fechta (? **F**echin of Fore +666) accompanied **M**o-Choemog (+654) to visit his pupil, who had just begun to construct his monastery, and had built only the church (v. *Mo-Choemog* 29); cured a chest illness of **L**asrian of Leighlin (+641) (31). Bought the freedom of a prisoner of the king of Tara (36). Discouraged pilgrimage (37), but himself saw Rome in a vision, with the help of **M**aedoc of Ferns (v. *Maedoc* 38). 'Archiepiscopus' Maedoc (+626) intended to go to Britain to visit his master **D**avid (+589), who was his confessor, but was persuaded by an angel to make Lugid his confessor instead (38, *cf.* v. *Maedoc* 20); Maedoc proposed to subject Ferns to Lugid, but king Brandub refused to let him (*2*, 32). Brandub came to Clonfert Mulloe, demanding entertainment for his 400 men on a Sunday, but did not get it till Monday (*2*, 51). Lugid was soul-friend to David, Mo-Choemog, Maedoc and Comgall, *M. Oeng.* He visited Erneas, head of **A**bban's monastery of New Ross, Wexford (*S 72*). He was delighted to hear of Gregory the Great's accession (590) (40). **D**aganus took Lugid's rule (*ASS* Aug. 1, 352) to Gregory (47), and later suggested Lacteanus as Lugid's successor (50). Lugid revived the wife and cured the son of **S**canlan Mor, king of Ossory (+646) (*3*, 27-28). (Scanlan's son and the queen of the Dessi, *2*, 52; 60.) He received the viaticum from **C**ronan of Roscrea (+640) and died on Saturday, Aug. 4; his relics were contested between Munster and Leinster, but remained at Clonfert Mulloe (52). The angel who visited **F**intan Munnu twice a week missed a visit because Heaven was welcoming Lugid (53; v. *Fint. M.* 25; v. *Mo-Chua* 5). Gregory (+604) *heard of his death* (54). Lugid was 'mitis ad omnes' (53), killed no bird or any living thing, *M. Oeng.* In contrast with Fintan's pride, Lugid 'nulli praesenti maledixit, nec absenti detraxit', v. *Mo-Chua* 5.

    Cuimine, **F**lannan, **L**asrian of Leighlin, **M**o-Chua of Timahoe.

    LUGID, *see* Mo-Luoc, Molocus.

    LUNAIRE, *see* Leonorus.

    LUPUS, bishop of Troyes, *c.*426-*c.*479, July 29. *BHL* 5087-5091. *DCB.* Friend and correspondent of Sidonius; accompanied **G**ermanus of Auxerre to Britain, 429. Friend of **C**onstantius, who wrote the vita *Germani, c.*480.

    MACARIUS of Mull, Argyll (*NM 63*) and Aberdeen (*NJ 9406*) VI L/VII E, Nov. 12. I;P. *BHL* 5736, lost Life, extracted in O'Donnell, v. quinta *Columbae* 3, 23-30, *cf.* 1, 13 (*TT* 435-6; 391) (1); *Brev. Ab.* PH 155-6 (2); *Mart. Ab., cf. Adam King's Calendar*, Nov. 12. (Forbes 136; 167) (3). Forbes 394 refers to an unpublished verse Life in Cambridge University Library. Mo-Chonna 'qui et Macharius et Mauritius' (*1*); 'Mauricius . . . apud Scottos Machorius . . . apud Hybernicos vero

Mo-Chrumma' (*3*). Son of *king* Fiachna, brought up in Connacht (*1*), baptised by Colman (of Dromore ?) (*2*). Joined Columba in Ireland, accompanied him to Iona as 'adolescens' (*1*); identified by Reeves, *Adamnan* 246 with To-Channu mocu Fir Cetea (Adomnán v. *Col.* App.), *cf.* (*2*) one of the 12 who crossed with Columba. Aroused the jealousy of the monks of Iona by writing late at night with a bright (miraculous) light in his cell; Columba therefore sent him away with 12 disciples, consecrating him bishop 'in Pictorum provinciam' (*1*) to Mula insula (*2*), to a river on the borders of the province whose course looped like his staff (*1*); he is the patron of Aberdeen cathedral, and of a few sites near Aberdeen; MacKinlay, *Ancient Church Dedications in Scotland*, 2, 95. Accompanied Columba to Rome, where Gregory the Great gave him the name Mauritius (*1, 2*). On the return journey, stayed at Tours, and there died (*1-3*), *being proclaimed bishop*, (*1, 2*; archbishop *3*). Columba brought from Tours a missal discovered in Martin's tomb (*1*; a gospel found in Martin's tomb preserved at Derry, *Lismore* 900; Columba also recovered the Gospel of the Angel from Patrick's grave, *AU* 552). Macarius borrowed seed from Ternan, *Brev. Ab.* PH 105.

MAC CAILLE, bishop of Croghan, Offaly (*N 43*) 492, Apr. 25. I;I. Tírechán *Coll.* 16. *Book of Leinster* 372, 1 = *VT* 310, 550; v. *Brigit* (1). *TT* 525 n. 11. Veiled Brigit.

MAC CAIRTHENN, bishop of Clogher, Tyrone (*H 55*) +505, Aug. 15. I;I. *BHL* 5105. *Sal.* 799 (1), *ASH* 737 (2). Tírechán *Coll.* 16. *cf. Add.* 8, *Bethu Phátraic* = Stokes *VT* 310; 338; 144, 156, 174-6 (3). Also named Aed, and Fer da Crich (man of two borders). Clogher and 'Dairinis' (unlocated ? Sligo, Hogan 329), of the family of Eochaid m. Muiredaig (Ulaid, Dal Fiatach) *M. Don.* Of Airgialla *M. Tal.* Uncle of Mael Ruan of Tallacht, *M. Oeng.* Baptised by Patrick (*3*), Patrick's champion (*3*). Uncle of Brigit (3).

Built his monastery 'in platea and regalem sedem Ergalliensium' (*1*, 1). Eochaid of Airgialla sent his son Cairpre (Domangart +512) to expel him, under pressure from his magi (druids) (2), and made a second attempt (3). When Eochaid's nephew Tigernach returned as a monk from Rosnat, Eochaid endeavoured to evict Mac Carthenn (Maenchatinus), and replace him with Tigernach, but Tigernach indignantly refused (v. *Tig.* 12).

MAC CR(E)ICHE V L/VI E, Aug. 11 (so Colgan's catalogue, *cf. VSH* x; probably by confusion with Mac Cridhe of Louth? Aug. 11. *M*). vita, Plummer, *MHH* 13 (Irish text), 53 (English translation).

The name means 'son of plunder' (Mac Creiche) or 'son of the border' (Mac Criche). Of Corcumroe, Co. Clare (1), baptised and taught by Mainchim (9). Ailbe (+528), on his way from Emly to Aran, was joined by Mac Criche; they founded several churches, and Mac Criche stayed behind at Tracht Ailbe (Ailbe's strand), the place from which Ailbe went to the Land of Promise to meet the seven of his men whom he had sent to sail westwards into the ocean (10-18; v. *Ailbe* 32, civitas Ultani, Cathir Ultan, Imokilly, Clare, *W 97*); Ailbe was high bishop of Munster (ardeaspocc), Mac Criche a bishop under him (18). Mac Criche protected the Ciarraige against plague (19), raiders under the king of West Munster, *Crimthann*, father of Aed Bennan (+621) (21-31). Visited Ailbe at Emly (34) and went with Luchtigern and Mainchin to secure a reduction of 'boroma' (cattle tribute) from the king of Connacht, *Aed (Abrat) m. Eochaid*, 557-578 (34-40); tributes of Corcumroe, Ciarraige and Eoganachta of Loch Lein assigned to Mac Criche, in verse (41-48). He defeated the plague, personified as a lake monster (49-67) and was assigned tributes (68-71).

He was one of the envoys, with Finnian and Erlatheus (+481) to secure the independence of Aran from the primacy of Pubeus (Kebi) (v. *Endei* 33). In old age, he was evicted from his cell on Iniscaltra in Lough Derg, Clare (*R 78*) by Columba of Terryglass (+551) (v. *Col. T.* 15). Well-known Munster and Connacht kings are introduced out of due time in interested stories about tribute. His connection with Ailbe and with Aran is echoed in their own traditions, and serves no local interest; his eviction in old age by the young Columba is an independent confirmation of his date; his active life will have been spent within the years *c*.475-*c*.535; died aged *180* (1). He was evidently a Kerry cleric of some importance, despite the figure of fun depicted in his folklore life. Luchtigern.

MAC CUIL (Macuil) maccu Greccae V M, July 30? I;Man. Muirchú 22, tyrannus . . . hi nDruim (Nendrum, Down, *J 56*) moccu Echach, intended to kill Patrick as 'seductor ille et perversor hominum', converted by a miracle, set sail in a boat without oars (*cf. ASC* 891), came to the Isle of Man, where he was welcomed by two bishops, Conindrus (Cynidr?) and Romulus (Rumilus), whom he succeeded as bishop of Man. The 'succession' to two bishops sounds like an elaboration of an original wherein two British bishops joined with Patrick in the canonical consecration of one of his converts as bishop in Man. He may be Cobair mac Cuill, July 30; (the entry has inspired the imaginary *Germanus* mac Guill). The cognomen may be identical with the name, but not the person, of Mac Cr(e)iche.

MAC CUILIN, bishop of Lusk, Dublin (*O 25*) +496, Sept. 6. I;I. *M.* Named Luachan *M. Oeng.*, Cuinnid, Cuinnigh, Cuindig, *M., Annals*; of the Ciannachta, *M. Don.* His Life, *BHL* 2987, 6 = O'Hanlon 9, 165-168 = *AB* 69, 1951, 338 (wrongly described as hitherto unpublished, p. 325) is an adaptation of a life of Findbar of Cork, itself conflating the Lives of more than one person, achieved by substituting the names Mac Cuilin and Lusk for Findbar and Cork throughout. A possible occasion of the adaptation is that v. *Findbar (VSH* 6) calls his Leinster cell, Cell mic Cathail, Gowran, Kilkenny (*S 65*), 'Chell inn Cantilir' (Irish), Cyllin cantiliz (Latin text), giving Cu(i)lin as the name of a monastery whose founder's Life was that of Findbar.

MACHARIUS, *see* Macarius.

MACHUTUS, *see* Malo.

MAC LAISRE, abbot, bishop of Armagh 612-624, Sept. 12. I;I. *Annals. Book of Leinster* 42ᶜ (sedit xviii, for xii).

MACLOVIUS, *see* Malo.

MAC MOIL VI M/L. I;B. v. *Cadoci* 11, 15, 58, Irish follower of Cadoc, came with him to Britain, built a church in Gwent, perhaps Macmoil, Bedwellty, Mon. (*SO 1600), LBS* 3, 394.

MAC NISSE (Angus), bishop of Connor, Antrim (*J 19*) +509, Sept. 3. I;I. *BHL* 5125. *Sal.* 925. Confused with Coeman Brecc (Sept. 14, born 529). Trained by Bolcan (Olcan) in Dal Araide (1-3), a little boy under Olcan, to whose ecclesiastical heritage he succeeded, in the time of Saran of Dal Araide (brother of Fiachra Lon, +482) (*Bethu Phátraic VT* 166). Visited 'Jerusalem terra reprommissionis' and Rome, where he ordained many bishops and was given vessels of precious metal (5-6). Cured lepers (6,8); foretold Comgall of Bangor to his parents (12); visited by Brigit

(13). Foretold Colman Elo (558?-613) who would be born of his own kin 60 years later (14). Colman Elo was of the southern Ui Neill of Meath, and in his youth visited Mac Nisse's tomb at Connor (v. *Colman Elo* 3). Colman of Dromore.

MAC TAIL, bishop of Kilcullen, Kildare (*N 80*) +551, June 11. I;I. Son of Eogan the smith, *M. Oeng.*, of Munster, *M. Don.* Placed at Kilcullen with *Iserninus* by *Patrick* *Bethu Phátraic*, Tírechán *Coll.*, *Add. VT* 186, 331, 350; a smith *Bethu Phátraic VT* 250.

MAEDOC (Aedan, Mo-Aed-oc) of Ferns, Wexford (*T 05*) +627, Jan. 31. I;B.I. *BHL* 184-7. *VSH* 2, 141 (1); 295 (2); *Sal.* 463 (3); v. *Cadoci* 22, 25, 70 (4); v. *David* 15, 35, 36, 42 (5).

Native of the Ui Briuin of Connacht, given as hostage as a boy to Ainmire, high-king 565-9 (4). Taught by Caillin of Fenagh (Leitrim, *H 00*. VI M, Nov. 13. *M. Don.*). Sodalis (? pupil) of Lasrian of Devenish (+563) (8), with whom he helped to resuscitate *(Cairpre) Domangart* (+511) of Airgialla, and with whose monastery he shared relics (10); v. *Lasrian* (20, 24). Left home, against the will of Aed Finn, king of the Ui Briuin to study under David (+589) in Britain (11; 5). When sent by David's economus with a waggon to haul timber from afar, left his open book in rain that did not wet it (12; 5, 35); while fetching beer, his cart had an accident, without damaging the beer or the oxen (14); he cured the son of British king, blind, deaf and dumb (15); his prayers routed an English army invading Britain, so that the enemy dared not return while he was in Britain (17), *cf.* Finnian of Llancarfan, *c.*580? Blinded Saxon raiders (2, 18); a 'potens homo' (rex de Saxonibus 2, 18) pretended to be deaf and blind, was made so for his deceit (18). Returned to Ireland, 'fully instructed, his failings purified' (5, 36), 'with the blessing of his master David' (*1*, 19). He wished to retain David as his confessor, but was persuaded by an angel to take Lugid instead (20; v. *Lugid* 38). Established a monastery among the Dessi (21-22), where his mill supplied flour to a man of Ossory (23). Colman of Dromore (VI M) helped to revive king Brandub of south Leinster after an enemy attack. Founded many monasteries among the Ui Cennselaig of south Leinster, one of them under a Dicuil (24) Clonmore, near Enniscorthy, Wexford, *S 93* (Hogan 267), which he defended miraculously against the invading army of Aed m. Ainmirech, king of Ireland, who withdrew (24), perhaps the campaign of Mag Ochtair (Cloncurry, Kildare, *N 84*, Hogan 528), 590 *Annals*; or the invasion of 600, when Brandub of Leinster killed Aed's son at Dun Buchat (Hollywood, Wicklow, *N 90*, Hogan 378); Aed again invaded, with 24,000 men, but was killed (24; 55) at Dunbolg by Brandub who then fell sick, and was cured by Maedoc; he gave him Ferns (Guernin 5, 36) where both Brandub and Maedoc were later buried, and convened a synod where he decreed that Ferns should be the archbishopric of all Leinster (26); Coemgen's Glendalough, near Brandub's royal seat, had previously been the principal ecclesiastic site in the kingdom. Friend (v. *Colman-Elo*, *Sal.* 39), patron (v. *Lugid* 3, 36) of Brandub, archiepiscopus (55; v. *Moling* 8, v. *Lugid* 38). Visited David in Britain just before his death (589) (32). Visited Fintan Munnu at Taghmon and cured his sick monks, but consented to Munnu's prayer that they should fall sick again, since 'virtue is perfected in sickness' (29) *cf.* 52. Gave a plough and oxen to a newly-founded house for women (31). Prayed that no Leinster prince who sat in his see, and no monk who deserted him, should sit with him in heaven (33). Rescued captives of his kin in Munster (35). Cured Guaire Aidni of Connacht (+663) 30 (40?) years before his death (37). Showed Rome in a vision to Lugid (38); offered Ferns to Lugid, but was prevented by Brandub (v. *Lugid* 2, 43; *3*, 36); helped Mo-Chua with seed corn (40). Cursed the hand of comes Saran who murdered **B**randub (44) (608), and prayed for his soul with Colman Elo (v. *Col. E.*, *Sal.* 39). He lent his architect Gobban, with men and oxen, to help Mo-Chua build Lochre (48). With **L**ugid, revived a nun of Ita (+570) (49). Grew fruit trees (54; v. *Lugid 2*, 66). Cured a paralytic from Rome (56). Died (59), succeeded by Mo-Chua (34) and **M**oling (58).

In early Welsh tradition, Maedoc is a major saint. The 'chief leaders' (principales proceres) of the 'three parts of the country' are David and **T**eilo (in Demetia), **I**lltud and **D**ochou (in Morgannwg and Gwent), **C**ynidr and Maedoc (in the upper Usk and Wye) (*4*); in Carmarthenshire tradition he is bracketed with Teilo (*LL* 101 'Teliaus et Maidocus . . . non figmenta poetarum nec veterum historias, immo Jeremie prophete lamentationes [legentes]'). The traditions are early, for **C**ynidr's church in Radnor, and Madoc's principal Welsh foundations, the extinct Llanmadoc in Cwmteuddwr in Radnor (*SN 9667*) and Llanbadoc Fawr (not from a hypothetical 'Padoc') in Monmouth (*SO 3700*) had lost all importance when these texts were written; no later interest explains or justifies a tradition that puts their founders on a par with the great saints of Morgannwg and Demetia. His sites in Ireland are unusually numerous (O'Hanlon 1, 575). His name is common and widely distributed in Welsh place-names, some of which are listed *LBS* 3, 395, matching with names in Cil- and dedications to Brigit, with two or three instances in Pembrokeshire and western Gower, in Monmouthshire, and 10 or 12, with as many Cil- names, along the route of the Roman road from Brecon to Chester, with another eight or nine instances in Gwynedd, including Anglesey. Its frequency in these defined areas is as marked as its total absence elsewhere. Some of the northern sites may however take the name of **M**atoc Alithir.

In the south, the explanation clearly lies in Maedoc's connection with David, and in his influence at St. David's in the 40 years of his life after David's death (589). The vita *David* claims (42) that 'a third or a quarter of Ireland served "David Aquilento" (Aquaticus, water drinker), where Maedoc was'. David left no native successor. As bishop, Teilo installed **I**smael at St. David's. As head of the monasteries that obeyed David, Maedoc was his successor. *M. Oeng.* has a sharp story of Maedoc and St. David's. A bishop and 50 *bishops* (monks) of Cell Muine (St. David's) came to Maedoc at Ferns. From David's time meat had not been brought into the refectory of Cell Muine until 'comarba Moedog' brought it. There was dispute, so the monks came to Ferns, in Lent. Maedoc offered them cakes, whey and leeks, which they refused, demanding pork and beef. Maedoc gave them meat, but reproved them. The bishop answered 'the pig drank its mother's milk, the ox ate nothing but nature's grass; but that cake consumed 365 labours' (i.e., needed a year's agricultural labour). The accounts of Irish saints contain several stories (**C**omgall, **F**intan, etc.) of pressure brought on ascetics to relax rigorous rules akin to David's, and the tradition of Maedoc contains no echo of David's severity, though Maedoc was his pupil. The story, whose author evidently disliked vegetarianism, makes Maedoc reluctantly sanction its discontinuance at St. David's. The Book of Leinster (285b = Best, *et al.* 5, 1243) also makes Maedoc 'coarb' (successor) of David, and the story of *M. Oeng.* presumes the effective monastic authority of Maedoc in St. David's. The popularity of Maedoc is therefore likely to have been spread by monks of Demetia in the half century or so after 589. The Modoc names of Scotland, Forbes 403, may be due to one of his followers, or to another Aed. The Breac Mogue (Aed = Hugo; Mogue = Mo Hugo) in the Royal Irish Academy Museum is one of the oldest Irish reliquaries.

MAEL (Mel), bishop of Ardagh, Longford (*N 26*) +486, Feb. 6. B;I. *Bethu Phátraic*

VT 82-88 and Patrician legend; v. *Brigit*. First named of Patrick's bishops, his *nephew*. British-born bishop, *veiled Brigit* at the request of his disciple **Mac** Caille, v. *Brigit* (Ultan 18 and other lives affected by the Patrician tradition; Brigit veiled by Mac Caille, Cogitosus 3, without mention of Mael). *ECMW* 10 Llanfaelog, Anglesey (*SH 3373*) Mailis (i), appears to be fifth-century and is perhaps Irish, Jackson *LHEB* 329 n. 1.

MAEL and Sulien VI M/L. A;B. Companions of **C**adfan, *ByS* 20. Their sites are Corwen, Mer. (*SJ 0743*) and Cwm, Flint (*SJ 0677*).

MAELDUBH of Malmesbury, Wilts. (*ST 9387*) VII M. I;E. Maildufus, Bede *HE* **5**, 18, *cf.* Plummer 2, 310. Irishman, founded Malmesbury, and taught its most famous pupil, **A**ldhelm, *c.*660, who later returned as its abbot. He may or may not be identical with one of the numerous Maeldubs recorded in Ireland. Leland, *Coll.* 1, 102, cited Forbes 385, dates the foundation of Malmesbury to 642.

MAELOC of Anglesey V L. B;I.B. v. *Kebi* 5, 10. Accompanied **K**ebi to Ireland. Names Llanfaelog, Anglesey (*SH 3373*) with its adjacent lake and spring, *LBS* 3, 404.

MAELOC of Bretoña, Spain +572. *Conc. Hisp.* 3, 206, cited *HS* 2, 99. Mailoc, 'Britonensis ecclesiae episcopus', present at the second Council of Braga.

MAELOC of Llowes, Radnor (*SO 1941*) VI M/L? Nov. 14. B;B.A. v. *Gildae (R)* 2 *Son of Caw, brother of Gildas*, 'venit Lyuhes in pago Elmail ibique monasterium aedificans'. He names a couple of sites near Gildas' in Brittany, and several in Radnor, Brecon and adjacent counties, *LBS* 3, 404 (but is nothing to do with Mo-Chelloc, *M. Oeng.* March 26).

MAELRUBHA of Applecross, Ross (*NG 7144*) 642(Jan. 3)-722, Tuesday April 21. I;P. *Annals* (birthday, weekday of death *AT*; age 80) *M. Annals. Brev. Ab.* PE 89, translated and summarised Forbes 383. Of the Ui Neill (Cenel Eogain), his mother a relative (*sister*) of **C**omgall. Monk of Bangor (abbot) *Annals, M.*; possibly 668-671; but his name is not included in the list of abbots in the *Antiphonary of Bangor*, Kenney 706, *cf.* 265, drawn up under abbot Cronan 680-691 (and he was over young at 26 for the abbacy), crossed to Scotland 671, founded Applecross 672, *Annals*; and a score of other sites, Forbes 383. He is entered in Scottish Calendars under Aug. 27.

MAENCHATINUS, *see* Mac Carthenn.

MAGLORIUS of Dol VI M/L, Oct. 24. B;A. *BHL* 5139-5147. Cousin and successor of **S**amson, soon resigned in favour of Budoc, founded a monastery on Sark, dispossessing its previous possessor, Loescon. Raided by a Saxon fleet (*c.*580/590?). Originally his rule was teetotal and vegetarian, but was relaxed at the request of an angel. **T**yssilio.

MAGLOS, *see* Mael.

MAGONUS, *see* Patrick.

MAIAN, abbot of Plouguin, near Ploudalmazeau, *D 2* (Achm) VI M. B;A. Brother of **G**oueznou, visited by **H**oernbiu; present at his funeral.

MALO (Maclovius, Machutus, Machutes, etc.) of St. Malo (Aleth) *R 1*, VI M/L (+559, or 604?), Nov. 15. B;A. *BHL* 5116-5124. 'Plaine et de la Borderie', *Vie de St. Malo*, Rennes, 1884, 170. The fullest Life (1) is by Bili of Aleth, *c.*870. Native of

Gwent, *cousin of **S**amson*. Pupil of ***B**rendan of Clonfert*, at *Nantcarvan* (1); learnt his alphabet in a day (3; *cf.* Machutus the intellectual, *M. Gor., cf. M. Don.*). Ordained by Brendan (13). Sailed with Brendan and a crew of 95 in one ship on a seven-year voyage to the Island of Yma (16 ff.); encountered an island that looked like a mirror, or glass (quasi speculum aut vitrum), an iceberg (20). Reached Yma on the seventh Easter, landed, found a small path that led to a distant fountain, and then found nearby a two-headed bush (sentem, glossed 'acanthus', *cf.* Du Cange), whence they drank (23-25), perhaps a cactus. Celebrated mass on the back of a whale (26), returned home, to plant his bush at Nantcarvan (28). Made a first unsuccessful voyage in an 'aplustralis navis' (ship with a rudder), failed to find Yma, but reached the Orkneys 'and other northern isles' (*2*, 7); on a second voyage saw the iceberg, but failed to find Yma (*2*, 9-13). Left Nantcarvan, sailed to Brittany, to 'insula September' (Cesambre in the Rance estuary, *R 1*) (30-39) 'Claruit' Sigebert *Chron.* a. 561=558. Went to Corseult, near Dinan (*Q 2*), revived a corpse and celebrated mass in the presence of '**C**onmor, dux Domnonicae regionis' (+560) (74-76); the order of events is given by a lost Life epitomised in Leland, *Coll.* 1, 430, cited *LBS* 3, 431; *cf.* 1, 298; 'Machutus venit ad Corsult . . . Conmor dux tunc temporis Domnonicae regionis; una die petierunt palatium Philberti (Childebert I) regis VII Britonum episcopi, videlicet Sampson, Machu, Paternus, Courentinus, Paulus Aurelianus (MS. Ninanus), Pabu (MS. Fabu) Tutwallus, Briomelus (Brioc). Lupercus quidam . . . coram Filiberto . . . terras suas dedit sedi Machutis. Machutus Romam petiit. Canalchus insula, nunc S. Machuti. Machutus venit ad Leontium episcopum, fugiens a suis quos propter scelera maledictione mulctaverat'. Came to Aleth, a civitas long deserted, founded many cells and monasteries in the city and the neighbouring islands and places (40). Helped by his disciple **R**ivan (41 *cf.* 55); took over the cell of Domnech, who had received land, yoke and oxen from **M**eliau, regens in pago Alet (44); made bishop by king **J**udicaelus, consecrated at Tours (48-49), took over the cell of the hermit **A**aron (Ilot d'Aaron, St. Malo) and spent 40 years (*cf.* 90) in Aleth (53). The throne was seized, after Judicaelus' death, by Rethwalus, who killed all Judicaelus' sons except Hailoc, including one to whom Malo gave sanctuary, and himself died three days later (60). Hailoc attempted to destroy Malo's church, but was blinded and cured, and gave Malo 'the best land' and 'much gold and silver' (*2*, 19). While walking by the river, a man accused him of looking for a woman, took his cloak, and used it as a blanket on his bed; when he returned it, Malo gave it to the poor, considering that 'a cloak that had been used by rustics was not fit for him to wear' (79). He aroused considerable opposition. One well-born girl protested 'You foreigner, your own country could not stand you, so you have come to turn us out of our own land' (*2*, 18). When Hailoc died, the 'impia generatio' rose against Malo, complaining that he owned so much land that he virtually owned the whole country, leaving nothing for their children to live on in the future; they beat up his pistor Rivan, and tied him to a horse's tethering-post below high-tide mark, and told Malo to fetch him; Malo rode down and rescued him, leaving his own horse tethered, with the crowd jeering, 'Keep your horse in your own stable' (*2*, 21; *1*, 55). Malo decided to emigrate, stayed for a few days at Luxodium with **C**olumban (after 590) (*2*, 21; *1*; 56); sailed round Brittany to the region of La Rochelle (93 ff.) in the time of *bishop* *Leontius* of Saintes (he was bishop 614/660); he may have been a priest of Saintes before becoming bishop; it is possible that 'papa Leontius' who rebuilt the basilica of Eutropius at Saintes (Fortunatus *Carmen*, *1*, 13) before 614 (Fortunatus died well before 614, since his second successor as bishop of Poitiers was then in office) was a priest, the future bishop, rather than bishop Leontius of Bordeaux (+*c.*573/576), to whom most of the hymns headed Leontius are addressed, since in the others Leontius of Bordeaux is styled episcopus; the usage of 'papa' was not yet fully fixed.

Recalled, after seven years (101), receiving Pleguier from Bili on the way (102), but soon returned to where he died, aged *133*, on Sunday evening (106), Nov. 15 (2, 30). The mathematics appear to fit the year 599 or 604. His head and right arm were restored to St. Malo as relics under Childebert (III, 695-711) when Roiantwor was *comes* (1, ii, 5-9), the rest of his body in the time of king Alan of Brittany (c.888-907), *BHL* 5124.

He has some 25 sites in Brittany, a score in Normandy, Picardy, Artois and Ile-de-France, eight in the Saintonge, one each in Orleans, Nevers and Anjou (*BHL* 5116, Plaine et Borderie 19 ff.), with three in Monmouthshire *LBS* 3, 433; and in the later Middle Ages was believed in Tenerife to have reached the island in his voyages with Brendan. He also has a dedication at Wulwerghen in Flanders, that is not known to derive from the importation of relics (Plaine et Borderie, 27). Gurwal, Tyssilio.

MANCHAN Sapiens of Liath Mor (Lemanaghan, Offaly, *N 12*) +664, Jan. 24. I;I. *M.* Of the Ui Neill, Cenel Conaill Gulbain; compared with Jerome for learning, *M. Don.*

MANSUETUS of northern Gaul +461. B;Gaul. *Mansi* 7, 451. 'Mansuetus episcopus Britannorum interfui et subscripsi', at the first Council of Tours, 461. The bishops attending were those of Lugdunensis Tertia, without Brittany, and of Rouen, Chalons, Bourges and Clermont-Ferrand. The tenth-century tradition of Toul, near Metz, calls its first bishop Mansuetus, assigned to the early or mid-fourth century, a 'Scot' from 'Ireland' (cited *HS* 2, 289); in the tenth century ecclesiastical foreigners from the British Isles were assumed to be Irish. The name also occurs in the early unconfirmed lists of the adjacent sees of Meaux and Senlis, north of Paris, at much the same date; and in a list of bishops of Trier, to the north of Toul, which also incorporates names annexed from the list of Tongres, north of Trier. (Duchesne, *Fastes episcopaux*, 2, 476; 3, 117; 3, 32; 3, 36). Otherwise, the name is not known among Gallic bishops. It is possible that the dispersed immigrant British population whom Mansuetus served included settlers at Senlis, where a British bishop, Conotigernus (*cf.* Kentigern), was elected in the next century, and that the list of Meaux borrowed from that of Senlis. The Toul tradition of a bishop from the British Isles might derive from a similar group of settlers, or might also be a borrowing from Senlis. The Toul tradition also knew the tombs of St. Mansuy and of his 'successor' Amon, a name also known in Britain as the father of Samson.

MAOINEANN, *see* Mo-Nenn.

MARIANUS SCOTTUS (Moel Brigte) 1028-1082. I;Germany. Irish Chronicler, of Moville, exiled by his abbot 1056, settled at Cologne, Fulda and Mainz. Kenney 614.

MARIANUS SCOTTUS (Muiredach Mac Robartaig [Rafferty]) of Ratisbon +1088. I;Germany. Relative of Domnall Mac Robartaig, comarb of Columba of Iona at Kells (1062-1098), who made the case of the Cathach of Columba of the O'Donnells (Kenney 629); founded St. James of Ratisbon on the Danube, 1076, whence his successors established the Schottenkloster of Vienna, Eichstatt, Constance, Nuremberg, Wurzburg and Kiev. A prolific scribe. Kenney 616.

MARUANUS, *see* Rumon.

MARTIN of Tours +397, Nov. 11. *BHL* 5610-5666. Sulpicius Severus' Life was published before Martin's death. Son of a Pannonian soldier, drafted into the army, discharged as a conscientious objector by Julian *c.*358; settled as the first western hermit near Poitiers, under Hilary. A group of citizens of Tours, disliking both officially nominated candidates at the episcopal election of 372, tricked Martin into coming to the city, where he was enthusiastically proclaimed by the electors, to the distaste of established bishops. Established a monastery, with a school, at Marmoutiers, two miles from the city. The first to preach to peasants and found rural churches; impressed public opinion by his disregard of the majesty of the emperors Valentinian I and Maximus; tried to prevent ecclesiastical prosecutions for heresy in lay courts. His best-known pupils were Amator of Auxerre and Victricius of Rouen. Ciaran of Saigir; Ninnian; Senan.

MATERICUS presbyter Sosani episcopi ecclesiae Britaniensis subscripsi *Conc. Hisp.* III 449, cited *HS* 2, 100, eighth Council of Toledo.

MATHEUS, *see* Matoc.

MATOC Elithir (pilgrim, =? foreigner) VI M/L, Apr. 25. B;I. Son of Deichter, d. of Muiredach Muinderg, king of the Ulaid (+492), who was also mother of Sanctan (son of the British late sixth-century king Samuel Pennisil) *M. Don.*, son of the British king *Canton*, *M. Tal.* Matoc (footnote Elithir) distinguished from 'Elithir', *M. Gor.* Glossed 'Matheus', *M. Don.* alphabetical table, p. 438. British, like his brother Sanctan, came to Ireland before Sanctan, settled at Inis Matoc (Templeport Lake, Co. Cavan/Leitrim border, *H 11*), Sanctan's hymn composed while journeying there from Clonard. His monastery continued into the eighth or ninth centuries, since a St. Gall codex of Priscian contains a gloss by a scribe connected with Inis Madoc (O'Curry 27, citing Zeuss, *Grammatica Celtica*, 1853). He, rather than Maedog of Ferns, may be the origin of many of the numerous places in Wales that bear the name Madoc. It may well be that he both recruited monks from Britain at Inis Madoc, and sent back pupils to Britain.

MAUCANUS (Moucan) VI M. B;B. Vir sanctus, on an angel's instruction, upbraided Maelgwn of Gwynedd for his cruelty in invading Gwynllwg (Monmouthshire) (*c.*540). Maelgwn ignored him and was blinded. Maucanus was sent with Maelgwn's envoy Argantblad to Cadoc, who cured Maelgwn, and was granted *refugium* for himself, and also for 'David in Rosina Valle' v. *Cadoci* 69. Maucanus' name occurs at St. Maughans and Llanfeugan (Monmouth, *SO 4617*; Brecon, *SP 0924*), *cf. LL* 323 'ecclesia de Maucheyn', with several other sites in south Wales, Cornwall and Brittany, *LBS* 3, 452; 497, with widely varying feast days.

MAUCENNUS of Rosnat V L. B;B. v. *Endei* 6-7 (1); v. *Eugenius Ardstraw* 1 (2); v. *Tigernach* 3-4 (3); v. *David* 2 (4); *Bethu Phátraic VT* 137 (5). Maucennus, *1*; *4*; Nennyo qui Maucennus dicitur, *2*; Mo-Nennus, *3*; Maucen magister, *5*, of Rosnat, *1*; *2*; *cf.* v. *Darerca* 25; Rosnat, alio nomine Alba *3*; 'Maucenni monasterium . . . nunc . . . Depositi monasterium vocatur', *4*.

The date implied is *c.*460 for *1*, *c.*470 for Darerca; *c.*500, *2*; *3*; *c.*500 or soon after, *4*. *2*, *cf. 3* implies that he was abbot of a monastery whose founder was Nennyo; Nynias is Bede's name for Ninnian. Frequent statements in the Lives that a saint studied, e.g. 'in scola S. Kierain abbatis', mean, in their first form, 'at Clonmacnoise' but are often understood by mediaeval editors to mean 'under Ciaran' personally, rather than 'at Ciaran's monastery'.

He and Mugentius are the only abbots of Rosnat known to Irish or British tradition; Maucennus is placed in late V by *1*, *2*, *3*; Mugentius in mid VI. The 'Maucenni monasterium' of v. *David*, will have been founded by *c*.500, or soon after, since David seems to have studied under one of Maucennus' successors, Guistilianus. Maucennus was therefore perhaps the great teacher (librarius) from the 'far north' who established a monastery situated three days' journey from the home of Samson's parents in Demetia, at the time of his birth (*c*.495/500), when the teacher was himself believed to be there present. Distinct from Mugentius and from Maucanus.

MAUDETUS (Mawes, Modez) VI M/L, Nov. 18. I;B.A. *BHL* 5722-3, *cf. LBS* 3, 441. *AG* 722. Irish prince, son of Erc(leus) and *Gentlusa*, became heir to the throne when the plague (*c*.550?) killed the rest of his family; renounced his inheritance, crossed to Brittany by way of Cornwall, in the time of Childebert (+558) and Daeg (? Deroch) of Leon. His disciples Bothmael and Tudy; monk under Tudwal at 'Lexobium' (Tréguier). He has some 60 sites in Brittany, *LBS* 3, 447, citing *AG* ed. Thomas; with St. Mawes, Co. (*SW 8433*). The name Daeg suggests an Irish original behind the Life; the author of Tudwal *2* says that he used an Irish language Life, written 'barbarica Scotigenarum lingua'.

MAURITIUS, *see* Macarius.

MAWES, *see* Maudetus.

MAWGAN, *see* Maucennus.

MAXIMUS of Asturia VI M? B?;Spain 'Ad sedem Britonorum (Bretona) . . . (pertinent) . . . ecclesiae quae sunt intra Britones, una cum monasterio Maximi, et quae in Asturiis sunt'. Council of Lugo, 569, *Conc. Hisp.* 3, 188, cited *HS* 2, 99. It is probable that the migration to Spain formed part of the third British migration in the 540s, possible that it began earlier; but since Spain is well chronicled, and its records refer a dozen times to the British settlement from 569 onward, it is likely that any significant earlier settlement would have left some record.

MEL, *see* Mael.

MELLITUS, archbishop of Canterbury, 619-624, Apr. 24. Italian;E. *BHL* 5869-5901. Bede *HE* **1**, 29, 30; **2**, 2-7; **3**, 22. Sent by Gregory the Great to Augustine. Bishop of the East Saxons at London, expelled after Aethelbert's death, went to Gaul, returned, settled in Canterbury when London refused to receive him back; succeeded Laurentius as archbishop. Paulinus of York.

MELLONIUS III L/IV E, Oct. 22. B;Gaul. *BHL* 5899-5902. Believed to have been first bishop of Rouen; all the Lives call him British, but all are very late. Avitianus, his successor in the early episcopal catalogues, attended the Council of Arles in 314. The tradition is probably pre-Conquest, since St. Mellons, Cardiff (*ST 2281*), which bears his name, was probably a Norman foundation.

MELORIUS VI M, Aug. 28 (Oct. 1. *translatio*; Jan. 3, arbitrary). A;A. *BHL* 5903-6. Young son of Meliau, *dux* who was deposed and killed by his *brother* Rivodius, who pursued Meliau, and had him killed. 'Nobilis comes Commorus' had him honourably buried. His sites *LBS* 3, 471-2.

MERNOC, *see* Ternoc.

METOPIUS 633, Spain. 'Britaniensis ecclesiae episcopus', fourth Council of

Toledo, prescribing the Celtic Tonsure, *Conc. Hisp.* 3, 386, cited *HS* 2, 100. This text contains the most exact description of the tonsure.

MEUTHI VI E. I;B. v. *Cadoci* 1-7. Irish hermit, baptised **C**adoc, in the name of **C**atmail, educated him from the age of seven for 12 years, 'Donato Priscianoque nec non aliis artibus' in a town. Probably **T**atheus of Caerwent (Meuthi = Mo[ta] Theus). Named Llanfeuthin at Llancarfan, S. Meuthin *c.* 1200, *LBS* 3, 483.

MEVEN VI L/VII E, June 21. B;A. *BHL* 5944-6. *AB* 3, 1884, 142 (1) *AG* 323 (2) Conaidus (qui et) Mevennus, son of Gerascenus, of 'Orcheus pagus (Orkh, *2*) in Guenta provincia' (Ercig), whence also came **S**amson's mother. Accompanied Samson (of Yorkh, *2*) 'illius regionis fidelium dominus et magister' to Letavia. When Samson had settled in Dol, he sent Meven to **G**ueroc. He was received by **C**advonus, who established him at St. Meen in Montfort (*Q 4*), west of Rennes; and aided by king **J**udicael, who later became a monk of his. He specialised in sheep-farming. He miraculously freed a prisoner of Judicael's predecessor **H**aelo. Visited Rome; on his way back, threw a dragon into the Loire near Angers, and founded a monastery near St. Florent le Vieil (*X 8*, midway between Angers and Nantes). Died and succeeded by **A**ustolus, who died soon after. He has numerous sites in Brittany, and named St. Mewan (*SW 9951*) by St. Austell and Mevagissey (*SX 0144*) in Cornwall. The same person cannot have accompanied Samson to Brittany in the 540s and also have been Judicael's abbot in 640. It is likely that Conaidus founded a monastery that his second successor, Meven, made famous. The Life regularly terms him Conaidus in connection with Samson and Haeloc, Mevennus in connection with Judicael.

MICHOMERUS, *c.430.*

MIDA (Mo-Ite), *see* Ite.

MILBURGA of Wenlock, Shrops. (*SO 6398*) VI L/VII E (+*c.722*), Feb. 23. E;E. *BHL* 5959. *NLA* 2, 188. Daughter of Herewald (king of the **M**agonsaetan, north Herefordshire and south Shropshire), *son of Penda* and of *Dompneva*, sister of Ermenburga, cousin of the king of Kent, sister of **M**ildred and Milgitha, a nun of Eastrey, Kent. Founded Wenlock after her father had been converted by a Northumbrian priest, Edfrid.

MILDRED of Thanet, Kent VI L (+*c.700*), July 13. E;E. *BHL* 5960-4; *NLA* 2, 193. Sister of **M**ilburga, founded Thanet.

MOBHI Clarainech (Flatface) of Glasnevin, Dublin (*O 13*) +544, Oct. 12. I;I. v. *Columba Iona* (O'Donnell) 43-48 (1); v. *Columba Iona, Lismore* 866 ff. (2); v. *Fin. Cl.* 19 = *Cat.* 5 (3); v. *Fin. Cl.* 9 (4); v. *Fin. Cl.* 11 (5); *M.* Mobhi *1-3*; Biteus *4-5*.

Of the Lugne of Connacht, *M.* Also called Berchan, 'prophet and poet' *M.* Pupil of **F**innian of Clonard with Mo-**G**enoc and others (*3*). Discouraged by an angel from visiting Rome, with Finnian and *Cathmael* (*4*), confusing Finnian with Finnian of Llancarfan. Returned from Britain with Finnian and Genoc (*5*). Established at Glasnevin when **C**olumba left Finnian to join him, in a community of 50, that included **C**ainnech, **C**omgall, and **C**iaran (of Clonmacmoise) (*1, 2, M. Don.*), the poor huts of his monastery lying west of the river, the church across the river. Held a 'colloquium' on the future of the monasteries, at which Ciaran put emphasis on church services, Cainnech on books, Comgall on medicine, Columba on gold and silver for church ornament and charity (*1, 2*). Dispersed his monastery because he foresaw the plague (*1, 2, M.*). Columba went to Derry, but did not accept the site given by his cousin king Aed until Mobhi's death (*1, 2, M. Don.*). Prophet and poet, *Book of Lecan* 52a5 = Book of Ballymote (*Genealogies of the Saints*, cited *CS* 541 n.), *A. Tig., CS*; 'supposed to be called in English Merlyn' *AC*; died in the 'Blefed', *Annals*.

MOBHI of Iniscourcey (Inch), Down (*J 44*) VI L/VII E, July 22 (July 29 *M. Tal.*). I;S. Mo-Biu, Mobi, *M. Oeng.* Biteus, i. Mo-Biu, *M. Don.* Bite, *M. Tal.* Mo-Biu, *M. Gor.* Mo-Biu episcopus, *Kal. Drummond.* (Do-Bius), Dabius, v. *Mo-Chua, ASH* 788. Dabius, Davius, David, Moveus, Forbes 320, *cf.* O'Hanlon 7, 293.

An Ulsterman, born when **Mo**-Chua of Balla (+640) was a youth, *ASH* 788. He has several sites in Bute, Mull, and south-west Scotland. *David of Armagh*.

MOBHI maccu Alde VI L/VII E. I;I. v. *Col. T.* 13 = *Fintan Cl.* Ed. 3. When Columba of Terryglass (+551), with his young disciples **F**intan of Clonenagh (Leix) (+606), Mo-Cumma of Terryglass, and Coeman of Antrim, Leix (*S 29*) were seeking a site on the borders of Leinster, Columba warned his pupils that the site was reserved for Mobhi, who was not yet born. Maccu Alde is also the kin of **B**rendan of Clonfert, whose natal name was said to be Mobhi (v. *I. Brendan C.* 3ⁿ), perhaps by confusion between two saints of the same kin, dates forbid identification. Mobhi, from Brendan's homeland of Kerry, evidently had a house in Leix, when the Fintan tradition was formed, that did not survive to preserve his memory.

MO-CHOE (Caelan, Coelan) of Nendrum, Mahee Island, Strangford Lough, Down (*J 56*) +498, June 23. I;I. Converted by **P**atrick, who gave him a gospel (the first to receive a gospel *M. Don.*), a table and a crozier, the 'Eteach Mochai', vita II, 32, 77, 14, *Bethu Phátraic VT* 41 = *Lebor Brecc Homily VT* 453, etc. Taught letters to **C**olman of Dromore (VI E/M), v. *Col. D.* 3; Finnian of Moville studied at Nendrum, under *venerabilis senex Coelanus*, about thirty years after his death. He had 450 monks, *Litany AB* 77, 1959, 318 ff., no. 38; built his first church of wood, with 140 monks, *M. Don.*; Mocae an ceoil (the musician) listened to angels who sang in the form of birds, and the song lasted thrice 50 years, so that he returned in the time of his great grandchildren, *Irish Poem, AB* 49, 1931, 42, *cf.* 47, 1929, 98; *M. Don.*

MO-CHOEMOG (Coemgen), Pulcherius, of Laithmor, Leighmore (Leamakev-oge), Tip. (*S 25*) +654, March 13. I;I. *BHL* 5975. *VSH* 2, 164. Son of Beoanus, a Connacht 'artifex in lignis et lapidibus ... audax in milicia' who emigrated to Munster, and married a Dessi woman, Ness *sister of **I**ta*, becoming Ita's smith. His mother's milk cured the blindness of saint Fachnan of Ross Carberry (Cork, *W 33*), who maintained a 'magnum studium scolarium', five days' journey (55 miles due south as the crow flies) from Killeedy. Named Coemgen, Mo-Choemog was brought up 'in moribus honestis scientiaque literarum' by Ita (+570) *for 20 years* (*cf.* v. *Ita* 18), and sent to **C**omgall (+605) at Bangor. Founded Antrim, Leix (*S 29*), surrendered it to saint Coeman, and moved to Munster (Eile). Welcomed by the pious dux Coemhan, who had a church in his castellum at Raith Eanaidh (Rathenny, Clonlisk, Offaly, *R 98, VSH* 2, 338), who offered the royal fort to Mo-Choemog, and, on his request for a desert site in place of a royal seat, gave him Liath Mor. Coemhan's successor Ronan tried unsuccessfully to evict him, but the monastery became the royal cemetery of the south Eile rulers; Mo-Choemog tried without success to mediate between Ronan's son and nephew (18, *cf. CGH* 384 *LL* 325c33), and all were buried at Leighmore, against the opposition of **C**ainnech and other abbots. With his friend and immediate neighbour, bishop Colman of Derry-more, prevailed against the arrogant fornicator, king Failbe Fland of Munster (628-

639). Visited by Cainnech of Aghaboe, a full day's journey (18 miles) away; visited Cronan (+640), v. *Cron.* 19; taught Dagan (+641), whom he revived after decapitation by robbers, with the help of Cainnech. When Colman of Ossory sought to extract an enemy who had sought sanctuary at Leighmore, Mo-Choemog withdrew his curses because Colman was protected by Cainnech and Fachnan (28. *cf.* v. *Cainnech* 39-41). With Cainnech (+603), Molua (+612) and Fechin of Fore (+666) visited the monastery of one of his pupils while under construction, the church and refectory built but still unroofed, the cells not yet built, and were miraculously protected against rain and wind. When a Dessi *comes* broke a peace he had sworn before him, and defied him with the claim 'I do not care what you do, Mo-Choemog, because Cuimmine Foda (+661) has blessed me', Mo-Choemog cursed his castle and horses and wife and daughter, whose afflictions were repealed on the *comes'* submission. He and Fursey (+649) protected a young *dux.* Revived a dead man to give him the viaticum; revived a monk who had died at Emly, whose body the archbishop refused to surrender; restored the sight of the virgin Cainer; died, *aged 413* *M. Don.*, buried at Leighmore. Outlived Fintan Munnu (+637), v. *Fint. M.* 29.

MO-CHONOC, *see* Conoc.

MOCHTA, *see* Mocteus.

MO-CHUA (Cronan) of Balla, Mayo (*M 28*) (584)-640, March 30. I;I. *ASH* 788 (= *ASS* Jan. 1, 47). Ulsterman, son of Beccan, pupil of Comgall (+605), sent out as a missionary by Comgall, visited Fechin of Fore (+666), while Fore was being built, cut a channel from a lake to work a mill (*cf.* v. *Fechin* 14). Came to Connacht at the age of 35 (i.e., 619), established Balla, which was confirmed by king Cellach of Connacht (+703) and his *successor* (predecessor) Cennfaelad (664-680), both made *his contemporaries*. Died at the age of 56. Mobhi of Inch.

MO-CHUA of Timahoe, Leix (*S 59*) (566)-656, Dec. 24 (Jan. 1. *ASS*). I;I. *BHL* 5977. *VSH* 2, 184. Son of Lonan, a Luigne warrior, tonsured at the age of 30 (596), burnt a villa bequeathed by an uncle, lest he should inherit the alms and property of a sinner, and founded Tech Mochua (Timahoe). Expelled a demon of pride and ignorance from Colman Elo (+613); cured Fintan Munnu of leprosy in 619 (seven years after the death of Mo-Lua, 612). Helped *Cianan* (+491) build Duleek, a story perhaps adapted from a Life of Mocteus. Built 30 churches and 120 cells in Ireland and Scotland; removed to Derinish, Lough Oughter, Cavan (*H 30*) in 626 (30 years before his death); died, aged 90, on Dec. 24. He is possibly bishop Caranus of the Aberdeen Breviary, Dec. 23, Forbes 297.

MOCHUDA, *see* Carthacus.

MOCTEUS of Louth (*H 90*) +533, Aug. 19. B;I. *BHL* 5976. *Sal.* 903. Born in Britain, emigrated to Ireland in infancy, with his parents and their relative, the 'magus' Hoam (conceivably Lomman) (1). Learnt 'literarum elementa' with a 'ceraculum' (wax tablet) provided by an angel, visited Rome, *consecrated* (2), returned 'with the blessing and authority' of the pope, with 12 disciples, one of them named (A)edan (3). Built a monastery at Kell Mor Ydan (Kilmore, Monaghan, *H 53*) (4), expelled by the inhabitants, settled at Louth, 'magorum tunc possessio' (5). Pupils flocked to him from all parts, so that he is said to have trained 100 bishops and 300 priests; he sent out saints like swarms of bees, fathering many monasteries (6). He is perhaps *Mo-Chua* who helped Cianan of Duleek.

He and Patrick discussed their primacy and deferred to each other, deciding that the first to die would yield primacy to the other; on Patrick's death, he *held the see of Armagh for a few days before resigning it to Benignus*. The insertion is marked with the words 'Repetamus ordinem narrationis' (7). He described himself as a follower of Patrick; 'sic ipse scribsit in epistola sua; Mocteus peccator prespiter, sancti Patricii discipulus, in Domino salutem', *A. Tig.* etc.; 'proselytus Brito homo sanctus sancti Patricii episcopi discipulus Maucteus nomine ita de nostro profetizavit patrono (de Columba Iona), sicuit nobis ab antiquis traditum expertis compertum habetur', Ad. v. *Col.* pref. 2; hence *Bethu Phátraic VT* 226, 264, *cf.* 266, 574 'Mochta, Patrick's priest'. 'Discipulus' does not imply that he had known Patrick, but that he honoured and accepted him, and presumably intended acceptance of the episcopal authority of Armagh.

Revived Hoam's daughter (8), and bride, Brigit (9), a robber executed by King Ailill (of Airthir) (10), his disciple Fintan the priest, enemy of Kebi (11). His pupils included Ibar (12; *cf.* v. *Ibar 1*, 5; *2*, 13), brought to him by Corbanus, and Dagaeus (20; v. *Dag.* 2-4), who gave him the viaticum (21). He declined an estate offered to *him* (to Columba) by Aed m. Colcan (king of Airthir +612), prophesying that it would belong to Columba (16; Ad. v. *Col.* pref. 2); his monasteriolum and Columba's were separated by a hedge (Ad. v. *Col.* pref. 2). There is no surviving trace of a Columban house at Louth or Kilmore; the story presumably concerns late seventh-century houses, one of which escapes record. He never uttered an idle word or ate fat (19; *M. Don.*). He maintained a school of '80 psalm singing nobles' (*M. Oeng.*), '60 psalm singing seniors' (*M. Don.*), whose time was wholly devoted to study, without agricultural labour. He is the earliest annalist cited in existing texts, for the events of 471, 511, 527 (*AU*). Died at the age of 300 (19; *M. Don.*, etc.).

His 'papal authority', his adherence to Patrick, and his protection of Fintan the priest, suggest that he may have been involved in the dispute between Enda and Kebi (Pubeus) about British authority over Aran (and doubtless much of the rest of the Irish church) at the end of the fifth century, and opposed the British claims, asserting the independent episcopal authority of Armagh, at least in the north; his pupil Ibar is said to have been the principal southern opponent of Armagh claims. Fintan Crimthir; Lomman.

MODANUS VI/VII? Feb. 4. I;S.P. *BHL* 5979. *ASH* 252. *Brev. Ab.* PH 51. Forbes 401. Irish missionary in the Dumbarton and Stirling areas.

MODEZ, *see* Maudetus.

MODWENNA VII M/L? July 6. E;I.E.P. *NLA* 2, 198. Confused with Darerca, her story embedded into the Life of Darerca. Abbess of Faughart, Louth (*J 01*), friend of 'Alfred' (Aldfrith, the future king of Northumbria, Fland Finn); returned to England when her monastery was pillaged, established by Aldfrith at Whitby. Founded Burton-on-Trent, Staffs. (*SK 22*); Polesworth, War. (*SK 2602*); possibly accompanied Aldfrith's sister Osthryd when she went to marry Aethelred of Mercia. Founded churches at Longforgan (*NO 3430*), by Dundee, at Dumpelder (Traprain Law, East Lothian, *NT 5874*) and other sites in Scotland, Forbes 406, presumably after the English occupation of the Lothians and southern Pictland, together with Ronan (of Drumisken in Louth, probably Ronan Scottus, an early advocate of the Roman Easter among the Irish in Britain, before the Synod of Whitby).

MOEDHOG, *see* Maedoc.

MO-GENOC, *see* Genoc.

MO-LAISSE, *see* Lasrian.

MOLING (Dairechellus) of Luachair, of Tech Moling, St. Mullins, Carlow (*S 73*) +696, June 17. I;I. *BHL* 5988. *VSH* 2, 190. *Sal.* 819. Of south Leinster (1); founded St. Mullins with a few disciples (2), appointed as bishop both of Glendalough (6) and Ferns (8), the two earlier sees of Coemgen and Maedoc of south Leinster, but continued to live principally at St. Mullins. Dug a mile-long canal to supply water to his monastery (9), used the tides to float logs for building (10), made roads by moving rocks (11), made a 'horologium' (? sundial) from a large stone with circular marking (13). Constrained his own Leinster king to restore booty taken from Ossory, but induced Ossory to acknowledge Leinster supremacy (16). Put out a fire in a locked and bolted house whose owners were away, that threatened to spread throughout Ferns (17). Induced the high-king Fianachta (674-694) to remit the Boruma (cattle tribute of Leinster) (19), against the opposition of Adomnán (Irish Life, cited Reeves, xlix); tamed and fed wild animals as God's creatures (23 ff.); friend of abbot Oiblan (29). Died and buried at St. Mullins (30). He became a principal saint of south Leinster, the subject of numerous legends, O'Hanlon 6, 712 ff.; 719 ff. Llanfyllin, Montg. (*SJ 1419*) bears his name and observes his day, *LBS* 3, 489. Abban.

MO-LUA, *see* Lugid.

MOLUCUS, *see* Mo-Luoc.

MO-LUOC (Lugid), Molocus of Lismore Island, Loch Linnhe, Argyle (*NM 8440*) +593, June 25. I;S. *BHL* 5989. *Brev. Ab.* PE 5. *TT* 481. Forbes 409. Pupil of Brendan of Clonfert; and perhaps identical with Luan, pupil of Comgall, who founded 100 houses in Scotland and Ireland (Bernard, v. *Malachi* 6). Came to Lismore from Melrose; visited Tyle (? Iceland). He has a score of sites in Argyle and the islands, Forbes 410, O'Hanlon 6, 792 ff.; Lismore became the episcopal see of Argyle. He is wholly absent from the tradition of Columba of Iona; there is no reason to connect him with any of the monks called Lugbeus, Mo-Lua, Lugid by Adomnán. His work, therefore, appears to have been complementary to and independent of Columba.

MO-NENN of Cloncurry, Kildare (*N 84*) VI/VII? Sept. 16. I?(B?);I. Monenn, Moennen, Maoineann, Moninn identified with Ninnian, *M. Gor.*; lost Irish Life of Ninnian, cited Ussher, 351, reproduced *AB* 77, 1959, 165.

MO-NENNA, *see* Darerca.

MO-NENNYO, *see* Ninnian, Maucennus.

MO-NINN, *see* Mo-Nenn.

MO-NINNA, *see* Darerca.

MORAN (Modera[m]nus) VII L/VIII E, Oct. 22. A;B.A. Flodoard 1, 20. *AG* 642. vitae cited *LBS* 3, 499. Duchesne, *Fastes Episcopaux* 2, 346. Armorican, came to Britain to prevent his father's bigamous marriage, returned, bishop of Rennes, visited Italy 715/720, retired to a monastery. Lamorran, Cornwall, by Truro (*SW 8741*) bears his name.

MORWENNA of Morwenstow, Co. (*SS 2015*) VI? July 5. B?;B. *LBS* 3, 490. She has the same day as Darerca, who is confused with the English Modwenna.

MO-SINU, *see* Sinell of Bangor.

MU-, *see* Mo-.

MUGENTIUS VI M. B;B. v. *Finnian* of Moville (Frigidian) *1*, 1; *2*, 6 (*ASH* 634; 638; *cf.* 438). 'Magister ... in civitate quae dicitur Candida'; in 'Futerna' (Whithorn, *cf.* App. *L.*, Rosnat) *Hymn of Mugint*, Preface, Liber Hymnorum 1, 97, *cf.* Kenney 263. Taught Finnian of Moville, used physical force in attempting to discipline him after he was involved in an escapade with a Pictish princess, and was himself physically attacked. He is distinct from Maucennus, and Maucanus. The name might be Mo-Gind(oc).

MUIRCHÚ maccu Machtheni VII L, June 8. I;I. Medran and Murchon, two brothers, in Cell Murchon among the Ui Ailella (Ceis Corainn in Connacht, Keschorran [*G 71*], SE of Ballymote, Sligo, Hogan 206, *cf.* 72); Medran and Murchú, two sons of the Ui Machtene, and I know not where they are, *M. Oeng.* Muirchú mac Ua Maichtene, Meadhran mac Ua Machten, *M. Don., cf. M. Tal.*; Medardus (for Medran), Muirchú mac Ua Mactain, *M. Gor.* of the Ui Faelain (found in Leinster, Munster, Ulster and Connacht) (Hogan 670), *Lebor Breac* notes to *M. Oeng.*; 'in Killmurchu in regione de Hi Garrchon' (Wicklow, Leinster, Hogan 672, where, however, no Kill Murchú is known) *Cashel* Calendar, cited *AB* 1, 1882, 542-3. 'Haec pauca de sancti Patricii peritia et virtutibus Muirchú maccu Machtheni, dictante Aiduo Slebtiensis civitatis episcopo, conscripsit', contents table, *Book of Armagh* 20vo. There was a Tuath Mochtaine in Mag Macha (by Armagh) in Ulster, Tuath Mochthuinde *RC* 20, 338 (Hogan 652). 'Pater meus Cogitosus', a previous writer, Armagh contents table preface, 20ro, presumably to be identified with Cogitosus, biographer of Brigit of Kildare, Leinster, whose church he knew and served. Muirchú of Connacht, father of Colman, author of a hymn to the Archangel Michael (lib. Hymn [T] 8; 'Francsic.' 22); Kenney 269 (trans. O'Hanlon 6, 252), abbot of Moville, +736. The name Muirchú is otherwise not known, and it is therefore probable that these contemporaries are all one person. The family was possibly of Ulster-Armagh origin; Cogitosus lived in Leinster and his son Muirchú was a disciple of Aed of Sletty in Leinster, establishing his own church in Connacht, presumably later, whence his son Colman returned to Moville, near the original family home in Ulster. Present with Adomnán and Aed of Sletty, at the synod of Birr, 697, which approved the *Cain Adomnain* (Kenney 246).

Muirchú's *de Patricii peritia* is extant in three MSS. (Bieler, *Codices Patriciani* Latini 18). The Book of Armagh (diplomatic edition, ed. John Gwynn, Dublin, 1913) begins with Muirchú, its first entry: a folio is missing, the text beginning in the middle of chapter 6, continuing to the end of chapter 25, followed by the words (7ro), 'Finit primus, incipit secundus liber', and continues with a separate work, beginning with a different list of contents, concluded (8vo) 'Finit. Amen', commonly described in modern literature as 'Muirchú Book II', though there are no MS. names and authors; words 'primus ... secundus liber' distinguish the first two books incorporated into the Book of Armagh, without asserting that they are the works of the same author. Armagh later (20ro), after a blank page, gives the contents table of Muirchú 1-28, with its preface, placing Muirchú's signature at the end of 28. The second MS. (Brussels, from the Irish monastery of Wurzburg) omits the contents table, begins with a preface to the Life, and gives chapters 1-28 only. The third, Novara MS. (thirteenth-century?) (*PRIA* 52 C, 1948-50, 179) without prefaces or contents tables, runs together the texts of the first two books in Armagh as a single work, without naming any author.

The Brussels MS. has not been printed. Hogan, *AB* 1, 1882, 545 and vita *S. Patricii* 1882, 17, print the Armagh MS., supplemented by the Brussels text of the chapters there missing, preface 1-6, 26-28, and numbers the chapters. Stokes, *VT*

269 prints the Armagh contents table and text, taking from Brussels only the missing opening words of chapter 6, omitting 1-5 and 26-28; Novara, and apparently Brussels, insert Armagh's closing chapter (2, 13) after 1, 11, on which it is plainly a gloss.

Though confusion will remain until the texts are collated and properly edited, it is plain that two distinct works are concerned. The preface, contents table, prologue, and chapters 1-28 bear the signature of Muirchú, and constitute a straightforward vita *Patricii*, unaware of any particular claims of Armagh. Armagh Book 2, omitted in Brussels, runs on to Book 1 in Novara, with its separate title page in Armagh, is a *de Miraculis Patricii*, that turns the human Victoricus of Patrick's *Confessio* and Muirchú to the 'angel Victor', as in Tírechán, and includes advanced Armagh claims. No source ascribes it to Muirchú; it might be a later work of his, bearing a similar relation to Muirchú's Life as Sulpicius Severus' *Dialogues* to his vita *Martini*, or it might be the work of a separate author. Linguistic analysis, not yet attempted, might indicate whether or not it is likely to be the work of the same author. But, whoever the author, it is a distinct work with a different purpose: Muirchú's own work knows nothing of the claims advanced by Tírechán; Armagh Book 2 is well acquainted with them.

MUNDUS, Munnu, *see* Fintan of Taghmon.

MUNGO, *see* Kentigern.

MUNNU, *see* Fintan of Taghmon.

NAILLE of Kinnawley, Ferm. (*H 23*) and Inver(naile) Don. (*G 87*) VI L, Jan. 27. I;I. Plummer, *MHH* 100 (Irish Life of XVII). (Confused with Natalis *ASH* 169). Son of *Angus m. Nadfraech of Munster* (+492). Established by Columba of Iona at Inver, successor (?) of Mo-Laisse (Lasrian) (+563) at Devenish (*M. Don.*), established a compact with Maedoc (of Ferns, *M. Don.*, of Breifne, *vita*). Ferns was probably founded in the 590s. The Life, largely concerned with his bell, whose handle survived as a relic, with his pupil Luan, and with tributes due from local rulers and lesser houses, is a fair specimen of the Irish language Lives that have escaped the extravaganzas of the storyteller, but have been engulfed in monastic poetic fancy.

NATALI(U)S of Kilmanagh, Kilkenny (*S 35*) V M/L, July 31. B?;I. Abbot, teacher of Senan, v. *Senan* 10 ff. (296 ff.); like many Munster saints, *son of Angus of Munster* (+492), *cf. ASH* 169 (where he is confused with Naille). His date and Roman name suggest that he came from Britain or Gaul, *cf.* Virgilius Maro.

NECTAN of Hartland, Devon (*SS 2624*) VI E? June 17. I?;B. *AB* 71, 1953, 397 (MS. Gothanus, hence Wm. of Worcester, Leland, *Coll.* 4, 153). *Eldest son of Brychan of Wales*, inspired by 'Antonium . . . et alios . . . patres Egipiacos' crossed the sea to Hartland, received two cows from the pious *Huddon* (of Huddisford), four leagues (east-north-east) from Hartland. Nectan was killed by robbers who stole his cows. His 24 brothers and sisters met annually at Hartland on December 31. For his Cornish dedications, *cf.* Doble, *Life of St. Nectan*, Cornish Saints, 25, *cf.* 48; *LBS* 4, 1-2; *AB* 71, 391; Breton dedications, *AB* 71, 392. He is sometimes confused with the south Cornish St. Neot (*SX 1867*), *BHL* 6052-6, king Alfred's ninth-century Glastonbury relative (so the contemporary account of Asser), whose relics, translated in the tenth century, named St. Neots, Huntingdonshire (*TL 1860*), whose Cornish dedications are listed Arnold-Forster, 109, *cf. LBS* 4, 6 ff.

NEMNIUS, *see* Nennius.

NENNIDIUS, *see* Ninnidh.

NENNIUS VII L/VIII E. B;B. Known only from his works. The *Historia Brittonum* exists in some 30 MSS. of which the most important are Harley 3859 (*H*), probably eleventh/twelfth; *Chartres* 98 (*Ch.*), probably ninth/tenth (incomplete); Cambridge University Library Ff.1.27 (*Ca.*), twelfth; *Vatican* Reginensis 964 (*V*), eleventh/twelfth. *Ch.* is headed 'Exberta (i.e. excerpta) fi(li)i Urbaoen' (usually identified with Urien Reged, +*c.*580), and perhaps bears the date *c.*800 (*RC* 15, 177). *H*, without heading, bears dates that are probably 829, with a copyist's date of 858 (ch. 4, '831 AD'); ch. 16, discussed *BBCS* 7, 1935, 384 ff., probably 829 (anno 4 Mermini regis [825-844] and 858); *Ca.* includes the contents table, and a double preface, by 'Nennius S. Elboti (+809, bishop of Bangor [archbishop of Gwynedd] *ACm*) discipulus' dated *858* equated with 'xx vero quarto Mervini regis (anno)', where 'xx' is probably a copyist's error, since Mervin reigned only 19 years, dying in 844, for an original 'anno 4 Mervini: = 829'. *V*, apparently dated 944 (*BBCS* 11, 1941, 45 ff.) is ascribed to 'Mark the Anchorite', presumably the copyist. Most other MSS. attribute the work to *Gildas*. The best edition is Mommsen's, *MGH AA* 13 (Chron. Min. 3, 1), 1894, 111 ff. The fullest is *MHB* 47. Faral, *La Légende Arthurienne*, Paris, 1929, prints *H* and *Ch.* in parallel (see also my edition and translation, *Arthurian Period Sources*, vol. 8). For emendations to Mommsen's variants from *V* (his *M*), *see BBCS* 11, 1941, 43. For discussion of the text, *see* Kenney 152, *LHEB* 47-8 and sources there cited. The modern discussion has concentrated almost entirely on the relation between the various MSS., with less emphasis on their content. All versions contain interpolations by later copyists.

The work is a collection of historical documents, not a history. Nennius' preface accurately states 'coacervavi omne quod inveni', 'I have made a heap of all I found'. The separate documents are slotted together in roughly chronological order, but retain their identity. The contents are preface, contents table, and the following:

I.	(chs. 1-4) *World Chronology*, based on Jerome-Eusebius, Prosper, Isidore and Bede, with discordant dates.
II.	(chs. 7-18) *Early British History*
	A. Topography, extracted from a lost *Notitia Britaniarum*, also used by Gildas, *de Excidio* 3. (chs. 7-9, with 67.)
	B. Foundation of Britain by Brutus the Trojan, descended alternatively from Noah or from Numa Pompilius and Anchises (chs. 7; 10-11; 17-18).
	C. Origins of the Picts and Scots, mainly from Irish tradition (chs. 12-15), with notes on the coming of Cunedda, of Patrick and of the Saxons (chs. 15-16).
III.	(chs. 19-30) *Roman Britain*, incorporating two conflicting traditions, in one of which the empire defends the province against Picts and Scots, while in the other the British nation patriotically defeats and expels the Romans (28). The main accounts are supplemented by evidence drawn from a variety of sources, from native tradition (Maximus' settlement in Gaul, 27); by references to Britain abstracted from a lost *Breviarium* (20-27), similar to, but not identical with Eutropius and Victor; extracts from *Annals* (e.g. 29), evidently including a chronicle using consular year datings that began in 375 (31, *cf.* 26); and from the deliberate use of inscriptions as historical evidence, e.g. 21, where

CIL XIII, the monument of Ti. Claudius Drusus at Mainz is assigned to the emperor Claudius, Moguntiacum (Mainz) is confused with Mogantia (Moganza), Lombardy, indicating a written source for the text of the inscription; 25, where an inscription of Constantine at Caernarvon is interpreted as his tombstone; and citations from Virgil, Prosper, Orosius, etc. Though Nennius here makes mistakes that seem ludicrous to better-informed ages, the method of his scholarship is far in advance of his European contemporaries and successors.

IV.   (chs. 31-56, with 66.) *The Fifth Century*

    A. A vita *Germani*, devolved, of British origin (chs. 32-35; 39; 47-48); *cf. SEBC* 112-115.

    B. A *Mabinogi*, story-teller's romance, of Embreis Guletic and the two dragons (chs. 40-42).

    C. The *Kentish Chronicle*, a straightforward account of the campaigns of the British Saxon wars fought in Kent in the period 440-460, rational, coherent, free of miracles, quite different in concept and treatment from other known accounts of the distant past composed in Britain or Gaul in the seventh and later centuries; the style and content are unlikely to have been composed later than the sixth century, and might possibly be late fifth (chs. 36-38; 43-46).

    D. The descent of Fernmail of Builth ('who now rules', *c.*750/800) from Vortigern (ch. 49).

    E. A vita *Patricii*, abridged from Muirchú and Tírechán (chs. 50-55).

    F. *Arthur's Battles*; the mistranslation of 'iscaut' (ysgwyd, shield) as 'ysgwydd', shoulder, argues a translation into Latin from a Welsh original, probably a poem of 12 stanzas, of which four concerned a single engagement on the river Dubglas (? Witham) in Lindsey, with a note that the mass migration of the English, and the movement of their dynasty from Germany to Britain, was a consequence of his victories (ch. 56).

    G. The *Chronographer* (the 'Computus'); elaborate calculations establishing the arrival of the English in Britain in 428 (ch. 66). A few notes inserted into these texts are mainly concerned with equating British and English names for the same places.

V.   (chs. 57-65) *The Sixth and Seventh centuries in the North.*

    A. Five groups of Anglian genealogies, in eight branches, six ending in the late seventh, two extended to *c.*800 (chs. 57-61).

    B. The *Northern Chronicle*, events *c.*550-690 (chs. 62-65), probably composed in the early or mid-eighth century, *cf.* Jackson, *Celt and Saxon* 21 ff.

VI.   Preserved in the Harleian recension, is omitted by Nennius himself on the advice of his magister, Beulanus presbyter, who considered the English records 'inutiles'.

VII.   (chs. 67-75 [68-87]) *Miscellanea.*

    A. The *Wonders* of Britain, Mona and Ireland, with additions and omissions in various versions.

    B. *National Characteristics*, the good and bad qualities of numerous peoples.

    C. Two *Poems*, an alphabetical encomium addressed by Nennius to Samuel, son of his master Beulan, and a three-line satire on an unnamed scribe.

D. *Colophons*; 'AD 858, xx vero iv Mervini regis Britonum haec historia a Nennio Britonum historiografo composita est' (=? 829, *cf.*
above), with additional scribal dates of 909 and 1166 on various
MSS.

VIII. Additional matter in the Harleian recension.

A. *Annales Cambriae* 453-954, whose exceptionally full entries of 814
and 816 suggest an initial version at that date.

B. Twenty-nine British genealogies, to the mid-ninth century, two of
them extended to 954.

It is possible that both these texts formed part of the material used by Nennius
in 829 and his editor in 858, and received additions in 954. Nennius' other works
include a joke alphabet devised in vaguely runic characters (*BBCS* 7, 1935, 381 and
fig. A [facsimile]) in the *Liber Commonei* (*BBCS* 5, 1930, 226 ff.), headed 'Nemnivus
istas reperit literas . . .'; perhaps a parallel text of part of Deuteronomy, in the Old
Latin and in the Greek text in Latin characters, *BBCS* 7, 1935, 389; and possibly
the whole of the *Liber Commonei*, largely concerned with weights and measures,
offered 'meo patre Commoneo . . . simul ac magistro' in 820. The text of this MS.
(Bodleian Auct. F. 4. 32) does not yet seem to be fully published. Nennius' Latin
has not yet attracted linguistic study; few of the documents he assembles, other
than the *Northern Chronicle*, have been separately examined; it is therefore not yet
possible to suggest how far these texts retain the language of their separate authors,
or how far the idiom of successive editors has adapted them. Casual observation
suggests that there may well be significant differences in the style and Latinity of
the several authors, complicated by the tendency of some editors to modernise
Welsh and English personal and place-names.

NENNIUS, *see* Ninnidh.

NEN(N)YO, *see* Ninian.

NEWLYNA, *see* Noyala.

NINIAN of Whithorn, Wigtown (*NX 4440*) V E, Sept. 16. B;P. *BHL* 6239-6241.
Bede *HE* **3**, 4 (1); vita, by Ailred of Rievaulx, Forbes, *Historians of Scotland* 5, 137
= Pinkerton, ed. Metcalfe, *Lives of the Scottish Saints*, 1, 9 (2). Hence *NLA* 2, 218
etc. Ringan, Trinian, etc., in place-names.

'Australes Picti . . . fidem . . . acceperant, praedicate . . . Nynia episcope . . . de
natione Brettonum, qui erat Romae regulariter fidem et mysteria veritatis edoctus,
cuius sedem episcopatus, sancti Martini episcopi nomine et ecclesia insignem, ubi
ipse etiam corpore una cum pluribus sanctis requiescitiam nunc Anglorum gens
obtinet. Qui locus . . . vulgo Ad Candidam Casam, eo quod ibi ecclesiam de lapide,
insolito Brettonibus more fecerit' (*1*). The time was 'multo ante (Columbae, 563)
tempore'. Patrick (*Epistola* 2; 15) twice describes the Picts as 'apostates', in the mid-
fifth century; some missionary had therefore converted some Picts, some of whom
had lapsed, considerably earlier, hardly later than the beginning of the century.
That missionary was evidently Ninian; if he were not, it would be necessary to
suppose two distinct major missions, one of which left no trace at all, the other
abundant trace.

Son of a *king*, in western Britain where two estuaries separate the Scoti and
Angli, i.e. Alclud (*2*, 1); studied 'pluribus annis' in Rome, on his way home visited
Martin of Tours, who lent him masons (cementarios) (*2*, 2), who built the stone
church at Witerna, which since Martin died (397), 'in eius honore studuit dedicare'

(*2*, 3). Cured the blindness of king Tuduvallus (the retention of the second syllable suggests an early source for the name) (*2*, 4); miraculously absolved a priest falsely accused of paternity by a pregnant girl (*2*, 5), possibly an adaptation of the mischances of Martin's successor Briccius (Greg. Tur. *HF* 2, 1 ff.). Converted the southern Picts (*2*, 6). Died and buried at Whithorn (*2*, 11); his miracles (*2*, 7-10; 12 ff.). A verse text of his *miracula* existed at York *c*.782/804 (Alcuin, *Ep.* 273, *MGH Epp.* 4, 431); it, or a similar text, is published (*MGH* Poetae Latini aevi Carolini 4, 943, *cf.* 452, *cf. Ant.* 14, 1940, 280, and references there cited), and may or may not be the 'liber de vita et miraculis eius, barbario scriptus' which Ailred 'barbarico . . . exaratam stilo, a sermone rustico . . . in lucem Latinae locutionis educam' (pref. *cf.* prolog.).

Ninian has some 70 sites in Scotland (*2*, [Forbes], p. 13; Forbes, *Kalendars*, 424), including Glasgow (v. *Kentigerni* 9) with probably Wooler, Northumberland (*NT 9928*), and Brougham, Cumb. (*NY 5328*). Arnold-Forster 2, 224; *cf.* also *Cumb. West Trans.*, 36, 1936 (Bampton). An early stone church that could well be Ninian's has been excavated at Whithorn (*Trans. Dumfries* 27, 1950; 34, 1957) and has occasioned an extensive literature, animated and controversial, largely concerned with expressions of belief or disbelief in the statements of Bede and Ailred. Patrick and Bede are the authorities for the approximate date; it is likely that a British ecclesiastic returning from Rome visited Tours, whether or not Ailred had authority for his statement. The date he gives coincides with the visit to Britain of Martin's pupil Victricius, the advocate both of monasticism and of preaching to barbarians, then novelties. Whithorn, an episcopal see in Bede's time, can hardly have been so in *c*.400; Ninian may have been bishop of Carlisle. The monastery is prominent in late fifth-century tradition, *cf.* **M**aucennus and **R**osnat. Irish tradition confused him with Mo-Nenn. **K**entigern. **V**olocus.

NINNIDH of Inishmacsaint, Lough Erne, Ferm. (*H 15*) VI E, Jan. 18. I;I. *ASH* 111. Of the Ui Neill (Cenel Endae, *M. Don.*; Laeguri, *M. Oeng.*). Pupil of **B**rigit (+525), gave her the viaticum. Pupil of **F**innian of Clonard, *Cat.* 5, v. *Fin. C.* 19 (Naynnid Lamderc), teacher of **C**iaran of Clonmacnoise, v. *Ciar. C.* 20, variant (Nynnidius); Ninnidius, Nennius, v. *Brigit*. The martyrologies know several other saints named Ninnio.

NINNOCA VI M, June 4. B;A. *BHL* 6242. *Cart. Quimperlé* 55. *AG* 361. *Daughter* of Brochan (**B**rychan) and Meneduc *Daughter of king Constantine*. Baptised by *Columba of Iona* in the name of Ninnoc Guenngustle. *Taught by* bishop **G**ermanus (of Auxerre; in central Wales) sent *from* Ireland *by* St. Patrick (i.e. who sent Patrick to Ireland). Crossed to the Vannetais with bishops Morhed and Gurgallonus and Ilfin (Elfin) Gur Kentelua (commander of the bodyguard), husband of Guennargant, relative of Meneduc. Given Ploemeur (*J 6*) near L'Orient, by **W**aroc. Her cult, *LBS* 4, 19, in the Vannetais.

NOCHATH, *see* Rochath.

NONN (Nonita) VI E. B;B. Mother of **D**avid, v. *David* 2 ff., hence v. *Gildae* (CL) 4 etc., with a number of sites in southern Wales, Cornwall, and Brittany, *LBS* 4, 23 ff., Arnold-Forster 2, 175.

NOTHELM, priest of London, archbishop of Canterbury, 735-739. E;E. Informant of Bede, *HE* dedication, preface.

NOYALA of Newlyn, Co. (*SW 42*) and Noyal-Pontivy, Morbihan VI? July 6.

B;A. Known only from inscriptions formerly painted in her churches, reproduced *LBS* 4, 11; came from Britain to Morbihan, beheaded by the tyrant Nezin.

OFFA VIII E. E;Rome. Son of Sigehere, king of Essex, and of Osgytha. Abdicated 709, with king Coenred of Mercia, became a monk in Rome, Bede *HE* 5, 19. Inherited extensive estates in Mercia, presumably from his mother Osgytha.

OFTFOR VII L. E;E. Bede *HE* 4, 23. Pupil of Hilda, sent to Rome by Theodore, bishop of the Hwicce 'multo tempore' from *c*.691 under king Osric (of the Hwicce).

OMER (Audomarus) of Therouanne +*c*.670, Sept. 9. Gaul;Gaul. *BHL* 763-776. *MGH SRM* 5, 753. Monk of Luxeuil, bishop of Therouanne, teacher of Winnoc. Named St. Omer.

OSGYTHA VII L, Oct. 7. E;E. The vitae summarised *DCB*, *cf*. Finberg, *Early Charters of the West Midlands*, 181 ff. A Mercian, daughter of Frithewaldus, *subregulus* of Surrey, who founded Chertsey with Erconwald, bishop of London, 674-693, Birch *CS* 33, 34, 39. With Modwenna at Burton-on-Trent and at 'Streveshal' (? Streneshalch, Whitby; the early spellings of Stramshall, Staffs. *DEPN*, do not suggest 'Streveshal'). Wife of Sigehere, king of Essex, *c*.663-683; founded St. Osyth (*TM 1113*) near Clacton, Essex; mother of Offa.

OUDOCEUS of Llandaff, Cardiff (*ST 1578*) VI L/VII E, July 2. B;B. *BHL* 6408-9, vita *LL* 130. *Son of Budic son of Cybr Dan(iel?), pupil of Teilo*, *his uncle*, founded Llan Einiaun (Llan Oudocui, Llandogo, Mon., *SO 5204*), bishop of *Llandaff*, vita. Bishop of Theodoric (son of Budic) and of his son Mouricus, *LL* charter memoranda, *passim*, *cf*. index. 'Vir bonus et iustus et totius Britanniae Historiographus *Gildas* sapiens', while living as a hermit in Echni, stole the timber Oudoceus had cut for Llan Einiaun, vita.

OUEN (Audoen, Dado) of Rebais, east of Paris +686, Aug. 24. Gaul;Gaul. *BHL* 750-762. *MGH SRM* 5, 553. Son of a Frankish noble; in infancy blessed by Columban at his father's villa at Ussy on the Marne, with his brothers, Jonas, v. *Columban* 1, 26. Referendarius of king Dagobert I. With his brothers founded Rebais *c*.635; bishop of Rouen (640-686). His pupil Philibert (+684), after study at Luxeuil and Bobbio, founded Jumièges (on the Seine below Rouen), *c*.655, and Noirmoutier in the Loire estuary, dedicating an altar to Columban and enrolling Irish men among his monks. The vita was written within a few years of his death.

PADARN, *see* Paternus.

PALLADIUS V E, July 6. Italian?;B.I. *DCB*. *BHL* 6417. Prosper, *Chron*. 429 (1); 431 (2); *Contra Collatorem* (name omitted) 21 (*PL* 51, 271) (3); Muirchú 7-8 (4), and subsequent Patrician literature, *passim*.

Agricola Pelagianus, Severiani episcopi Pelagiani filius, ecclesias Britanniae dogmatis sui insinuatione corrupit, sed ad actionem Palladii diaconi papa Caelestinus (+432) Germanum Autisiodorensem episcopum vice sua mittit, ut deturbatis haereticis Britannos ad catholicam fidem dirigat (*1*); Ad Scotos in Christum credentes ordinatur a papa Caelestino Palladius, et primus episcopus mittitur (with MS. variant 'moritur' for 'mittitur', conceivably resting on an original 'Mittitur et moritur') (*2*); Coelestinus . . . ordinato Scotis episcopo, dum Romanam insulam studet servare catholicam, fecit etiam barbaram Christianam (*3*); Palladius archidiaconus pape Caelestini . . . ordinatus et missus fuerat ad hanc insolam . . . Neque hii fieri et inmites homines facile receperunt doctrinam eius, neque et ipse longum voluit transegere tempus in terra non sua (Novara MS. 'in cassum longum' for 'in terra non sua'); sed reversus ad eum qui missit illum. Revertente vero eo hinc et primo mari transito coeptoque terrarum itenere in Britonum (MS. variant 'Pictorum') finibus vita functus (4).

The deacon whose 'actio' caused Celestine to send Germanus to Britain was almost certainly a principal deacon of Rome, very possibly archdeacon. He was therefore an ecclesiastic of great importance in Italy; the next archdeacon was Leo, afterwards Pope Leo the Great, apparently appointed before the death of Celestine (Gennadius *DVI* 62, Cassian's *de Incarnatione* prompted by archdeacon Leo). The consecration of a senior churchman of Rome to a barbarian border episcopate was an extraordinary and unprecedented appointment, necessarily a matter of high importance to the whole western church; Prosper (*3*) explains the motivation, primarily to keep Britain Catholic, by extirpating Pelagianism, secondarily to convert Ireland. It is likely that the 'Scoti credentes', already converted, will have been Irish settlers in Britain, strongest in Demetia, with perhaps some of their relatives in southern Ireland. The appointment established a powerful orthodox champion among the heretical British bishops, but its terms of reference also entailed missionary work among the Irish. Prosper's claim of success, though contemporary, is clearly an untruthful exaggeration, acceptable in Italy; Muirchú's story of failure is accurate. Had he been alive when Prosper published the *Contra Collatorem*, c.435, it is scarcely probable that his name would have been omitted; Muirchú's statement of an early death is therefore probable. Leo was very possibly his successor, c.431/2, either because he had left Rome or because he was dead.

Later Irish tradition equated him with Torannan of Sligo (*cf.* Ternan of Leinster) and the Picts (*M. Oeng.* etc.) and with 'Old Patrick', placed at an unspecified date before 432 (Tírechán 56), associating him with a few Leinster sites; Pictish tradition (*Brev. Ab.* PE 24, etc.) brought him to the Mearns and killed him at Fordun, evidently building on the equation with Ternan; hence MS. variant (*4*) 'Pictorum'. The majority manuscripts' tradition is plainly earlier, that died in (southern) Britain, on the normal route to Europe. Modern suggestions that he was a Gaul, based on Sidonius' rhetorical 'Palladiorum stirps' (*Ep.* 7, 9) are hagiographical fancies (*cf.* Grosjean, *AB* 63, 1945, 76). The probable origin of a Roman deacon is Italian.

PANDIANA VI L/VII E? Aug. 21. I;E. Irishwoman at Eltisley, Cambs. (*TL 2759*), between Cambridge and St. Neots.

PATERNUS of Avranches +c.560, April 15 (16). Gaul;Gaul.A. *BHL* 6477. Vita, by Fortunatus (contemporary) *MGH AA* 4, 2, 33. Native of Poitiers, founded St. Pair, near Granville, Cotentin, and many monasteries in the dioceses of Coutances, Bayeux, Le Mans, Avranches, Rennes and Britannia, consecrated bishop of Avranches at the age of 70, died 13 years later. As bishop he attended the council of Paris c.557 (with Samson and Conotigirnus [? Kentigern] Mansi 9, 743). He is perhaps also Paternus of Fortunatus, *Carmina* 3, 25; 7, 23. On the festival and monastic site, *cf. AB* 67, 1949, 385 ff.

PATERNUS of Llanbadarn Fawr, Card. (*SN 6080*) VI M/L, April 15. A;B. *BHL* 6480-1; *VSB* 252 (1); *AG* 244 (2), Lectiones of Vannes, *AB* 67, 1949, 398 (3). Born in Armorica, son of Petranus (Petrwn, *ByS* 21) and Guean (Julitte Guen *2*). Soon after his birth, his father became a monk and emigrated to Ireland, leaving him with his mother. Accompanied 'caterva sanctorum' who went from Brittany to Britain under Ketinlau, Catman (Cadfan) and Titechon, with 847 monks. Founded the monastery of 'Mauritana' (? Maritima Ecclesia). Visited his father in Ireland,

and pacified two kings. Returned to Britain, to Maritima Ecclesia, founded monasteries throughout Ceredigion, placing over them Samson, Guinnius, Guppir, and Nimannauu, who came from Brittany. Maelgwn, in the course of a campaign against the southern British, accused him of stealing his treasure, was blinded, cured and gave the site of Llanbadarn and Aberystwyth. Accompanied David and Teilo to Jerusalem (so also v. *David* 44; v. *Teilo* 9 [*LL* 103]), where the Patriarch consecrated them; on their return they divided Britain into three episcopates. 'Tirannus regiones altrinsecus, Arthur nomine' tried to seize his tunic, but was swallowed up by the earth, and forgiven, accepting Paternus as his patron. Caradauc Vreichvras of Britain annexed Armorica, and took Paternus with him to Vannes, where he built a monastery. Summoned to attend Samson, granted the independence of Vannes from tribute to Samson's episcopacy. Attended an Armorican synod 'in uno monte' (? Menex Bre), harassed by false brethren, confirmed unit as the seventh of the principal saints of Armorica. Abandoned Armorica, died among the Franks. Third named of the Armorican saints who accompanied Samson and Malo to Childebert *c*.556/7.

There is nothing to suggest that the tradition of Llanbadarn had ever heard of the fifth-century Paternus of Vannes, known only from a Council signature; but there is confusion with Paternus of Avranches, whose mother was named Julitta, and who was certainly with Samson in Paris, *c*.557, when his close friend Albinus of Angers accompanied Tudwal to Paris. It is possible that Paternus of Avranches' foundations in 'Britannia' included a house at Vannes; not impossible that an Armorican monk of Paternus of Avranches accompanied Cadfan to Wales, and used his teacher's name for his foundations. But the name is common, and an Armorican Paternus who moved to Wales is quite possible. For his Welsh sites, *LBS* 4, 49-50; Breton sites, Doble, *St. Patern* (Cornish Saints 43); Cornish Petherwins, by Launceston, may relate to Paternus rex Cornubie, father of St. Constantine, *Brev. Ab.* PH 67; vita *Thuriau*, cited Doble 41. Malo.

PATERNUS of Vannes V M/L. Consecrated 461/490 (? *c*.465), Mansi 7, 951; his successor was in office in 511, Mansi 8, 347.

PATRICK +459, March 17. B;I. *BHL* 6492-6518. *Codices Patriciani Latini* (*CPL*) L. Bieler (Dublin, 1942, *cf. AB* 63, 1945, 242 ff.) (1-32). Plummer, *MHH* 59-61; 159-172; 291-2. The principal texts are reproduced in the *Book of Armagh*, diplomatic edition J. Gwynn (Dublin, 1913; facsimile of Patrician documents, E. Gwynn, Dublin, 1937), in W. Stokes, *Tripartite Life* (*VT*), 1887, London (Rolls Series), *cf. Bethu Phátraic*, ed. K. Mulchrone, Dublin, 1939; Colgan, *TT*. The principal modern studies are J. B. Bury, *St. Patrick*, London, 1905; Eoin MacNeill, *St. Patrick*, ed. J. Ryan, Dublin, 1964; and the Irish writers who maintain the existence of two Patricks, or of a 'late Patrick', notably T. F. O'Rahilly, *The Two Patricks*, Dublin, 1942 (given as a lecture in 1942); James Carney, *Patrick and the Kings*, in his *Studies in Irish Literature and History*, Dublin, 1955, 324 ff. (given as a lecture in 1949). D. Binchy, *Patrick and his Biographers*, in *Studia Hibernica*, 2, 1962, 7-173, with the references there given, *cf.* below, vol. 6 pp. 111 ff., with many other books and periodical articles, notably in *AB*.

The sources consist of those which incorporate the claims advanced on behalf of the see of Armagh in or after the later seventh century; and those which do not. The texts free of Armagh claims are Patrick's own works, the *Confessio* (1) and *Epistola ad Coroticum* (2) (*CPL* 1-2, ed. L. Bieler, Dublin, 1952; ed. N. J. D. White, *Libri S. Patricii*, 1905 [*PRIA* 25 C7]; *VT* 2, 357; 375; and ed. L. Mac Philibin, *Mise Padraig*, F.A.S., Dublin, 1960); with a parallel text translation into modern Irish

HS 2, 296; Muirchú (Book I), *CPL* 18; *AB* 1, 1882, 545; *VT* 2, *PRIA* 52 C, 1948/
50, 179 (Novara MS.) (3); written in the second half of the seventh century.
The extending claims of Armagh begin with Tírechán (*CPL* 17; *AB* 2, 1883, 35;
VT 2, 302) (4); 'Muirchú Book II' (*CPL* 18, etc.) (5), with its appended notes, *AB*
584 (6); all written at, or soon after, the end of the seventh century; and the
Additamenta to Tírechán (*CPL* 19; *AB* 2, 1883, 213; *VT* 2, 334) (7), eighth century,
whence the *Book of the Angel*, Probus, etc. The *Hymn of Secundinus* (*CPL* 16; *TT* 211;
HS 2, 324) (8) might be late fifth-century or later. None of the synods and canons
(*HS* 2, 328 ff.) (of which *CPL* 4 and 5, Synodus I and Armagh Canon [referring to
'cathedra archiepiscopi Hibernensium, id est Patricii', at Airdmacha] are referred
to in *CPL* and earlier writers to the fifth century) can be anything like as early as
Patrick's time. K. Hughes' dating of Synodus I to the sixth century rests on the
assumption that 'more Romano capilli tonsi' (6) refers to a close-cropped haircut
rather than a tonsure, and that pagan practices had been eliminated from Ireland
by the seventh century (*CEIS* 44 ff.). Almost the whole of the rest of the literature
is eighth-century or later, coloured or inspired by Tírechán and his successors, with
the possible exception of Synodus II (*CPL* 6), which may be late seventh. The Life
excerpted by Colgan as his vita secunda, *TT*, apparently still unpublished, is
probably not early in its present form, but does seem to be exceptionally free of
Armagh influence, and may therefore embody traditions earlier than the devices of
Tírechán and his successors.

'Patrem habui Calpornium (i.e. Calpurnium) diaconum, filium quondam Potiti
presbyteri, qui fuit vica Bannavem Taberniae villulam enim prope habuit, ubi ego
capturam dedi; annorum eram tunc fere xvi' (*1*, 1); 'qui et Sochet vocabatur' (*3*, 1;
also Imigonus) (Mavonius; Magonus [*4*] and Contice [Coirtice] [*3*] prolog., Brussels
MS.); Bannauem Thaburniae, chaut procul a mari nostro, quem vicum . . . conper-
imus esse Ventre (Nentre), matre . . . Concessa nomine (*3*, 1). In captivity, 'pecora
pascebam' (*1*, 16), for six years, escaped by a 200-mile journey overland, to a ship
(*1*, 17). Made land after a three-day journey, journeyed 28 days 'per desertum'
(*1*,19). 'Post paucos annos in Brittaniis eram', urged by his parents never to leave
home again after his past troubles, but dreamt of 'virum venientem quasi de
Hiberione, cui nomen Victoric(i)us', with letters that recalled the voices of those
who lived 'iuxta silvam Focluti quae est prope mare occidentale' urging him to join
them. The Lord fulfilled their request 'post plurimos annos' (*1*, 23); then aged 30,
he set out for Rome (*3*, 4). Later, he longed 'usque ad Gallias visitare fratres et ut
viderem faciem sanctorum Domini mei' (*1*, 43), suggesting old acquaintances. 'Non
parva tempore demoratus' with Germanus of Auxerre (*3*, 5) *for 30 or 40 years*,
constantly visited in dreams by 'ille antiquitus amicus valde fidelis Victoricus' (*3*,
7); 'istum (Patricium) . . . Gallia nutrivit, tenet ossa Scottia felix', poem of Cellanus,
abbot of Peronne 675-706, correspondent of Aldhelm, *Ériu* 5, 1911, 110.

'Timorem Dei habui ducem iteneris mei per Gallias atque Italiam, etiam in
insolis quae sunt in mari Terreno' (i.e. Lerins) (*6*, *AB*, 585, *VT* 301, *Dicta Patricii*,
possibly genuine) 'Coeptum ingreditur iter ad opus in quod ollim preparatus fuerat,
. . . et missit Germanus seniorem cum illo, hoc est Segitium prespiterum' (*3*, 8). He
had not yet been consecrated by Germanus, because Pope Celestine had sent
Palladius to Ireland (*3*, 8). At 'Abmoria' (perhaps Avriolles, *mansio* north of Auxerre,
Grosjean, *AB* 63, 1945, 75, *cf.* 75, 1957, 166) heard of Palladius' death from his
returning disciples, Augustinus and Benedictus; *consecrated* (ordained?) by
bishop Amathor(ex) 'in propinquo loco habitantem' (Amator, predecessor of Germanus, +418); came to Brittanias with Auxilius, Iserninus and others (*3*, 8). In
Britain, 'multi hanc legationem prohibebant, etiam inter se ipsos pos tergum meum

narrabant et dicebant "Iste quare se mittit in periculo inter hostes qui Deum non noverunt?", non ut causa malitiae, sed ... propter rusticitatem meam' (*1*, 46); against the opposition of 'aliquantis de senioribus meis' (*1*, 37), his great friend 'mihi ipse ore suo dixerat'. 'Ecce dandus es tu ad gradum episcopatus' (*1*, 32). 'Patricius peccator indoctus scilicet Hiberione constitutus, episcopum me esse fateor' (*2*, 1).

Patrick's statements on his consecration are not in narrative order; he is emphatic that he resolved to go to Ireland long before he actually did so; that his appointment aroused considerable opposition among British clerics, but that one of them formally proposed his consecration, and that he was consecrated bishop to Ireland. The consecration was evidently endorsed, after controversy, by a British synod. Muirchú adds that he studied at Auxerre, and that Germanus sent him, still a priest, before Celestine sent Palladius (431), 'to begin the journey to the long prepared work'; the project was resumed, with different companions, on Palladius' speedy death. Celestine had established a new bishopric, appointing his deacon in an unsuccessful attempt to curb the British Pelagians. Patrick, intent only on an Irish mission, not on reforming British heresies, was accepted after debate by the British clergy as Palladius' successor. His arrival in Ireland is dated by *Annals*, and all sources, to 432.

Patrick wrote the *Confessio* when he was about forty-five or fifty years old (*1*, 27; a childhood sin committed when he was about fifteen, confessed before he was a deacon, was brought up against him after 30 years). He had then been a considerable time in Ireland; he had converted 'populi multi' (*1*, 38), established 'clerici ubique' (*1*, 38; 40), been imprisoned once for a fortnight (*1*, 52), once for two months (*1*, 21; 37), made 'filii Scottorum et filiae regulorum monachi et virgines Christi' (*1*, 41), enrolled slave girls as nuns (*1*, 42), paid 'regibus' the 'mercedem filiis ipsorum qui mecum ambulant' as well as 'praemia' (*1*, 52), and paid out as much as the price of 15 men to 'illis qui iudicabant per omnes regiones quos ego frequentius visitabam' (*1*, 53), penetrating 'ad exteras partes, ubi nemo ultra erat et ubi numquam aliquis pervenerat qui baptizaret aut clericos ordinaret aut populum consummaret' (*1*, 51).

In Muirchú's account he coasted Ireland northwards to settle at 'Orreum Patricii' (Sabhall Phadraig, Saul, Downpatrick, *J 54*), and set out at once to seek his former master Miliucc, near Slemish (Antrim, *D 20*) among the Cruidneni (Dal Araide), who committed suicide on his approach (*3*, 10-11). He then set out to celebrate his *first* Irish Easter at Tara (Meath, *N 95*) 'quae erat caput Scotorum', the residence of Loegaire, son of Niall, 'imperator barbarorum'; the 'magi' and 'aurispices' and 'incantatores', headed by Lothroch (qui et Lochru) and Lucetmael (qui et Ronal), who denounced his 'doctrina molesta' from overseas as 'regna subversurum', his followers as 'turbas seductorum', were overcome in a contest of magic; Patrick was aided by 'puer Bineus' (Beninnus) and finding support from Ercc filius Dego of Slane, and Feic of Sletty, 'adoliscens poeta', pupil of 'poeta optimus', Dubthach Maccu Lugir (3, 9; 12-19). Among the Ulaid, Patrick converted the tyrannous Mac Cuil, who became bishop of Man (*3*, 22), forbade Sunday work on rath construction near Saul (*3*, 23), and was given the site of Armagh (*H 84*; near the ancient capital of Emain, Navan) by Daire (*3*, 24).

The purport of the *Confessio* is Patrick's refusal to abandon his work and come to Britain (*1*, 43), after a 'defensio' had already been held in Britain in his absence, and his old friend had turned against him (*1*, 32). The implication is that a second British synod had claimed authority over him, called him to account and summoned him to Britain. Patrick's statement that he would personally like to visit not only

Britain, but also to see the brethren in Gaul (*1*, 43) suggests a warning that he
might appeal over the heads of the British clergy. The 'probatio Patricii' by Pope
Leo (440-461) entered in *Annals* 440, with no understanding or explanation, means
that during his pontificate Leo 'approved' Patrick, thereby disapproving his critics.
Since much of Leo's energy was directed to lessening the authority of metropolitans
and provincials, and asserting the direct authority of Rome over individual sees,
the probable context is a papal decree freeing Patrick and his Irish converts from
dependence on the British church, and substituting the immediate supremacy of
Rome. The notices of Muirchú are limited to the north-east of Ireland.

The *Letter to Coroticus* (Coirthech rex Aloo [Alclud], Muirchú, contents table 28)
followed a previous letter delivered by 'sancto presbytero quem ego ex infantia
docui' (*2*, 3) and was therefore written some twenty years or more after Patrick
reached Ireland, in the 450s, not long before his death. It protested against a British
raid that had killed some 'crismati neophyti in veste candidi' (*2*, 3) and carried
over others who were sold as slaves to the 'Scotti atque Picti apostatae' (*2*, 2; 12;
15). Raiders from the Clyde troubled north-eastern Ireland; the Picts to whom they
sold their booty lived on their borders in northern Britain, and so probably did the
Scotti, either Dal Riada settlers, whose king Fergus transferred his dynastic seat to
Britain half a century later, or other settlers elsewhere. Coroticus died soon after,
after listening to a minstrel (*3*, 28).

Died 459, *Annals* etc., *cf.* below. For two centuries Patrick 'was not entirely
forgotten, but . . . his memory had slipped into the background of old and far-off
thing' (Kenney 324). He frequently refers to priests whom he had ordained, but
says nothing of other bishops, and Muirchú does not credit him with consecrating
any in Ireland. His death therefore left a problem of succession which only Rome
could resolve. A strong southern Irish tradition, attached to Ailbe, Ciaran of Saigir,
Declan, Enda, and Ibar, and to Docco and Kebi, assigns the creation of four
southern sees to Pope Hilary, Leo's successor, 461-7, with the admission of British
supremacy over at least the monasteries of central Ireland. Muirchú had heard of
late fifth-century bishops at Sletty in Leinster, and Slane near Tara, but did not
attribute the establishment of their sees to Patrick. The *Annals* record half-a-dozen
late fifth-century northern bishops, several of whom, including the most prominent,
Mel, were British, and also lists successors of Patrick at Armagh, indifferently
described as abbots or bishops. Such bishops can only have been consecrated on
the authority of the British church or of Rome. The traditions of Enda, Kebi, and
Mocteus' disciple Fintan concern the rejection of British authority, thanks to a
delegation sent to Rome, that included Erlatheus, probably of Armagh, late in the
fifth century. The bishop of Armagh is named first in Pope John IV's letter of 640
to the Irish clergy (Bede *HE* **2**, 19), and was therefore then regarded by the papacy
as the senior bishop in Ireland. Mocteus, who called himself Patrick's disciple,
according to Adomnán and the *Annals*, may well have asserted thereby the episcopal
primacy of Patrick's successors at Armagh over north-eastern Ireland, in opposition
to British claims. Patrick is not again mentioned in any context outside the later
Armagh tradition until the beginnings of the Easter controversy early in the seventh
century, save for a tradition, *Bethu Phátraic VT* 60, that Columba of Iona (+597)
and Colman m. Lenin (+606) wrote on Patrick's miracles. A colophon in the Book
of Durrow (App. *T* Gospel Books) may refer to Patrick, and may be dated before
or after the development of the Easter controversy. More certain references re-
appear in southern and central Ireland from the beginning of the Easter controversy.
The letter of Cummian (Cuimine, ? of Durrow), *c.*633, lists among the known Easter
cycles that brought to Ireland by Patrick, 'noster papa'. Ultan of Ardbraccan,

Meath (*N 86*), +655, wrote a 'scripta Patricii', (*4*, 1; hence probably the prologue
added to Muirchú in the Brussels MS. *3*, p. 548 *AB*) and 'nutrivit' Tírechán (*4*,
18) perhaps a Munsterman. Muirchú himself wrote 'dictante Aiduo Slebtiensis'
(**A**ed of Sletty in Leinster, active *c.*670-700) (*3*, contents table 28, p. 545; 548 *AB*;
269; 271 *VT*).

None of these texts claim any primacy for Patrick; he is one saint among many,
a bishop located by Muirchú in Down. The first wider claim 'Patricii, ut ita dicam,
totius Hiberniae episcopi doctorisque egregii' is advanced in the story of 'Moneisan
Saxonissa' (*3*, 26, *cf.* contents table), added to the original text of Muirchú (Bieler
218), perhaps soon after its original publication; even Patrick's connection with
Armagh (*3*, 24) appears to be a similar addition (Bieler 217). The tales go together,
since 'Moneisa' is probably a variant of Mo-Ninna (**D**arerca).

Before the middle of the seventh century, Patrick was remembered as a northern
bishop, the earliest such bishop known to have received papal approval, accepted
as patron by those who rejected British claims. His tradition was revived in the
south and centre in the middle of the century by the advocates of conformity with
Rome. Conformity required not only acceptance of a Roman Easter and a Roman
tonsure, but the adoption of a continental episcopal hierarchy, with a metropolitan.
The first such metropolitan claim was advanced by Muirchú's father, **C**ogitosus, on
behalf of **B**rigit's bishop, **C**onlaed of Kildare, styled 'archiepiscopus Hibernensium
episcoporum'. The claim found no support, and is not echoed elsewhere; though
high claims might have gained credence for Brigit, had she been a man, her chaplain
and his successors were not acceptable in the south or the north. The south, where
a number of principal abbots were also bishops of regional kingdoms, required a
nominal metropolitan whose actual authority need not intrude; the north still
rejected conformity and had no need of a metropolitan. Aed, Muirchú's patron, is
the first southern abbot known to have placed his house under the patronage of the
bishop of Armagh, regarded as Patrick's successors. The southern advocates of
conformity with Rome sought northern support by acknowledging the authority of
the senior northern see, whose distance protected them against unwelcome practical
interference. The promise of acknowledged metropolitan supremacy was an induce-
ment to Armagh to accept conformity with Rome, and thereby to give a lead to the
north.

The difficulty was that the vast majority of Irish Christian communities knew
well that they originated from monastic founders of the sixth century, or occasionally
late fifth, who had nothing to do with Patrick. The difficulty was overcome by the
remarkable work of Tírechán, whose adult activity lay within the limits *c.*650-*c.*710,
and who probably wrote nearer to 700 than to 650. Though neither Patrick nor
Muirchú makes any reference to the consecration of bishops in Ireland, Tírechán
asserted that he consecrated 450 bishops (*4*, 6) and named some fifty. He admitted
that this claim was not accepted by his contemporaries 'quia video dissertores et
archiclocos et milites Hiberniae quod odio habent paruchiam Patricii' and urged
the bishop of Armagh to press his claim, for 'if the heir of Patrick should claim his
paruchia, he would be able to reduce almost the whole island to his parish . . . for
all the primitive churches of Ireland are his'; 'si quaereret heres Patricii paruchiam
illius, potest pene totam insolam sibi reddere in paruchiam, quia . . . ipsius sunt
omnes primitivae ecclesiae Hiberniae' (*4*, 18). He surveys the seventh-century Irish
church in geographical order. His method is simple; almost all old-fashioned
churches that do not depend on known and major monastic founders are made
direct foundations of Patrick; founders believed to have lived before *c.*540, out of
living memory, are made disciples of Patrick, or are visited by him and authorised

by his episcopal authority; later founders were foretold by Patrick, or those who baptised or taught them are made his disciples.

Tírechán's claims were adopted by the church of Armagh, and found growing acceptance during the eighth and ninth centuries, after the north had accepted conformity with Rome; and the large corpus of Patrician literature elaborates his theme. The honorary primacy of Armagh matched the requirements of European ecclesiastical hierarchical organisation without subjecting the monasteries to unwelcome episcopal control. Tírechán and his colleagues provided the Irish church with an organisation as appropriate to its needs as that which Theodore provided for the English church. His text gives a full and accurate account of the traditions entertained about their original by virtually all Irish Christian churches outside the main monastic paruchiae in the later seventh century; all that is invented is the connection between their founders and Patrick. The traditions are themselves often not much more than a century old when he recorded them, only just outside the threshold of living memory; and in the north, it is in fact likely that those who are independently dated to the fifth century were either converts of Patrick or their disciples. Later, Tírechán's concepts were intruded into the Saints' Lives. Patrick appears in very many Lives, often out of due time, always adventitiously; he never plays an integral role and does not take the saint as his pupil or companion at an establishment of his own for a period of time; instead he visits the saint, or meets him by chance, blesses him, baptises him or his teacher or baptiser, or foretells his future greatness; and often, particularly in the south, the saint politely yields primacy to Patrick, either willingly or grudgingly, at the bidding of an angel, or else establishes a demarcation of rights.

A by-product of Tírechán's work was a troublesome confusion of dates. The figures available to Muirchú, presumably derived from Ultan, were that Patrick was 30 when he visited his parents in Britain (*3*, 4), an interpretation of the *Confessio*, captured at 16, enslaved six years, visited Britain 'post paucos annos' (*1*, 1; 17; 23). He was therefore then about thirty. It was then 'plurimos annos' (*Confessio* 1, 23) before he came to Ireland; Muirchú (*3*, 6) supplied the arbitary figure 30 (MS. variant 40) to 'plurimos', making him 60 when he landed. To this age was added a figure discovered by Constans (*c*.670) 'in Gallis' that he 'taught for 60 years', perhaps originally that he lived for 60 years and taught (lx vixit et docuit) (*6*); the figures are corrupted in the text; read, supplying the figures from the *Confessio* 'xv (MS. xx, for xvi) captus est, v. (MS. xv, for vi) servivit, xl legit, lx (MS. lxi) docuit; tota vero aetas eius cxx (MS. cxi)'. The overall age of 120 is repeated in 'Muirchú II' (*5*, 6) and Tírechán (*4*, 53) and numerous other texts, with varying corruptions in the detail figures that make up the total, and is compared with Moses by Tírechán. The age of 120 years posed a problem to the early *Annals*; they produced two solutions, presumably by different scholars; 120 was subtracted from the death date of *c*.457/460 to give birth date of *c*.337/340; and 60 (or variants of 62, 65, and the like) were added to Patrick's accepted date of arrival, 432, to give an additional death date in the 490s: *AI* combines the traditions by giving a death date 459/464, entered under 496. Two death dates created a further problem, and suggested two Patricks. The first to distinguish them was the author of the penultimate note appended to Tírechán (*4*, 53), who identified the first Patrick with Palladius, 'Patricius secundus' with Patrick, the author of the *Confessio*, 'ab angelo Dei, Victor nomine et a Celestino papa mititur', who taught 60 years in Ireland after 432. This is the two-Patrick theory, revived in modern times in Ireland, but not outside, with discordant views on which Patrick was which at what date. The problem which these theories seek to explain does not exist unless it is believed that Patrick attained the Mosaic age of 120.

Ailbe, Attracta, Breaca, Cuimine of Durrow, **Darerca, Declan, Enda, Fingar, Finnian** of Clonard, **Foirtchernn, Germanus** of Paris, **Ibar, Lasrian** of Leighlin, **Lomman, Mac Tail, Mo-Choe, Mocteus, Ninnoca, Senan, Winwaloe,** etc.

PAUL, abbot of Llancarfan, VI L. B;B.*LL* index.

PAUL AURELIAN VI M, March 12. B;A. *BHL* 6585-7. vita (dated 884 [ch. 1], from an older original, by Wrdisten, monk of Landevennec under abbot Wrmonoc, author of the vita *Winwaloe*) *AB* 1, 1882, 209 = *RC* 5, 1881-3, 417. (1); *AG* 191 (2).

Son of *comes* Perphirius of Penychen, in the region of Brehant; brother of Notolius, Potolius and Sitofolla (1, 3), probably Sativola, Aug. 2, of Exeter, daughter of 'Benna', Leland, *Itin.* 3, fo. 35 (1, 230, ed. Smith), Sidwell, Sidwella, sister of Bana, *Eadwara*, Wilgitha (= Wulvella) and Iuthwara (v. *Iuthwara, NLA* 2, 98), probably identical with (H)Aude (2, 11) of Brittany.

Studied in insula Pyrus in Demetia (Caldey Island, Ynys Byr, Pemb., *SS 1496*) under Illtud, with *David* (Devius), Samson and Gildas as fellow pupils, at Llan Illtut (Iltuti Monasterium) (2, 6-3, 9; in v. *Samson*, Caldey is a separate monastery under Pyro, but evidently an offshoot of Llantwit). Guarded the crops against birds. At the age of 16, he wished to leave the monastery to live as a hermit; Illtud warned him that all such propositions might have three possible origins: from God, from the Devil, or from ourselves, 'when we recall naturally what we have done or heard', and gave him time to think it over, and make sure that the call came from God, and let him go when he persisted (6, 17-7, 20). After some time in a hermitage on his ancestral estates, he was summoned to the court of king 'Marcus, quem alio nomine Quonomorus vocant' (Conomorus, +560), 'ad locum qui lingua eorum Villa Bannhedos nuncupatur' (glossed 'nunc . . . Caer Banhed' *AB*), but declined to become his bishop (8, 22-23). The place, whose name appears to be given in British, rather than Welsh, in a form scarcely later than the sixth century, is Castle Dore by Fowey, Co. (*SX 1251*), where Conomorus' name is still legible on his son's stone, *CIIC* 487, etc. Emigrated to Brittany, after settling the problems of his sister's estate, circumscribed on one side by 'evil co-heirs', on the other by the sea, by persuading the sea to recede a mile, and marking its boundary by stones, still visible, called 'Paul's Path' (9, 24-10, 32); a very similar tidal embankment is described in his boyhood at Llantwit, 3, 10, where the piled-up pebble embankment, protecting wet meadowland from the tide, at the mouth of the Hodnant (Col Hugh river, *SS 9567*), is nowadays very visible. Landed on Ushant with 12 named disciples, including Quonocus (? Conoc), Iahoevius, Tigernmaglus, Woednovius, Winniavus, Boius and Lowenanus, most of whom named places in north-western Brittany, and with 12 relatives, lay nobles, and 'sufficient slaves' (sufficiens manicipium) (11).

Crossed to the mainland, 'devenit ad quamdam plebem pagi Achniensis, quam antiquo vocabulo Telmedoviam (Plou-Dalmezeau, *D* 2) appellant. Ipse vero pagus (Achm) Domnonensis patriae quaedam pars est, occidentem versus constituta. In ea . . . plebe . . . repperit quemdam fundum qui modo . . . una ex tribubus eius, quas centum numero . . . habet (*cf.* 19, 61 "ex duobus pagis, Agnensi [Achm] Leonensi, centum numero tribus idem rex [Childebert] cum tituli praescriptione in perpetuam diocesim eidem pro hereditate regni coelestis consecravit sancto") . . . et in ipso fundo . . . locum . . . Ipse vero locus modo dicitur Villa Petri qui, ut fertur, consobrinus ei erat' (12, 36-7).

The monks, 'praedictam tribum in circuitu peragrantes', established their sepa-

rate 'habitacula'; Vivehinus, 'perlustrato eodem fundo' found a suitably pleasant
spring, built a 'praeparvo tuguriolo', at Lampaul, two miles north of Plou-Dalma-
zeau, but needed Paul's help to tame a wild ox that attacked his hut (13, 38-39).
Paul moved on to Plebs Lapidea (? Grouannec Coz, *E 2*) and villa Wormavi
(? Plou-Guerneau, *D 1*, two miles north-east), where, the monks 'saltus in circuitu
perarantes', Paul tested the ground with his staff until he found the well (14, 40-
42). There he discovered that the ruler of the district was named Withur (Victor)
and set out to seek him, along the 'via publica' that led westward (wrongly, for
eastward) to the 'city that bears his name' (15, 43). The city was 'then surrounded
by a fine earthen bank, but a large part of it is now fortified with a stone wall. Like
an island on all sides but the south, it is stretched like a bow on the British sea,
most attractive because its southern aspect catches all the radiance of the sun from
sunset to sunrise' (15, 44). The description fits, not the modern St. Pol de Leon,
but Roscoff, two miles to the north (*G 1*); on the sand hills east of Roscoff, the late
Professor J. B. S. Haldane discovered, in July 1961, the debris of a 'proto-Roscoff',
and subsequent investigations by the University of Rennes have found potsherds,
apparently Roman. The site was inhabited only by pigs, bees and a bear, with
some wild cattle (15, 44-45). Paul then crossed to the island of Batz, opposite
Roscoff, where found that *comes* Withur was both his cousin and an admirer of the
monks, and where he expelled a dragon (16, 46-18, 56). Withur and his people
begged him to become their bishop, and sent him with a letter, with 12 disciples
and sufficient slaves to Paris to king Philibert (Childebert), who gave him episcopal
rank (i.e. granted estates) and 100 tribus (19, 57-61). Accompanied Samson to
Paris, *c.*556, *cf.* Malo. He founded many churches and monasteries, and, as he
grew old, appointed disciples to discharge his episcopal functions, Iahoevius and
Tigernmaglus (whose name is given in sixth-century spelling), each of whom died
after a year's office, and then Cetomerinus (20, 62); Judual, cognomento Candidus,
dux of a large part of Domnonie gave him a territory (20, 63), and he retired to
Batz, leaving Cetomerinus as bishop (20, 64). Foretold the future destruction of
Batz by the Normans (20, 65-66), died on March 12, in Batz, after directing that
his body be buried on the mainland for the convenience of future pilgrims; the body
was so buried, after fierce dispute between the 'insulani' and the 'oppidani' (22,
67-23, 71). His sites are numerous in north-western Brittany; he and Sidwell have
churches at Exeter, Wulvella at Gulval by Penzance (*SW 4831*), the sisters several
sites in the Camelford area *LBS* 1, 188. 'Oxismorum ecclesiae episcopus' v. *Gildae*
(R) 3. Arthmail; Gouezno; Goulven; Iaoua.

PAULINUS of Cynwyl Gaeo, Carm. (*SX 6537*) (near Dolau Cothi) V L/VI E,
Nov. 22 (Demetian Calendar, cited *LBS* 4, 73). B?;B. Pupil of Kebi, v. *Kebi*, 5;
disciple of *Germanus* v. *David* 10. Taught David, v. *David* 10; and Teilo, v. *Teilo*
4 (*LL* 99). Perhaps intended by 'bishop Paulinus', who caused David to be summoned to the Synod of Brefi, v. *David* 49. 'Servatur fidaei patrieque semper amator,
hic Paulinus iacit cul(t)or pientisim(us aequi)', hexameter inscription, *ECMW* 139,
found with two others (140-141), both with Irish names, presumably therefore from
a cemetery, probably monastic, at Cynwyl Gaeo, which may bear a name derived
from Docco. It seems probable that Kebi's pupil and the teacher of David and
Teilo are identical with one another and with Paulinus of the inscription. He is
perhaps also the teacher of Bivatigirnus 'famulus Dei, sacerdos, et vasso (servant)
Paulini, Andoco (? Audoco) gnatione (of Anjou?)', who buried his wife at Llantrisant, Anglesey (*SH 3483*) early (*cf. LHEB* 446) in the sixth century, *ECMW* 33. He
is probably not connected with Paulinus Marinus Latio (of Latium?) *ECMW* 315,

Pembrokeshire, probably late fifth (*LHEB* 610) or Paulinus, father of Cantusus, *ECMW* 258, Port Talbot, neither of whom appear to have been ecclesiastics.

PAULINUS, first archbishop of York, +664, Oct. 10. Italian?;E. *BHL* 6553-4; Bede *HE* **1**, 29; **2**, 12-14, 16-18, 20; **3**, 1, 14; **4**, 23; **5**, 24. *ASC* 601, 625, 644. *NLA* 2, 312.

Sent by Gregory to Augustine in 601 with **M**ellitus, **I**ustus and Rufinianus; described to Bede by an eye-witness as 'tall, slightly bent (stooping), dark haired, thin faced, with a thin hook nose, venerable at the same fearful to look upon'. Consecrated 625, 'antistes', Bede; bishop, *ASC*; Gregory had, however, previously designated the see of York as metropolitan, with the right to ordain 12 bishops. Converted **E**dwin, his family, **H**ilda, and the witan, baptised in the Glen at Yeavering, and in the Swale, and Trent; evangelised Lincoln and there consecrated **H**onorius; withdrew to Kent on Edwin's defeat, leaving **J**ames the deacon in York, succeeded **R**omanus, in Rochester and there buried.

PEHTHELM of Whithorn VII L/VIII E. E;E. Bede *HE* **5**, 13, 18, 23. Monk and deacon of **A**ldhelm, friend and correspondent of Bede, correspondent of **B**oniface, bishop of Whithorn 731.

PELAGIUS *c*.420/430. B;Italy. *DCB*; *cf.* vol. 6, below, pp. 17-51. A Briton, a monk, settled in Rome by *c*.401. An outstanding theologian, a polished Latinist. Opposed Augustine's dogma of original sin, defended the action of God's grace. Attacked by **A**ugustine, acquitted by a synod in Jerusalem, condemned by an African synod. Pope Zosimus refused Augustine's request to condemn him unheard, but Augustine (418) secured an edict exiling him and his close associate **C**oelestius from the civil authorities, accusing them of responsibility for the socially disturbing views advanced by the **S**icilian Briton. His extant works, *Commentaries on the Epistles of Paul*, Migne (*PL* Supplement 1, 1110 ff.) and his *Letter to Demetrias* (Migne *PL* 30, 3; 33, 1099, published as *Hieronymus* *Ep.* 1) substantiate the comments of his contemporaries on the elegance of his Latin and forcefulness of his character, but show little trace of the social outlook of the Sicilian Briton. The controversy was fundamental to the evolution of the western church, since upon Augustine's premise rested the concept of the necessity of the intervention of the priest and the sacraments between God and man, while Pelagius' tenets appealed to Christians who sought a direct relationship of man and God, including ascetic eremitic monks and the later tendencies which ultimately evolved Protestant thinking. The controversy did not become acute until after 410; the edicts of 418 did not therefore command force in Britain, and there is little sign that Augustine's views won converts in Britain on any scale, despite the efforts of Pope **C**elestine, **P**alladius, **G**ermanus of Auxerre and others to instil them; and in the early seventh century Pope **J**ohn IV found the views of the Irish church Pelagian (Bede *HE* **2**, 19). Some 70 Pelagian works are extant, preserved in mediaeval monasteries, usually disguised under the names of Augustine, **H**ieronymus, and others, whereas virtually no writings of any other major heresies are preserved, save in quotations cited by orthodox theologians in their attacks upon them. The history of this manuscript tradition has not been studied; a considerable number were preserved and copied in Irish monasteries in Europe.

PERRAN, *see* Ciaran of Saigir.

PETROC of Bodmin, Co. (*SX 0767*) VI M, June 4. B;I.B. *BHL* 6639-6640. *AB* 74, 1956, 145 (Gotha MS.) (1), *cf.* 137, *cf.* 188, genealogy (2); 166 (vita metrica)

(3); 487 (*cf.* 470) translated Doble 4, 137 (4); *NLA* 2, 317 (5); Leland, *SB* 61 (6). Son of Glivis, brother of **Gwynlliw** (*cf. 1*, 2). **E**telic, **P**aul Penychen, etc. (*2*; = v. *Cadoci* pref.); son of Clemens, chief in Cornwall (twyssauc o Gernyv) (*ByS* 39). Shared the kingdom with Gwynlliw (*1*, 2), preceded him (*3*, 4, 4; *3*, 15, 3). Studied in Ireland (3) for 20 years (4); taught **C**oemgen of Glendalough (+618) from his seventh to his twelfth year, lost Life (Ussher, *Brit. Eccl. Ant.* 1687, 292, cited *1*, p. 143). Returned to Cornwall (4) with **D**agan (6); his disciples Credanus, Medanus, Dachanus, buried at Bodmin (Peterborough MS., *de Sepultura Sanctorum Anglorum*, cited 6, hence Bale, *1*, p. 143). Landed at Portus Reu, two miles from Petroxstowe (Padstow), (preter Heyle flumen, Padstow estuary *3*, 30, 2, probably Daymer Bay, Rock; St. Enodoc) (5), received by bishop **W**ethenoc, evicted **S**amson from his oratory nearby, who after an episcopate of two years in 'Anglia', emigrated to become archbishop of Dol (5). Wethenoc made over his cell to him; he built an oratory and mill at Nant Funttun (Little Petherick by Padstow) (*SW 9172*) (6). Visited Rome, returned to found 'Watune' (Nova Villa *4*, 8, Newtown St. Petrock, Devon, *SS 4112*) (7); after a second visit to Rome, Jerusalem, Arabia, Persia, and India, lasting seven years (8), returned after the death of the tyrant Teudor (**T**heodoric), in his son's time (9). Wethenoc returned, and to avoid quarrels, Petroc withdrew to Little Petherick with Petrus and Dator, working manually 'more Antonianum' and establishing a rule (10), placing Peter as dominus over his 80 monks (*4*, 10), each living in separate timber cells, some in caves (11). Baptised the tyrant **C**onstantine (12), visited by Wethenoc (15). A powerful pious 'provincialis', Kynan, built an oratorium in his honour (Bodkonan, Boconion, north of Bodmin) (16). After *60* years at Padstow and Petherick, moved with Dator alone to Bodmin, which he took over from the hermit Wronus (19-20) (Guron 6; Bodmin granted to Petroc by the reguli Theodor[ic]us and Constantine [*6*], who moved a day's journey to the south [i.e. to Gorran, *SX 0041*]); Bodmin was therefore probably identical with Duneurin, the seat of 'Kenstec, humilis . . . (ad) episcopalem sedem in gente Cornubia in monasterio quod lingua Brettonum appellatur Dinuurin elec-tus' who submitted obedience to Ceolnoth of Canterbury, 833/870, *HS* 1, 674. At Bodmin he was visited by Peter, while constructing a stone and mortar cell (21). A few years later, while visiting the brethren at Padstow and Petherick, he died at Treravel (near Petherick) (23).

His sites were very numerous in Cornwall, Devon, Wales, and Brittany, Doble 4, 160-165; *LBS* 4, 101-2; Arnold-Forster 3, 444. The Life is plainly much concerned with the mediaeval possessions of Bodmin; an Exeter charter, dated 938, Kemble, makes Athelstan grant Newtown to Petroc, and it belonged to Bodmin in 955, 1272, 1317 (Doble 4, 153); the charter, genuine or otherwise, is sufficient reason to bring Petroc to 'Watune'. It is, however, clear that Petroc's main centre was Padstow; Bodmin appears to have retained the name of its original founder in the mid-ninth century, and to have become Petroc's principal house later. But the wide spread of Petroc sites outside Cornwall suggests the continuing dispatch of missionary monks from Padstow, which was the principal port for travel from southern Ireland and south Wales to southern Dumnonia and Brittany. **D**occo.

PHERPHEREN, *see* Thynoy.

PIALA (Ciara) of St. Phillack, Hayle (*SW 5537*) VI E, Nov. 20. I;B. Sister and companion of **F**ingar.

PIRAN, *see* Ciaran of Saigir.

PUBEUS, *see* Kebi.

PULCHERIUS, *see* Mo-Choemog.

PUPEUS, *see* Kebi.

PUTTA VII L. E;E. Bede *HE* 4, 2, 5, 12. Bishop of Rochester, 670-676, withdrew to Mercia when Ethelred of Mercia sacked Rochester, given a church and a little land by Sexwulf, bishop of the Mercians. He may or may not be identical with Putta, first bishop of Hereford, +688 Fl. Worcester. Florence's list of the division of the Mercian see into five dioceses in 679 (HS 3, 128, Worcester, Lichfield, Leicester, Lindsey, and Dorchester) does not include Hereford; but if the small border territory had acquired its own bishop two or three years before, it would not form part of the division of 679. Equally, if Hereford was a priest's charge, not a bishopric, the fact that Putta was himself a bishop would justify Florence's words.

QUERANUS, *see* Ciaran.

QUONOCUS, *see* Conoc.

RADEGUND 519-587, Aug. 13. Thuringian;Gaul. *BHL* 7048-7054; her biographers Fortunatus and Baudonivia (*MGH SRM* 2, 364; 377, *MGH AA* B 38, *cf. Carmina, passim*, index 124) and Gregory of Tours (*MGH SRM* 1, *passim*, index 905) were her contemporaries and friends. Daughter of king Berthacarius of Thuringia, wife of king Clothaire I of the Franks; abandoned her marriage, *c.*550, escaped from her husband's territory, and with the help of the British recluse John of Chinon and of Gregory of Tours, went on to found her monastery near Poitiers.

RENAN, *see* Ronan of Locronan.

RINGAN, *see* Ninian.

RIOC, fellow pupil of Finnian of Moville at Whithorn, *c.* 550.

RIOCH (Riochatus?) VI M, June 21 (Feb. 12). A;A. Pupil of Winwaloe, visited and revived his mother; gave Winwaloe 'rura mea . . . *possessa parentis'*, v. *Winwaloe* 2, 22, *cf.* contents table (Rihocus); 2, 18 (Riochus), evidently a native of Armorica. His sites include Lan Riec near Concarneau, *H* 6; St. Roch, Achm, *C* 2; and similarly-named places, *I* 6, *K* 4, *L* 2, *L* 4, *N* 1, *M* 6/7, with Ker Riec *H* 6, Ker Roch *F* 5; as St. Rigat he is patron of Trefiagat, *F* 6 (feast June 21), *LBS* 4, 120. Son of *Elorn* of la Roche Maurice near Landerneau, an elderly hermit when he entered Winwaloe's monastery, *AG* 29 (Feb. 12). The forms Rihocus and Rigat point back to British Rigocatus, Riochatus by the fifth century, Jackson *LHEB* 457; the shortened form is scarcely possible (as 'Rigoc') until the disappearance of the 'g'.

RIOCH of Inch Bofin, Lough Ree, West Meath (*N 05*) V L, Aug. 1. B;I. *M.* *Brother* of bishop Mael of Ardagh (+486), and himself a bishop, *Bethu Phâtraic* (*VT* 82, 85, *cf. Book of Leinster* 372, 1, cited *VT* 550); 'carrier of Patrick's box' *Bethu Phâtraic* (*VT* 152) = Joscelin, v. *Patrick* (6, 84, *TT* 84), 'custos codicum . . . natione Brito, gradu tunc diaconus'. Aed m. Bricc (+589) visited Inch Bofin, and was received by *Rioch*, v. *Aed* 31. Three ancient churches on adjacent heights above the Nore by Kilkenny are named after Saints Patrick, Mel and Rioch (anglicised St. Rock's), O'Hanlon, 8, 6 ff. He is also named in the Scottish Drummond Calendar (Forbes 20, Aug. 1) and the Salisbury Calendar (with Mel, Feb. 6). The name, as with Rioch of Armorica, is probably a shortened form of Riochatus. He was a contemporary of Sidonius' Riochatus, like him a Briton, a monk and bishop, and a carrier of books, in traditions that knew nothing of Sidonius, and may therefore be identical with him. He is probably distinct from Rochatus.

RIOCHATUS antistes et monachus V L. B;B.I? Carried books, including recent publications of Faustus of Riez, which he concealed during a two-months' stay at Clermont-Ferrand, to the British, c.475, Sid. Ap. *Ep.* 9, 9. He is possibly identical with Rioch(atus), a Briton who became a bishop in Ireland and was remembered as 'custos codicum' in late V. If so he will have brought the first recorded contemporary theology to the Irish episcopate, including the 'semi-Pelagian' theses of Faustus. A British bishop in Ireland, who visited Provence and the Auvergne, is likely to have journeyed to Rome; the time was soon after the establishment of the southern bishoprics, during the dispute between Fintan Crimthir and Kebi, whose disturbed withdrawal route passed 10 miles south of Inch Bofin. The visit may therefore have involved discussion of these problems with Pope Simplicius.

ROCHATH (variant Nochath) V L. B?;I. With Enda and Pubeus (Kebi?) on Aran, v. I. *Brendan* 71. Possibly identical with Riochatus, who may also have been concerned with Enda and Kebi, if the spelling of the name is faulty in the MS. But the name Rocatus exists independently, of quite different origin (*CIIC* 500, Isle of Man, late-fifth century, Ogam and Latin); the name, if both British and Irish, should be a spelling of Rogadus (*LHEB* 187, *cf.* 173), evidently the African Latin name Rogatus. The MSS. give no authority for an emendation of the spelling.

ROCK, *see* Rioc.

RODANUS, *see* Ruadan.

ROMANUS VI M. Italian?;E. Kentish priest of Eanfled, daughter of Edwin and queen of Oswy, Bede *HE* 3, 25.

ROMANUS, bishop of Rochester, Kent (*TQ 76*) 624-*c.*628. Italian?;E. Bede *HE* 2, 8, 20. Consecrated to Rochester 624 by Iustus, on his promotion from Rochester to Canterbury. Sent by Iustus (+627) to Rome, drowned in the Italian sea. His successor Paulinus was consecrated by Iustus' successor Honorius.

ROMANUS, *see* Rumon.

ROMULUS, *see* Rumilus.

RONAN VI M. I;E. 'natione quidem Scottus, sed in Galliae vel Italiae partibus regulam ecclesiasticae veritatis edoctus; acerrimus veri Paschae defensor', against Finan of Lindisfarne, Bede *HE* 3, 25, possibly Ronan of Dromiskin, *cf.* Modwenna.

RONAN of Kingarth, Bute (*NS 0956*) +737 (? Feb. 7). I;S. *AU* 736 (737), perhaps identical with Ronan of the Scottish Calendars, Feb. 7, Forbes 441, with numerous sites, *cf.* O'Hanlon 2, 395, Watson *CPNS* 309.

RONAN of Locronan, Douarnenez, Cornouaille (*F 4*) V L, June 1. I;B.A. *BHL* 7336 (1); 7337 (2); *AB* 71, 1953, 393 (translated Doble 2, 120) (Gotha MS.) (3); *AG* 286 (4); Leland, *Coll.* 4, 152 (cited Doble 2, 120) (5).
Irishman (*1-5*) of modest birth (*4*), sailed to Britain for baptism because in Ireland his parents and schooling were pagan (*4*); crossed to Brittany (*1-5*), in the time of Gradlon (*1-5*). Identified with Rumon in *3* and *5*. His sites are very numerous in Brittany, Gougaud, *Saints Irlandais* 159, Doble 2, 121, under the name Ronan or Renan.

RONAN m. Berach of Dromiskin, Louth (*O 09*) +666, Nov. 18. I;I. *BHL* 7338 (*AB* 17, 1898, 161). Of the Ui Neill, encountered the son(s) (+664) of Aed Slane, founded Dromiskin. Possibly **R**onan Scottus, probably **R**onan, associated with **M**odwenna.

RUADAN of Lothra (Lorrha), Tip. (*M 90*) +587, Apr. 15. I;I. *BHL* 7349-7350. *VSH* 2, 240. *Sal.* 319. Son of Birra of the Eoganachta (of Munster), resident in Ossory (1), a huge man, *12* feet tall, and handsome (30). Pupil of **F**innian of Clonard (1; *Cat.* 5; v. *Fin. C.* 19). Established Lochra (2-3), near a cell of **B**rendan of Clonfert (4); founded houses in northern Ireland (5-9). Cured the wife of a Leinster chief (12). Revived the son of a British king, drowned when one of Brendan's ships sank in the Shannon estuary (13). His monks lived in idleness, occupied with prayer alone, without agricultural labour, thanks to the cultivation of a wonderfully sweet drink made from the juice of the lime tree (? lime tea, tisane, or possibly a distilled liquor), which became so popular that it attracted many monks from other houses. Under pressure from indignant abbots, Finnian constrained Ruadan to end production and to practise arable agriculture 'like other monks' (14; v. *Fin. C.* 24-26). Ruadan and Brendan of Birr compelled the high-king Diarmait to release Aed Guaire, sentenced for killing a royal official, and thereby 'ruined his kingdom' (15-18; *AC*, pp. 85-88, *cf.* ch. 7 above, pp. 133-4).

Visited **C**olman Elo (558-613) (24), and **C**iaran of Saigir (+*c.*530) (v. *Ci. S.* 33), helped by **C**olman m. Daire of Daire Mor (+VII E) (25). These visits, though all just possible if a very old man met a very young man, probably echo traditions of later relationships between their respective houses. With **C**olumba of Iona struggled with demons for the soul of the impious Aed Engach (the Innocent) to whom **A**ed m. Bricc (+589) had promised heaven; Columba gave him his splendid gold-coloured pen, and later reclaimed it when **B**aitan visited Ireland (29; Irish verse tale, *AB* 49, 1931, 99; Irish Life, Plummer *MHH* 173b); the same tale is told in v. *Cainnech* 22, where Columba and Cainnech aided **E**ugenius of Ardstraw in an aerial combat against demons, Columba leaving with Cainnech his 'graffium', which Baitan recovered on a subsequent visit to Ireland. Visited Clonard at the same time as Dagaeus (+589) (v. *Dagaei* 11). Findbar (VI M?) gave a site to two of his pupils (v. *[Find]barri* 12). Died, buried at Lothra (30). He is alleged to have published books 'Against king Diarmait', 'The Miraculous Tree' and 'The Wonderful Springs of Ireland' (O'Hanlon 4, 164); a Book of St. Ruadhan is said to survive (O'Hanlon 4, 165); his head was preserved in a silver reliquary until the dissolution of the monasteries (O'Hanlon 4, 165), and a bell found in a well at Lorrha, still extant, is venerated as the bell that he rang at Tara against Diarmait (O'Curry 337). **B**ec m. De; **C**iaran of Saigir; **C**olman m. Daire; **L**uchtigern; **S**enach.

RUAN, *see* Rumon.

RUMILUS V M. B;Man. British bishop. With **C**onindrus and **P**atrick, consecrated **M**ac Cuil to Man, *Muirchú* 22. The name is perhaps a corruption of Romulus.

RUMON of Tavistock, Devon (*SX 4874*) VI E/M? Aug. 30. I?B?;B.A. Also patron of Ruan Major and Minor (Lizard, *SW 71*) and Ruan Lanihorne on the Fal (*SW 8331*) in Cornwall, all three S. Rumoni ecclesia in the thirteenth and fourteenth centuries, *DEPN* 395; and other Cornish sites (brother of S. **T**udwal; Doble 2, 124), and in Devon, p. 133, with two sites in Finistère, Gougaud, *Saints Irlandais* 166. Leland, *Coll.* 4, 152, citing a lost Life seen at Tavistock, and the Gotha MS. (vitae *Ronani 3* and *5*) identify him with **R**onan of Locronan. It is possible that 'Maruanus' who came from Ireland with **B**reaca is Mo-Ruan, conceivably identical with Rumon; there is a village named Ruan in Co. Clare (*R 38*) in Ireland. Rumon is a British form of Romanus, Jackson *LHEB* 289, *cf.* 299; *M. Gor.* (hence *M. Don.*) have Roman

Ruanaid (the strong?) at Nov. 18, distinguished from Ronan m. Beraig. Rumon (Romanus) may therefore be British or Irish; but is distinct from Ronan, a normal and common Irish name.

RUN (RHUN) m. Urien VII E. B;B. *ACm* 626: 'Etguin (Edwin) baptizatus est. Et Run filius Urbgen baptizavit eum'. (1). Hence Nennius 63 'Run map Urbgen baptizavit eos' (Edwin's Northumbrians) (2). The Chartres MS. of Nennius begins 'Incipiunt excerpta (MS. exberta) (Run) f(il)ii Urbagen (MS. Urbaoen) de libro sancti Germani inventa' (3). In *1* the first sentence and the date occurs in the Irish Annals (*AC* only; there is no sign that *AC* or any other Irish Annalist borrowed from *ACm* or *ASC*); the second sentence is a British addition thereto, an assertion that Run baptised Edwin. In *3* the form Urbagen (variant Urbeghen) preserves an exceptional survival of the composition vowel, scarcely later than the seventh century (Jackson *LHEB* 648 ff.); and therefore probably derives from a text nearly contemporary with Run and Edwin. The statements of the texts are that Run excerpted a vita *Germani* and that he baptised Edwin; that attachment of the baptism to the annal of 626 is later than the statement itself. A statement apparently so close to the event cannot be lightly dismissed; Edwin was a refugee in Gwynedd; the belief that he was baptised by Run is likely to rest on a tradition that he was baptised while in exile, some 15 years before Paulinus baptised his people.

These traditions refer to an ecclesiastic, not to a layman. There is no tradition of a secular Run m. Urien, apart from a few late pedigrees (e.g. *Peniarth* 131, B 114, cited *CLH* 3, 39 c note) which add a Run to the sons of Urien, evidently on the strength of the tradition of Run m. Urbgen. The Run of the Urien poems is not described as m. Urien, and is probably identical with Run Ryvedvawr. It is not at all unlikely that a son of Urien became an ecclesiastic and settled in Gwynedd; it is probable that the clerics of Cadfan's court attempted to convert the exiled English boy, and that they claimed success; it is possible that Edwin accepted baptism in boyhood in exile at a Christian court, and disregarded it on his return to seek his throne among his pagan countrymen, probable that the Gwynedd Christians claimed his conversion, whether or not they achieved it. The uncertainties are scarcely greater than those which surround, in a vastly better documented age, the alleged conversion of king Charles II to Catholicism.

SAMSON of Dol *c*.563, Jul. 28. B;B.A. *BHL* 7478-9 = R. Fawtier, *Vie de St. Samson*, Paris, 1912 (1); *BHL* 7480-5 = *AB* 6, 1887, 79, *cf.* 12, 1893, 56 (2); *BHL* 7486 (auctore Balderico) (3), prologue published in (2), text, unpublished, a variant of (2); (*BHL* 7486 a) = *Liber Landavensis* 6 ff. (4); *NLA* 2, 350 (5); *AG* 409 (6); *Pietro de Natali*, 1514 (*cf.* 1, p. 4) (7); *Vincent de Beauvais*, 1473 (*cf.* 1, p. 4) (8); (*cf.* v. *Ailbe* 17) (9); *Dubricii*, LL 80-81 (10); *Gildae (R)* 3 (11); *Illtud* 11, 14-15 (12); *Maglorii* 2 (13); *Mevenni* 2-7 (14); *Pauli Aureliani* 3 (15); *Paterni* 24 (16); *Petroci* 5 (17); Mansi, *Concilia*, 9, 743 (18); etc.

Vita (*1*) was written within living memory. The author, in Brittany, had known an octogenarian nephew of Samson's cousin Henocus (Enoch), who had brought a written life to Brittany, and supplemented it by verbal recollections (2). The name of the bishop to whom the work is dedicated, then living, Tigernomalus is scarcely later than early VII (*cf.* Jackson, *LHEB* 446, 464-5, *cf.* 40). Vita (*2*) is of late IX (*1*, p. 14-15), (*3*) and (*4*) are of XII, (*5*) to (*8*) of XIV to XVI.

Samson is described as an old man, but not as an octogenarian or older; and was therefore probably born not much before 490. Son of Ammon and Anna, landed proprietors in Demetia (1), after the prophesy of a 'Librarius' (*Dubricius archiepiscopus* in *4*, 7) who 'lived in the far north', three days journey from Demetia (2-5), *cf.* **M**aucennus. At the age of five, sent to the school of Eltutus (Illtud) (7, *cf.* 11-12, 15) who rebuked his excessive fasting at the age of 15 (10). Ordained deacon (13) and priest (15) by papa Dubricius; incurred the jealousy of Illtud's nephews, moved to 'insula quaedam nuper fundata a quodam egregio viro ac sancto presbitero Piro nomine' (Ynys Byr, Caldey Island, Pemb., *SS 1496*) (20-21). Refused to visit his ailing father, protesting 'I have left Egypt . . . God can cure the sick', and was rebuked and ordered to go by Piro (22-24). On the journey, killed a witch with a curse (26-28); Ammon recovered, and the whole family took monastic vows except a worldly sister whom Samson rejected (29-30). On his return, bishop Dubricius, on his customary annual visitation to Caldey, commended his 'humane and loving care' for his parents, held an inquiry into the death of the witch, acquitted Samson and appointed him *pistor* (baker) (33-35). Piro, wandering 'in tenebrosa nocte et, quod est gravius, ut aiunt, per ineptam inebrietatem, in claustra monasterii'; fell down a well 'unum clamorem ululatus emittens', and was rescued but died the same night. Samson was elected abbot in his place, and instituted a strict rule, but resigned after 18 months, since the brethren considered him 'more of a hermit than a community monk' (36). He left with some learned Irishmen who stayed at Caldey on their way home from Rome, effected cures in Ireland, and founded a monastery, over which he placed his uncle Umbraphel, returning from 'arce Etri(de)' with a north wind (37-40). There was a church of Samson at Ballygriffin, Dublin, and there is also a Ballysamson in south Wexford, according to *LBS* 4, 148, and a Kil Sampson in Co. Tyrone, *H 74*, near Armagh. Withdrew, with his father and six others, to a deserted *castellum* on the Severn, thence to a woodland cave, where 'now is' a much venerated oratorium 'where Samson sang mass and came to communion every Sunday' (40-41). *LBS* 4, 150 locates the cave at Stackpole (*SR 9896*) on the strength of the name Sampson in St. Petrox (*SR 9797*), a mile-and-a-half to the north. A synod constrained him to accept the abbacy of a monastery said to have been founded by Germanus (*cf.* Samson of Llanilltud below). Soon after the annual council where bishops were consecrated on the Feast of Cathedra Petri (Feb. 22), Dubricius consecrated him bishop (42-44) (in succession to himself, 6, 9) in 'Yorkh' (App. *L* = Orkh, pagus Orcheus, Ercig; whence an antiquarian tradition made him 'archbishop of York'). Following a vision one Easter he abandoned his diocese after two years (17), crossing the Severn Sea, visiting his mother and aunt and excommunicating his adulterous sister, sailing to the monastery called Docco (Docto, Doccovi), probably St. Kew in Trigg, Co. (*SX 0276*), Doccuin in bishop Grandison's Register (45). Samson asked permission to stay, but abbot Winniavus (2, 15; Iuniavus *1*, 46) regretted that his stay would not be 'conveniens', since as a 'melior' he would condemn the monks of Docco who had 'relaxed their earlier rule'. Samson 'stupefactus super doctrinam eius' packed 'spiritualia utensilia sua atque volumina' on his 'plaustrum', harnessed the 'two horses he had brought from Ireland' to his 'currus', and proceeded to the 'mare quod Austreum vocant, quidquid ad Europam ducit' (46-47). But he spent some time in Tricurium pagus (Trigg), disrupting the rural rites of the subjects of 'comes Guedianus' by carving a cross on a standing stone on a hill top, and curing a boy thrown to the ground while 'equos in cursu dirigens' (48-49). He killed a dragon, refused to stay as bishop, but founded a monastery (50); in Cornish tradition, he was evicted from Trigg by Petroc (*17*). He then settled his monasteries and sailed to Europe; a chapel at Castle Dore by Fowey bears his name (St. Sampson, Golant). The deaths of Illtud and Dubricius are placed in *2*, i, 18-19, before he left Britain. In *6*, 10 the occasion of his migration was the plague of *c.*547-550. He was accompanied by **M**evennus (*14*) and his cousin **M**aglorius (*13*) who succeeded him, and founded Dol

(52). Learning that Jonas, praesul (53; imperator *2*, ii, 3; comes, *4*, 21) had been killed by a violent and unjust 'externus iudex' (dux Conmorus *2*, ii, 3; comes Commotus *4*, 21), and that his son Judualus was in captivity (so also *4*, 21; refugee in Francia *2*, ii, 3) he convened a council (*16*) at Menez Bre (q.v., named in many Armorican lives) against Conomorus, and went to Childebert (+558) in Paris (53-59), first-named of seven Armorican bishops, Leland, *cf.* Malo. Met Germanus of Paris (*c.*555-576) (*2*, 2, 10 ff.). His signature is extant on the minutes of the third Council of Paris, *c.*557 (*18*), with Kentigern and other Gallic bishops. Founded a monastery on the Sigona (Seine) (58-59) at Pentale (*2*, ii, 9, *cf.* *2*, ii, 22; *1*, 38). The king, Clothair (558-561) (the vitae were unaware that Clothair had replaced Childebert at Paris) sent him back with Judwal, and gave him the Channel Islands (Lesia Angiaque) (59) where he distributed 'numismiuncelli auri' (*2*, ii, 25), and secured by prayer Judwal's victory and Conomorus' death (Dec. 560). On a second visit to Paris founded Rotinson (*2*, ii, 21-22). Died at Dol (61), aged *120* (*2*, ii, 25). *Ailbe* (+528) visited him at Dol (*9*). He names a few places and churches in Wales, Ireland (see above), Devon, Cornwall, Dorset, Gloucestershire, Cresage, Shropshire, Wiltshire, at York (*cf.* Yorkh) (Arnold-Forster 3, 445-6), and Brittany, but very many in Normandy, Picardy, and some in Belgium, some of which are listed in Doble, *Dedications to Celtic Saints in Normandy* ('Old Cornwall', Summer, 1940, 1) and apparently by F. Duine, *cf.* *LBS* 4, 170, *cf.* Atrium Samsonis, v. *Cadoci* 49. **A**ilbe, **A**rthmail, **A**ustolus, **D**aniel, **E**thbin, **T**yssilio.

SAMTHANNA of Clonbroney, Longford (*N 27*) +739, Dec. 19. I;I. *VSH* 2, 253. Of Ulster birth, brought up among the Cenel Cairpri, succeeded Funecha, the foundress, as abbess of Clonbroney; encountered half-a-dozen early eighth-century kings and saints (*VSH* 1, lxxxvii); at Devenish met *Lasrian* (26, but not 10); with **A**ttracta and **U**ltan, she is added to the names of the assessors of ***B**erachus* (+VII E), v. *Ber.* 19, presumably due to the later interests of the houses concerned. **V**irgilius.

SANCTANUS of Kilnasantan, Dublin (*O 11*) (on the Dodder) VI M/L? May 9. B;I.B. Bishop of Cell da les or Cell espuic Sanctain i n-Uaib Cellaig i n-airther Laigen, *M. Oeng.*; of Cell da les, other martyrologies. The Ui Cellaig territory of southern Co. Dublin (Hogan 664) includes Kilnasantan (commonly corrupted to Kill Saint Anne), identified with Cell da les by Hogan 188. Sanctan mac Samuel Cheinnisil, epscop, o Chill da les. Deichter, ingen Muiredaigh Muindeirgh (+492) ri Uladh a mathair, acus mathair Matoc ailithir *M. Don.* Samuel Penissel (Low Head) (Penuchel, High Head, *ByS* 13, v. *Cadoci* 16), late VI, son of Pabo Post Prydein of the Coeling dynasty of the Pennines, is made father of **A**ssa(ph) in *ByS*, and was confounded by Cadoc in Glamorganshire. Reputed author of a hymn in the *Liber Hymnorum* held to have been composed during a journey from Clonard to Inis Matoc, both he and **M**atoc being described as British. Royal ancestry is a fiction ascribed to most British and many Irish saints, but in Britain often indicates a general date, here of the sixth century; the exceptional inclusion of a British-named prince in Irish tradition suggests tht he was remembered in British tradition. The reference to Clonard indicates a belief that he lived after its foundation, not earlier than the mid-sixth century. Since both he and Asaph are given the same father, his connections are probably with north Wales; he is therefore presumably the patron of Llansannan, Denbigh (*SH 9365*) (fair day May 7, *LBS* 4, 194), and Sannan of Llantrisant, Anglesey (*SH 3483*), perhaps also Sannan of Bedwellte, Mon. (*SO 1600*). His tradition is possibly also the origin of 'deacon Sannan, brother of

St. Patrick' of the notes to the Franciscan *Liber Hymnorum, VT* 412. He may possibly be identical with Sanctinus (? Sanctanus) of Bodafon, but *cf.* Sanctanus, June 10.

SANCTANUS VI? June 10. B?;I. *M.* Bishop. Perhaps of Mount Sanctan (Cill Sanctan), Antrim, near Coleraine (*C 83*), *cf.* O'Hanlon 5, 143-4. Possibly connected with the Welsh Sannan, whose day is June 13 in some Welsh calendars, *LBS* 4, 193-4; he may be a duplicate entry of Sanctanus of Kilnasantan. The Roman name suggests a British origin.

SANCTINUS (Sanctanus?) of Bodafon, near Llandudno, Caern. (*SH 7980*) VI E? (Jackson, *LHEB* 406), Sept. 17? B;B.I?. *ECMW* 83 (plate viii) 'Sanctinus sacer (-dos) in p(ace)'. A cross bar, evidently deliberately carved, joins the I and N of SANCTI-NVS, but both strokes are vertical, not joined at the top; epigraphically, *Sanctinus* is the more probable reading, but *Sanctanus* cannot be excluded. He is perhaps Sanctin, Sept. 17, *M. Gor.*; *M. Don.*; or possibly identical with Sanctanus of Kilnasantan.

SANE, *see* Senan.

SANNAN, *see* Sanctan.

SARAN VII M. I;I. Addressed by Pope John in 640, Bede *HE* **2**, 19; probably identical with Saran Ua Critain sapiens, +661 *Annals*, perhaps with Saran, Jan. 20. *M.* of the Delbna of Dal Cais, of Tigh Saran (Tisaran near Clonmacnoise) *M. Don. cf. M. Tal.*

SATIVOLA VI M/L. B;B. Sister of Paul Aurelian; lost Exeter Life, summarised Leland, *Itin.* 3, 35, Toulmin Smith 1, 230.

SATURN, abbot of Llandough, VII M/L. B;B. *LL* index.

SCELLANUS VII M. I;I. Addressed by Pope John in 640, Bede *HE* **2**, 19; perhaps identical with Scellan the Leper of Armagh, *M. Don., M. Gor.*, Sept. 1. Emendations of the text to Sillan, Stellan, etc. *cf.* Plummer, *Bede* 2, 113, seem unwarranted and unnecessary.

SEBI VII L. E;E. Bede *HE* **3**, 30; **4**, 6, 11. King of Essex, *c.*663-694; longed for a monastic rather than a royal life throughout his reign; resigned his crown, tonsured, *c.*694, died soon after in London; buried in a stone coffin in St. Paul's.

SECUNDINUS (Sechnall) +448, Nov. 27. Gaul?;I. Pupil of Patrick, Tírechán and derivative sources, *VT* index. *AB* 60, 1942, 26. Aged 75, *Annals*.

SEDULIUS VIII E. I;B. 'Britanniae episcopus de genere Scotorum', attended a church council in Rome in 721, with 'Fergustus episcopus Scotiae Pictus', Mansi 8, 109. The *Annals* note several Irish Sedulii, the martyrologies a few abbots in Ireland named Siadhal, *cf. ASH* 315, 'Britannia' here probably means Alclud.

SEGENE, bishop of Armagh, 660-688, May 24. I;I. *Annals, M. Book of Leinster* 42ᶜ (sedit xxvii), o Achad Chlaidb (? near Armagh, Hogan 7). Received Sletty from Aed, Tírechán *Add.* 16.

SEGENE, abbot of Iona, 624-652, Aug. 12. I;S. Adomnán 1, 1; 1, 3; 2, 4. Bede *HE* **2**, 19; **3**, 5. Informant. of Adomnán; received Cummian's letter on the Easter controversy *c.*633; sent a monk as bishop to the Northumbrians *c.*635, soon replaced him by Aedan. Addressed by Pope John, *c.*640.

SENACH, bishop of Clonard, +589, Aug. 21. I;I. Pupil of Finnian of Clonard,

Cat. 5 = v. *Fin. C.* 19. Sent by Finnian to enquire into the work and preferences of his other monks, v. *Fin. C.* 20; remained with Finnian when his other monks left him, v. *Fin. C.* 24. Bishop in Muskerry, brought up by Ruadan's sisters, handed over his cousin Aed Guaire, who sought sanctuary from king Diarmait, to Ruadan, v. *Ruadan* 15. Bishop of Clonard, *Annals* 589, Aug. 21, *M. Tal., M. Oeng.*; of Clonfoda, Aug. 21, *M. Don., M. Gor.*, based on *M. Oeng.* scholiast. Left with Finnian at Escayr Branain (Ardsallagh, Meath, *N 86*) as a boy by robbers, Finnian's successor as abbot, v. *Fin. C.* 17, not named; named, v. *Fin. C. (Lismore)* 2632.

SENACH, abbot of Armagh, 601-612. I;I. Book of Leinster. Identified with Senach Garb of Clonfert +621 (Sept. 10); Senach the Smith (May 11), of Kilmore (Nov. 2).

SENACUS of Anelog, Lleyn, Caern. *(SH 1527)* VI E/M. I;B. *ECMW* 78. Senacus pr(e)sb(iter) his iacit cum multitudinem(sic) fratrum, *cf.* 77, Anelog Veracius p(re-s)b(ite)r hic iacit. The stones, near Aberdaron, on the tip of Lleyn, opposite Bardsey, indicate a monastic cemetery; if the date (Jackson *LHEB* 279, 291, 518) is right, the monastery will be one of the earliest in Gwynedd. The name is common in Ireland, not used by the British; Jackson's equation with Henocus (Enoch, a biblical name also not otherwise used in Britain), Samson's relative, while philologically plausible, seems therefore improbable. Irish settlement is attested by the place-name Gwyddel a mile-and-a-half to the south, on the extreme tip of the peninsula.

SENAN of Inis Cathaig (Scattery Island), Clare *(Q 95)*, in the Shannon estuary, V L/VI E, March 8 (March 1). I;I.B. *BHL* 7573-4. *Sal.* 735 in doggerel verse, with much conscious satire (1); *ASH* 530 (misnumbered 612) (2); *Lismore* 1775 (Irish) (3); Leon Breviary, *AB* 66, 1948, 225 (*cf.* also pp. 209; 217) (4); *AG* 61 (5). (2) is a Latin translation of an abridgement of (*3*). Son of Erchanus (*1*; Ergindus *2*; Gerrgenn *3*; Hercanus *4, 5*) and Coemgella (*1*; Comgella *2*; Coimgell *3*; Cogella *4, 5*) of the Corco Bascin (Clare, north of the Shannon), named Senan (*1-4*; Sanus, Sane *5*). Foretold by Patrick, born at Mag Locha (*R 05*), four miles north-east of Kilrush, opposite Scattery (Hogan 523). Conscripted into his chief's army, ran away and hid in a pile of wheat in enemy territory, escaped; because he fell asleep (*2, 3*), because he was scared (*1*, 201 'illuc venit pavidus'; omit *4, 5*, accused of idleness and cowardice *5*). Tonsured by abbot Cassidan of Irrus (Erris; extreme west of Co. Clare [near Killaha, *Q 74*] Hogan 472) who sent him to abbot Natali(us)s in Ossory in whose mill he worked (*1*, 267; 290 ff.; *2*, 11 ff.; *3*, 1954, 1958; omit, *4, 5*); his family migrated to Munster, *5*. Visited Rome, on his return stayed at Tours, meeting *Martin* and visiting *David at Menevia* (*2, 3, cf. 1*, 24 [817-9], David ... ut diximus ... evidently referring to the missing portion at line 477). Founded Enniscorthy, Wexford (*S 94*) before his pilgrimage, met *Maedoc of Ferns*, founded Ard Nemidh, near Lismore, Waterford (*X 09*) and Inishcarra, Cork (*W 57*) on his return (*2, 3*). To Inishcarra came a ship from 'Letha' (abroad, 'Latium') with five decades of perfect men, who chose five Irish patrons, Findia (Finnian of Clonard?), Senan, Brendan (of Clonfert), Ciaran (of Clonmacnoise) and (Find)Barr (of Cork), bishops Iohann and Mula settling with Senan, passing thence to Findia, Brendan and Ciaran (*2, 3*). Visited Brittany, founding numerous named churches (*5*); 'Breaca venit in Cornubiam, comitata multis sanctis, inter quos fuerunt Sinninus abbas, qui Romae cum Patricio fuit', lost Life of Breaca, Leland *Itin.* 3, 4 (Toulmin Smith 1, 187). 'Gallos apperit' hymn appended to *1*. Refused tribute to the king of Raithlenn, *3*, citing a long poem attributed to Colman m. Lenin, founded several monasteries in Munster, leaving bishops and abbots in each (*2, 3*), revived a washerwoman's son drowned by the curse of the monk Finnan (*1*, 20) (676 ff. the monk Libren *3*, 2158 ff.; Libernus and 'Sedna seu Sedonius episcopus', *2*, 24).

Founded Inis Cathaig at the behest of the archangel Raphael, expelling therefrom a ferocious beast (*2*, *3*, *cf. 1*, 14 [479] 'bestia', referring to missing portion at line 477). King Mactail of the Ui Fidgenti (*cf. CGH* 392, *LL* 327 f. 7) tried unsuccessfully to expel him with the aid of his magus and of Senan's brothers Coel and Liath (*2*, *3*, *cf. 1*, 14). Established on the mainland a house for women under the daughters of king *Brennan* of the Ui Fidgenti (*3*, 2148). Refused to permit the aged virgin Canair (Kynrecha) to land on the island, protesting 'quid feminis commune est cum monachis?' (*1*, 18 [628]), but was persuaded to allow her burial on the shore (*1-3*). Visited by Brendan (of Clonfert) and Ciaran 'eius individuus comes semper ac socius' (*1*, 21 [714]), whom he fed miraculously, in the time of king *Nectan Cennfoda* (*son of Brennan*) of the Ui Fidgenti (*2*, *3*), and to whom he offered passage in a skinless coracle. They took him as their 'soul-friend', since he was their senior and a bishop (*3*, 2350). Ciaran gave him his cloak, and the story is retold in v. *Ciaran Clonmacnoise* 22, *cf.* 29. Ciaran 'comes semper et socius' is, however, scarcely the short-lived Ciaran of Clonmacnoise (511 [515]-548), but rather Ciaran of Saigir (*c.*440-*c.*530); the cloak, sent floating down the Shannon on its own in v. *Ci. C.* 29, was sent in *1*, 23 (772 ff.) by Senan's pupil Dermicius, who is probably 'Dermicius . . . qui et Iustus' who baptised Ciaran of Clonmacnoise.

Archipontifex, *1*, 23 (778); died on March 1, buried a week later (*2*, 42-43). Joint patron of the Ua Conaill (Gabra, of the Ui Fidgenti) with Ita, v. *Ita* 8. His Irish sites, O'Hanlon 3, 253 ff.; in Britain, he names Sennen, Lands End (*SW 3525*), in Brittany Plouzané, Leon (*D 3*). The Sannan churches of Wales, *LBS* 4, 193-4, plainly relate to **S**anctanus rather than to Senan; the Scottish dedications listed Forbes 444 to a Senach, and the identification with Kessog, Forbes 374, derives only from a relatively recent anonymous misreading of *M. Oeng. AG* 64 and Gougaud *Saints Irlandais* 167 give additional Breton sites, *cf.* Doble, *Cornish Saints* 15, unhappily omitted from Doble 1, 145. The surviving tradition of Senan is more devolved than that of most major Irish monastic founders; the one Latin Life, in addition to its peculiar bias, is heavily contaminated by timeless stories from the Irish Lives, which may owe their name to **S**enan of Leon.

The Irish tradition knows no close date, but places him early, his childhood previous to the traditions of the later fifth-century bishops of southern Ireland; in later life he is made senior to Ciaran, probably of Saigir, and encounters the hostility of kings who still depend on magi; and he is said, exceptionally, to have been much respected by saints who lived abroad. In Cornwall, the Life of Breaca makes him her principal abbot, *cf.* **S**inninus; in Brittany, the Breviaries explicitly identify Sane with Senan. Whether he personally visited Britain or Brittany, on his pilgrimage to Rome or on another occasion, is relatively unimportant; the essence of the tradition is that he was regarded as a patron of the forceful emigrants who accompanied **B**reaca and **F**ingar at the beginning of the sixth century; the occasional use of his name in Cornwall and Brittany is sufficiently explained by the immigration of persons held to have been his followers, naming churches in honour of their teacher. **C**airnech Coem; **E**rc of Kerry; **F**ingar; **I**ta.

SERVANUS of Culross, Fife (*NS 9885*) VI E? July 1. Gaul?;P. *BHL* 7609-7610 v. *Kentigerni 1*, 4; *2*, 8 (1). *Brev. Ab.* PE 15 (2), PE 25 (3); vita, Pinkerton, *Lives of the Scottish Saints*, ed. Metcalfe, 2, 119 = *CPS* 412 (4); Angus, *Mothers of the Saints*, Ballymote 212 a (text reproduced Watson, *CPNS* 209, 2) (5).

Servanus of Culross 'sacras literas plures docebat pueros'; 'legem clericos docebat

Christianam' in the childhood of Kentigern (VI E), taught Kentigern (*1*); conse-crated by *Palladius* (V E), (*2, 3*) teaching at Culross (*3*), at Dysart, Fife (*NT 3093*) (*2*). A Scot (*2*); Serb of Culross, between the Ochils and 'sea of Guidi' (Firth of Forth), son of Alma, daughter of the king of the Cruithne (Picts) and of Proc, king of the Canaanites of Egypt (*5*); Servanus, son of Obeth, king in terra Chanaan and of Alpia daughter of the king of Arabia (*4*). Crossed the sea of Icht (English Channel), received by abbot Edheunanus (Adomnán) at Inchkeith (*NT 28*), given Fife as his sphere, established Culross against the opposition of king Brude m. Dagart (? m. Derile 696-706, rather than m. Feredach, *c*.843), lived in a cave at Dysart, received pilgrims who came from the Alps (*4*). Killed a dragon at Dunning in Strathern, Perth (*NO 0114*) (*2; 4*). *Brev. Ab.* distinguishes the earlier Servanus the Scot of Dysart and Dunning from the later Servanus, an Israelite, in the time of Adomnán, of the island of 'Petmook' (? Inchkeith) (*2*).

Most of these curious notices either derive from the storyteller or serve a later monastic interest. Those which do not are the connection with Kentigern, for Glasgow tradition does not gain by making Kentigern the pupil of an obscure saint of Fife, and the tradition that an island hermit had a foreign or Mediterranean origin. These traditions concern a Servanus of Culross and Dysart early in the sixth century; and a Servanus of Inchkeith, Petmook, Dysart and Culross befriended by Adomnán and attacked by his contemporary Brude, *c*.A.D. 700. It is likely that they concern one person, that the stories of Adomnán and Brude concern a dispute about Culross, *c*.A.D. 700, misplaced to the time of its founder; possible that the traditions concern two persons of the same name. Palladius is introduced to give apostolic authority to a very early monk, for whom no consecrating authority was known.

SETNA VI E. I;I. Pupil of Ibar.

SETNA VI M, March 10. I;I. 'Sedna seu Sedonius episcopus', pupil of Senan, v. *Senan 2*, 24; Setna Ep. March 10, *M. Tal., M. Gor., M. Don.*; episcopus Saigir (successor of Ciaran) nomine Setna, friend and visitor of Lugid (534-612, Aug. 4) v. *Lugid* 35. Perhaps named Sithney, Co. (*SW 6320*), near Helston, festival Aug. 3 (*LBS* 4, 201), sanctus Sydinus, 1270, *DEPN* 423, *cf.* Sezni.

SEVERUS, bishop of Trier, V M. Gaul;B. v. *Germani* 2, 2; v. *Lupi*; = Bede *HE* 1, 22, accompanied Germanus on his second visit to Britain *c*.445. Otherwise known only from the catalogue of bishops of Trier, Duchesne, *Fastes* 3, 36.

SEXBURG of Ely VII L, July 6. E;E. *BHL* 7693-5. Bede *HE* 3, 8; 4, 19, *cf.* 22. *NLA* 2, 355. Leland, *Coll.* 3, 164. Daughter of Anna, king of East Anglia, queen of king Earconbert of Kent, mother of king Hlothere of Kent, of Ercongota, abbess of Brie, of Ermengild, queen of Wulfhere of Mercia. Veiled by archbishop Theodore at Sheppey (*Liber Eliensis* 76, cited Plummer, *Bede*, 2, 239), succeeded her sister Aethelryd as abbess of Ely, *c*.679, re-buried her sister at Ely *c*.695 in a marble sarcophagus taken from a (Roman) cemetery outside the walls of Cambridge. Succeeded as abbess by her daughter queen Ermengild, sister of Aedilberg of Farmoutiers.

SEXWULF, bishop of the Mercians, *c*.674-705. E;E. Bede *HE* 4, 6, 12. Birch *CS* 22. *ASC* 656; 675; 705. Founder and first abbot of Peterborough (Medeshamstead), 664, bishop of the Mercians, presided over the division of the diocese, gave a church and land to Putta on his removal from Rochester.

SEZNI VI E? March 6, Sept. 19. I;A. *AG* 528. Chapters 1-4 are a devolved transcript of v. *Ciaran Saigir 4* and *5*; *cf. AB* 59, 1941, 220 ff. Chapter 5 lists his sites in Leon. The name corresponds to the Irish Setna, Sedna, Middle English Sydni(us), of Sithney, Co. (*SW 6329*); and he may therefore be identical with Setna of Saigir, but *cf.* Sinninus. Received the servant of a lord named Gerran (3); the name Geran occasionally occurs in Ireland, but might be a version of Gerennius (Gerontius), and may derive from a tale originally set in Cornwall.

SICILIAN BRITON V E. B;Italy. Anonymous author of two letters and four tracts, C. P. Caspari, *Briefe, Abhandlungen und Predigten eines Unbekannten*. Christiana, 1890; R. S. T. Haslehurst, *The Works of Fastidius*, Society of SS. Peter and Paul, Westminster, 1927 (with an English translation); Migne *PL* Supplement 1, 1687 ff. (Letter I, assigned to an unknown author); 1375 ff. (Letter II and the tracts, assigned to Pelagius, following G. de Plinval, *Pelage*, Lausanne, 1943). The works are certainly by the same writer (Caspari, introduction; Morris *JTS* 16, 1965, 26 ff.), who is neither Pelagius, nor any other known named writer. He wrote in Sicily (Letter I, 5), whither he had recently come from Rome. He was a young man, a native of Britain, since he equates 'in omni Barbaria' with 'in Francia et in Saxonia' (Letter I, 1), a location appropriate only to northern Gaul and Britain, and twice explains that his journey had involved a difficult and dangerous sea crossing (Letter I, 2, 5). The first of the tracts, *de Divitiis*, is cited by Augustine (*Ep.* 156) in 414, as a recent publication, circulating in Sicily. It is probable that the author joined the considerable evacuation of well-to-do urban Romans to Sicily, on Alaric's capture of the city in 410, and published in the years 411-413. Two related works are the *de Virginitate* (Migne *PL* 30, 162; 18, 77; 20, 227; 103, 671, published as *Hieronymous* *Ep.* 13), described by Gildas (38, citing *de Virginitate* 6) as the work of 'quidam nostrorum', a Briton; the author might be the Sicilian Briton, but is probably a nameless colleague; and *de Divina Lege* (Migne *PL* 30, 104, published as *Hieronymous* *Ep.* 7), written in an urban Roman senatorial milieu, equally by a nameless sympathiser of the Sicilian Briton, whose nationality is not revealed.

The outlook of the Sicilian Briton can only be described as socialist. Some of his tricks of speech, notably his use of triad form and invocations like 'Quaeso, diligenter advertas' ('Look you now carefully, I pray you'), and 'Lector, attende', are alien to continental Latin, and recall the idiom of later Welsh and Cambro-Latin. A comparative study of the language of British, Gallic, Italian and African Latin texts of the early-fifth century, long overdue, might help to show whether such superficial similarities and differences have or have not substance.

SIDONIUS APOLLINARIS, bishop of Clermont-Ferrand, 471-489. Gaul;Gaul. Born 431, of an outstanding senatorial family, son of a praetorian prefect, grandson of a praetorian prefect of Constantine III, cousin and brother-in-law of the emperor Avitus. His letters and poems, *MGH AA* 8, 1-264. *See also* Columban, Constantius, Faustus, Lupus, Riocatus.

SIDWELL, *see* Sativola.

SIGBERT +636/640. E;E. King of the East Angles, exiled to Gaul, converted *c.*630, brought Felix to East Anglia, abdicated, monk 'multo tempore', recalled to the throne on Penda's invasion, killed. Bede *HE* 2, 15; 3, 18-19. Finan of Lindisfarne.

SILLAN, abbot of Bangor, +612, Feb. 28. I;I. 'MoSinu moccu Mind i. Sillan abb Bennchair', *M. Tal.*; 'MoSinu maccu Min, scriba et abbas Benncuir, primus Hibernensium compotem a Graeco quodam sapiente (i.e. Dionysius) memoraliter dedicit. Deinde Mo Cuoroc . . . alumnus . . . hanc scientiam literis fixit', Wurzburg

MS. (eighth-century), Kenney 218, *AB* 64, 1946, 215; probable author of the *Computus* of 607, passed off as the conclusion of the letter of Cyril of Alexandria of 419, and the accompanying *Disputatio Morini*, *AB* 64, 1946, 225 ff. The production of these works presupposes a formidable learning, and also a formidable library; presumably Mo Cuoroc (*cf.* Youghal, Cork, *X 07*), obtained the books that Sillan lacked. Mo Cuoroc was perhaps also author of the poem 'Nonae Aprilis' (*MGH* Poet. Lat. 4, 670), rendering Dionysius into a short verse abstract easily memorised, *AB* 63, 1946, 244. The *Computus* of 607 was a first attempt to introduce into Ireland an Easter reckoning acceptable to Rome, and cannot be independent of Columban *Ep.* 3, seeking papal approval of the Irish date for the Easter of a year that is probably 607 (*cf.* *AB* 63, 1946, 209), since Columban was himself a former monk of Bangor. The controversy which Columban raised in Gaul and Italy touched Bangor, whence he drew his practice and his theory, on the authority of Comgall (+605). Sillan, Comgall's second successor, reacted promptly, and was evidently anxious to avoid controversy with the church of Europe; he must have known Columban well, and foreseen the lasting tensions that his simple intransigence was likely to produce.

SILLAN, bishop and abbot of Moville, +621, Aug. 25. I;I. *Annals. M.*

SINCHELL the elder of Killeigh, Offaly (*N 31*) +551, Mar. 26. I;I. *Annals. M.*, aged *330* *FM*.

SINCHELL the younger of Killeigh, Offaly VI L, June 25. I;I. *M.* His school, Kenney 475, K. Meyer, *Hibernica Minora*, Oxford, 1894, 41 ff., an eighth-century text describing his rule. Fintan of Clonenagh.

SINELL, bishop of Moville, +670, Oct. 1. I;I. *Annals. M.*

SINNINUS abbas VI E. I;B. First-named of the companions of Breaca, Leland, *Itin.* 3, 4 (Toulmin Smith 1, 187) 'qui Romae cum Patricio fuit'. Three of Breaca's six companions name adjoining parishes by Helston; Doble, *Parish of Crowan*, 1939, 4, assumed that the lost Life concocted the companions out of the names of neighbouring parishes and that therefore the other three must have named neighbouring parishes whose dedications have changed, and therefore equated Sinninus with Sithny (Sezni) adjoining Breage, to whom the words 'Romae cum Patricio' are apt, since the v. *Sezni* appropriates the vita of Ciaran of Saigir, who is said to have met Patrick in Rome. But Breaca's party formed one half of the powerful armament headed by Fingar, whose members include numerous followers of Ciaran of Saigir, Findbar of Cork, and Senan of Scattery, all three associated with one another in their native traditions in Ireland, and whose sites spread widely over south-western Cornwall, and include the neighbouring parishes of Burian, Sennan, St. Just and Madron. Sinninus transliterates Sennan, but requires emendation to equate with Setna. Sennan was also at Rome in the mid- or late fifth century, and, though Patrick does not meet him there in surviving tradition, where he foretells Senan, already conceived, he does meet Ailbe, Declan and several other southern saints in Rome, whence the story reached the Ciaran-Sezni Life; and the story is likely to have been inserted into any Sennan text which omitted the pre-natal prophecy, but retained the visit to Rome. Sinninus is therefore better identified with Senan and with the parish of Sennen.

SITH, *see* Ita.

SITHNEY, *see* Setna, Sezni.

SOCHET, *see* Patrick.

SOMRE, abbot of Llantwit, VII L. B;B. *LL* index.

SONA VII M. B;Spain. 'ecclesiae Britanensis indignus episcopus', 646, signed the seventh Council of Toledo *Catal. Conc. Hisp.* 423, *HS* 2, 100.

SOSANUS VII M. B;Spain. 'episcopus ecclesiae Britaniensis', 653, represented at the eighth Council of Toledo by his priest Matericus *Catal. Conc. Hisp.* 449, *HS* 2, 100.

SUIBNE, bishop of Armagh, 725-730, June 21. I;I. *Book of Leinster* 42ᶜ (sedit xv). Of the Ui Niellain (Newry/Dundalk). Flaithberthach, high-king of Ireland, entered Armagh as a monk in 730, *Annals*.

SUIBNE, abbot of Iona, 652-655, June 22. I;I. *Annals. M.*

SULGEN (Sulyen) VI M/L, Sept. 2. A;B. Companion of Cadfan and Mael. *ByS* 20 and late texts cited *LBS* 4, 203. His sites, *LBS* 4, 204 ff., *cf.* Bowen *SCSW* 93 in Powys and perhaps Cardigan. The name is easily confused with Silin, the Welsh form of Giles, and with Julian.

SULGEN, abbot of Llancarfan, VII M/L. B;B. *LL* index.

SULGEN (Sulien), monk and abbot of Llandough, VII E/M. B;B. *LL* index.

SULIAU, *see* Tyssilio.

SULIEN, SULYEN, *see* Sulgen.

TAGU, *see* Thynoy.

TANEU, *see* Thynoy.

TATA, *see* Aedilberg.

TATBERT VII E. E;E. Pupil of Wilfred, abbot of Ripon, Eddius, pref. 1, 63, etc.

TATFRID VII L. Monk of Whitby, trained by Hilda, elected bishop of the Hwicce, *c*.690, died before consecration. Bede *HE* 4, 23.

TATHAN, *see* Tatheus.

TATHEUS of Caerwent, Mon. (*ST 4690*) VI E, Dec. 26. I;B. *VSB* 270. *NLA* 2, 361. Son of T(u)athalius, an Irish king, studied letters, renounced his inheritance, crossed to Britain in a boat without sail or oars, with eight followers, landed 'in ostio vocato ex advenienti vocabulo gentis', perhaps Portskewett, Mon. (*ST 4988*), south of Chepstow, who had prepared a bath, 'as he usually did on Saturdays', entertained him (4). Caradoc, son of Ynyr (Caradocus rex, 5; Caradoci regis filii Ynyrii nobilissimi donatione, 6; possibly Ynyr son of Caradoc) king of both Gwents, invited him to establish a school in Caerwent, where he taught the seven sciences to scholars from all parts; and founded a church in honour of the Trinity, with 12 canons *with the authority of the bishop of Llandav*. The 'presbiteri Tathiu' still signed grants, as the clergy of Caerwent, with the clergy of Llandaff and the archdeacon of Gwent, in the eleventh century, *LL* 270. The fee of one pupil was a cow (7). After conflict with king Gwynlliw, Tatheus accepted his son Cadoc as a pupil (12). He is therefore probably identical with Meuthi, Cadoc's Irish teacher who had the same quarrel with Gwynnliw, v. *Cadoci* 1, 4, 6-7, and taught him

'Donato Priscianoque nec non aliis artibus per annox xii^cim'. Founded a chapel in honour of his shepherdess Machuta, killed by robbers, and buried her in Caerwent church. Miraculously provided water for the swineherd Tecychius, defended the pigs against wolves, kept tame pigeons. Died, buried in Caerwent church. The 'Ecclesia de sancta Tathana' *LL* 320, 325, 331, St. Athan, Glam. (*ST 0168*) may owe its name to him, the gender confused by forgetfulness of its origin, or to an otherwise unknown Tathana; Llanfeuthin by Llancarfan (*ST 0571*) bears the name of Meuthi, perhaps devolved from Mo-Thotan or the like. 'Tangusius', teacher of Beuno, VI L/VII E, was perhaps a successor.

TEILO (Teliauus, Eliud) of Llandeilo Fawr, Carm. (*SN 6322*) VI M/L, Feb. 9. B;B.A. *BHL* 7997-8. *LL* 97. *NLA* 2, 364. Born at ecclesia Gunniau (124: 255) perhaps Penally, Pemb. (*SS 1199*) (opposite Caldey Island) which was his 'hereditarium ius' (116). Taught by **D**ubricius (patron of Caldey) (*cf.* v. *Dubricii, LL* 80) and **P**aulinus (of Cynwyl Gaeo) where he was a fellow student of **D**avid (98-99). The princeps (Baia [Boia] Scottus, v. *David* 16) of sea-borne *Pictish* invaders set his women to tempt Teilo and David (99-100). Teilo and **M**aedoc 'non figmenta poetarum nec veterum historias immo Ieremei prophete lamentationes (legentes)' miraculously provided stags to carry firewood (101-2). Teilo, David and **P**aternus visited Jerusalem (103-5); (v. *David* 44-48; v. *Paterni* 20). On their return, they divided Britain into three episcopates (v. *Paterni* 20, omit, v. *David*, v. *Teilo*), being the territories of Seisil, Rein and Morgant (v. *Paterni* 30), *L* Reinawc. David and Teilo were consecrated bishops, Paternus was recognised as 'egregius cantor' (106). The tradition of v. *Cadoci* (22, *cf.* 25; 70) recognised three paruchiae of David and Teilo (Demetia with Carmarthen), **I**lltud and **D**ocheu (Glamorgan), **C**ynidr and **M**aedoc (Ercig) (variant Cannou for Docheu); Cadoc gave a principal villa each to David, Teilo and Doguin (v. *Cadoci* 22).

Teilo was consecrated to *the church of Llandaff with all its parochia as successor to Dubricius* (107), but could not stay there because of the Yellow Plague which killed Maelgwn and destroyed his patria (107). The saints withdrew to distant places, Ireland or France, Teilo to Brittany (108). On the way, he became the confessor of king Gerennius in Cornwall (108); on arrival he was received by **S**amson of Dol, also a pupil of Dubricius, and stayed with him (109). The plague abated in Britain, and Teilo sent messengers to recall the numerous British who had fled to France and Italy, filling three very big ships. But king **B**udic, with a large Armorican army, asked his help in expelling a pestilence, in the form of a dragon; which he did (110). Budic and Samson therefore invited him to stay and assume the bishopric of Dol; he blessed the Armorican cavalry so effectively that 'even today' the Armoricans are seven times as victorious as cavalry than as infantry (110-113). Hearing that Gerennius was dying, Teilo returned to Cornwall to shrive him (113-4). He then returned to his see (unnamed), as 'princeps of all the churches of all southern Britain', and convened a synod of all the disciples of Dubricius, which regulated the church. Appointed **I**smael as bishop at Menevia (St. Davids), after David's death in 589 (115). Teilo revived the dead and cured the sick; 'reguluus Guadam' who violated the sanctuary of Llandeilo Fychan was struck dead (116). On Teilo's death, three churches claimed his body, Penally, Llanteilo Fawr and Llandaff; God solved the dispute by giving him three bodies, which were interred in the three churches (116-7).

In the vita he is connected with Llandaff only in the single sentence interpolated on p. 107, that he was consecrated to Llandaff, but was unable to stay there; his relics are admitted to lie in Penally and Llandeilo. In the vita *Oudocei* and other

Llandaff texts (*LL* index) he is regularly treated as bishop of Llandaff, successor of Dubricius, treated as founder of the see, succeeded by Oudoceus. The grants appended to his Life were made by Idon, son of Ynyr Gwent (VI), Aircol Lauhir (VI E) and *Margetud* (+796) of Demetia, none by rulers of Glamorgan. In the Life his principal association is with David, secondly with Paternus. His sites have the same association (Bowen *SCSW*, figs. 12-15, pp. 50-56; Doble, *St. Teilo* [Welsh Saints 3], Lampeter, 1942, 40; *LBS* 4, 238; *LL* 124; 255), centred on Ystrad Tywi and eastern Demetia (30 sites), with two in Gower, one in Brecon, one (Merthyr Mawr) in Glamorgan, three near Abergavenny, as well as Milton Abbot, Devon, *SX 4179*, with Constantinus rex Cornubiensis. There was also upland distribution in the lands most heavily settled by the Irish, avoiding the Roman villa lands of Morgannwg, whose see in later centuries was Llandaff.

In the ninth century, the paruchiae of David and of Teilo were one. The Gospel Book of Teilo is known as the 'Book of Chad' because it was looted, in or after the late ninth century, by the Mercians, and has ever afterward remained at Lichfield, the see of Chad. It contains the signature of the Mercian bishop Wynsi (974-992). It also contains a number of eighth- and earlier ninth-century marginalia, reproduced by Evans in *LL*, *cf.* Gospel Books. The signatories include the son of bishop Saturnbiu, bishop of St. David's, died 831; and Nobis, bishop of St. Davids, 840-873, who signs as 'episcopus Teiliau', bishop of Teilo, evidently at Llandeilo Fawr. Nobis was a relative of Asser, king Alfred's biographer, who reported that king Hemeid of Demetia (+892) 'plundered the monastery and parochia of St. Deguus (David) and . . . expelled archbishop Nobis, my relative, and myself'. Nobis perhaps signed himself as bishop of Teilo after his expulsion; his signature is followed by that of 'Saturnguid sacerdos Teiliau'. But he regarded himself as bishop of Teilo as well as of David; Teilo is said to have appointed David's successor as bishop; Asser, Nobis' kinsman and contemporary, calls him 'archbishop', though in his memoranda he is content with 'bishop'. The claim presumably extended to a title to supremacy over several other Welsh bishops, and was doubtless asserted only while he remained at St. David's. But at Llandeilo he calls himself bishop of Teilo, while he was at the same time exiled bishop of St. David's. The Carmarthenshire territory of Llandeilo had belonged to Demetia; and the Demetian bishop was heir to both David and Teilo.

Teilo has, however, no connection with Llandaff before the eleventh century (*cf.* Bowen *SCSW* 48, 57). From the time of the foundation of Morgannwg under Theodoric and Mouricus in the late sixth century, the kingdom had its bishops; some are recorded on inscriptions at Llantwit; nothing but repeated insertions into *LL* suggest that Llandaff became the seat of the Morgannwg bishops before the time of Morcant Hen (930-974). *LL* claims the authority of Teilo for the foundation of Llandaff because the bishops of Teilo and David had in the past claimed the status of metropolitan, which from the eleventh century Llandaff also claimed. It is likely that the Mercian raid which carried off the Book of Teilo to the cathedral of Chad in Lichfield also ended the pre-eminence of Llandeilo, and enabled Morcant Hen's clergy to lay claim to the revenues and traditions that it had formerly asserted.

Teilo also has an extensive cult in Brittany, *cf.* Doble, *Teilo* 44, *LBS* 4, 234; the story of the shriving of king Gerennius also occurs in the Life of Thuriau, a purely Armorican Life, and may have been adapted therefrom, or vice versa.

TENENAN (*Tinidorus*) of Leon VI M/L, July 16. I;A. *BHL* 7999. *AG* 400. Son of an Irish prince, educated by 'Karadocus ou Karentec' (Cairnech Coem? V L), who cured him of leprosy, sent to the court of the king of Great Britain at

London (evidently derived from a story of attendance at the court of king Arthur, as in vita *Illtud*, suggesting a lost mediaeval British Life as source). Escaped the advances of the 'Countess of Arundel' by praying successfully to catch leprosy. Returned to Ireland, where Karantec cured him. Crossed to Brittany with the priests Senan and Quenan, in the episcopate of Goulven of Leon; repelled by his prayers an attack by barbarian *Danes*. Succeeded Goulven as bishop of Leon, consecrated at Dol by (arch)bishop 'Genevee ou Gennou', succeeded by Houardon. His followers included Kennen, Armen, and Glanmeus. His principal monastery was at Plabennec *E 2* (north of Brest). His relics were preserved with Gurthiern's on Ile de Groix, v. *Gurthiern* (*Cart. Quimperlé* 46); other Breton sites, *LBS* 4, 249. The episcopate of Leon is probably a hagiographic contrivance. **V**ougay.

TERNAN of Banchory, Kincardine (*NO 6995*), south-west of Aberdeen VI M/ L, June 12. I;P. *Brev. Ab.* PH 105 (1); *Mart. Ab.* June 12 (2), both evidently deriving from a lost Life. Irishman from 'provincia Myrma' (? Momonia, Munster). Baptised (*1, 2*) and taught (*1*) as an adult (*2*) by *Palladius* (*1, 2*). Visited Rome (*1, 2*), stayed seven years (*2*), *consecrated by Gregory the Great* (*1, 2*), who gave him a gospel in four volumes, bound in gold and silver, of which the Matthew volume is still preserved at Banchory (*2*); gave him a bell (*1*). Converted king 'Convecturius' (conceivably a corruption of Gartnait, 548-555 or 584-603), gave seed to Macarius (*1*), his contemporary (*2*). Terrenanus archipresul, buried at Banchory (*2*), heremi cultor devotissimus (*2*). Probably identical with Torannon of 'Bennchor', and Tulach Fortceirn (Tullow, Carlow, *S 87*) in Leinster, and of Drumcliff (Sligo, *G 64*), *M. Gor., M. Don.*; Mo-Thoren of Tullow and Drumcliff, identified with *Palladius*, *M. Oeng.*, also June 12; Torannan, the far-voyager, buried at 'Leconium' in Alba, poems cited Forbes 451. The surviving tradition pointedly ignores Columba; in invoking Palladius, it claims an authority and date independent of Columba, and earlier than him. The loan of seed to Macarius also implies that he was established before the arrival of Macarius, Columba's first-known Aberdeenshire missionary. 'Post Ninianum sanctum Pictorum Australium veluti apostolus', Camerarius, Forbes 238. His sites, O'Hanlon 6, 641; Forbes 451.

TERNOC (? of St. Ernan's, Don., *G 97* and of Iceland?) VI M/L. I;I. v. I *Brendan of Clonfert* 13 (Ternoc; Mernoc v. II *Br. C.* 3; the name is To- (or Mo-) (Ernanoc). 'Frater' of **B**arrfind (Barrinthus). Barrinthus 'de quadam occeani insula dicens' related that Ternoc found 'insulam quandam in mari contemplationi celestium satis aptam . . . post multum temporis ceperunt multi monachi undequaque ad illum confluere'. When Barrinthus visited him, Ternoc and his monks came to greet him 'cumque a loco eorum itinere trium dierum distassem'. The island was therefore presumably large enough for Ternoc's monastery to be some 30 or 40 miles from the port where Barrinthus landed. The monks emerged 'ex diversis cellulis', for 'multe . . . eorum ibi mansiones . . . et una ecclesia, et una refectio' (many separate cells, a single church and a single refectory). When the others had retired for the night, Ternoc and Barrinthus strolled to the shore on the west coast. They sailed westward through fog banks to reach the Land of Promise, returning after a 40-day voyage to Ternoc's island, named Insula Deliciosa. Barrinthus later told the story to **B**rendan, who repeated the voyage. Ternoc had made the voyage before he accompanied Barrinthus; his monks complained of his frequent absences, for a day, a fortnight, a month; though they recognised the 'sweet smell of paradise' that clung to his garments for some weeks after his return, they did not themselves know where the island was. The very large island in the ocean, Insula Deliciosa (*cf.* v. I *Br. C.* 25; 66) is probably Iceland. Ternoc is presumably one among the numerous saints named Ernan, Ernen, Mernoc, Ternoc listed in the Calendars. One of them named St. Ernan's island in Donegal Bay; perhaps Ternoc of Iceland, since Donegal Bay (Slieve League, *B 57*) was the starting point for a westward voyage to the Land of Promise recommended by Fintan Munnu to a British monk (v. *Fintan M. 2*, 31 [*Sal.* 412] = *1*, 28 note [*VSH*]).

TERNOC mac Reithi VI? Oct. 3. I;B.A. *M. Gor.*; Tearnog *M. Don.*; Mac Reithi *M. Tal.*; Ternoc, *Tréguier* and *Leon Calendars*, Oct. 3. *LBS* 4, 295. Named Landerneau, east of Brest, *F 2*, Llandyrnog, Denbigh (*SJ 1064*), perhaps also St. Erney, Co. (*SX 3759*), Landrake, west of Plymouth; he is perhaps St. Torney of Northill, Co. (*SX 2776*), *LBS* 4, 260 (confused in *LBS* both with Tigernach and Tenenan; Llandyrnog kept a festival on April 4, Tigernach's day, in the eighteenth century, *LBS* 4, 260, and the name might evolve from Tigernach . . . Teyrnog).

THANEY, THENEU, *see* Thynoy.

THEODORE, archbishop of Canterbury, 669-690, Sept. 19. Cilicia;E. *BHL* 8083. Bede *HE passim, cf.* index, especially 4, 1 ff. *NLA* 2, 368. Born in Tarsus, *c.*602, educated at Athens, an elderly scholar living in Rome, trained in eastern Mediterranean theology and monasticism, recommended to Pope Vitalian by abbot Hadrian, ordained sub-deacon 667, consecrated in Rome, March 26, 688, reached Canterbury May 27, 669, accompanied by Hadrian and Benedict Bishop, aged 67. Reconstructed the church of England, devasted by the plague of 664 and the Synod of Whitby, and left with no regularly consecrated bishops. His tact and firmness reconciled the hierarchical episcopal organisation of Rome with the simple fervour of the Anglo-Irish monasteries. 'To put it shortly, in his episcopate the English churches initiated such spiritual progress as had never before been within their power' (Bede *HE* **5**, 8). He rejected the prelatical concepts and organisation of Augustine and Wilfred; the flexible structure which he devised for the English church has since required only detailed modification, and has proved able to survive both the investiture controversies of the Middle Ages, and the Reformation. Died 690, aged 88, buried in SS. Peter and Paul, Canterbury.
Agilbert; Albinus; Cuthbert; Leutherius; Oftfor; Sexburg; Tobias; Winfrith.

THEON(IA), *see* Thynoy.

THOMAS, second bishop of the East Angles, *c.*647-*c.*652. E;E. Bede *HE* **3**, 20. Deacon of archbishop Honorius, Canterbury. Native of the Gyrwe (about Peterborough); he is the second native-born bishop after Ithamar of Rochester (644).

THURIAU VIII E/M? July 13. A;A. *BHL* 8341-3. *AG* 395 (1). Bull. Soc. Arch Ile et Vilaine, 1912, 1-48 (cited Doble *St. Teilo* 22) (2). Born at Lanvollon *M 1*, near St. Brieuc, a dependency of Dol. Moved to Dol in childhood, took service as a shepherd with a citizen of Dol, who allowed him several hours a day released from work, to study under a cleric. Noticed by Tiarmaillus or Armahel, then archbishop of Dol, who took him into the monastery. Succeeded Armahel as archbishop; forced the submission and repentance of a powerful lord, Rivallon, who burnt and pillaged a dependent house of Dol. Lived *705-749*, his relics taken to Paris after the late ninth-century Norman invasion (*1*). Shrove his friend Geren, across the sea (*2*), the story identical with that told in v. *Teilo*, where Geren is a Gerennius of Dumnonia; one Life has plundered from another; Teilo, a Briton visiting Armorica, is more likely to have been acquainted with a Dumnonian king, but the v. *Thuriau* (*2*), said to be of the later ninth century, is a much earlier text. A twelfth-century list of archbishops of Dol drawn up in opposition to the claims of Tours (Duchesne, *Fastes* 2, 386) names Samson's successors as Maglorius, Budoc, 'Genevius', 'Restoaldus', Armel, 'Iumael' and Thurian. Armel, Armahel or Tiarmaillus in (*1*), may well be a corruption of Tigernomalus, bishop in office when v. *Samson* (1) was written in VII E. More will be known when (*2*), said to reproduce place- and personal names in 'archaic' form, and to be full of detail, is published in an accessible periodical.

Turianus, metropolitan, presided over a council in the presence of the comites Juthael of Rennes and Budic of Cornouailles, which granted an estate to Lan Ninnoc, v. *Ninnoc* (*Cart. Quimperlé* 63) in the time of Guerech (Waroc). Substituted for Teilo as the companion of David and Paternus on pilgrimage to Jerusalem v. *Pat.* 2, 9 (*AG* 246).

THYNOY VI. B;B. Thynoy d. of Lewdwn Llyudyauc (of the Hosts) 'o Dinas Eidyn (Edinburgh) yn y Gogledd' (in the north), mother of Lleudat Sant yn Enlli (Bardsey), Baglan yg Coet Alun (Llanfaglan, Caern., *SH 4669*), Eleri of Pen Nant Gwytherin (Denbigh, *SH 8761*), yn Rywynnyauc, and of Thygwy and Thyuriauc in Keredigyawn Is Coet, sons of Dingat m. Nud Hael, *ByS* 18. Pherferen d. of Lewdwn Lluydauc o Dinas Eidyn yn y Gogledd, mother of Beuno m. Hywgy (of Powys) *ByS* 30, *cf.* v. *Beuno* 1; Beren verch Lawdden. Tagu wife of Ludun mother Cynan Colledauc, of Cornwall and Brittany, *AG* 675. 'Dinoi filia Lidinin regis qui tenuit principatum totius Britanniae maioris', mother of Gurthiern (of Brittany), son of Bonus of Gloucester, v. *Gurthiern, Cart. Quimperlé* 42. Thaney d. of Leudonus, 'vir semipaganus, a quo provincia quam regebat Leudonia (the Lothians) nomen sortita in Brittania septentrionali', mother of Kentigern, son of Ewen filius Erwegende (Ewen filius regis Ulien [Urien]), v. *Kent.* 2, 1; unnamed d. of cuisdam regis, secta paganissimi, in septentrionali plaga Britanniae principantis, v. *Kent. 1*, 1; Dinw d. of Lewdun Llyudauc mother of Kyndeyrn Garthwys m. Owein m. Vryen, *ByS* 14. Unnamed mother of Findbarr of Cork, son of Amargen ferrarius, v. *Findbarr* (*VSH*) 1, *cf.* *Brev. Ab.* PE 115 (reprinted *AB* 69, 1951, 337), etc. Theon(ia), abbess of Gwytherin, v. *Wenefred* (Robert of Salisbury *BHL* 8849). *Brev. Ab.* PE 34. Dina, d. of a 'Saxon' king, mother of Cynauc m. Brychan, and of ten other saints, sons of Brychan, Aengus, 'Mothers of the Saints', cited *ASH* 312.

Raped, v. *Kent.* 2; wholly ignorant of how she conceived, just as in Genesis (19, 31 ff.) Lot, when drunk, did not know that he had lain with his daughters, v. *Kent. 1*; the father of Amargen slept with his daughter when drunk, like Lot; the dux issued an edict that no one should marry a girl he desired for his concubine, but Amargen married her, v. *Findbarr* (*VSH*); the king promulgated an edict that no one should sleep with his virgin daughter, nevertheless 'miles quidam' seduced her, v. *Findbarr* (*Brev. Ab.*). Sentenced to be stoned, thrown off the high cliff of Traprain Law in a cart, landed unharmed, set adrift in a boat without oars, rescued by St. Servan, v. *Kent.* 2, 4 ff., *cf. 1*, 3 ff. Sentenced to be burnt at the stake, saved by the protests of the infant within the womb, v. *Findbarr*.

The wide spread of this legend cannot be explained by the interest of particular monasteries; its peculiarity is the lurid sensationalism preserved in the Kentigern and Findbarr versions, which prompted the biographers of other saints to adapt it; the names remain, the improper story omitted, in surviving later and shortened versions, including the *lectiones* of Kentigern and Thynoy (printed with v. *Kentigerni*) in the Aberdeen and Edinburgh breviaries. Its most likely centre is Denbighshire, where Theon and one of her 'sons' appear in distinct traditions, near to St. Asaph, to whom Kentigern is annexed. Leudonus emerges from (or evolves into) Llew m. Cynvarch (brother of Urien Reged), ruler of Lodoneis, father of Gwalchmai

(Gawain), *cf. TYP*, p. 422. Thynoy, corrupted to Theneuke, names St. Enoch's church (and railway station) in Glasgow, perhaps also Llandenoi, Llanreithan, Pemb. (*SM 8628*), *LBS* 4, 250.

TIARMAILLUS, *see* Tigernmalus.

TIGERNACH of Clones, Monaghan (*H 52*) +548, Apr. 4 (5). I;I. *BHL* 8287. *VSH* 2, 262. *Sal.* 211. Son of a Leinsterman, grandson of Eochu of the Ui Crimthann, king of the Airgialla of Clogher (Tyrone, *H 55*). Baptised by Brigit's Conlaed. Captured by pirates and taken to the king of the British, whose queen sent him to study under Mo-Nenn (Maucennus) at Rosnat ' . . . alio nomine Alba' (Whithorn). ('Tigernacus, puer tunc tenellus', captured by pirates, taken to Britain with Eugenius of Ardstraw, studied under Maucennus at Rosnat, taken prisoner by pirates who came 'from Gaul to Britain', with Eugenius and Coirpre of Coleraine, served in the mill of the 'king of the Gauls' in Armorica, who freed them and sent them back to Ireland, v. *Eugen.* 1-2). Went from Rosnat on pilgrimage to Rome, returned by way of Tours in the company of Ciaran m. Echach of Tubbrid (in Munster). Revived Ethne, daughter of the king of Munster (Eochu 492-526), newly-married wife of the king of the British (Ethni Wyddeles, wife of Tutagual Tutclit, mother of Rhydderch of Alclud [+*c*.600]) who thereafter 'in utriusque hominis castitate Deo devote servivit'. In Munster, destroyed an idol 'from which a demon gave responses'. Returned 'ad patriam suam' (Leinster), founded a monastery on land given by Fiachra (? m. Crimthainn Ua Cennselaig). Migrated to the territory of his grandfather, who offered to expel bishop Maenchatinus of Clogher, and make over his see and monastery to Tigernach; Tigernach refused indignantly and withdrew to a mountain cell. 'Maenchatinus' is evidently Mac Carthenn of Clogher, +502. Revived Du(bth)ach of Armagh (498-512, rather than 534-547). Founded Galloon, Newtown Butler, Fermanage (*H 42*), near Clones (with Eugenius, v. *Eugen.* 5), where later he secured the release of hostages held by Aed m. Cormaic (of Clogher), one of whom subsequently fathered Fechin, and Romanus abbas (perhaps intended for Ronan m. Aeda of Achadh Furcha in Meath, *M. Don.* Dec. 23). Leaving his disciple, Comgall, in charge of Galloon, founded Clones where he spent the last 30 years of his life (i.e. 518-548). Llandyrnog, Denbigh (*SJ 1064*), feast April 4 in the eighteenth century, *LBS* 260, may derive its name from him, or from Ternoc mac Reithi. Ciaran.

TIGERNMALUS VI L/VII E. A;A. Bishop of Dol when the vita I *Samson* was written in the late sixth or early seventh century; perhaps identical with 'Tiarmaillus' (Armahel), predecessor of Thuriau.

TINIDORUS, *see* Tenenan.

TÍRECHÁN VII M/L, July 3. I;I. *M. Gor., cf. M. Don.* His *Collectanea* (Book of Armagh, 9 r° = *VT* 300 = *AB* 2, 1883, 35, *cf.* Kenney 329) begin 'Tirechanus episcopus haec scripsit ex ore vel libro Ultani (of Ardbraccan, +655) cuius ipse alumpnus vel discipulus fuit', written (25) 'post mortalitates novissimas' (the great plague of *c*.666 rather than the famine and foot and mouth disease of 700, as MacNeill, *Patrick*, 139). The words 'servi sumus Patricii' (15) in relation to Tirawly, Connacht, suggest the location of his bishopric rather than of his birth. Since the name is virtually unique he is very possibly the Tyrechanus whose mother obtained the aid of Fechin of Fore's prayers to bring him home safely from a pilgrimage to Rome to join her in Cashel in Munster (v. *Fechin 2*, 14); Fechin and Ultan were close neighbours, and close colleagues (v. *Fechin 2*, 29).

TOBIAS, bishop of Rochester, c.696-726. E?;E. Bede *HE* **5**, 8, 23. 'Latina, Graeca et Saxonica lingua atque eruditione multipliciter instructus', pupil of Theodore and Hadrian, succeeded by Aldwulf (+739). His nationality is not stated; known by a biblical ecclesiastical name. He may, like Thomas of the East Angles, have been English.

TOCHANU, *see* Macarius.

TOMMENE mac Ronain, bishop of Armagh, 624-660, Jan. 10. I;I. *M. Bk. Lt.* 42ᶜ (sedit), lxxxiii (for xxxvi). First-named of the bishops addressed by Pope John in 640 (Tomianus), Bede *HE* **2**, 19.

TOQUONOCUS, *see* Conoc.

TORANNAN, *see* Ternan.

TORNEY, *see* Ternoc.

TOWEDOCUS, *see* Goueznou.

TRINIAN, *see* Ninian.

TRUMBERT VI L. E;E. Bede *HE* **4**, 3. Pupil of Chad (Ceadda) and teacher of Bede, the only teacher named by Bede.

TRUMHERE, bishop of the Mercians, 659-662. E;E. Bede *HE* **3**, 21, 24, 30. English-born, relative of Oswin, consecrated by the Irish, abbot of Gilling.

TRUMWINE, bishop of the Picts, 678-685. E;E. Bede *HE* **4**, 12, 26, 28. His see at Abercorn, West Lothian (*NT 0879*), retired to Whitby when the Picts killed Egfrith, there died; also called Tuma.

TUDA, bishop of the Northumbrians, +664. E?;I.E. Bede *HE* **3**, 26-27. Educated and consecrated among the southern Irish, observing the Roman tonsure and Easter, came to Northumbria in the episcopate of Colman, succeeded him after the synod of Whitby 664, died of the plague. The name is English rather than Irish.

TUDWAL, bishop of Tréguier, Leon (*L O*) VI M/L, Nov. 30. B;A. *BHL* 8350-3; A. de la Borderie, *Les Trois Vies anciennes de S. Tudual*, Paris, 1887. The first Life (also *RC* 1884) is identified by the editor with the Life by Tudwal's disciple Lovenan, cited *3*, pr. *3*, 6, and assigned to the sixth century; wrongly, for the language can hardly be earlier than the eighth century, and is more probably ninth or later (*1*, 1 and *3*, pr. however both cite Lovenan) (1-3). *AB* 8, 1889, 161 (4); *AG* 783 (5).

Son of Pompaia, sister of Rival, the first of the British to emigrate, in the time of Childebert (+558); followed later, in the time of his cousin Deroch. Landed in Achm, founding Lan Pabu in plebe Macoer (Trebabu in Ploumoguer, *C 3*), Trepompé in Morlaix, *H 2*, and Tréguier. Troubled by Ruhut, minster Conemor (+560) 'regis Francorum praefectus'; went to Paris with Albinus, bishop of Angers (+c.560), to secure confirmation as bishop; Pabu Tutwallus, named sixth of the seven bishops who accompanied Samson and Malo to Paris, c.556/7. Went on pilgrimage to Rome, *where he was elected pope, for two years, as Leo Britigena, 'ut Romanus catalogus narrat'*. Died at Tréguier, succeeded by Ruilinus, who was forced to yield three paruchiae to archdeacon Pebrecatus. 'Alias multas invenit ram in Britannia quam in regione Gallorum' (*1*, 2). His sites in Wales and Brittany, *LBS* 4, 273. Gonerus, Rumon, Winwaloe.

TUDWG, *see* Tudy.

TUDY VI M/L, May 11 (Sept. 3 Cornwall). B;A. Disciple of Maudetus, Winwaloe and Tudy, heirs of Corentin; possibly identical with Tethgo, pupil of Winwaloe; in v. *Winwaloe* 2, 19 'Tutualus' is perhaps an error for Tudi. Named St. Tudy, Co. (*SX 0676*), north of Bodmin and numerous sites in Brittany, *LBS* 4, 278, together with those assigned to *Tudwg*, *LBS* 4, 275-6.

TUMA, see Trumwine.

TUNBERT, bishop of Hexham, 681-684. E;E. Bede *HE* **4**, 12, 28. *Hist. Abb. anon.* 2, 3. Abbot of Gilling, moved to Ripon, bishop of Hexham, deposed (and succeeded by Cuthbert), 'pro culpa cuiusdam inobedientiae', vita *Eatae*, cited Plummer *Bede* 2, 268.

TUROG VI L/VII E, June 26. B;B. Wrote the 'Tiboeth', the lost Gospel Book of St. Beuno, said to have been in existence in 1594, *LBS* 4, 279. Named Maentwrog, Mer. (*SE 6640*) and several other Welsh sites, *LBS* 3, 281.

TYDECHO of Llanymawddwy, Mer. (*SH 9019*) VI M, Dec. 17. A?B;B. Verse Life, epitomised, with references *LBS* 4, 283. Lived with Dogfael and Tegfan in Pembrokeshire, relative of *King Arthur*, brother of Tegfedd, moved to Mawddwy, annoyed by Maelgwn and by Cynan (of Powys?). Perhaps identical with Titecho, who came with Cadfan and Padernus from Brittany, v. *Pat.* 4, *ByS* 22.

TYSSILIO of Meifod, Denbigh (*SJ 1513*) VI L/VII E, Oct. 1. B;B.A. Unpublished Life, cited *LBS* 4, 296; *AG* 603 (Suliau). *Son* of Brocmael Yscithrog of Powys, entered Meifod under abbot Guimarchus, whom he ultimately succeeded. Visited at Meifod by Beuno, v. *Beuno* 9. Brocmael was succeeded by his brother Iago (Jacob; unknown to the genealogies, perhaps of Gwynedd), who died two years later; his childless widow Haiarme seized the government and persecuted Tyssilio, who emigrated to Brittany. He landed at the mouth of the Rance, met St. Malo and established St. Suliac (*S 2*), seven or eight miles upstream, where he was visited by Samson. He protected his fields against cattle by planting hedges on high banks. Maglorius rescued his cook from a conger eel. Two monks of Meifod, *Pellibesten and Caramanien* asked him to return; he refused, but gave them a Gospel Book; and died soon after. His sites *LBS* 4, 301, perhaps also those assigned to *Tyssul* *LBS* 4, 305. Represented by Cyndelw as present at the battle of Maes yCogwy (Cocboy, Maserfelth, 642), *RBH* 1165 = *MA* 2, 177, 4, 8, cf. *BBCS* 3, 1926, 59.

ULTAN of Ardbraccan, Meath (*N 86*) +655, Sept. 4. I;I. *M.* mac Ua Conchobair, *FM* 656, *M. Tal.* Ultanus episcopus Conchuburnensium (in Deisib Breg, Hogan 288, whose territory probably extended as far north as Ard Bracca), *Tírechán* 1. Maintained some hundreds of children orphaned by the plague, *M. Oeng., M. Don.* With his left hand stayed a great fleet of foreign invaders, in the time of Diarmait *m. Cerbaill* (and Blathmac 655-664, therefore *c.*655). *M. Oeng.* Replaced Fursey (+649) as abbot of Louth (perhaps by confusion with Ultan, brother of Fursey) *M. Oeng.* Collected the miracles of Brigit and gave them to his disciple Brogan Claen to turn into verse, *M. Oeng.*, whence Ussher and Colgan (*TT* 542) ascribed Colgan's *vita tertia*, of the ninth(?) century, to him. At Fore, prayed with Fechin (+666) and Ronan m. Berach (of Dromiskin, Louth) that Ireland be spared famine, plague and foreign invasion, v. *Fechin* 2, 29 (*ASH* 136). His book on the miracles of Patrick, and his verbal information was used by Tírechán, *Tir.* 1. Berachus, Samthanna.

ULTAN of Lindisfarne *c.*740, Aug. 8. I;E. *SD* de abbatibus, Aethelwold 1, 274, hence *ASH* 109. Scottus, 'polite atque concinne libros sacros coenobii usum exscribere solebat'; after his death, his hand availed to cure sick brethren.

The tenth-century colophon says that the Lindisfarne Gospels were written by abbot **E**adfrith, 'in his own hand', *SD* 2, 12, perhaps literally accurate, *cf.* facsimile, Olten 1960, 5 ff. If the work was delegated, Ultan, remembered as the fairest scribe of his day, is the most likely author; if not, he evidently continued Eadfrith's work in texts that have not survived.

ULTAN of Peronne and Fosses (near Namur) +*c*.675/680, Apr. 27. I;E.Gaul. Bede *HE* **3**, 9. Kenney 505. Brother of **F**ursey and **F**oelan, accompanied his brothers to East Anglia and Gaul, succeeded Foelan as abbot of Peronne and Fosses.

ULTAN m. Maelsnechta VI/VII? May 1. I;S. Perhaps the Ultan whose relics were preserved on Sanda Island, off the Mull of Kintyre (*NR 5907*).

VALENS, bishop of Mursia in Pannonia, *c*.332-*c*.370, *DCB* pre-eminent Arian leader, intimate adviser of Constantius II.

VANDRILLE (Wandregislus) of Fontelle +668, July 22. Gaul;Gaul. *BHL* 8804-8810. *MGH SRM* 5, 13. Kenney, 494. Count of the royal palace, related to the Merovingian dynasty, inspired by the example of **C**olumban of Bobbio, wished to visit Ireland, imitated Irish asceticism, founded Fontenelle, on the Seine below Rouen, *c*.648.

VAUK, *see* Vougay.

VENNIANUS, *see* Finnian.

VENNOCUS, *see* Winnocus.

VERGILIUS, *see* Virgilius.

VICTORICUS Patrick, *Confessio* 23 'vidi in visu noctis virum venientem, quasi de Hiberione, cui nomen Victoricus' (hence the angel Victor of later Patrician legend, and Tirechan's 'bishop Victoricus') ('In a dream I saw a man named Victoricus, who seemed to come from Ireland'.) The form *Victoricus* occurs only in the Armagh MSS.; but has found its way into almost all modern printed texts. Six MSS. read *Victoricius*, a form unknown and linguistically improbable. The remaining MS. (St. Vaast, Arras Bm 450, printed *ASS* Mart. 2, 530 ff. ed. 2, the relevant passage now mutilated) reads *Victricius*. All editors have agreed to reject the majority reading *Victoricius* as improbable; and are therefore left with a straight choice between the Armagh *Victoricus* and the St. Vaast *Victricius*, each given in one MS. only. Recent convention has preferred the Armagh reading, because the MS. is available in Ireland, and is not, as the St. Vaast MS., now damaged. Victoricus is, however, a name virtually confined to Roman Africa (Victoricus of Therouanne is an eighth-century invention, Duchesne, *Fastes* 3, 147 ff.); Victricius (of Rouen) is a name closely connected with Patrick, a person whom Patrick was likely to see in a dream, *cf.* Grosjean *AB* 63, 1945, 99; and his name is corrupted, in some MSS. of Innocent *Ep.* 2, to 'Victoricius'. 'Victoricus' is therefore probably identical with **V**ictricius of Rouen.

VICTRICIUS, bishop of Rouen, *c*.388-*c*.408, Aug. 7. *DCB* His *de Laude Sanctorum* (Migne *PL* 20, 443) describes his visit to Britain (*c*.396); pupil of **M**artin of Tours (Sulp. Sev. *Dial.* 3, 2); correspondent of Paulinus of Nola (esp. *Ep.* 18; 37, *PL* 61, 239, 353) who praises his missionary work among the heathen in the territory of the Morini and Nervii, and of Innocent I (*Ep.* 2, *PL* 56, 519; *cf.* 18, 4, *PL* 61, 239) in 404, who rebuked interference in other dioceses. He brought to Britain the precepts of the martyrs, monasticism, the cult of martyrs, preaching to the heathen, confounded his opponents and taught the teachable, evidently in a British synod concerned with Martin's monastic innovations; the assertion of some modern writers that he was concerned with 'Pelagianism' is quite untenable; Pelagius had not yet expressed his views, and they did not become heretical until 20 years after Victricius' visit. He is probably the Victricius (or *Victoricus*) who appeared in a dream to Patrick and encouraged him to preach to the heathen Irish, since Victricius is the only known ecclesiastic to have advocated or practised missionary work among pagans on or beyond the frontiers at this date. His visit was followed by the establishment of the first-known martyr cult in Britain (St. Alban's), the first-known monasteries, St. Albans and Whithorn, and the first mission to barbarians (Ninnian's); and may well have inspired them.

VIGEAN, *see* Fechin.

VINNIANUS, *see* Finnian.

VIRGILIUS, bishop of Salzburg, +784, Nov. 27. I;Austria. *BHL* 8680-6. Kenney 523 ff. Grosjean, *AB* 78, 1960, 92 = MG Neci Serm. 2, 1907, 27. An Irishman, Alcuin *MGH* Poet. Lat. Aevi. Karol 1, 340, CIX, xxiv (Kenney 526, 329, vii); died 784, Annales Iuvanenses maiores, Salisburgenses, *MGH SS* 1, 87; 89; 785, Annales Ratisponenses, *MGH SS* 1, 92; 11, 6 ff. 789 (=784). Fergil, abbot of Aghaboe (Ossory) (of Cainnech), *AU*; (five years late with ecclesiastical dates in mid-VIII). 784, Fergil the geometer, abbot of Aghaboe, died in Germany in the thirteenth year of his episcopate, *FM*. Sent to Salzburg, *c.*742, after Pippin's defeat of Duke Odilo of Bavaria; abbot of St. Peter of Salzburg, administered the diocese with the help of a subordinate bishop Dobdagrecus (Dub-da-crich), consecrated in 755, after the death of Boniface; accompanied by Sedonius (Setna), subsequently bishop of Passau. Supervised the conversion of the Carinthian slavs. Compiled the *Liber Confraternitatis*, listing Irish abbots, in Iona, Ireland and Germany, *c.*760. Accused of teaching that another inhabited world, with another sun and another moon, existed 'under' the earth (more probably implying the existence of another universe in space than inhabitants of the Antipodes). Modern speculations, doubting the identity of Fergil of Aghaboe and Virgilius, making him a monk of Iona, of Samthann, author of the fantasy Geography of Aethicus Ister (Kenney 145) etc., are discussed by Grosjean. The name, unknown to the martyrologies, first appears in the eighth century; among clerics it is always spelt Ferghil, and is rare, confined to four or five individuals, of whom the earliest, Ferghil of Kilmore +770 *AU*, 765 *FM*, and Fergil m. Feradaig of the Clann Enna m. Loegaire m. Neill (Connacht) vir sanctus, eighth century, INL 700, are contemporaries of Ferghil of Aghaboe. Virgilius, transliterated from Ferghil, is plainly the abbot of Aghaboe, for the name is very uncommon; Austrian, Bavarian and Irish Annals record his death at the same date; Irish Annals are not otherwise known to have borrowed from German Annals, and only rarely notice Irishmen abroad. His sites in Carinthia, Gougaud *Saints Irlandais* 171.

VIRGILIUS MARO V/VI? Gaul;Gaul. Kenney 143, *cf. ZCP* 9, 118; Grammarian, pioneered experimental Latinity, akin to but differing from the language of Gildas, anticipating the fashions that begot the *Hisperica Famina* and the style of Aldhelm; acquainted with the Irish language and with Irish names, his work became popular in mediaeval Irish monasteries. Wrote probably in Aquitaine. His date is uncertain; if he were fifth-century, his connection with Ireland would be a solitary illustration of the otherwise unconfirmed statement of a *Leyden glossary* (VI/

VII, Kenney 142) that after the fifth-century invasions of the Huns, Vandals, Goths and Alans 'all the learned men this side of the sea fled to Ireland . . . and increased the learning of its inhabitants', cf. Kuno Meyer, *Learning in Ireland in the Fifth Century*, Dublin, 1913, and J. N. Hillgarth, *PRIA* 62 C, 1962, 167, for continuing Visigothic literary contact in the sixth and seventh centuries. Though Visigothic Latinity, and the works of Isidore, affected Irish metre and Irish thinking, in its early stages, Irish scholarship soon surpassed the mediocre attainment of the Visigothic lands in the fifth and sixth centuries. The statement that 'all the learned' emigrated to Ireland in the fifth century is patently absurd as it stands; apart from Virgil, no others are known. Doubtless some emigrated; Natalis, Boecius and a few others might have been immigrants from Europe, but the available evidence does not suggest that their numbers or influence were considerable.

VOLOCUS V E? Jan. 29. Gaul?B?;P. *Brev. Ab.* PH 44. *BHL* 8729. Soon after A.D. 400, Volocus, a foreigner, came to preach to fierce barbarians in Mar, who knew nothing of Christ and paid little attention to him. He lived in a wattle hut. The slender story, unconnected with any known monastic establishment, may be an echo of one of Ninian's monks.

VORTIGERN, *see* Foirtchern; Gurthiern.

VOUGAY (Vio) VI E/M, June 15. I;A. *ASS* June 2, 1060. *AG* 296. Irishman, *canon and archbishop of Armagh*, crossed to Brittany, founded Lanvenoc, *E 3*, opposite Brest and St. Vougay, *G 2* by Plouzebde, where, after his death, Tenenan (VI M/L) erected a chapel in his memory. His relics at Penmarch (headland) *E 6* in Treguennec, the south-western tip of Brittany. The mediaeval Litany of St. Vougay, *AG* 299, names no Irish saints but himself (as Becheve), Brigit and Fintan Munnu. He may be identical with St. Vauk, patron of Carn, Wexford (*T 10*) the south-eastern tip of Ireland, O'Hanlon 6, 668. In Brittany he is invoked to still the savagery of coastal storms.

WALDHERE, bishop of London, 693-*c*.725. E;E. Bede *HE* 4, 11. Successor of Erconwald, accepted king Sebbi of Essex as a monk, present at his death; received a grant from Swaefred 704, Birch 111; wrote to archbishop Bertwald 705, *HS* 3, 274, Birch 115; signed charter of Aethelbald 723 or 729 (if genuine). His successor Ingwald was in office by 731, *ASC*.

WASNULPH VII M/L, Oct. 1. I;Gaul. *M*. Usuard and Belgian etc. Calendars, O'Hanlon, 10, 1. Irishman, settled at Conde in Hainault, north of Valenciennes, now the French frontier town (Dep. du Nord) opposite Mons.

WENEFRED VII E/M, Nov. 3. B;B. *BHL* 8847-8854. *VSB* 288 = *BHL* 8847, by Robert of Salisbury, *ASS* Nov. 1, 708 = *BHL* 8848. *NLA* 2, 415 = *BHL* 8853. Daughter of Teuyth of Tegeingl (Flint) in the time of Cadfarn of Gwynedd (*c*.620-630). Beheaded by a would-be royal suitor, Caradauc f. Alauc, Beuno replaced her head. Went on pilgrimage to Rome, attended the Synod of Wenefred, where diverse houses agreed a common rule, discouraging anchorites (*VSB*). Lived under Deifer at Bodfari, Flint (*SJ 0970*) and Sadwrn at Henllan, Denbigh (*SJ 0268*), then with Eleri at Gwytherin, Denbigh (*SH 8761*), where she succeeded his mother Theon(ia) *Thynoy* as abbess and died. The place of her decapitation is Holywell, Flint (*SJ 1875*). Her relics were translated to Shrewsbury in 1138. Her later legends, *LBS* 3, 185 ff.

WERBURGA of Ely VIII E, Feb. 3. E;E. *BHL* 8855-7. *NLA* 2, 422. Said to have been daughter of Wulfhere, therefore niece of Aedilthryd. Abbess of Sheppey and Ely, she names a dozen major houses, mostly in Mercian lands. Her relics, translated to Chester, name its cathedral. Ermingild.

WETHENOC and Iacutus (James) VI M, Feb. 8. B;A. Unpublished Paris Life, (extract, A. de la Borderie, *Les deux Saints Caradec*, Paris, 1883, 23), *LBS* 3, 200; 3, 332; twins, brothers of Winwaloe. Their sites in Brittany, *LBS*.

WETHENOC VI E/M, Nov. 7. B;B. Bishop at Padstow, Co. (*SW 9175*) when Petroc arrived, maintained himself with difficulty in face of Petroc, v. *Petroc, passim*. Named St. Wetheney, Padstow, Bishop Stafford's register, 1415, cited *LBS* 4, 351. St. Enodoc, Rock. Daymer Bay, opposite Padstow, Gwinedoci in 1434, Guenedouci in 1607, is scarcely his.

WIHTBURGA of East Dereham, Norfolk VII L? March 17. E;E. *BHL* 8979-8981. *NLA* 2, 468. Said to have been a daughter of Anna, king of the East Angles, and therefore sister of Aedilthryd and Sexburga of Ely; brought up at Holkham, Norfolk, said to have been formerly known as Withburgstow (Arnold-Forster 2, 371). Founded East Dereham, south of the episcopal seat of Elmham, in her youth, lived there to a great age; her bones stolen by the monks of Ely in the tenth century.

WILFRED of Hexham and York, 634-709, April 24. E;E. *BHL* 8889-8896. Bede *HE passim*. Eddius, v. *Wilfred* (translation J. F. Webb, *Lives of the Saints*, Penguin, 1965). Summary, Plummer, *Bede* 2, 316. Nobly-born Northumbrian, entered Lindisfarne 648; pilgrimage to Lyons and Rome 653, 654-7 at Lyons. Summoned home by Alchfrith in 658, given Stanford and Ripon, 661, ordained by Agilbert, *c*.663. Led the Roman party at the synod of Whitby 664, elected bishop, consecrated at Compiègne, returned 666, to find Ceadda installed as bishop. Retired to Ripon, 666-669. Installed at York by Theodore 669; began to build Hexham, *c*.674. Expelled 678, went to Rome by way of Frisia, stayed with Dagobert II of Austrasia and Perctarit of the Lombards. 680 returned to Britain, imprisoned by Egfrid. 681-6 in Sussex, 686-9 restored to York, acts as bishop of the Middle English. Excommunicated at a Northumbrian synod in 702, in Rome 704. Recovered Ripon and Hexham 705, died at Oundle 709. Acca; Aebbe; Agilbert; Ceolfrid; Dicuil; Hilda.

WILGITHA, *see* Wulvella.

WILLIBRORD of Utrecht +739, Nov. 7. E;Frisia. *BHL* 8935-8945. (The earliest extant Life, by Alcuin, itself near contemporary, rests on a lost Irish original). Bede *HE* **3**, 13; **5**, 10-11, 19. Eddius 26. Born *c*.658, son of Wilgils, who soon after became a hermit in Northumbria; entered Ripon, studied in Ireland 678-691 under Egbert and Wichtbert, who had tried unsuccessfully to convert the Frisians. Sailed to the Rhine mouth, with 11 disciples, ill-received by the Frisians, withdrew to Frankish territory under Pippin II, went to Rome, consecrated by Pope Sergius I, 695. Returned to Frisia, ill-received by king Radbod, hostile to Frankish domination, tried unsuccessfully to evangelise the Danes under king 'Ongendus', returned towards Frankish territory with 20 Danish boys; on his way desecrated a heathen sanctuary on Heligoland, 'an island on the frontier between the Danes and the Frisians'. Deported by king Radbod. On Pippin's death (714), when Charles Martel subdued the Frisians, established himself at Utrecht. Built Echternach, and died there.

WINE, bishop of Winchester and London, *c*.674. E;E. Bede *HE* **3**, 7, 28; **4**, 12. King Cenwalh of Wessex, intolerant of the 'barbarica loquela' (presumably Frankish) of **A**gilbert, bishop of Wessex with his seat at Dorchester, 'subintroduced' Wine, 'suae linguae episcopus', 660 *ASC*, and established him at Winchester, having him consecrated in Gaul, without consulting Agilbert, who withdrew indignantly, leaving Dorchester vacant. Consecrated **C**eadda (Chad), with two British bishops, being himself the only duly consecrated English bishop, 664. Expelled from Wessex, bought the see of London from Wulfhere, held it to his death, *c.*674. **H**aedde.

WINFRITH, *see* Boniface.

WINFRITH, bishop of the Mercians, 672-*c.*674. E;E. Bede *HE* **3**, 24; **4**, 3, 5-6. Deacon of **C**eadda (Chad), 'vir bonus ac modestus', consecrated as his successor by **T**heodore, 672. Deposed by Theodore 'post annos . . . non multos', *c.*674, 'per meritum cuiusdam inoboedientiae', succeeded by **S**axul, retired to the monastery of Ad Baruae (? Barrow-on-Humber, Lincs. [*TA 0721*] opposite Hull), there died.

WINNEL, *see* Gwenael, Winwaloe.

WINNIAVUS, *see* Iuniavus.

WINNINUS, *see* Finnian.

WINNINUS of Kilwinning, Cunningham, Ayrshire (*NS 3043*) VI? Jan. 10. I?;B. *Brev. Ab.* PH 38 'Scotica provincia ortus', came by sea to Cunningham. Erected a marvellous stone cross at Kilwinning, there buried. He was probably an Irish Finnian; he was certainly not **F**innian of Moville, but it is possible that the story derives from the place-name, and that the place was named by a disciple of Finnian of Moville. He is almost the only Irish saint said to have preached among the British of Alclud.

WINNIOCUS VII E. Gaul.B?;Gaul. Local priest (presbiter ex parrochianis), father of Bobbolenus, later abbot of Bobbio, joined **C**olumban at Luxeuil, cured by Columban when an oak fell on his head during tree cutting, marvelled at Columban's miraculous acquisition of grain, Jonas, v. *Columban* 1, 15; 1, 17. The name is probably British.

WINNOC(HUS) +588. B;Gaul. Winnochus Britto came to Tours 'a Britanniis' (from Britain) on his way to Jerusalem in 578, wearing nothing but sheep skins; impressed by his extreme abstinence, Gregory ordained him priest, in order to keep him at Tours. In 586, the priest Vennocus Britto, 'whom we mentioned above', who had lived so ascetically that he ate nothing but uncooked vegetables, and when he took a cup of wine, imbibed so little that he seemed to kiss the cup rather than drink, gradually became ill, and took to drinking the whole cup immoderately. When drunk, he attacked men with a knife, or stone, or any kind of weapon, chasing them with insane fury, so that he had to be kept in chains for two years until he died. Greg. Tur. *HF* 5, 21; 8, 34 (incompletely reproduced with a wrong reference, *HF* 2, 78).

The pathetic consequence of prolonged undernourishment explains the intemperate violence attributed to some saints in the Irish and British Lives, and also the reason why a majority of monks opposed, and ultimately suppressed, the early ascetic practices of **D**avid, **R**uadan and others. The clothing, diet and pilgrimage to Tours and Jerusalem are contemporary instances of practices frequently reported in the Lives, which, seen in isolation, might overhastily be set aside as the invention of later hagiographers.

WINNOCUS of Wormholt, south of Dunkirk, Dep. Nord. +717, Nov. 6. A;Flanders, *BHL* 8952-6. *MGH SRM* 4, 769. Son of king Iudicael of Domnonie, +*c*.650, pupil of Audomar (**O**mer) of Therouanne (+670), himself a monk of Columban's Luxeuil. Came, with his disciples Quadanocus (Danoc?), Ingenocus and Madocus, to the territory of the Morini (Flanders), founded Wormholt and other sites under the protection of abbot Bertinus. Named his monastery in honour of Martin of Tours, died. His cult is widespread along the Belgian coast.

WINNOCUS, *see* Genoc.

WINWALOE of Landevennec (*F 3*), in the Faou estuary, the southernmost inlet of the Rade de Brest VI M/L (?583 or 594?), March 3. B;A, *BHL* 8957-8967. *AB* 7, 1888, 172, by Wrmonoc, abbot when Wrdestan wrote v. *Paul Aurelian*, in 884, in two books.

Son of Fracanus, 'Catovii regis Britannici . . . consobrinus' and Alba, brother of Weithnocus (**W**ethenoc) and Iacobus, who crossed to Brittany, landing at the mouth of the Gouet (Sangris) 'in portum . . . Bracke' (St. Brieuc, *N 2*) (1, 2) where Winwaloe was born, his mother being pregnant on the journey (1, 3). Placed as an infant in the monastery of Budic Arduus in insula Lurea (? Brehat islands, *M 1*) (1, 4-5). After childhood virtues and miracles (1, 6-13) returned to his parents and cured the wounded eye of his sister Chreirbia (1, 14). Fracanus 'fundum quendam reperiens non perparvum, sed quasi unius plebis modulum, silvis dumisque undique circumsaeptum, modo iam ab inventere nuncupatum' (Plou-Fragan (*N 2*), a mile south of St. Brieuc) had established himself on an estate surrounded by woods (1, 2); evidently the lands of a former Roman property, not yet wholly reverted to woodland. Cured his disciple Thetgonus of snake bite (1, 15). Protected the flock of Woedmonus, shepherd of Quonothedus (1, 16). Fracanus and Riwal, dux of Domnonia, arranged a match, to test the speed of their horses; they mounted the 'lightest boys', and several horses entered. Fracanus' horse was leading, but threw its jockey, Maglus son of Conomaglus, who fell among sharp stones, and was taken for dead. Fracanus was blamed. Some of the bystanders said, 'This son of yours Winwaloe, who is a holy man, can revive Him'. He told the crowd to stand back and clear a space, saying, 'The boy is not dead, but sick', and revived him (1, 18). The forms of the name 'Maglos, son of Conomaglos' cannot be much later than the sixth century; the story is near contemporary, and is almost the first account of a point-to-point horse race, the horses ridden by light jockeys with no carts attached. He formed the intention of visiting the holy places of Ireland, but St. Patrick appeared to him in a dream and told him to seek a site in Brittany (1, 19). So he decided to leave his master (1, 20-22). Set out with 11 disciples and came to Theopepigia (Tibidy, near Landevennec) in Cornugilensium confina (2, 1-3), thence to Landevennec (2, 4-8). His temper was equable, he wore goatskins, ate barley bread and vegetables, with a little fish on Fridays, but no meat and no fat, drinking water or apple juice, but no wine, like the Egyptian monks (2, 9-12). This rule was observed from the time of Gradlon to the fifth year of the emperor Louis (818) (2, 12-13). Visited king *Gradlon* of Cornubia, who had sunk the keels (cyulis) of five enemy chiefs on the Loire, poem inserted (2, 15-17); accepted the estates of his pupil **R**ioc, poem (2, 18, *cf.* 2, 22, *cf.* contents table). He, *Courentin* and **T**udwal (? for **T**udi, since Tutwal was not active in Cornouailles) are the three saints of Cornubia, king Gradlon its founder, poem (2, 19).

With his young deacon **E**thbin, who served the church a mile from Landevennec, cured a leper (2,22). Confounded the sons of Catmaglus, who robbed the monastery at midnight (2, 24). After various miracles (2, 25-27), died on Ash Wednesday, March 3, in the first week in Lent (2, 29); the complex mathematics suggest the year 583, or possibly 594. His numerous sites in England and Wales as well as Brittany, *LBS* 4, 361, include, exceptionally, several in East Anglia, at Norwich, Wereham, Norfolk (*TF 6801*), with Downham market nearby (*TF 6103*), and Winnell's Grove, Barley, Herts. (*TL 4038*), 'capella' near Royston. S. Winwaloei in 1387 *EPNS* 175. *LBS* cites a Norfolk rhyme, still used, of the March winds on the first three days of the month:

> First comes David, then comes Chad,
> Then comes Winnell roaring mad.

In a radio broadcast in 1956, I recited this rhyme and asked for information about similar local verses; six replies from different parts of the country gave variant versions of the same rhyme, all said to have been heard in Norfolk. The portion of the Icknield Way near Royston was called 'Wynewalestrete', *c.*1470 *EPNS* 175. Winwaloe's successor **G**wenael is said to have spent some years in Britain, seven years after Winwaloe's death (either just before or just after the landing of St. Augustine in Kent), and to have founded at least one monastery in Britain. His visit may be the occasion of these remarkable place-names, bestowed in honour of his master; his own name would give the same English form, Winnell, as Winwaloe, but would not give the fourteenth-century form Winwaloeus of the Royston site. **C**onocau; **I**diunet; **T**udy.

WIRO of Roermond, Limburg, Holland, on the Meuse north of Maastricht VII L/VIII E, May 8. I;Holland. *BHL* 8973-4. *NLA* 2, 444. Irishman, established in Limburg with the backing of Pippin.

WOEDNOVIUS, *see* Goueznou.

WULVELLA (**Wilgitha**) VI M. B;B. Sister of **S**ativola (Sidwell) and of **P**aul Aurelian; named Gulval, Co. (*SW 4 3*), near Penzance. Her other Cornish sites, *LBS* 4, 363.

WYMERUS, *see* Guiner.

WYNNER, *see* Guiner.

YWIUS, *see* Iwi.

LAYPEOPLE

(alphabetically listed)

LAYPEOPLE

[John Morris had, at the time of his death, drafted only a few specimen-entries for this section.]

AELLE	CUNORIX
AMBROSIUS	EDWIN
AMBROSIUS AURELIANUS	MAELGWN
ARTHUR	ODOVACER
BOIA	SAMO
BRIDEI	SERYGEI
BUILC	THEODORIC
CANINUS	VORTIGERN
CAUUS	

AELLE, k. Sussex, c.457 (symbol? c.495).

'Aelle and his three sons, Cymen and Wlencing and Cissa, came to Britain with three ships at the place called *Cymenes Ora* (*cf.* SELSEY, *below*) and there slew many Welshmen and some they drove to flight to the wood called *Andredesleg* (the Weald)', ASC 477 (= c.457).

'Aelle fought with the Welsh near *Mearc Redes Burnan stede* (Frontier Treaty River place)', ASC 485 (c.465).

'Aelle and Cissa besieged *Andredes Cester* (Anderida, Pevensey, the Roman Saxon Shore fort east of Eastbourne) and slew all who were therein, nor was there any Briton left', ASC 491 (= 471).

The archaeological and place-name evidence explains these entries. Fifth-century English cemeteries concentrate in the Downs between Brighton and Eastbourne in the east of the county, with a few, notably Highdown, west of Brighton. No pagan cemeteries have yet been discovered west of the Arun, that which meets the sea at Littlehampton, and the Chichester region has as yet provided no evidence of Saxon settlement before the seventh century, save for a single sixth-century brooch from the Roman cemetery. Unless and until such evidence is discovered, the existing evidence must be accepted, that the fifth-century Saxons settled in east Sussex, and did not cross the Arun before the second Saxon revolt at the end of the sixth century.

The place-name evidence concurs. Chichester bears the name of Cissa (*EPNS* 10, *cf.* xiii); it is not named 'Elchester' from Aelle. The wording of ASC 477 names Cymen, a normal personal name first, Cissa third; in between comes 'Wlencing', a place-name, Lancing, meaning 'the people of Wlenca' (*EPNS* 199). The story of Aelle's three sons therefore evidently developed. Cymen might have been drawn from the place-name, but at some date there certainly was a Cymen who named it. Since it was the traditional first landfall, it might have earned its name from a person who actually landed there, a companion or possibly a son of Aelle, and have retained it while the place was not in English hands. Wlencing, not a person, is plainly an addition. The last name in any set of brothers in a pedigree is always most likely to be an addition; and Cissa is therefore likely to have lived considerably later than Aelle. He may have been the king who occupied Chichester in or about the late sixth or early seventh century.

The ASC entries record three events: first a landing at Selsey, a battle, when only 'some' of the enemy fled to the Weald; second a battle at the *stede* (root meaning, a fixed place, *static*, in later usage a place in general) by a frontier treaty river; the name implies a previous treaty (Mercred is not a normal name, and rivers rarely bear the names of people) which fixed a frontier on a river. The archaeological evidence suggests that it was the Arun. The English settled the countryside in the east, but the British held the walled fortress of Pevensey fourteen years later. The frontier battle is not claimed as a victory. The British record of the Kentish Chronicle (s.a. 449E) also held that Sussex was ceded by treaty, about the mid 450s. The ASC record suggests that the British of Chichester did not respect the treaty made by Vortigern.

Bede (HE 2, 5) calls Aelle the first English king to hold *imperium* over 'all the southern English', like Aethelbert of Kent a century later. The meaning cannot be that the *imperium* was acquired by conquest, since the small isolated kingdom of Sussex did not subdue Kent, East Anglia, the middle Thames, and Leicestershire in the fifth century. The *imperium* can only have been one conferred by agreement among allied English kings. It is likely that the occasion was Badon, and Aelle, if still alive, was then the senior English king. The traditions of Kent and Wessex place the deaths of their commanders, Aesc and Cerdic, at about the time of Badon, in the middle 490s.

Bede's tradition implies that Aelle was appointed supreme commander of the army that marched to Badon; the coincidence of dates suggests that it included contingents from Kent and Hampshire. No relevant traditions survive from the English on and north of the Thames to indicate whether any of them also took part.

AMBROSIUS

Guorthigirnus . . . urgebatur . . . a timore Ambrosii, Nennius 31; *a regno Guorthigirni usque ad discodiam Guitolini et Ambrosii anni sunt XII* (= 425 + 12 = 437) *quod est Guoloppum, id est Catguoloph*, Nennius 66. Emrys Wledic exiled to Armoria by Vortigern (with his brother Uther Pendragon).

Vortigern's contemporary cannot be Ambrosius Aurelianus (below), who was in his prime 30 years later. He may be his unnamed father, *purpura indutus*, emperor (Gildas 25), called *de consulibus Romanicae gentis*, Nennius 42. *T* 51 makes him 'son' of Custennin Vendigeit, who is probably evolved from Constantine III. The substance of these tales is that he belonged to the high Roman aristocracy of early fifth-century Britain, and was a ruler of the island, emperor, dispossessed by Vortigern.

AMBROSIUS AURELIANUS

After the migration of the late 450s those who remained (*reliquiae*) rallied *duce Ambrosio Aureliano, viro modesto, qui solus forte Romanae gentis tantae tempestatis collisione, occisis in eadem parentibus purpura nimirum indutis, superfuerat*, Gildas 25. His unworthy descendants were living in Gildas's time. He is not otherwise mentioned except in medieval legend (Mabinogion Culwch ac Olwen; BBC 31, 63, etc.; Nennius 41 ff.). Some of these references evidently allude to lost poems and stories, which doubtless occasioned the naming of hills (e.g., Dinas Emrys). His name may also be preserved at Emricorva (perhaps Chepstow) *cf.* LL 158, and possibly in the chapel of St Ambruxca or Ambrose at Crantock in Cornwall (*LBS* 1, 151).

The name was occasionally used in early Wales, *cf.* e.g., Emris (LL 226, dated to the early sixth century), Ambrus (LL 32, undated); but it was not common. The more recent popularity of Emrys derives rather from the Mabinogion stories than from a direct memory of Ambrosius.

A personal name Ambres is common in English place-names: examples are Ambresdene and Ambresmedwe (*EPNS* county volume reference given) in the west country, Ombresley (SO 8563), and a lost name near Feckenham (SO 9862) (Worcs. 268), Amberley in Hereford (SO 6547) (*DPNS* 9) and in Gloucestershire (SO 8501) (95); Amesbury in Wiltshire (SO 1641) (359) and Ambrosden in Oxfordshire (SO 6019) (161); elsewhere only in Sussex at Ambersham (SO 9120) (97, but not Amersham in Bucks 29), Amberley (TQ 0213) (146), and Amberstone (TQ 5911) (435); and, most common of all, in Essex, Amber near Debden (TL 5633) (524), Stebbing (TL 6724) (632), Walthamstow = Folly Lane (TQ 3691), Marching (TL 5313), and Wickham Bishops (TL 8413) (106), and at Ambersbury Banks (TL 4300) in Epping Forest (TL 4109) (22) (where, however, the name is first attested in the seventeenth century). I have not been able to locate, or see the early spellings of Amsbury in Kent (cited as from Wallenberg, *PNK* 161).

The editors of the several volumes have advanced a wide variety of discordant guesses for the meaning of this name. The earlier suggestion of an unrecorded 'pet form' of Eanbeorht was rightly dismissed in WO 268; instead the 'archaic Vandal' *Ambri* was substituted, frequently repeated under the less exact description of Old German. No such name is known in England, and it does not seem likely that so many places were named after an archaic Vandal unknown to English tradition. Other guesses include a species of sorrel (Ess. 524), various birds (Gl. 5; *DEPN* 9 Amberden), an imaginary Celtic *ambr*, supposed to mean a river because Latin *imber* means a shower of rain (*DEPN* 9 Amber, rejected Db. 2), and further imaginary English names, as Eamha (Sx. 436). Since so many early English names are known, invented names never used by known Englishmen are doubtful explanations.

The diligent attempts to find an English derivation for 'Ambres', as a personal name or as a topographical term, have not succeeded; the explanations proposed are contradictory and unconvincing. No relevant topograpical term in any other language has been observed. Linguistically, the obvious, simple and unexceptionable origin is a personal name 'Ambres' or 'Ambros'. This was the earliest explanation advanced, in Camden's *Britannia* (1594) 186 (repeated *LBS* 1, 150); and the only known person of that name is Ambrosius. The explanation has been ignored, not through any philosophical objections, but because the historical conclusion was not superficially obvious.

This explanation implies that these places were called by some form of the name Ambrosius before the English overran them, in or after the late sixth century, and acquired an English termination, as Dunwich in Suffolk is the 'wic' of a British (or Irish) Domnoc. They are unlikely to be the personal estates or residences of Ambrosius, as, for example, a Paulignac in parts of France denotes the estate of a Roman Paulinus, since such names are not known in England.

The explanation must be sought in some other habit of Roman place-name formation. A frequent usage was for military stations to be known by the name of their garrisons, as, for example, the modern Passau was called *Batavae* because its garrison was a cohort of Batavians (*AA* p. 53). In the later Roman Empire army units known by personal names were normally those raised by emperors: 'Theodosiaci' or 'Theodosian', 'Honoriaci' or 'Honoriani' are frequently used, meaning troops named after the Emperors Theodosius and Honorius. The most likely native origin of 'Ambros' is therefore that the places so named were the stations of units raised by and named after Ambrosius Aurelianus, styled 'Ambrosiaci' or 'Ambrosiani'.

The naming of a place from its garrison implies a long residence by that garrison. Such places therefore suggest the permanent homes in which the units were placed after the wars, not necessarily their location during the fighting. Their distribution is striking. In general, they are confined to the central regions of the fifth-century wars, between Norfolk and the Severn valley. In particular, they comprise three main groups. One surrounds and protects (or contains) the *civitas* of the Dobunni. Three such places are poised around the confines of the English of east Sussex: the third group, the densest concentration of the three, lines the valley of the Lee and Stort, well sited to shield London against East Anglian attack down the Roman roads from Cambridge, complementary to the fortress of Colchester (see pp. 76-77) whose situation covered the more easterly approaches from East Anglia to London.

The surviving 'Ambres' names are likely to be no more than a proportion of those which may at one time have been in use. Their explanation, as British military posts of the early sixth century, appears to be the most logical inference from the peculiar name; and as such must take precedence over fanciful and discordant philosophical guesses, and over the obvious truism that we do not certainly know the explanation. It is, however, tentative, and can stand only until new evidence or new considerations suggest a more logical inference.

ARTHUR
Poems

CA 1241-2 (Gododdin) *gochore brein du ar uur / caer ceni bei ef Arthur*, translated Jackson *Ant.* 13, 1939, 29, 'a warrior glutted the black ravens of the ramparts of the city (i.e., by making corpses of so many Englishmen), though he was no Arthur', at the battle of Catraeth, *cf. Annals* 598. The substance of the poem is probably of the early seventh century (*CA* introduction, Jackson *Ant.* 13), its latest additions of the later seventh. The Arthurian verse probably belongs to the original core of the poem. The poem was written probably within a century of Arthur's lifetime, just within living memory. It praises its hero for his exploits, 'though he was no Arthur', and thereby asserts that there had been a hero named Arthur in the recent past whose exploits overtopped those of the late sixth-century warriors.

Marwnad Gereint (Elegy of Geraint) line 20, *BBC* 72, 9 = *RBH* 14, 8 (FAB 267: 38 and 275; translated Gwyn Williams, *Burning Tree* 43) described the death of Geraint of Dumnonia while fighting against the English at Llongborth (probably Portchester by Portsmouth) under the emperor (Ameraudur) Arthur. The surviving text is of the eighth or ninth centuries, but its content and form ally it with the bardic elegies of the late sixth century, the earliest surviving Welsh poems, which mourn the death of patrons the poet had served and known. The poem is likely to be a modernised version of a lost original. It has fewer detailed signs of early Welsh orthography. A poem of the late fifth century could not, however, have been composed in Welsh, since the British language had not yet turned into Welsh. A later Welsh version was therefore necessarily more ruthless, amounting to a translation rather than a normal modernisation.

Nennius 56 reads, *Tunc Arthur pugnabat contra illos* (the Saxons under Octha [Ossa,

Oesc] in the late fifth century) *in illis diebus cum regibus Brittonum, sed ipse dux erat bellorum*, following with a list of 12 battles, the second, third, fourth and fifth on the river Dubglas in Linnuis (the Witham in Lindsey? *cf.* AA p. 112), the last of them Badon. The text is a translation from a Welsh original, since it contains the rendering (repeated *ACm* 516) that carried the 'image of the Virgin Mary' (cross of Jesus Christ, *ACm*) *super humeros suos*, on his shoulders, mistaking *ysgwyd*, shield, for *ysqwydd*, shoulder. The original was probably a poem, which devoted four stanzas to the battle on the Douglas, *cf.* AA p.112 above. This or a similar poem is perhaps also echoed in the later poem *Kadeir Teyrnon*, referring to Arthur's 'armoured legion' (*leon luryc*) and 'red purple' (*goch gochlessur*) *BT* 36, 16; 34, 18. The northern British tradition that makes Ossa Gyllelfawr (Big Knife), Oesc of Bernicia and Kent fight Arthur at Badon may have the same origin; and English tradition hints that Cerdic of Wessex and Aelle of Sussex may have allied with Oesc.

The Welsh bards also knew a third Arthurian poem. The paragraph in the *Welsh laws* on the 'Chief of Song' (*Pencerdd*) in the Gwent Code (1, 37) contains the ruling that:

6. When the king wishes to hear a song, the Pencerdd shall sing two songs . . . one of God, another of the kings . . . the household bard (*bard teulu*) shall sing the third.

7. When the queen wishes a song in her apartment (*ystauell*), the bard (of the household, MSS. variant) shall sing (three songs, MSS. variant) of Camlan (kerd of Camlan), not loudly, that the hall (*neuad*) be not disturbed.

In the Demetian Code (1, 25) the bard of the household is to sing the queen 'three elaborate songs' (*gerd vangaw*), while the Venedotian Code (1, 41) omits the queen's song.

The manuscripts are late, but it does not seem probable that the queen's song is a post-Norman addition. Rather, the variation in the Demetian and Venedotian Codes suggests that it was an earlier rule, later dropped.

The Myrddin Cycle contains allusions to two or three other lost Arthur poems, and there were doubtless others. One at least was translated into Irish, and became a standard tale. The *Book of Leinster* (*c.*1130) lists the title of a lost Irish tale of Arthur, that all true *filid* should know 190a 40 (4, 837).

These notices indicate that there was at one time a Historical Cycle of at least half-a-dozen Arthur poems, that was forgotten early. There are reasons why some poems were remembered and others forgotten. The territories that the northern princes of the late sixth century ruled remained British-speaking for 500 years. Heirs of these dynasties took refuge in Wales or on the Clyde, preserving the poems that honoured their personal ancestors, and these poems were first composed in Welsh.

Contemporary poems about Arthur were necessarily composed in British. They concerned localities whose rulers spoke English from the seventh century, and Arthur left no descendants. But the essential reason is that Arthur was victorious. The early verse that medieval Wales preserved is a literature of defeat: the victory songs sung in the sixth century in honour of Maelgwn, and doubtless of others, have also not been preserved. The two Arthurian poems whose theme is known, that were preserved, in Welsh translations, later than the eighth century, were both songs of Arthur's defeats at Llongborth and Camlan. The poem, known to Nennius or his source, and probably the Irish story, were songs of victory.

Annals

ACm 516 (= *c.*495) *Bellum Badonis* (*cf.* **P** Badon) *in quo Arthur portavit crucem Domini nostri Jhesu Christi tribus diebus et tribus noctibus in humeros* (= shield, *cf.* Nennius 56, note above) *suos et Brittones victores fuerunt.*

ACm 537 (= *c.*516, *cf. Annals* 537) *Gueith Camlann* (unlocated) *in qua Arthur et Medraut corruerunt.*

These two notices are the only British entries, apart from the birth of David, in the Cambrian Annals before 573. In deciding where to integrate them into his text of the Irish Annals, the compiler had to work out their position for himself. It seems probable that he had before him some indication of the interval between Badon and Camlann, perhaps a synchronism of the type common in Ireland, instanced for Wales in *CPS* 161, but had no indication of absolute date.

Saints' Lives

v. *Cadoci* prolog. *hero strenuus* who helped Gwynnllyw repel invasion by Brachan.

23. *hero fortissimus*

22. *rex illustrissimus Britanniae* who invaded south-east Wales from beyond the Wye, in pursuit of *Ligessauc* (sea farer) *Lauhir filius Eliman, dux Britannorum fortissimus*, who had there sought refuge after killing three of Arthur's *milites*, when none would shelter him for fear of Arthur.

v. *Gildae* (CL 5) *rex totius maioris Britanniae, rex universalis Britanniae* killed Hueil (Cuill) of the upper Forth who feared no king, not even Arthur.

v. *Iltut* 2 *Iltutus . . . audiens . . . Arthurii regis . . . magnificentiam, cupivit visitare tanti victoris curiam*, where he served. Later, Poulentus of Penychen in Glamorganshire made Iltut his 'magister militum' because he had been *curialem . . . militem atque honorabilem.*

v. 1 *Carantoci* 4 *Cato et Arthur regnabant in ista patria* (Dumnonia; near Minehead, Somerset, **E** Cairnech) and offended the saint, but Arthur granted him his site. Cato ruled Dumnonia, then perhaps including Dorset, Wiltshire and Hampshire; Arthur appears as his sovereign.

v. *Paterni* 21 (near Aberystwyth) *deambulat quidam tirannus regiones altrinsecus, Arthur nomine* who offended the saint and was pardoned.

The incidents are unhistorical, all but the first placed after Arthur's time. The attitude to Arthur is their tradition. It contains two statements: he is an all-powerful king of the whole of Britain, superior to the regional kings of the south, his power feared by all; and in Wales and Scotland he is a foreigner, lecherous, violent, cruel, coming from abroad to assert his authority in the highlands.

The Name

Artorius is a normal Latin *nomen*, family name, comparable with Calpurnius (father of Patrick, **E**, with Quintillius, Catellius, etc., in the genealogies, with Pumpeius and Turpillius in inscriptions (*ECMW* 198; 43). He is likely also to have had a *cognomen*, personal name. These names, proper to the early empire, survived in the fourth and fifth centuries, principally among the local landowning classes of the western provinces.

The name was popular in the sixth century, given to their sons by Aeden, king of the Irish Scot settlers in Dal Riada, in Argyle, and by his son Conang (Adomnán, v. *Col.* 1, 9); by king Peter of Demetia (BD); Bicoir the Briton (**A** 626); Coscrach of Leinster (CGH 78. R 125 a 41, probably late sixth century), and possibly by Pabo of the northern Pennines (BN). Thereafter it is not again recorded until prince Arthur, murdered by king John in the twelfth century (the letters 'Artr' in the old

Welsh Towyn inscription *ECMW* 287, probably of *c*.700 A.D., Jackson LHEB 668, n. 1, are not likely to be a form of Arthur). Prince Arthur and subsequent Arthurs were certainly named after the Arthur of legend: the half-dozen British and Irish rulers who gave the name to their children a few decades after Arthur's death will have named them after the recent king, the hero celebrated in the *Gododdin*. This isolated crop of Arthur names at this date, among the Irish and British, indicate a great ruler whose name was widely honoured in both countries, who lived about the year 500.

Place

The tradition of the Saints' Lives puts Arthur outside Wales and Scotland, and therefore in the lowlands (and/or the Pennines), in what is now England. Arthur's popularity in later ages caused him to be localised by Welsh tradition in Wales. The Norman romances do not share this tradition. Their tradition is to be preferred, because they had no axe to grind, and because they occasionally show that they had access to accurate information. Chritien correctly located king Mark at Castle Dore by Fowey, in the hundred of Lantyen in Cornwall, though he did not know that Mark was also called Conomorus, or that his name was there extant upon an inscription (**E** Paul Aurelian). Arthur's knights live in Logres (Lloegr, England), not Wales. They name many identifiable places. Apart from Avalon, Tintagel and the purely Norman Cardigan (Welsh Aber Teifi), they make him hold court in Camelot (*Chevalier de la Charette* 34, Vulgar Lancelot, etc.), Car(d)ueil (Carlisle) (*Erec 4515, Marie de France, Lanval,* etc.), Carlion (*Charette* 32), Caruent (*Erec 2315*), Cestre (*Erec 1721, 2690*), Evroic (York) (*Erec 2131*), Gloecestre (Gloucester) (*Erec 1935*). These are all major Roman towns, *coloniae, civitas* capitals, or legionary fortresses. Whatever their source for these names, it is plain that the one site among them not readily identified, Camelot, is to be sought among places of the same kind as its fellows, in a major Roman city whose name was something like Camelot. The place intended can hardly be other than Camelodunum, Colchester. The archaeological evidence suggests that Colchester may have been a place of some moment in the Arthurian period. Its gates were twice burnt and forced, the most likely historical contexts being the first and second Saxon revolts; and it held one massive well-built wall constructed over a Roman street, with a medieval street above it. Outside the castle (the temple of Claudius, possibly a fortified point in the late Roman period) a small chapel was built, out of alignment with the castle, but before the Norman bailey was added. Nothing is known of its date, save that it lies between the Romans and the Normans, save that its successive footings suggest that it was rebuilt at least twice, and therefore had a long life; and that, in one of its periods, at least part of its internal walls seem to have been faced with marble gates (*cf.* the drawings and sections, Hull, *Roman Colchester*).

Insula

The History: The poems, with battles in Hampshire, Lincolnshire and the border counties, the tradition of the Saints' Lives and of the Norman romances make Arthur a supreme ruler, emperor, of the whole of the former Roman province of Britain. No other direct memory is preserved, beyond a name, a defined territory, and a mighty legend of lost power and glory. Many other notices describe the events and persons of Arthur's reign. Gildas does not name him. He names no names at all save those of the five kings he denounces, and Ambrosius Aurelianus, whose descendants he attacks, and does not even name the one good king he praises, Agricola of Demetia. But he also praises the government of Arthur's day, when

'kings, public and private persons, bishops and priests, each kept their own station'
(26), in contrast with the degeneration of his own day, and says something of its
institutions. Incidental evidence suggests that Arthur and his subordinates employed
Irish commanders in lowland Britain, at Wroxeter, Silchester, Winchester, Goths
and German against the Irish (cf. Boia;Theodoric); Roman emperors commonly
employed barbarian captains, with or without forces of their own countrymen. The
evidence for events that relate to the time of Arthur are discussed above.

The Legend

Arthur is more prominent in Welsh medieval story than any other individual,
named in two dozen Triads, cf. TYP 294, the Mabinogion, especially *Kulhwch ac
Olwen* and Twrch Trwyth, the Verses of the Graves, and many other poems, cf.
references in TYP 276-7, R. S. Loomis, *Arthurian Literature in the Middle Ages*, 1959,
J. D. Bruce, *Evolution of Arthurian Romance*, 1923, etc. Though many of the Welsh
stories survive only in late form, it is more probable that the core of this legend
was shaped long before the Norman romances, who make incidental use of it.

The Norman legend takes two main forms. Geoffrey of Monmouth's Arthur is a
conqueror who made the name of Britain great. To the poets, he is the champion
of justice, the pattern of strong, fair, royal government that restrained mighty lords
from wronging the weak and unprotected, especially the damsels. His reign had
been a golden age, destroyed by disunity. The story caught the imagination of the
literate wherever the Normans went, and Arthur's name became the most widely
sung among all great kings of the past who slept until they should return to free
mankind from evil. Arthur left a son in Welsh legend, but the son is little celebrated;
he is made nephew of Ambrosius Aurelianus and son of 'Uthyr Pendragon', but
this is not developed. Arthur himself sleeps in Richmond Castle, Sewingshields on
Hadrian's Wall, Cadbury Castle in Somerset, Manchester, Mount Etna, in Savoy
and in Arabia, and in many other places. In Britain he names a large number of
hills, rocks and the like. It is unlikely that any of the hills or rocks bore Arthur's
name before the legend became popular; several of them are doubtless corruptions
of names that contained the common place-name and personal element *arth*. A little
evidence suggests that some of the sleeping places in England may have been
connected with Arthur before the legend was duly developed. Manchester (Mancun-
ium), is the likely origin of 'the king of Magounz' of *Le Lai du Cor*, a place-name
turned to a person, as 'Evrawc' (York) becomes the 'father' of Peredur (Perceval).
Excavation has shown Cadbury Castle to have been a stronghold during the Arthurian period (*Ant. Jl.* 47, 1967, 70; 48, 1968, 6; cf. *Ant.* 41, 1967, 50).

The detail of the transmission of the legend from the sixth-century Arthur mem-
ories to the Norman romance is unknown, but not mysterious. Welsh legend wove
stories about Arthur, and was to a limited extent utilised by the Norman poets,
and in its turn borrowed back a few of their names and stories. But it had a wholly
different idiom and purpose. Almost nothing whatever is known of the secular
literature, oral or written, of Cornwall or Brittany in the intervening centuries.
There is no reason to suppose that the numerous fifth-century British-speaking
settlements in Normandy had wholly abandoned their language by the twelfth
century. The silence of French writers gives no indication: there is little enough to
be found in modern French literature to show that Breton is still spoken, or in
modern German records to show that the Slavonic tongues, Sorb and Wendish, are
still spoken in parts of Saxony and elsewhere. It is likely that versions of the Arthur
story were remembered in Brittany and Normandy, just as English folk songs are
occasionally recovered in the Alleghany mountains in the U.S.A., after several

centuries of migration. It is also likely that in the very different conditions of the British of Brittany and Normandy, the content of the Arthur legend will have taken a different form from the Welsh. But since nothing whatever is known of the songs and stories of the British in Gaul, it is not possible to guess their content, possible only to indicate that such stories are likely to have been available, constituting the *Leis*, '*matiere de Bretagne*', rendered into French by Marie de France and her successors.

BOIA

v. *David*, 16-19, *Baia . . . Scottus . . . satrapa; Buched Dewi, Boya ac Yscot oed*; tempted David's monks by parading naked women before them, and tried to kill David; the same story attributed to *Picta gens subdola . . . ilius gentis princeps* v. *Teilo LL* 100.

The name Boia is not otherwise recorded: Boia is a Germanic name, not uncommon among the English (Searle *Onomasticon* 110, *cf.* also Bodmin Gospels, Manumission 20 [*HS* 1, 679] *Boia diaconus*, signing with other priests with English names).

Both forms occur in place-names immediately by St Davids, at the isolated rock of Clegyr Boia (*SM 7325*), which has an early fortified *castell*, and at Caer Fai (*SM 7524*).

Boia was killed by *Lisci filius Paucaut*, perhaps an Irish Losc m Pichain, *cf.* Porth Llisky (*SM 7323*) also by St Davids. The stories may have been invented to explain the names, or the places named from the story; but either way, the Germanic name Boia is present at St Davids.

BRIDEI

k. Picts 554/6-584. *Venit autem Brittaniam Columba, regnante Pictis Bridio filio Meilochon, rege potentissimus, nono anno regni eius*, Bede *HE* 3, 4. The chapter begins *anno . . . DLXV . . . Venit de Hibernia . . . presbyter et abbas . . . Columba Brittaniam, praedicaturus verbum Dei provinciis septentionalium Pictorum*. Adomnán (his evidence summarised Reeves, p. 310, Columba) gives the date of Columba's arrival as 563, and is followed by the *Annals*, in Bridei's eighth year, Chron. Pict. *CPS* 7. Adomnán was a careful scholar, earlier than Bede, and much better informed. His date must prevail. Bede's information was that the express purpose of Columba's migration was to convert the Picts, which considerably oversimplifies; his subject is the Picts, and his source is either Scot or north British. It is likely that the date he gives is that of Columba's first visit to Bridei, and that he assumed that Columba had crossed in the same year. If 563 was his ninth year, his reign began 554/5; if his eighth 555/6; if 565 was his ninth, 556/7.

In Britannia Bridus rex Pictorum effecitur, Marcellinus continuator, 1. 557 cited Plummer *Bede* 2, 131. He is the only fifth- or sixth-century king in Britain to be noticed in a continental chronicle by name. Reigned 30 years. 'Son of Meilchon', put the Scots to flight, *Annals* 560; died 584, *Annals*.

Received Columba, at first unwillingly, at his fortress down the river Ness from Loch Ness, i.e., near Inverness; king of the Picts, the king of Orkney his client, powerful king of the Picts, Adomnán, v. *Columbae, passim, cf.* index, Reeves 120-1.

His name is Brudeus in 21 MSS. readings, in half-a-dozen mentions of the name, in Adomnán, Brudeus in one, Brudenus in one, in Pictish texts in *CPS* Bridei (7), Bruide (28, 399), Brude (173, 286), Brudenus (399). Bede's spelling Bridius is probably earlier, since Meilochon retains the composition vowel, suggesting a source text considerably earlier than Bede's time, *cf. LHEB* 647-8; Maglocunus-Maelgwn is not among the category of names where the composition vowel remained, in words where the syllables were somewhat harder to pronounce without it. Commonly Bruide in the *Annals*.

Meilochon is Maglocunos-Maelgwn, and is British. Bede does not expressly identify him with Maelgwn of Gwynedd, and theoretically he might be another man of the same name who lived in the same generation. But the name is very rare, with only three or four instances known from all texts and inscriptions. The man whom the Picts elected as king was not the son of an obscure person; since the Pictish succession passed through the women, a Pictish princess must have married Bridei's father or grandfather, and the princess is equally unlikely to have been married to any but another royal. Welsh tradition allots Maelgwn to an 'Irish' Pict mother, and unless the so-called 'Gwydyl Fichti' are to be accepted as fact, the tradition must be held to relate to a normal Pict. There is therefore little reasonable cause to doubt that the Bridei whom the Picts selected was the son of the great king of Gwynedd. Since he is the first recorded foreigner to occupy the Pict throne, his choice was a deliberate political decision of considerable importance. The Pictish regnal lists show a divided kingdom before his accession, and the *Annals* record another king in his last years, presumably a rival, named Galam Cennaleph, who was killed in southern Pictland in a civil war among Picts (*AT*).

He sufficiently impressed future generations to cause three seventh-century successors to be given his name (usually preserved in spelling Bredei, Brude), and to cause the compilers of the Pictish lists to name a group of 30 imaginary kings of the centuries B.C. 'Brude', distinguished by epithets in pairs, Brude Pant, Brude Urpant, Brude Gant, Brude Urgant, and the like. The spelling of Adomnán, Bede, and the Pictish lists suggests that the name may be the same as the Powysian Bredoe, Brittu, Brydw. Since Maelgwn is given a Powysian wife, it is possible that she was his mother and passed to him a Powysian name.

The number and nature of references to him single him out as the greatest of the early Pictish kings, but give little information on what he did to earn his fame. To Bede he was the king converted to Christianity, and also *potentissimus*. Slight evidence, principally of place-names, suggests that in the early sixth century, under his predecessors, the Scots of Dal Riada had annexed a large portion of southern Pict territory in Strathmore and that his victory over Gabran in 560 recovered all or most of it, uniting the Picts. He appears to have held them, for Adomnán makes no reference to wars between him and Aedan of Dal Riada. He was killed by a rebellion by the southern Picts. The *Annals* date Aedan's expedition to the Orkneys and his wars in southern Pictish territory to the years after Cennaleph's death in 581, before and after Bridei's death in 584, but no source names Bridei as Aedan's enemy.

The *Annals* do not indicate whether Bridei's immediate successors ruled from Inverness or from southern Pictish territory, but they report successive rulers with little sign of division between the two territories. The English annexed southern Pictland for a generation in the seventh century; king Bredie f. Bili who expelled them is called king of Fortrenn, the southern Picts, but since his body was brought to Iona for burial (v. *Adomnani*), he probably also ruled the north. It is probable that, at least from his time, the main seat of monarchy lay in the south.

BUILC

Nennius 14 (immediately before the sentence cited above, Kidwelly) *Builc autem cum suis tenuit Euboniam insulam et alias (regiones) circiter.* Eubonia is here more probably Anglesey (Mon) than the Isle of Man, *cf.* index. 'Other regions' would therefore mean Gwynedd. Builc (Bolg) recalls the Fir Bolg, one of the ancient 'pre-Gaelic' peoples of Ireland, but is exceedingly rare as a personal name, or epithet. A Carthach mac Deirg of the Ciarraige is glossed 'is e Bolgc Druince in sin' (CGH 299: R 159 b 51); Bolg mac Decci *quem Patricius baptizavit*, of their neighbours across the Shannon, the Corco Baiscinn (CGH 380: LL 324 g 51) is assigned to the later fifth century, somewhat late for the Nennius context; Crundmael Bolg Luatha, king of Leinster (*ca* 629), is much too late and is never named as plain Bolg; but Aengus Builg king of the Corco Laigde in south-west Munster about Bantry Bay, father-in-law of Corcc, king of Munster in Patrick's time (CGH 195: R 148 a 25; *cf*. 262-3: R 115 b 11-24), dates to about 400 and is much more prominent. He is the only Bolg who appears as an ancestor, and therefore in the genitive case, in the available genealogies; and Nennius' British source, employing an Irish genitive as a Latin nominative, presumably rests on a genealogy. None of these people are connected with Britain in the Irish sources, unless Aengus Builc be equated with Aengus ri Alban; but they are the only persons called Bolg (or Builc) that I have been able to observe, and all of them belong to west Munster. Settlement in Anglesey might of course be more readily expected from Leinster or Meath, but I have not noticed the name Bolg in either province at a possible date.

CANINUS

Aurelius Caninus (*catule leonine*) is named by Gildas (ed. Winterbottom, 1978, 30) between Constantine (*leaenae Damnonia*) in the south-west of England and Vortepor (*Demetarum tyranne*) in Dyfed (south-west Wales) and so his territory is generally assumed to lie in between these two; thus Somerset, Gloucester and Glamorgan may have formed the nucleus of his kingdom.

His name is not attested elsewhere, and whether or not the *Caninus* is a pun on *Cynan* to enable the (insulting) epithet *catule leonine* ('lion whelp') to be applied remains imponderable.   R.B.W.

CAUUS

Cauus of Arecluta (Alclud) (MS. Caunus for Cauus, Jackson [*LHEB* 306], father of Gildas, v. *Gildae* [R] 1). The names are preserved, in a late life, in a spelling of the sixth century, scarcely later than Gildas's lifetime, Jackson *LHEB* 306-7, *cf*.42.

Later texts call him Caw Prydein, and locate him 'beyond Bannauc', probably about the Upper Forth, in the Menteith region, about 20 miles north of Glasgow. But Gildas lived his life in Wales and was there schooled (**E**); before or after Gildas's birth, *c*.495 the family moved from the Clyde to Wales. The genealogies locate Gildas's relatives in southern Powys, in or near Roman forts.

The recorded occasion of a late fifth-century movement from southern Scotland to central Wales is the migration of Marianus, grandson of Cunedda to Merioneth. This migration appears to have included a Cauos. *ECMW* 282, Llanfor (*SH 9436*), near Caer Gai (fifth/early sixth century) reads *Cavo(s) Seniargii* (*filius*) (or alternatively, but less probably, *Cavoseni Argii*, *cf*. *LHEB* 521). An inscription from Caer Gai gives the name of the fort at that date *ECMW* 283, Caer Gai (*SH 8731*), reads *Hec iacet Salvianus Burgo Cavi, filius Cupetiani* (or Burso Cavi) (fifth/early sixth century). 'Burgus' is normal later Roman army titulature for a small fort; and, since Cavo(s) is buried nearby, it is probable that he named the fort.

Three other inscriptions appear to concern Cupetianus. *ECMW* 284 Llanymawddwy (*SH 9019*), Merioneth, seven miles south of Caer Gai, reads *Filiae Salvia(ni)ni(etti) hic iacit Ve(tti) . . . maie uxsor Tigirnici et filie eius Onerati* (uxsor ia)*cit Rigohene . . . oceti . . . aci*. *ECMW* 285, Tomen-y-Mur (*SH 7038*), the next Roman fort on the road from Caer Gai to Caernarvon, reads *D M Barrecti Carantei (filius)* (fifth century). One inscription from Scotland gives the same names. *CIIC* 514, *cf. PSAS* 70, 1935-6, 33, Liddel Water, 'between Newcastleton and Hawick', i.e., between *NY 4887* and *NY 5696*, on the borders of the Selgovae and Votadini reads *Hic iacit Caranti fili Cupitiani* (late fifth to early sixth century, LHEB 290).

The names Carantus and Cupetianus are unique. All the inscriptions in Wales were found in or near Roman forts; the relatives of Gildas who are placed in the genealogies are also placed in or near forts, one 10 miles north-east, and one 10 miles south-west of Caer Gai, on the Roman road from Chester to Dolgelly, two at Caersws, one by Clyro, and near Gobannium (Abergavenny), further south.

If the persons named on inscriptions are identical, the two Cupetiani, the two Caranti, the two Salviani, the relationship, taking the dates assigned by Nash-Williams and Jackson to the stones, would be:

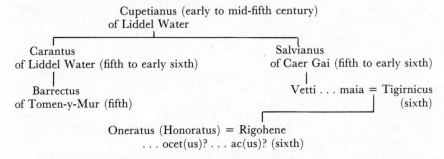

Cupetianus (early to mid-fifth century)
of Liddel Water

Carantus
of Liddel Water (fifth to early sixth)

Salvianus
of Caer Gai (fifth to early sixth)

Barrectus
of Tomen-y-Mur (fifth)

Vetti . . . maia = Tigirnicus
(sixth)

Oneratus (Honoratus) = Rigohene
. . . ocet(us)? . . . ac(us)? (sixth)

The meaning of the pedigree is that one of Cupetianus's sons went south, in the fifth century, and lived on to succeed Cavos at Caer Gai. The other son died at home, his son Barrectus emigrated with his uncle, or joined him later, and was established in the neighbouring fort of Tomen-y-Mur.

The inscriptions and the saints' pedigrees between them name 10 persons from two families, who moved from Scotland to Roman forts in Powys and Merioneth at the end of the fifth century. The date coincides with that given to Marianus; and to the renewed Irish invasion defeated by Catwallaun Lauhir, father of Maelgwn.

Legend turned Caw (Cauus) to a giant, because *cawr* means 'giant' in Welsh. Cadoc was made to resurrect his bones in the middle of the sixth century, in his homeland (v. *Cadoci* 26), and he is prominent in later fancy, *cf. TYP* 301 ff., not primarily as the father of Gildas, but in his own right. He also is given a son, who stayed home in Scotland, Cuil, who is said to have died fighting against Arthur.

CUNORIX
A funerary inscription from Wroxeter reading
    CUNORIX MACUS MAQI COLINE
and dated (on linguistic grounds) to A.D. 460-475 from an unstratified and thus unknown context. The inscription can be translated '(the grave of) CUNORIX son of the son (by dedication) to COLINI'.

COLINI contains *colinos*, 'holly' and is presumably the eponymous ancestor of CUNORIX's people. Other eponyms containing trees include hazel, yew, oak and rowan. The use of an apparently pagan eponym such as this does not necessarily mean that the man was not a Christian.

See R. P. Wright and K. H. Jackson, 'A Late Inscription from Wroxeter', *Ant. Jl.*
48 (1968), 296-300.   R.B.W.

EDWIN

Bede *HE* 2, 5. Edwin *maiore potentia cunctis, qui Britanniam incolunt, Anglorum pariter et
Brettonum populis praefuit, praeter Cantuariis tantum; nec non et Mavanias Brettonum insulas,
quae inter Hiberniam et Brittaniam sitae sunt, Anglorum subjecit imperio* cf. 2, 9 *quod nemo
Anglorum ante eum omnes Brittaniae fines. Quin et Mevanius insulas . . . subiugavit.* Bede's
statement that Edwin conquered Anglesey and Man has no confirmation, but must
be accepted. Some fragments of Welsh tradition seem to remember a campaign in
Anglesey in his later years. This short-lived conquest affords the only plausible
explanation yet advanced for the surprising name of Anglesey, 'island of the English'. No campaigns are recorded against the southern English; his *imperium* over
them would appear to amount to a formal acknowledgement that he was the greatest
king. The conception of the *Bretwalda* (ASC 827, etc.), rendered as holder of *imperium*
by Bede is matched by Adomnán's use of the title *imperator* for Oswald. It perpetuates
the political concepts of the Welsh *Guletic*, keeping alive a tradition that the self-
contained island of Britain had had, and, at least in some men's views, should
have, a single supreme ruler. The fact that successive holders of *imperium* were
acknowledged as paramount sovereigns, if only for parts of their lifetime, is not to
be doubted.

MAELGWN

Mailcun(us), Nennius 62; LL 118, Mailconus, v. *Teilo* LL 107, Maglocunus, *Gildas*
33 ff. Meilochon, *Bede* 3, 4; Maelicon, *CS* 560; Maec(h)on *A Tig* 142, 4, 1542; *AU*
557, 559, 584; Milc(h)on, *AC* 563, 4, 584; Maelgwn.

Has as his *praeceptor* the *paene totius Britanniae magistrum elegantem, Gildas* 36; *in
primis adolescentiae annis* killed *avunculum regem*; when his proud reign (*regni fantasia*)
ended, he took a monk's vow, and put away his wife; later he returned to power,
killed his first wife and his brother's son, and married his widow, *Gildas* 34-5;
becoming *insularis draco, multorum tyrannorum . . . supradictorum depulsor,* 'greater than
almost all the commanders of Britain in rule as in statute' (*cunctis paene Britanniae
ducibus tam regno . . . quam statu liniamento editior*), *Gildas* 33.

Rex Guenodotie, v. *Kebi* 17; *AC* 547, etc. Nordwallie, *DSB* 12, 9, etc., rex
Borealium Britonum, v. *Pat. 15*; rex Dyganwy, Kentigern charter *Red Book of St
Asaph* 119 (*LBS* 4, 384) (*cf. BT* 33, 19-20 = *FAB* 275, 154 imprisoned Elphin at
Deganway, etc.). Maelgwn of Mona, *BT* 40, 7 = *FAB* 538, 164; *wledic pendefic gwlat
hed*, 'noble sovereign of the land of peace', imprisoned Elphin (*BT* 40, 14-15 = *FAB*
539, 164). Chief king of the Cymry after they lost the crown and sceptre of London
and lost England, *AWIL* 5, 2, 1, 2 48-50 = *FAB* 1, 64-5 = *TYP* 439-40, etc., the
continuation of the story, that, thanks to the ingenuity of Maeldav (his grandfather,
of Penardd in Arfon, *AWIL* 14, 4, 4; 2, 584; Chirk Codex) he ruled from Aberffraw
in Anglesey over the Earls (Iarll) of Mathravel (Powys), Dynevwr (south-west),
and Caerleon (south-east), describes the political geography of the ninth and later
centuries (early traditions do not place his main centre in Anglesey). *Imperavit in
tota Britannia*, v. *Cadoci* 23, cf. 69.

Blinded, and cured, by numerous saints, e.g., v. *Paterni* 19; Kentigern, *Brev. Ab.
PH* 29c; v. *Cadoci* 69, etc.

Exacted an annual tribute of 100 cows and 100 calves from each pagus in Britain,
v. *Cadoci* 69; seized cattle in Merioneth, *Cywydd Tydecho Sant* (fifteenth century),
cited *LBS* 4, 283; exacted census in Gwynlliauc (eastern Glamorgan) v. *Cadoci* 23.

Invaded the southern British v. *Paterni* 15; introduced trial by ordeal, v. *Paterni* 18. Married Sanant of Powys, *DSB* 12, 9; married Walldewen, verch Avallach, Achau'r Mamau, cited TYP 502; son of Caswallaun Llauhir. Father of Run; Bridei, *Bede* 3, 4; *Annals* 560, 584; Alser, TYP 42; Eurgain, wife of Elidyr Mwynfawr (of York? *cf.* Elidyr).

Died of the Magna Mortalitas *Annals* 551 (*ACm* 547); of the Yellow Plague (*pestis flava*), v. *Teilo*, LL p.1-7; Yellow Spectre (i.e., plague), Jesus College MS. 61, cited *Ant.* 15, 1941, 285[n], etc.; court at Rhos near Deganwy, buried in the church of Rhos (Dingestow Brut and other references, cited TYP 438-9).

Cf. Nennius 61-3 *Ida filius Eobba, tenuit regiones in sinistrali parte Brittanniae . . . Tunc Outigirn . . . fortiter dimicabat contra gentem Anglorum . . . Mailcunus magnus rex apud Brittones regnabat, id est in regione Guenedotae . . . Adda, filius Ida, regnavit annis VIII.* The passage, *cf.* Arthurian Period Sources, Vol.8; *Nennius* pp.78, 79, is an insertion into the account of Northumbria; it links Maelgwn with Ida in time, and its inclusion in this context may be due to lost traditions connecting Maelgwn with wars against the northern Angles.

Maelgwn was remembered in the northern poems as an outstanding military commander; e.g., *CT* 11, 37 = *BT* 17-18 = *FAB* 338, 150 (Gwallawc), where a north Welsh king of the next generation (Owain, grandson of his cousin Cuneglassus) is honoured as 'Owein Mon Maelgynnin'; *BBC* 1, 8; 4, 4 = *FAB* 368, 369, 6, *cf.* A. O. H. Jarman, *Ymddiddan Myrddin a Thaliesin*, Cardiff, 1951, where the succeeding, and probably the preceding, verses are fragments from the Arderydd saga. Whether or not the north Welsh were involved in the battle, their forces are known as 'Maelgwn's' a generation after his death. A number of other references in later Welsh verse are cited TYP 440-1. He is also named in TYP 1, 46, 69.

The name is genitive in form; and the genitive was already used as a vocative, and therefore presumably also nominative, in Gildas's (and his own) day, *cf. LHEB* 624. The nominative form survives as Meilyg. (Maelgwn) *ECMW* 353 (= *CIIC* 446) Nevern, Pembrokeshire; MAGLOCUN(I) FILI CLUTORI, Ogam MAGLI-CUNAS MAQI CLUTA(RI), V to early VI.

ODOVACER

Chief of the Saxons of the Loire, led them to subdue the Alamanni in Italy, in the 460s, Greg. Tur. *HF* 2, 18-19. Visited St Severinus in Noricum, Eugippius, 7 *cf.* 32, while a 'tall youth', then clad in rags. Chosen to lead a mixed Germanic force of Heruli, Turcilingi and others, occupied Italy 476, discontinued the appointment of western emperors, ruled as king. Killed by Theodoric the Ostrogoth 493.

The name is characteristic of the Anglo-Saxon group of peoples; the elements (Searle, *Onomasticon*, Odo, -wacr) are sufficiently common, but unique in combination. He was a son of Edeco, perhaps in German Eadwig, a notable at the court of Attila. The suggestion that Edeco was by birth a Hun rests principally on the fact that he had to talk to the Constantinople eunuch Chrysaphius through the Hun interpreter Bigilas (E. A. Thompson, *Attila*, 11[2]); but Bigilas ought to have known German, and any German in long-service with Attila must have learnt Hunnic, but not Greek. Odovacer's conquest of Italy can hardly have followed immediately on his march from the Loire; he was a wanderer without an army when he visited St Severinus in Noricum. Strong evidence would be needed to argue that there were two separate barbarian chiefs called Odovacer in Italy in the same decade, since the name is unique.

SAMO

Natione Francos de pago Senonago (unidentified) *plures secum negutiantes adcivit, exercendum negucium in Sclavos coinmento Winedos perrexit* (*sic*). Such was his *utilitas* when the Wends rebelled succesfully againt the Avars (623), that he became their king, reigning 35 years and begetting 37 children by 12 Wend wives; Fredgearius 4, 48 (*MGH SRM* 2, 144-5). The *pagus* has not been identified in Frankish territory. It recalls the Senones, who left their name to territories in northern Gaul and north central Italy, and, like the Boioi, may also have settled and named parts of Bohemia. But, in the spelling of Fredegarius, it also recalls Semnones.

In 632, the *Sclavi coinmento Winidi* (of Bohemia) *in regno Samone* killed some Frank merchants. King Dagobert sent envoys to *Samonem regem Sclavinorum*, and, failing to obtain satisfaction, sent his army, and defeated Samo (Fredegarius 68). To the author (in 871) of the *Conversio Bagoariorum et Carabtanorum* (4; *MGH* SS 11, 7) *Samo homine quidam Sclavus manens in Quarantinis fuit dux gentis illius* suffered defeat by Dagobert. Fredegarius's words imply that Samo ruled other Slavs besides the Winidi. If the Carinthian tradition is right in claiming him as their ruler, his empire was extensive.

SERYGEI

Serygei fought Catwallaun at Cerryg y Gwddyl, Irishman's Rocks, in Mon., *TYP* 62. The name survives at Trefdraeth (*SH 4070*) at the head of the Malltraeth Sands, where the natural route (and modern railway) finds firm ground to cross the marshes towards Aberffraw and Holyhead. But the description 'Rocks' might fit others among the Cytiau's Gwyddelod. Catwallaun and his cousins slew Seregri at Llan y Gwyddyl (Irishman's monastery) at Caer Gybi (Holyhead), destroyed the 'Gwyddyl Ffichti' (Irish Picts) completely, and drove them from Anglesey (North Welsh genealogical triads, 4, *TYP*, pp.256, 258).

The name Serrach exists, and there is no need to assume a corruption let alone to turn it into Norse 'Sitric' (Rhys, Meyer, O'Rahilly, cited *TYP* 508). The genealogy of Aed m. Serraig m. Cuind (*CGH* 424, *LL* 335 b 57) belongs to the Conmaicne, a subject people of Connacht, and, unless this pedigree relates to the small outlier of the Conmaicne Bec of Meath, this Serrach is unlikely to be concerned with Britain, especially as the uncertain dates of the Conmaicne lists, resting of CGH 320 (R 161 b 18-19), would place him about a century later. But others will have borne the same name. The Aberdeen Breviary (PH Propr, 25 c) makes St Kentigerna daughter of Seriacus, *Monchestree regulus*, and of his wife, the daughter of *Tyrennus* (i.e., *tyrannus*) *Laynensium regulus*, the tyrant of Leinster. As she was the mother of Fursey, died *c*.649, this pedigree would make Seriacus at least a generation later than Illan; but the pedigree of saints rarely makes chronological sense. The fragment preserves a tradition that there was a sixth-century, or earlier, Leinster chief named Ser(i)acus, made son-in-law to the king of Leinster.

THEODORIC

f. Theudebald, king in Wales and Cornwall, *c*.500-530.

Theodoric is recorded in the exceptionally devolved Brecon texts and also in half-a-dozen Cornish-Irish Saints' Lives. In *LL* 118 he is listed among Teilo's contemporaries, Idon, Gurcant, Mailcun, Aircol, Catgucaun Tredicil and Rein, whose dates vary from the beginning to the end of the sixth century.

In the Brecon texts (BB, DSB, of which CB is a variant) Brecheniauc was first named from Brychan. At the beginning of time Teuderic (son of Tuedfall [Theudebald]), son of Teidhrin (Teidtheryn, Teudur, variants perhaps Theodhere),

the king of that area, came to Garth Matrun, and then advanced with his generals
and elders (*ducibus et cenioribus*) and all his household (or war band, *familia*) and
went to Bran Coyn by Llan Maes. Teuderic said to his daughter Marchel, 'I will
send you to Ireland with 300 men to marry Anlac son of Coronac, king of that
country'. So Marchel set out with 300 men to Lan Semin, and there on the first
night 100 men died from the severity of frost. On the second night she came to
Methrum, and there as many died as before. On the third night she reached Port
Maur, a sunnier place. Then she crossed with the 100 survivors to Ireland, where
she married Anlac and became the mother of Brychan.

The story has a context. Demetia had been ruled by Ui Liathain kings from
Munster for nearly a century, the last of whom, at the end of the fifth century, was
Aed Brosc. 'Anlac' (Andach m Cormac) is elsewhere said to have 'subdued Britain'
in company with Briscus, and two other men with Irish names that belong to south-
west of Munster, at a date given as 493, in a tradition of Aberaeron (*SN 4562*),
halfway between Cardigan and Aberystwyth. An isolated chain of Irish place-names
reaches inland from Aberaeron down the Roman road as far as Llandovery (*SN
7634*), the Roman fort that commands the roads from Brecon to Demetia. The
names suggest that Aed Brosc received reinforcements from Munster, either endeav-
ouring to extend his kingdom, or, more probably, to defend himself against
threatened attack. Demetia was the only substantial kingdom in Wales which the
sons of Cunedda had failed to subdue in the fifth century. The date is about the
time of Badon, when Arthur, free of threat from the English, was in a position to
undertake the reduction of remaining settlements. Independent traditions bring
Irish forces to renewed intervention in Britain at the turn of the century in north
Wales under Catwallaun, and in Cornwall (*cf.* below), where Arthur is said to have
been personally present with king Cato. These numerous isolated statements, in
British and Irish sources, are each of them placed in a nonsensical context; but
they are independent of each other, and add up to a conclusion that Arthur
undertook a concerted campaign to reduce and expel the remaining Irish-held
pockets in Britain.

Several references in the Saints' Lives bring Arthur to Wales, to Aberystwyth
and to the south-east. All but one are set well after Arthur's lifetime. The exception
is a story, in the Life of Cadoc, that he helped king Gwynlliw, whose territory
stretched inland from the coast between Cardiff and Newport, to defeat Brychan
(about the year 500, since the occasion was Gwynlliw's abduction of Brychan's
daughter Gwladus, the mother of Cadoc, who was born *c*.500 at Bochriu Carn
(Fochriw, *SO 1005*, on the Roman road from Cardiff to Brecon half-way between
the Roman forts of Gelligaer and Pen-y-Darren [Merthyr Tydfil] at a point where
the Roman road passes within yards of a prominent cairn on the southern slope of
Mynydd Fochriw).

Theodoric is dated in the Cornish Lives, in three independent traditions, of
Cynan, or Petroc, and of Fingar and his fellows, to the first decades of the sixth
century. He was not Brychan's grandfather, but his contemporary, and a younger
contemporary of Arthur. He is first reported near Brecon, and Marchel's route runs
down the Roman road from Brecon to the Demetian coast. Garth Matrun is
probably Talgarth (*SO 1553*) (*HW* 1, 272 n. 246, *cf. Arch. Camb.* VI. iii, 1903, 82-4;
Wade-Evans, *Welsh Christian Origins*, 89), the principal seat of the future kings of
Brycheiniog, seven miles north-east of the town of Brecon. He came to Llan Maes
(*SO 0328*), on the outskirts of modern Brecon. Marchel's route went straight down
the Roman road for 25 miles to Lan Semin (Glasnevin, *SN 7328*), four miles south-
west of Llandovery, where 'a hundred men' were lost. The next stage was 30 miles

farther, to Methrum (Meidrum or Mydrim, *SN 2821*, where the second hundred
died). The exact course of the Roman road beyond Carmarthen is not known, save
that it passed through the Roman fortlet of Castle Flemish (*SN 0026*) in Pembrokeshire; but Porth Mawr (Whitesands Bay, *SM 7327*) is about 35 miles from Mydrim,
a mile and a half north-west of St Davids. The site is unexcavated, but has produced
a little material and is approached from the site of its harbour by an ancient road
made of huge slabs, while some of the large boulders lying within it are of the shape
and size of early Christian memorial cross-stones. It was also traditionally the
harbour whence Patrick sailed to Ireland (v. *David* 3), and since the last identifiable
stretch of Roman road, at Castle Flemish, 17 miles away, is pointing straight at it,
it is likely to have been a main port of embarkation for southern Ireland.

The route sounds like the route of a military force, and armies are normally
commanded by men. Four miles short of Porth Mawr, directly on the straight line
from the road at Castle Flemish thereto, is the village of Caer Farchell (*SM 7927*).
In Wales, Caer, normally a substantial earthwork, is rarely compounded with the
names of women, commonly with men's names. It is probable that Marchel was
originally a man, Marcellus, an officer despatched by Theodoric, turned to a
'daughter' for the convenience of the tale about Brychan's ancestry. The distances
given are too great for the day's journey of infantry, but they would fit a mounted
force. They might, however, originally have figured as the sites of engagements
fought during the campaign, for men were lost at each of the intermediate sites,
and the commonest way that soldiers are killed is in battle.

These places and persons are preserved only in absurd stories about the mothers
of saints. They are, however, the whole of the known fragments that could concern
expeditions in this area about the year 500. It is remarkable that they make
geographical and military sense. Aed Brosc of Demetia secured help from Munster,
and reached Llandovery, perhaps Brecon, blocking all roads that approach Demetia,
except that from Neath. From the east came a two-pronged attack. Arthur is said
to have struck towards Brecon from the direction of Cardiff; Theodoric approached
from the north-east, first mentioned at Talgarth, halfway between the forts of
Clyro and Brecon Gaer. He advanced to Brecon, and sent Marcell(us) forward to
Carmarthen and the main Demetian port, through which further Munster reinforcements might be expected.

Even if this exact detail of time and place were pure coincidence, some such
campaign has to be inferred. The Irish names in the list of Demetian kings end
abruptly about 500, and are replaced by men with Roman names and Roman titles.
Triphun (Tribunus) is given, perhaps correctly, as father of Agricola, possibly a
misreading of *Agricola tirbuius*, and Agricola's son Vortipor, elderly when Gildas
wrote about 540, is recorded on his tombstone, near Narberth, halfway between
Carmarthen and Haverfordwest, as 'Protector', a Roman military title that recurs
in the pedigrees of Demetia, and of Demetia alone. It is evident that a successful
campaign, a generation before Gildas's time, ousted the Irish dynasty, and replaced
it with men who used names and titulature more Roman than in most of Wales.
The Irish were not expelled, but assimilated, for Vortipor's memorial stone is
bilingual. So are many others, but when a king's memorial is bilingual, then his
government admits two languages.

A few years later Theodoric is recorded in Cornwall. The rarity of the name
makes it unreasonable to suppose two different persons with the same name in the
same generation. The name is not merely Germanic, almost unparalleled in Wales
and Cornwall. It is as yet distinctive among Germans, Gothic alone, and the great
Theodoric was still ruling in Ravenna. His name had also been used by Visigothic

kings in Gaul, but the first non-Gothic Theodoric, the future Frankish king, did not become king until 511. The name is Theodoric in the Life of Cynan and in the Anselmian and Armorican Lives of Fingar and Guiner, but is shortened to the familiar Tewder and Theodorus in Leland's sixteenth-century version of these Lives, and in the Gotha MS. of v. *Petroc*. Since the earlier texts of the same story give Theodoricus for Leland's Theodorus, there is no doubt that the unfamiliar form is the original.

Fingar sailed from Ireland with a force of 770 men, including a king, Germochus (Cermait?) and landed at Hayle Bay (St Ives). *Theodoricus rex Cornubiae* set a watch on his coasts, from his headquarters, *Revier* (Phillack, Hayle Bay, *SW 5638*) *castellum Theodori in orientali parte ostii Hayle fluvii, nunc, ut quidam putant, absorptum a sabulo* (Leland). He separated the Irish forces, fell on one party of 200 from the rear and cut them to pieces; another force of 300 surrendered and was massacred, while, in Leland's version, a part escaped.

In the Life of Cynan, Theodoric was a cruel tyrant who lived at Gudrun (Goodern, *SW 7843*, two-and-a-half miles west-south-west of Truro, where a substantial earthwork is the principal feature of the hamlet), and exercised authority in the Roseland peninsula across the estuary from Falmouth. Five miles south of Falmouth, on the Helford estuary, Lestowder (*SW 7924*) in St Keverne, 'Theodore's court', may preserve the shortened form of his name.

On the Gotha Life of Petroc, he was a cruel tyrant, dead, his son reigning, when Petroc returned from Jerusalem, and in Leland's version he and Constantine were pious kings, who gave Bodmin (*SX 0767*) to Petroc.

He is located in the tip of Cornwall, his St Ives and Truro strongholds being some 20 miles apart. At Bodmin, 25 miles north of Truro, he was associated with Constantine, Gildas's king of Dumnonia, evidently his sovereign. The date indicated is a decade or two after 500, a little later than that implied for Wales. These stories therefore say that he was settled with a small territory in Dumnonia after the successful conclusion of the campaign in Demetia.

He was also concerned with Brittany. The Fingar story says that Guiner's force intended to pass through Cornwall on its way to aid his 'uncle' Maxentius, whom Theodoric had 'defeated, and compelled to relinquish lands which he had recovered'. The name Maxentius is arresting. It is otherwise unknown to Britain or to hagiography, and is recorded only for one other secular ruler in Gaul in these centuries. About 520, the brothers Budic and Maxentius returned from Alamannia to recover their paternal inheritance of Armorican Cornouailles, and killed Marcellus. The name Marcellus is as unique as Maxentius: common enough in Roman history, it is not recorded for a lay notable in Gaul or Britain after the Marcellus whom the Roman nobility of Gaul tried to make emperor, apparently with Visigothic support in 456 or 467 (Sidonius *Ep*. 1, 11, 6, *cf.* C. E. Stevens, *Sidonius Apollinaris*, 41-4, *cf.* 181-5). Both names were occasionally borne by ecclesiastics, but it is more than coincidence that the only Marcellus and the only Maxentius are linked with the only Theodoric in the same generation, in the separate traditions of south Wales, of Cornwall, and of Brittany. The statements are that first Budic and Maxentius returned and killed Marcellus; secondly that Theodoric deprived Maxentius of part of the territory that he had regained. The implication is that Marcellus, from whom he took the territory, had received it after the Demetian war, as Theodoric had received his Cornish lordship. A fourth tradition from south-east Wales links Theodoric with the fortunes of Budic and Maxentius. Budic was exiled from Britain, evidently after his return and after the death of Marcellus. He took refuge with Agricola of Demetia, and was restored with the aid of a British force, and a fleet. The author of his exile is not stated. But in the neighbouring territory of Vannes, as in many other states of Gaul and Brittany, kings were exiled or killed by their brothers, and Maxentius is the likely enemy of Budic, whom the Demetians helped.

The Brecon legend suggests that Theodoric had helped Agricola to his throne. The story of Budic's exile does not say that Theodoric commanded the Demetian forces sent to help him. But he had some connection with a Theodoric. Gregory of Tours, his contemporary, says that he named his son Theodoric. The choice was extraordinary for an early sixth-century Briton, and implies that, in selecting such a name, he had some close connection with a contemporary called Theodoric, in whose honour he named the child.

A ruler who was active in Wales, Cornwall and Brittany, and who appears to have participated in the restoration of an Armorican prince from Demetia, is likely to have had a fleet at his disposal. Theodoric's name is Gothic. The only organised naval force known to have been maintained in the Atlantic in the fifth century was the Biscay fleet of the Visigothic kings of Aquitaine (Sidonius *Ep*. 8, 6, 13), presumably based in the Bordeaux area. In 507 Clovis the Frank destroyed the Visigoths of Aquitaine; their king, and what survived of his army, withdrew to Spain. The harbours of Aquitaine fell to the Franks. Nothing is recorded of what happened to their fleet, if it was still in being. It may have stayed in port to surrender; it may have hazarded a voyage round Gibraltar to the Mediterranean coast of Spain; or it may have joined Theodoric in Britain. If so, the Demetian campaign would date soon after 507, about 510.

The story that the notices of Theodoric tell is not in itself remarkable, as it was normal for a late Roman government to employ a Germanic commander against barbarians, and to reward him with large estates. What is remarkable is the manner in which these notices have been preserved. A large number of incidental references, almost all of them in very late tales, extremely devolved, most of them absurd in the context in which they occur, fall together in time and place to give a detailed reconstruction of two normal military campaigns, and the full career of one commander. There is no confirmation of any one of the incidents related; each step in Theodoric's career is an inference drawn from these isolated statements. In theory, it might be pure coincidence that all the detail fits, but it would be a most remarkable coincidence. It seems more reasonable to assume that these notices are broken fragments of reality, preserved more abundantly than usual.

VORTIGERN

Nennius 31 ff. *Superbus tyrannus*, Gildas 23. Frequently named in early medieval Welsh literature, *cf*. selected references in *TYP* 392. Began to rule in 425, Nennius 66; 40 years after Maximus, Nennius 31, who reigned 348 years after the coming of the Romans, Nennius 30. With his council invited Hengest and Horsa's success, Gildas 23, Nennius, 31, in 428, Nennius 66. His subsequent history is told in two distinct texts in Nennius, the rational Kentish Chronicle, and the devolved Germanus legend.

'Son' of Vitalis (Vitalinus) of Gloucester. The physical relationship is the inevitable form of the genealogist: the tradition linking Gloucester and Vitalinus is of more moment than the relationship. In place-name, Gwerthrynion in Builth perpetuates his name; also remembered in Caernarvonshire, Demetia, and Wiltshire (William of Malmesbury's *Wirtgernesburg* [*Hist. Regum* 1, 23] is apparently meant to mean Bradford-on-Avon, *cf*. H. M. Chadwick in *SEBH* 31). In Brittany, Gurthiernus 'rex Anglorum', son of Bonus son of Gloui, founder of Gloucester (*Cart. Quimperlé* 42 ff.) is apparently Vortigern turned to a saint.

The name 'over-king' or 'top tyrant', hence Gildas's pun, turning *superior tyrannus* to *superbus tyrannus*. It is not used of any other Briton, but is not uncommon in Ireland. It is found in various forms a dozen times in the genealogies (CGH index) and in Adomnán 2, 17, and twice on inscriptions (*CIIC* 97, Co. Cork, the second inscription of a palimpsest, and 297 Co. Waterford). The earliest known bearer of the name in Ireland is bishop Foirtchernn (Clonmacnoise) said to have been a son of king Laogaire's son Feidelmid and of the 'daughter of the king of the Britons'. Since she gave her son the then exceptional name of Vortigern, the king, who was her father, is likely to have been Vortigern, Laogaire's contemporary, of the right age to be her father, *cf.* H. M. Chadwick, *SEBH* 27. The suggestion of N. K. Chadwick, *SEBH* 38, that the name arises from a 'saga' is hardly tenable; no such 'saga' could have arisen by the time Foirtchernn was named. All dateable genealogies, Adomnán, and one of the inscriptions are later than the time of bishop Foirtchernn; the other names are undated. It is therefore probable that the use of the name in Ireland derives from the popularity of bishop Foirtchernn.

Foirtchernn filius Fedeilmtheo invenit (Lommanum Brittonem) evanguelium recitantem . . . et mansit cum illo donec mater eius quaerere eum parvenit; et laeta facta est in conspectu eius, quia Britonissa erat . . . Fedelmidius laetificabatur in adventu clerici, quia de Brittonibus matrem habuit, id est filiam regis Brittonum, id est Scoth Noe. Salutavit autem Fedelmidius Lommanum lingua Brittannica . . . Tírechán *Additamenta* 1-4, *AB* 2, 1883, 213-216; *VT* 334-336; and derivative texts. In other versions (e.g., *Bethu Phátraic*, ed. K. Mulchrone, 1939, 43) Foirtchernn m Feidelmid is the son of the British mother. In Tírechán either *matrem* is a mistake for *uxorem*, or Foirtchernn is to be understood as the subject of *habuit*. Feidelmid emigrated to Clonmacnoise and Foirtchernn 'gave away' (*distribuit*) the church of Trim to *Cathlaidus peregrinus*. Fortchern ep. Roscommon, v. *Finnian*.

Clonard 2: Finnian was to have been baptised by Fortchern, but Abban baptised him instead, evidently a conflict of traditions, since Abban's see replaced Fortchern's in importance in Leinster at the end of the fifth century. The name was particularly popular among the Dessi, of Waterford, CIIC 297 (Vortigurn), *cf.* also CGH 161. R 144 c 21, undateable (Fuirtgern, Furgern, Fortchern), with another inscription (CIIC 97 . . . 11 maqi Vorrtigurn) from Muskerry in Cork. The home of Columba's host Foirtgirnus (Adomnán 2, 17) is not identifiable. The unusual variety of spelling suggests that the name was unfamiliar to copyists, of alien origin. The British connection is emphasised by the one northern instance. Tigernach of Airgialla in the later fifth century named his two sons Catchern and Fortchern: Catchern, otherwise unknown in Ireland, is Catigirnus, the name borne by the son of the British Vortigern. The four dateable instances fall within the period 480/550 (Columba's host could be 540/590, but the incident, apparently in Ireland, is probably to be referred to the years 540/560, before Columba's exile). I have not observed later instances.

The literary tradition in the Gildas and both the Nennius stories is hostile to Vortigern. The widespread use of his name suggests that other tales were told wherein he was a hero; places are not normally named after villains, unless they actually were connected with the places. The Powysian tradition of the pillar of Eliseg, that he was blessed by Germanus, married to a daughter of Maximus, and the source of the legitimacy of the dynasty, is an echo of these favourable tales. *See also* **E** Foirtchern.